THE
FAITH
OF
MILLIONS

THE FAITH OF MILLIONS

The Credentials of the Catholic Religion

REV. JOHN A. O'BRIEN

REVISED EDITION

Our Sunday Visitor, Inc.

HUNTINGTON, INDIANA

Nihil obstat: Rev. Lawrence Gollner, Censor Librorum
Imprimatur: Leo A. Pursley, Bishop of Fort Wayne-South Bend
March 16, 1974

The Nihil Obstat and Imprimatur are official declarations that a book or pamphlet
is free of doctrinal or moral error.
No implication is contained therein that those who have granted
the Nihil Obstat or Imprimatur agree with
the contents, opinions, or statements expressed.

ISBN 0-87973-830-8
Library of Congress Catalog Card No. 74-82119

ADDRESS INQUIRIES TO:
Our Sunday Visitor, Inc.
200 Noll Plaza, Huntington, Indiana 46750

10 9 8 7 6 5 4 3 2 1

Introduction

The Faith of Millions is a splendid exposition of the doctrines and practices of the Christian religion. The clarity, thoroughness and friendliness with which these have been presented have won for it millions of readers of all faiths and have caused it to be translated into French, German, Italian, Spanish, Chinese, Japanese, Hungarian, Korean, Malayalam and account for its publication in a special British edition.

Priests, bishops and cardinals in many countries have singled out *The Faith of Millions* for special praise. To embody the numerous changes brought about by Vatican Council II and by the worldwide ecumenical movement, this new revised and ecumenical edition has been issued.

Having served as a consultant to the author in bringing out this new edition, I am confident that this thoroughly revised edition will enable *The Faith of Millions* to continue to minister to the needs not only of Catholics but of other faiths as well. It will give added impetus to the movement for Christian unity and help to bring Christ, His light and love into the minds and hearts of the millions of its readers.

> ✠ Edward L. Heston, C.S.C.
> Titular Archbishop of Numida and
> President of the Pontifical Commission for
> Social Communications
> Rome, Italy

Commendations of the First Edition

The Faith of Millions is up-to-date. Following in the footsteps of Cardinal Gibbons, Father O'Brien has adopted, not controversy, but exposition, and from personal experience in dealing with non-Catholics, particularly university students, he sets forth Catholic teaching on all the moot questions now occupying thinking minds in the matter of religion.

The reader will find that the chief qualities of Father O'Brien's exposition of Catholic truth are simplicity, clearness, cogency of reasoning and a sympathy for those who are groping after the truth. In an efficient manner it meets the needs of the day in matters religious and should have a wide circulation and yield a copious harvest.

✠ Dennis Cardinal Dougherty
Archbishop of Phildelphia

There is always a place for books which explain the doctrinal and sacramental structure of the Catholic Church. The truths of our faith are as old as the Church itself, but they need restatement from time to time for the countless inquiring souls who are seeking to find and understand the Church which Christ established on earth. The credentials of the true faith and the means by which it may be found are admirably presented in *The Faith of Millions.*

This book by Father O'Brien cannot fail to aid many within and outside the Church. I wish for it the large circle of readers which it merits and I pray that it may bring many to a fuller understanding of the life of the Catholic Church and a greater participation in the divine life which it diffuses.

✠ William Cardinal O'Connell
Archbishop of Boston

Author's Foreword

The purpose of this volume is to present in a simple straightforward manner the credentials and the teachings of the Catholic faith. It seeks to show that it is the duty of every person to endeavor to find out which is the Church established by Jesus Christ to guide him in attaining eternal life.

This is a question of prime importance, which must be answered to the best of one's ability, if one is to live an intelligent life. No amount of absorption in other matters can justify the lifelong neglect of this important matter. Upon the answer given to this question hinge consequences of far-reaching import — consequences that reach into eternity.

The appeal is not to the emotions and prejudices of the reader but to his reason and conscience. The author asks of the reader but a single favor: that he bring an open mind to the investigation of the most important matter which life presents. God never fails to give light to those who seek the truth with honesty and singleness of purpose.

In the preparation of this book, the author has had the valuable advice and counsel of cardinals as well as of many bishops and priests, whose names are too numerous to be mentioned here, but not too numerous to be treasured in his grateful heart.

The author hopes that this volume, which has been for him a labor of love, will prove helpful to his fellow countrymen and to the people of every land in their earnest search for "the church of the living God, the pillar and ground of the truth."[1] That it may be in some small way a "pillar of the cloud by day" and a "pillar of fire by night,"[2] guiding the groping feet of earnest pilgrims into the promised land of religious truth and certainty, where the mists no longer confuse nor the shadows obscure the vision of Christ and His teachings, is the author's daily prayer. If it leads but one soul into the bark of Peter and thus guides him safely to the feet of Christ, the author will be more than repaid for his years of labor in the completion of this volume.

*   *   *

Since writing the above foreword, the author is gratified to learn that the volume has gone through many editions, has passed the two million mark and has been translated into French, German, Spanish, Italian, Hungarian, Chinese, Japanese and Malayalam. He respectfully requests the prayers of the reader that the work may continue in a humble manner to assist truth seekers to find Christ who is "the way, the truth and the life" and to be to them a channel of divine grace. He expresses his profound gratitude to Bishop Leo A. Pursley and to the late Archbishop Edward L. Heston for their invaluable suggestions in the writing of this new and revised edition.

John A. O'Brien
Notre Dame, Indiana

1. Tm. 3:15
2. Ex. 13:22

How to Conduct
A Religious Discussion Club*

A religious discussion club is a group of persons meeting at regular intervals to improve their knowledge of religious matters by cooperative study and discussion. Members acquire information regarding some specific subject, and develop accuracy of statement and the power of self-expression, through discussion. Under the guidance of a discussion leader the topic of the paragraph is laid open to all. Each member is free to speak, as the very essence of the club is discussion. Members unconsciously develop from this experience an ease of expression.

The discussion method is simplicity itself. A suitable textbook is chosen and a copy is provided for each member of the club. The members in turn read aloud a brief passage from the text while the rest follow silently. The leader then encourages a retelling of the paragraph or passage by asking questions that bring out its obvious highlights. Discussion literally means "shaking apart." As this method shakes apart a reliable text, its chief feature is a practical analysis of the text.

The small group. The discussion group ordinarily has eight to twelve members, for only within a small group is spontaneous discussion possible. Where as many as sixteen persons apply for membership, it is well to form two clubs which will meet separately. A small group is informal and each member has time to express himself and enter freely into the discussion.

In a large group, on the contrary, the talking is usually done

* Excerpts from The Religious Discussion Club *(Confraternity of Christian Doctrine, N.C.W.C., Washington, D.C.).*

by a few, and not always by those best qualified. Congenial persons should be placed in the same group, to produce less restraint and better cooperation.

Officers

A Spiritual Director. The religious discussion club should always be under the guidance of a priest. The local pastor is usually requested to act as Spiritual Director, or to appoint another priest to do so.

When a question arises and the group does not agree on a decision, it is always referred to the Spiritual Director. However, discussion clubs are the laity; if they are to accomplish their purpose, the laity must do the work.

A leader need not be an expert. He also is a learner in this informal group committed to cooperative study and discussion. He should, however, acquire a clear knowledge of the subject matter, learn to direct the discussion, and hold it to the chief points of the assignments. *Do not overstress the requirements for leadership — it is a simple task.* The leader need not be further advanced in natural gifts or religious instruction than the other members of the club.

The leader should use the *Discussion Aids* (which follow each chapter) in conducting the discussion. He should see that every member is given an opportunity to take part, and should consider and respect every member's opinion on the subject.

A secretary (1) calls the roll; (2) reads the brief record of the previous meeting (mainly a digest of the chief thoughts developed in the discussion); and (3) records and refers to the Spiritual Director questions that cannot be decided by the group.

Who are members? The discussion club is not merely for exceptional laymen, experts and college graduates, but for all persons of high-school years and over, quite regardless of their degree of formal education. Anyone who can read and is willing to use his mind "in learning more of the things of our blessed Lord and of His Church" can profitably join a club without very extensive study or expenditure of time. Members should be urged to attend every meeting, even though they have made no preparation. If they have their texts they may profitably participate in the discussion even without previous preparation.

Every member too should realize that the success of the discussion club depends primarily upon his or her own individual preparation and responsiveness. Discussion (which will present and develop the subject) is the very nature of the discussion club.

Each member obtains a copy of the textbook adopted; this is necessary for efficient work. He feels personally responsible for attending every meeting, and for taking his text. People can discuss profitably only in such measure as they acquire correct information and a vocabulary to communicate it readily.

Frequent meetings for a short period. Two or three weekly meetings of an hour and a half, which begin and end promptly, are generally more satisfactory than meetings held less often for a longer period. Subject matter of the previous meeting is more readily recalled and related, and members cannot forget on which week the meeting is held.

The first meeting. Read and discuss the first lesson of the text, even though no preparation was made except by the leader. This will demonstrate the simplicity of the discussion method.

Select a name by which to distinguish your club from others in the parish or city. Saints' names are often used.

Discuss and decide the permanent day and hour of meeting during the session. Give the place of the next meeting.

Order of Meeting:
1. Begin promptly.
2. Open with prayer.
3. Roll call by secretary.
4. Brief review of previous assignment.
5. Reading and discussion of assigned text. Leader keeps the discussion within bounds of the assignment, and promotes participation by the members.
6. Assignment of lesson for the following meeting.
7. If meetings are held at different homes, announce the place of the next one.
8. Adjourn on time, closing with prayer.

Suggest that after discussion each member ask himself the following questions: (1) What are the leading ideas of the lesson?

(2) What new information have I gained? (3) Have any of my former ideas been changed? (4) What is my conclusion? (5) How shall I apply this knowledge practically?

When there are absentees, the meeting opens as usual and proceeds according to the "Order of Meeting." Valuable time need not be lost in wondering why persons are not present, and those attending can have a profitable meeting. There is no formal program dependent on the presence of certain people. Prior to the next meeting, remind absentees to come, or even ask members to call for and bring them to the meeting.

Dues and Expenses

Ordinarily, there should be no dues in discussion clubs. Each member purchases his own textbook, which becomes his property. The cost may vary from ten to fifty cents.[1]

TABLE OF CONTENTS

PART I

Which Is Christ's True Church?

The Answer of Scripture, History and Reason

CHAPTER 1

Basic Christian Doctrines

The Christian religion teaches that there is one God in three divine Persons, equal and distinct, the Father, the Son and the Holy Spirit. This is called the mystery of the Blessed Trinity, a truth not against our reason but above it. We believe it because it has been divinely revealed to us in Holy Scripture. God the Father is the Creator of the world, God the Son is the Redeemer of mankind, and God the Holy Spirit is the Sanctifier.

Our Christian faith teaches that Jesus Christ is divine in His personality and possesses two distinct natures, human and divine. "He is God of the substance of the Father, begotten before time," says the Athanasian Creed formulated in the fourth century, "and He is Man of the substance of His mother, born in time."

In order to redeem us from our sins the Son of God became incarnate, being conceived by the power of the Holy Spirit in the womb of the Virgin Mary, and was born in a stable at Bethlehem on Christmas day more than nineteen hundred years ago.

The first thirty years of His life were spent in comparative obscurity with Mary and Joseph in the humble home at Nazareth. Christ then began His public ministry, selecting twelve men who are called Apostles to assist Him in the propagation of His teachings. He "went about doing good," healing the sick, restoring sight to the blind, hearing to the deaf, cleansing the lepers and raising the dead to life. Throughout Judea the Savior went preaching a gospel of peace, justice, mercy and brotherly love that embraced even one's enemies.

After three years of public ministry, during which He schooled His Apostles in the truths He had come upon earth to teach, He was crucified on Mount Calvary. By His suffering and death He offered to the eternal Father atonement for the sins of mankind. "He was wounded for our iniquities: He was bruised for our sins . . . and by His bruises we are healed."[1]

To commemorate the day on which Christ died for love of us, we may abstain voluntarily from flesh meat on Friday. It is a little act of salutary mortification by which we endeavor to show our love and gratitude to our Redeemer and like St. Paul "to bear about in our body the mortification of Jesus, that the life also of Jesus may be made manifest in our bodies."[2]

We reverence the cross because it was the instrument of our Savior's crucifixion. It surmounts our churches and adorns our altars. "Far be it from me," says St. Paul, "to glory save in the cross of our Lord Jesus Christ."[3] We begin and end our prayers by making on our person the sign of the cross, while we say: "In the name of the Father, and of the Son, and of the Holy Spirit, Amen." That this is an ancient custom is evident from the words of Tertullian who lived in the second century: "In all our actions, when we come in or go out, when we dress, when we wash, at our meals, before retiring to sleep . . . we form on our forehead the sign of the cross. These practices are not commanded by a formal law of Scripture, but tradition teaches them, custom confirms them, faith observes them!"[4] In making the sign of the cross we profess our faith in the Trinity, the incarnation and in

18

the redemption — three of the basic truths of the Christian religion.

On Easter Sunday the third day after his death, Christ rose from the dead, thus giving the most striking demonstration of His divine power. After forty days, during which He appeared several times to the Apostles, instructing them further in the faith, Christ ascended into heaven from the Mount of Olives. Ten days later on the feast of Pentecost, or Whitsunday, our Savior sent the Holy Spirit upon the Apostles while they were assembled in prayer. The Apostles were thus divinely strengthened to fulfill the mission given them by Christ "to preach the gospel to every creature." It was on Pentecost Sunday that the Apostles began their sublime mission, and from that day we date the active life of the Church.

Christ taught that there is a heaven and a hell. "Come ye blessed of My father," said Christ, "possess the kingdom prepared for you from the foundation of the world."[5] "Eye hath not seen," says St. Paul, "nor ear heard, neither hath it entered into the heart of man, what things God hath prepared for them that love Him."[6] The supernatural happiness of heaven consists in the union of the soul with God through beatific vision. "Now we see in a mirror, obscurely; but then face-to-face. Now I know in part; then I shall know fully, even as I am known."[7] In the next life union with God is heaven, separation from Him forever is hell.

The suffering of hell, according to the common teaching of the Church's theologians, is twofold: the pain of loss and the pain of sense. The pain of loss consists in the eternal separation of the soul from God and the realization that this separation is due to one's own fault. This is the chief punishment of hell. "Perhaps the pain of homesickness," says Dr. J. M. Cooper, "is as near to this pain of loss as anything we suffer here on earth. Here we do not miss God, so to speak. We have on earth all sorts of distractions and interests. But at death we leave all such interests and distractions behind."[8]

Concerning the detailed specific nature of hell, says Father B. L. Conway, "The Catholic Church has defined nothing. . . . It is useless to speculate about its true nature, and more sensible to confess our ignorance in a question that evidently exceeds human understanding."[9] While our Lord did not see fit to disclose to us the specific details concerning the nature of heaven and hell, other than that the one means union with God and the other separation from Him, the fact of their existence cannot be denied without denying the authority of Christ Himself.

We have said that Christ came to redeem the world from sin. There are two different kinds of sin: original and actual sin. Original sin is inherited from our first parents, being the state into which we are born as a result of their fall. Original sin is, therefore, the privation of sanctifying grace.

Actual sin is any willful thought, word, deed or omission contrary to the law of God. Actual sin is of two kinds: mortal and venial. A mortal sin is a grievous offense committed with sufficient reflection and with full consent of the will. It is so called because it robs the soul of sanctifying grace, which is its life, and thus brings spiritual death to the soul. A venial sin is a slight offense, that is, the deed done is not seriously, grievously wrong or, if it is serious, it is performed without sufficient reflection or without full consent of the will.

For example, if a person steals a newspaper, he commits a sin of injustice. But as it does not constitute a grievous wrong, it would be but a venial sin. If, however, a larger amount, say, a hundred dollars, were stolen, that would constitute a grievous injustice and therefore a mortal sin.

Christ came upon earth to redeem mankind from all their sins; that is why He is called *Jesus*, which means *Savior*. He established a Church to propagate His teachings and to transmit to all mankind the blessed fruits of the Redemption. The marks which distinguish Christ's Church from all those founded by men are four — unity, sanctity, catholicity and apostolicity.

As the sailor out on the boundless deep has the compass and the North Star to guide him safely through the darkness of the night over the mighty expanse of sea into his true harbor, so the searcher after truth has marks to guide him out of the darkness of error into the Church founded by Christ. These guiding marks must be certain and plain, otherwise they might mislead the searcher after truth. Accordingly, Christ has invested the Church founded by Him with four unmistakable, characteristic marks whereby it might be known.

First, let us consider its unity. Christ founded His Church when He gave the great commission to His Apostles, saying: "All power is given to Me in heaven and on earth. Going, therefore, teach ye all nations, baptizing them in the name of the Father, and of the Son, and of the Holy Spirit, teaching them to observe all things whatsoever I have commanded you." That phrase, "all things whatsoever I have commanded you," demands faith in all His doctrines without exception. If there is an obligation on the part of the Apostles and disciples to preach the gospel, there is the corresponding duty on the part of the faithful to embrace it.

Christ makes this obligation explicit when He says: "Preach the gospel to every creature; he that believeth and is baptized shall be saved; he that believeth not shall be condemned." Furthermore, He tells them: "He that heareth you, heareth Me, and he that despiseth you, despiseth Me." St. Paul emphasizes the necessity of this unity of faith when he tells the Galatians: "But though we, or an angel from heaven, preach a gospel to you besides that which we have preached to you, let him be anathema. For I give you to understand, brethren, that the gospel which was preached by me is not according to man. For neither did I receive it of man, nor did I learn it; but by the revelation of Jesus Christ."[10]

This unity of faith is found in the Catholic Church throughout all the countries of the world — in her and in her alone. The Mass at which Catholics assist every Sunday is the same Mass that is celebrated in Europe, Asia, Africa, America, and everywhere else under the sun; for we are members of a mighty organization that encircles the globe, and all under the one visible head — the Pope of Rome, the Successor of St. Peter.

The second mark is sanctity. By this we mean that the Church is holy because her Founder, Jesus Christ, is holy and the source of all holiness; because her end is to make men holy; because her dogmas and her sacraments are holy in themselves and lead to holiness; and finally, because she has produced in all ages members distinguished by their eminent sanctity, some of whom have shed their blood in far-off lands for the faith of Christ. With her, sanctity is placed above all temporal goods, and men and women leave father and mother, brother and sister, home and lands and all that the world holds dear to carry the teachings of Christ to the far corners of the world. Here is the sacrifice sublime which surpasses the wisdom of the world, the living proof of the Church's holiness.

Moreover, St. Paul tells the Ephesians: "Christ loved the Church and delivered Himself up for it that He might sanctify it; . . . that He might present it to Himself a glorious Church, not having spot or wrinkle, or any such thing, but that it should be holy and without blemish."[11] This is the mark of holiness, which Christ has stamped indelibly upon His Church to draw all men to it.

The third mark of the Church is her catholicity. Catholic means universal. Since her foundation the Church has existed in all ages and among all nations and has everywhere taught the same doctrines. Here we have what, to my mind, is one of the most striking and unmistakable proofs of the divine origin of the Catholic Church in the cold historical fact that *for more than fourteen centuries after the death of Christ there was no Christian Church in existence save the Catholic Church.* The heretical sects that arose during that time, for the most part, withered and died away, while the Catholic Church *alone* existed throughout all Christendom. Of the many denominations that exist today, none of them can trace its origin back more than a few centuries at the most. Hence, it must be evident to all that they cannot have Christ for their Founder, since they did not even exist at that time, nor for more than fourteen hundred years after His death. This is a point that does not demand any subtle reasoning nor prolonged study to see; it is a plain historical fact which all who run may read.

I cite it not in a critical spirit, but in a friendly manner, as the most evident truth of history. The Catholic Church, on the other hand, has come down to us through all the ages, from the moment when Christ said to His Apostles, "Teach ye all nations," to the present time. The tide of time rolling down through the centuries has engulfed many a human institution and the rust of ages has eaten into all the edifices erected by the hand of man. Kingdoms, thrones and empires have risen, have grown strong and powerful, only to fall and lie buried in the dust of ages. But both the ravages of time and the wear and tear of cen-

22

turies stand powerless against the Catholic Church, ever ancient, yet ever fair and young.

Why is this so? Why is she the sole exception to all the laws of human decay? It is because she is not merely human, but *divine.* Divine in her foundation, divine in her teachings; she is human but in her membership. The Church has stood the test of ages and today in a world of changing fads alone stands immutable and unchanged because Jesus Christ has kept His promise when He said: "Thou art Peter, and upon this rock I will build My church and the gates of hell shall not prevail against her."

The historian, Macaulay, non-Catholic though he was, felt compelled by the facts of history to pay the following tribute to the Church's defiance of the laws of decay which have sung the requiem of the great institutions of the past: "There is not, and there never was on the earth a work of human policy so well deserving of examination as the Roman Catholic Church. The history of that Church joins together the two great ages of human civilization. No other institution is left standing which carries the mind back to the times when the smoke of sacrifice rose from the Pantheon, and when camelopards and tigers bounded in the Flavian Amphitheater. The proudest royal houses are but of yesterday, when compared with the line of the Supreme Pontiffs. That line we trace back in an unbroken series from the Pope who crowned Napoleon in the nineteenth century to the Pope who crowned Pepin in the eighth; and far beyond the time of Pepin the august dynasty extended till it is lost in the twilight of fable. The republic of Venice came next in antiquity. But the republic of Venice was modern when compared with the Papacy; and the republic of Venice is gone, and the Papacy remains. The Papacy remains, not in decay, not as a mere antique, but full of life and useful vigor. The Catholic Church is still sending forth to the farthest ends of the world missionaries as zealous as those who landed in Kent with Augustine, and still confronting hostile kings with the same spirit with which she confronted Attila. . . .

"She saw the commencement of all the governments and of all the ecclesiastical establishments that now exist in the world; and we feel no assurance that she is not destined to see the end of them all. She was great and respected before the Saxon had set foot on Britain, before the Frank had passed the Rhine, when

Grecian eloquence still flourished in Antioch, when idols were still worshiped in the temple of Mecca. And she may still exist in undiminished vigor when some traveler from New Zealand shall, in the midst of a vast solitude, take his stand on a broken arch of London Bridge to sketch the ruins of St. Paul's."[12] Such is the tribute of history.

Furthermore, the Church is apostolic. By apostolicity is meant that the doctrine is the same as that taught by the Apostles, and that the succession of rulers dates back to the Apostles and to their head, St. Peter. Apostolicity of doctrine follows as a logical consequence of the Church's unity of belief. Indeed, when that gifted scholar, John Henry Newman, then an Anglican divine at Oxford, set out to disprove the Church's claim to apostolicity of doctrine, he consulted the writings of the early Fathers of the Church, such as St. Augustine, St. Jerome, St. Basil, St. Chrysostom and others who lived in the first five centuries. He examined the writings of these early Christians on such points of doctrine as the sacraments, the Real Presence, the devotion to the Blessed Virgin, confident that he would find a disagreement between their writings and the teachings of the Catholic Church in England in his day.

What was the result? So striking was the agreement, yes, even the identity of doctrine which he discovered, that he perceived that there could be no shadow of doubt that the teachings of the Catholic Church were the teachings of the early Fathers, of the Apostles and of Christ Himself. It was this clear proof of the Church's apostolicity of doctrine that brought that brilliant mind into the fold, though it cost him the sacrifice of his friends and relatives, his high position and worldly gain. And with him came over such a distinguished number of Oxford scholars that the movement has gone down in history as the *Oxford Movement.*

These, in short, are the four marks which will guide the searcher after truth to the Church founded by Christ. These are the bright beacon lights that will guide the pilgrim in his search for truth into the true fold. Indeed, so clearly and so unmistakably are they the marks of the Catholic Church that she holds that any one who approaches this subject with an open, unbiased mind, and studies it carefully, can scarcely fail to be

24

convinced of the divine character of the Catholic faith. She asks no one to enter without first being convinced of the truthfulness of her claims, confident that Christ has stamped upon her the unmistakable sign of her divine origin and the indelible seal of His abiding presence. But when that truth is realized, may no temporal motive or fear of worldly loss keep the inquirer from entrance into the Church of Jesus Christ.

Discussion Aids

What is the teaching of the Church on the Trinity? How many Persons are in the Trinity? How many natures? Is belief in the Trinity against our reason? How many Persons are there in Jesus Christ? How many natures?

What was the mission of the Son of God among us?

What was the mission of the Son of God among us? Sketch briefly the background of His life on earth. Discuss the following in relation to the accomplishment of His mission: I. The Crucifixion: our reverence for the cross. II. The Resurrection (confirming miracle of divine power). III. Ascension (in order to send the Holy Spirit). IV. Pentecost (divine life instilled into Church). What is the teaching of the Church on heaven? On hell? On sin?

What are marks of the Church? Are they inherent in the nature of the Church or did Christ make them and superimpose them as labels? Could the Church be the true Church of Christ lacking any one of the marks? Discuss unity and catholicity together. Test the persistence of these two marks through 1900 years as a miraculous phenomenon. Can men sanctify themselves without divine aid? Is the finger of God evident in all four marks of the true Church?

Practices

Make the sign of the cross without haste and with reflection.

Make a morning offering of all your thoughts, words, and deeds in union with Christ for the salvation of the world.

Be regular and devout in going to the sacraments, thus displaying your faith in the teachings of the Church.

NOTES (Chapter 1)

1. Is. 53:5
2. II Cor. 4:10
3. Gal. 6:14
4. De Corona, C. iii
5. Mt. 25:34
6. I Cor. 2:9
7. *Ibid.*, 13:12
8. *Religion Outlines for Colleges,* Vol. 2, p. 21 (Catholic University Press, Washington, D.C.)
9. *The Question Box,* p. 388 (The Paulist Press, N.Y.)
10. Gal. 1:8-12
11. Eph. 5:25-27
12. Thomas B. Macaulay in his essay, "Ranke's History of the Popes," in *The Miscellaneous Work of Lord Macaulay,* Vol. IV, pp. 366-367 (G.P. Putnam's Sons, N.Y.)

CHAPTER 2

Is One Religion as Good as Another?

A Plain Answer to a Common Question

In maintaining that one religion is as good as another, regardless of how much the various religions differ from one another, the indifferentist makes an assertion which is opposed to the very first principle of logic and common sense as well. It is a law of logic that contradictory statements cannot be true at the same time. If one statement is true, then all the statements which contradict it are false. Deny this principle of logic and you deny all possibility of correct human reasoning.

Thus, for example, a teacher holds before a class of fifteen pupils a sheet of white paper, asking each pupil to state the color of the paper. He hears fifteen divergent answers. One says it is "blue"; another, "red"; another, "purple"; another, "yellow"; another, "green"; and so on down to the fifteenth pupil, who alone says it is "white." Let us suppose that the teacher has so much affection for every member of his class that he tells them that they are all correct, rather than that they are all wrong save one.

Suppose then that he were thus to address them after the fashion of the indifferentist: "Children, you are all equally correct. You, who say it is purple, you who say it is red, you who say it is green, and all the rest of you are equally correct with the pupil who says it is white. Each one of you is correct and no one of you is wrong." While one might not be disposed to question the affection and large-heartedness of such a teacher, everyone would be compelled to question his *sanity*. In giving full rein to the impulses of the heart, he stifles all the dictates of reason and common sense. He is able to agree with these fifteen divergent answers simultaneously only at the cost of intellectual suicide.

Is it not passing strange that people will recognize the validity of this elementary principle of logic in all the practical concerns of their daily life, and then upon entering the domain of religion promptly proceed to throw it overboard? Yet that is precisely what the indifferentist does. He attempts the same impossible mental gymnastics as the teacher above described.

Do not the various denominations differ from one another just as obviously and flagrantly as the pupils did in their answers? Thus in answer to the question, "How many persons are there in God?" the Unitarian replies, "Only one," while the Methodist answers, "Three: the Father, the Son and the Holy Spirit." Is it possible for any person to say in reply: "I agree with both of you. You are both correct"? Not without destroying all possibility of correct human reasoning.

This instance of difference in doctrine between the Methodist and the Unitarian can be paralleled on down the line among all the creeds. Each sect constitutes a distinct denomination only because it differs on some one or more important doctrines from all the other creeds. Thus Baptists reject infant baptism as invalid, while Lutherans regard it as valid. Catholics believe that the Holy Eucharist contains the body and blood, soul and divinity of our Savior, while Presbyterians regard Holy Communion as merely a symbol or reminder of Christ.

These are the differences which Pope Pius XI, in his encyclical on "True Religious Unity," points out as frustrating all efforts of Pan-Christians at attaining real unity. "Through what agreement," he asks, "could men of opposed opinions become one and the same society of the faithful? How, for example, can they who affirm that sacred tradition is a true source of divine revelation and they who deny it, become members of one Church? They who hold that an ecclesiastical hierarchy formed of bishops, priests and ministers is divinely constituted and they who assert that little by little it has been introduced through conditions of time and events? They who adore Christ really present in the Most Holy Eucharist by that wonderful change of bread and wine called transubstantiation, and they who say that the

Body of Christ is present there only by faith or through the sign and power of the sacrament; they who hold that in the Eucharist there is a true sacrifice as well as a sacrament, and they who say that it is only a remembrance or commemoration of the sufferings of our Lord? . . .

"In such great differences of opinions we do not know how a road may be paved to the unity of the Church save alone through one teaching authority, one sole law of belief and one sole faith among Christians. Moreover, we know how easy is the path to neglect of religion, to indifferentism and also to modernism which holds the very same error, to wit: Dogmatic truth is not absolute but relative, it is proportionate to the different needs of times and places and to the various tendencies of the mind since it is not based upon an unchanging revelation, but is to be accommodated to the life of men."[1]

From these fundamental differences in doctrine there flow practical corollaries of far-reaching consequences. If the Unitarian be right when he says Christ is a mere man, then the Anglican who esteems Him as divine and so adores Him becomes guilty of idolatry. By the same token, if the Anglican is right, then the Unitarian who denies His divinity, and refuses to worship Him as divine, but treats Him as a mere human, becomes guilty of blasphemy. In other words, the proposition of the indifferentist that all creeds are equally good, really means in its concrete significance that vice is as good as virtue, falsehood as good as truth, and idolatry as good as true worship. It means also the obliteration of all *objective* criteria for the determination of truth and the denial of all human reason.

There may be some, however, who will say that the principle of the indifferentists that one religion is as good as another is valid if applied only to the various denominations of Protestantism. Even this expedient will not avail. While the principle of private judgment is basic among all Protestant sects, yet they differ from one another in the objective doctrines which they believe. Thus the pathetic complaint of Theodore Beza, one of the early reformers of the sixteenth century, is as true as when he uttered it. "Our people," he bewails, "are carried away by every wind of doctrine. If you know what their religion is today, you cannot tell what it may be tomorrow. In what single point

29

are those churches, which declared war against the Pope, united among themselves? There is not one point which is not held by some of them as an article of the faith and by others rejected as an impiety."[2]

Thus it is seen that, when held up to the light of reason, indifferentism stands condemned as intrinsically repugnant, inasmuch as it obliterates all distinctions between truth and error. We would be justified in resting our case here after having secured such an indictment of indifferentism before the bar of *human* reason. Because of the importance of the issues involved, however, we shall lay the case before the tribunal of *divine* revelation; we shall ascertain if the voice of eternal truth speaks in accents different from the voice of human reason.

Time was when Christians were willing to follow the example of their divine Master and His Apostles in braving torture and death itself rather than deny or even modify the tenets of their religious faith. For their refusal to deny Christ and offer incense to the idols of pagan Rome, hundreds of Christians in the first three centuries were thrown into the Roman amphitheatre to be torn limb from limb by savage beasts of the arena, while many others were coated with pitch and tar and burned alive to illumine at night the courses for the chariot races of the Romans![3]

Still fresh in the minds of these early Christians was that memorable scene wherein Christ had set them the example of unswerving loyalty to the truths of supernatural revelation at the cost of life itself. The dramatic scene was enacted before the high priest, Caiphas, in the crowded courtroom of the Jewish Sanhedrin on the eve of His death. Rising from his seat, Caiphas addressed Christ with the challenging words: "I adjure Thee by the living God, that Thou tell us if Thou be the Christ, the Son of God."[4]

Now there was a law among the Jews that subjected to capital punishment the person who claimed divine honors. Christ knew full well that, if He answered that question in the affirmative, He was sealing His own death warrant. He knew also that if He would but deny His divinity, the Jews would have no legal charge against Him and He could escape the impending tragedy. In the face of this knowledge, without equivocation or evasion, but with rapier-like precision, the Master answered simply and clearly: "Thou hast said it." And forthwith they led Him out to be crucified.

Hence Christ went to His death upon the ignominious cross rather than save His life by modifying in the slightest degree one single tenet of His teaching. That was the example which loomed up before the minds of the Christian world for centuries, prompting them to an unfaltering loyalty to His teachings, and causing them to regard orthodoxy of faith as of supreme importance. It precluded the acceptance of the viewpoint that it is a matter of comparative indifference whether one accepts or modifies the teachings for which Christ died.

The procedure of Christ in refusing to soften or tone down His answer to the question of Caiphas to suit the prejudices of the Jewish Sanhedrin is typical of His manner of teaching during His entire public ministry. It is clear, therefore, that Christ Himself was no indifferentist.

Let us inquire now if Christ imposed the same obligation upon His disciples and all those who would come to the knowledge of the faith through their teaching. If Christ did this, then religious indifferentism stands condemned before the tribunal of divine revelation.

Let us examine, therefore, the very words with which our divine Savior establishes His Church and commissions the Apostles to preach the gospel. To obviate any objection from our non-Catholic readers, the texts which follow immediately are taken from the Protestant version of the Bible. These are the words of Christ to the Apostles: "All power is given unto Me in heaven and in earth. Go ye, therefore, and teach all nations, baptizing men in the name of the Father, and the Son, and the Holy Spirit, teaching them to observe all things whatsoever I have commanded you: and, lo, I am with you always, even unto the end of the world."[5] "And He said to them, Go ye into all the world, and preach the gospel to every creature. He that believeth and is baptized shall be saved; but he that believeth not shall be damned."[6]

From these words of Christ, a twofold obligation is evident. First, the Apostles are commissioned to preach the gospel to all nations without exception. Christ came to save the souls of all

31

mankind. He wanted His religion, therefore, to become the universal religion of the whole human race. If any race or even any individual would refuse to accept His religion, the aim and purpose of the divine revelation would to that extent be frustrated.

Secondly, Christ imposed upon the Apostles the obligation of teaching the same identical doctrines which He had taught them: "Teaching them to observe *all things whatsoever I have commanded you.*" In other words, the Apostles were not to teach different doctrines in accordance with the divergent whims and fancies of each individual. On the contrary, they were charged to teach "all things whatsoever" Christ had delivered unto them. They were given no liberty to teach one doctrine and reject another. Thus the entire Christian gospel hung together as one great organic whole: this, they were to impart, without omission or addition, without change or mutilation, to the whole world.

Having established the fact that Christ charged His Apostles to teach the same identical truths to all nations, the question may still remain in the minds of some as to whether Christ made the acceptance of the gospel message obligatory upon the hearers or left them free to accept, modify, or reject the same. It will become evident upon reflection, however, that Christ could not logically confer upon the Apostles the moral power and authority of preaching the gospel to the multitudes without placing upon the latter the correlative duty of accepting it; for every right implies a corresponding duty on the part of another to respect that right. Hence the solemn delegation to the Apostles of the moral power of teaching with authority would be meaningless and contradictory if Christ did not impose the corresponding obligation on the part of the hearers to receive their message.

We shall not content ourselves, however, with this answer to the question — an answer clearly implied in Christ's mandate to the Apostles. Christ Himself has put in explicit form the duty on the part of the hearers, which is implicit in His commission to the Apostles. After His charge to the Apostles, He clearly defines the duty of the auditors of the gospel message by adding immediately: "He that believeth and is baptized shall be saved; but he that disbelieveth shall be condemned."[7] From these clear words of our Divine Master it is apparent that He gave to the auditors no more freedom to reject the teachings than He gave to the Apostles to modify them.

He had come upon earth to reveal these supernatural truths, and He made it as mandatory on the part of the listeners to accept the revelation as it was mandatory for the Apostles to preach it. The exponent of the theory, that it does not matter much what a man believes, finds therefore that his theory is the direct opposite of the teaching of Christ on the necessity of believing the precise doctrine which He committed to the world through the teaching of the Apostles. Not only does Christ insist upon the acceptance of His divinely revealed truths by every hearer, but He makes it the indispensable condition for eternal salvation.

Christ did not stop, however, with commissioning the Apostles to teach His doctrines. To counteract any impression on their part that they were not able correctly to present His truths, and to remove any misgivings that might be felt by the hearers on the ground that the Apostles, being human and fallible, might unconsciously mislead them, the divine Master hastened to assure the Apostles of His abiding presence and ceaseless assistance, saying: "And lo, I am with you always even unto the end of the world."[8] "But the Comforter, the Holy Spirit, whom the Father will send in My name, He shall teach you all things, and bring to your remembrance all that I said unto you."[9]

Hence while the Apostles of themselves were fallible, Christ gave the assurance that in the mission of preaching His doctrines, He would be with them all days, safeguarding them from error and stamping their teachings with the seal of His own divine approval. In the same manner as the Father had commissioned, so He authorized them, saying: "As the Father hath sent Me so I send you."[10]

Moreover, "this same absolute oneness of faith and religion," as Otten points out, "implied in Christ's commission to His Apostles, is inferred with equal clearness from every reference which He makes to His Church. That Church He always speaks of as one, not as many. He speaks of it as one family, one fold, one city, one kingdom. He builds it upon one foundation, the rock, which is Peter. He appoints but one supreme pastor to feed His lambs and to guard His sheep; but one vicar to whom

He gives the keys of the Kingdom of Heaven. He seems to have multiplied illustration upon illustration, and figure upon figure, in order to impress upon His Apostles the absolute necessity of unity in the faith."[11]

Indeed, so insistent was Christ upon unity of faith that the gospels portray Him emphasizing this truth in season and out of season. Thus on the very eve of His passion, He made it the special object of His prayer: "Holy Father, keep them in Thy name which Thou has given Me; that they may be one, even as We are."[12] To make it apparent that He intended this unity not only for His Apostles but for all the countless multitudes who in the ages yet to come would believe in Him, Christ added the significant words: "Neither for these only (the Apostles) do I pray, but for them also that believe in Me through their word; that they may all be one."[13]

This dominant emphasis of Christ upon the necessity of unity of faith is reechoed by the Apostles in their teaching ministry. Faithfully indeed did they discharge the sacred mission entrusted to them. With steadfast loyalty to their divine Master, they exemplified that unity in their own lives and counselled their followers to hold fast to that same unity of faith. Thus the indefatigable Apostle of the Gentiles writes to the Ephesians: "I, therefore, a prisoner in the Lord, beseech you to walk worthily of the calling wherewith you were called. . . . There is one body and one Spirit, even as also ye were called in one hope of your calling; one Lord, one faith, one baptism, one God and Father of all."[14]

What can the modern advocate of religious indifferentism say, when confronted with the scorching condemnation of discord in doctrine and the lack of unity in belief, which St. Paul meted out to the Galatians, when he discovered some of them wavering in the faith which He had delivered unto them? "I marvel," he writes, "that ye are so quickly removing from him that called you in grace of Christ unto a different gospel; which is not another gospel; only there are some that trouble you, and would pervert the gospel of Christ. But though we, or an angel from heaven, should preach unto you any gospel other than that which we preached unto you, let him be anathema. As we have said before, so say I now again: If any man preacheth unto you any gospel other than that which ye received, let him be anathema. . . . For I make known to you, brethren, as touching the gospel which was preached by me, that it is not after man. For neither did I receive it from man, nor was I taught it, but it came to me through revelation of Jesus Christ."[15]

It is evident, therefore, that the great Apostle of the Gentiles, in common with the other Apostles, regarded a distortion or modification of any part of the divine revelation as deserving of the severest censures. Of the indifferentist who asserts that doctrinal differences are inconsequential as all creeds are about equally good, St. Paul says in effect: "Let a man who preaches to you a doctrine different from the gospel delivered to you by Christ and the Apostles, be shunned as a heretic, who would pervert your faith. Let him be regarded as a most insidious danger to your true faith, and if such a one after the first admonition still persists in his heresy, he is to be excommunicated from your midst." These words may sound stern, but they are no more so than the words of the gentle Jesus: "He that believeth not, shall be damned."[16]

Isn't sincerity of belief in any religious faith sufficient for salvation? One must distinguish between sincerity as a subjective quality, an attitude of the mind, and as a substitute for objective truth and for reasonable efforts to find it.

Sincerity, as a subjective quality, like the sentiment of good will and friendliness in the attitude of the religious indifferentist, is very commonly respected. But sincerity, like good will, must have eyes; it must be directed by intelligence; otherwise it will be led by blind emotion and serve merely to bolster falsehood. Sincerity, however, *as a substitute for objective truth and for reasonable efforts to discover it,* in the sense in which it is used by the religious indifferentist, is wrong and worthy only of condemnation.

If, because of prejudices which one cannot eradicate or because of other circumstances beyond his control, he does not find the true faith of Christ but believes in his own creed with sincerity and good faith, then he is not culpable in the eyes of God. Here is a case where sincerity is proved through earnest and reasonable effort to find the objective truth.

This is the clear teaching of Pope Pius IX, who in 1854 and

1863 declared: "We must . . . recognize with certainty that those who are in invincible ignorance of the true religion are not guilty of this in the eyes of God . . . and may, aided by the light of divine grace, attain to eternal life. God . . . by no means permits that anyone suffer eternal punishment who has not of his own free will fallen into sin. . . . And who will presume to mark out the limits of this ignorance and diversity of peoples, countries, minds and the rest?"

Reflecting the infallible teaching of the Supreme Pontiff, the Baltimore Catechism says: "They who remain outside the Catholic Church through no grave fault of their own and do not know it is the true Church, can be saved by making use of the graces which God gives them. Those who are outside the Church through no fault of their own are not culpable in the sight of God because of their invincible ignorance."

Contrary to the impression of many outside her fold, the Catholic Church is the most broad-minded and the most reasonable institution in the world. As an organization reflecting the mind of Christ and perpetuating His teachings, she would be bound to be the last word in kindliness and in reasonableness. Though she opposes every heresy, as Christ obliges her to do, she loves the heretic: though she fights sin with all her power and resourcefulness, she loves the sinner and never despairs of winning him to a life of virtue and holiness. She holds ajar the door of salvation for every human being; only he who acts contrary to the light of his own conscience and who refuses to investigate if he doubts closes the door upon himself.

A final question remains. "How is it, then," asks the person affected by the viewpoint of the indifferentist, "if membership in the true religion is so essential for eternal salvation, and therefore presumably for right living, that there are persons who are not members of the Church of Christ, but are professed agnostics who yet lead good lives and are highly respected citizens?" The answer is to be found in the fact that such persons living in a society permeated with Christian ideals are profoundly influenced, consciously or unconsciously, by the moral standards and the code of ethics inspired by the teachings of Christ. It will usually be found, upon analysis, that every trait which commends them in the eyes of their fellow citizens is traceable to the standards of conduct inculcated by the religion of Christ; they are good citizens not *because* of their agnosticism or atheism, but *in spite* of it.

Suppose a boy were to take his sled to the top of a hill two blocks long, and then coast down. After he has reached the bottom of the hill, his sled continues to travel rapidly along the level ground. If a person standing a block beyond the bottom of the hill were to see the youngster gliding rapidly over the level ground and did not raise his eyes to perceive the hill in the background, he might hold the following soliloquy: "What a marvelous invention that must be! A sled that is drawn by no horse, nor propelled by a motor, and yet travels rapidly along level ground!"

The mystery would fade away, however, when once he raised his eyes to the hill whence the sled derived its momentum and energy. Coasting along now on even ground, it is traveling on *borrowed* power. So it is with the irreligious person in a society saturated with Christian ideals and standards. He is running on borrowed power. Consciously or unconsciously he is influenced at every turn by the group standards which are in the main the result of nineteen centuries of leavening by the Christian religion.

Such a person is essentially a moral parasite. As Balfour in his *Foundations of Belief* observes: "Biologists tell us of parasites which live, and can only live, in the bodies of animals more highly organized than they. . . . So it is with those persons who claim to show by their example that naturalism is practically consistent with the maintenance of ethical ideals with which naturalism has no natural affinity. Their spirit life is parasitic; it is sheltered by convictions which belong not to them, but to the society of which they form a part; it is nourished by processes in which they take no share. And when these convictions decay, and these processes come to an end, the alien life which they have maintained can scarce be expected to outlast them."

Furthermore, when a person without any religious belief strays from the path of rectitude, the task of reclaiming such an individual is immensely more difficult than in the case of his religious neighbor. Why? Because there are so few functional incentives that can be brought to bear upon his conscience.

If the Ten Commandments be regarded as but temporary laws evolved out of the consciousness of the Semitic race, which become obsolete if God's existence is questioned and the fact of immortality is denied, what basis for the observance of the moral law remains? The individual knows that he can escape the penalty decreed by the civil law as well as the social opprobrium which generally falls only upon the culprit so awkward as to be detected in his misdemeanor.

With the person of definite religious faith, however, the story is different. Here there is an abundance of supernatural incentives which spring directly from the Christian religion. Unlike the ones decreed by civil legislation, and which are dependent for their efficacy upon clumsy, fallible human agents for their enforcement, the sanctions of religion are applied with unerring certainty by the all-seeing eye of Almighty God. The religious-minded individual may be said, therefore, to have a policeman always with him in the form of his own conscience.

It was this profound truth concerning the necessity of religion as a firm and enduring foundation for proper moral conduct which Washington voiced in his famous farewell address — a warning which needs to be kept always before the eyes of the people of America: "Let us with caution indulge the supposition that morality can be maintained without religion. Whatever may be conceded to the influence of refined education on minds of peculiar structure, reason and experience both forbid us to expect that national morality can prevail in exclusion of religious principle."

Hence a religious faith helps not only to restrain an individual from falling but also to reclaim him if he has violated a moral law in spite of the protests of his own conscience. "The true Christian," as that careful student of the religious life, Father Bertrand L. Conway, C.S.P., aptly points out, "may under stress of temptation fall into the worst vices of the pagan, and give the lie to his high profession. But no matter how low he may fall, he falls *from a standard*, and you may appeal to him. He has once climbed up the mount of God, and he knows that with God's help he can again reach the summit. But if a man feels confident that every lapse is due merely to the evil of environment, a taint in the blood, or the impelling force of a stronger

38

will, he will not answer your appeal to higher things. He calls evil good, and good evil."[17]

From what has been said it is evident that religious indifferentism has as its basic underlying principle the subjectivism which Martin Luther brought into the world by the establishment of private judgment as the supreme guide in one's religious life. It is the twentieth century harvest of the seeds of religious chaos and anarchy which were sown by the misguided reformers in the sixteenth century. Indifferentism has become the common philosophy of religion among the great masses of people in America. It serves as an unhealthy sedative, lulling the mind into a sense of false security, and deterring it from the vigorous restless search for objective truth.

Its falseness must first be exposed in order to gain a hearing for the claims of the Catholic Church to be the one true Church established by Christ and designed by Him as the Church of all mankind. When the implications of religious indifferentism are made clear, it becomes apparent that it is opposed both to natural reason and to divine revelation. It contradicts the elementary principles of logic and the dictates of common sense. Beneath its pleasant surface lurks a virus which is poisoning the American people and making them sick unto death.

It was therefore a timely note which our Holy Father, Pius XI, sounded in his encyclical on "Religious Unity" when he pointed out to the nations groping in the twilight of error and confusion, that true religious unity is to be achieved not by the external federation of churches while each retains its own doctrinal creed, but by the separated Churches returning to the fold of the Mother Church and embracing again the faith of their fathers. There is the tender note of a father's solicitude that echoes in his pleading for the return of the sheep that strayed from the true fold.

"Let these separated children,"[18] entreats His Holiness, "return to the Apostolic See established in this city which the Princes of the Apostles, Peter and Paul, consecrated with their blood, to this See, 'the root and matrix of the Catholic Church'[19] not indeed with the idea or hope that 'the Church of the living God, the pillar and ground of truth'[20] will abandon the integrity of the faith and bear their errors, but to subject themselves to its teaching authority and rule. Would that what has not been granted to Our predecessors would be granted to Us, to embrace with the heart of a father the children over whom We mourn in their separation from Us by evil discord. May God Our Savior 'Who will have all men to be saved and to come to the knowledge of the truth'[21] hearken to Our ardent prayer and vouchsafe to call back all the wanderers to the unity of the Church!

"In behalf of which lofty intention We invoke the intercession of the Blessed Virgin Mary, Mother of Divine Grace, Conqueror of all heresies and Help of Christians that soon there may dawn that longed-for day when all men will hear the voice of her Divine Son 'keeping the unity of the Spirit in the bond of peace.'[22] You know well how much We want their return; and We desire, too, that all Our children know it and not only they of the Catholic world but all who are separated from Us. If they who are separated from Us will ask in humble prayer the grace of God, there is no doubt but that they will recognize the one true Church of Jesus Christ and enter it united at last with Us in perfect charity."

Here is a consummation devoutly to be wished — the restoration of a united Christendom. In the achievement of that great objective, the healing of the breaches that for four centuries and more have divided the Christian world, there would be removed the sources whence issue much of the misunderstanding and rancors which keep the world in turmoil and unrest.

Discussion Aids

Analyze indifferentism in the light of human reason. Examine the doctrines of various denominations to show lack of logic.

Analyze indifferentism in the light of divine revelation.

Was Christ an indifferentist? Support your opinion with examples from His life.

Examine the great charter of the Church (Matthew 28: 18-20) for:

1. Twofold obligation imposed on the teaching Church.

2. Obligation of those taught to accept these teachings. (See also Mark 16: 15-16.)

3. Christ's infallible support of doctrine.

Give two additional examples of Christ's insistence upon unity of faith (John 17:11, 20).

Discuss St. Paul's teaching on unity of faith, analyzing especially Ephesians 4: 1-6 and Galatians 1: 6-13.

Define "body" of the Church; "soul" of the Church. What is the proper interpretation of "Outside the Church no salvation"?

What is a religious parasite? A moral parasite? Why is it harder to win an irreligious person than to reclaim a fallen-away?

Summarize the case against indifferentism and for unity as given in author's conclusion.

Practices

Form the habit of reading a chapter of the Scriptures daily, thus learning to know Christ at first hand.

Devote some of your material substance, saved preferably from the sacrifice of some pleasure, to a missionary cause.

When permitted your own choice for a term paper or shorter exercise, use a subject concerned with Catholic history or doctrine.

NOTES (Chapter 2)

1. Cf. I Tm. 2:5
2. *Epist. ad Aud. Dudit*
3. Aube, "Histoire des persecutions de l'Eglise," p. 99; de Rossi-Duchesne, "Martyrologium hieronymianum," p. 84
4. Mt. 26:63
5. *Ibid.,* 28:18-20
6. Mk. 16:15-16
7. *Ibid.,* 16:16
8. Mt. 28:20
9. Jn. 14:26
10. *Ibid.,* 20:21

11. B.J. Otten, *The Reason Why*, p. 300 (B. Herder Co., St. Louis)
12. Jn. 17:11
13. *Ibid.*, 17:20-21
14. Eph. 4:1-6
15. Gal. 1:6-13
16. Mk. 16:16
17. *Best Sermons*, 1926, p. 145 (Harcourt Brace & Co., N.Y.)
18. Encyclical on "Religious Unity"
19. S. Cyp. Ep. 49 and Cornelium, 3
20. I Tm. 3:15
21. *Ibid.*, 2:4
22. Eph. 4:3

CHAPTER 3

Which Is Christ's True Church?

Evidence So Clear That He Who Runs May Read

When a person, after careful consideration, comes to perceive the fallacy of the common saying, "All religions are equally good and true," and realizes that it does "matter what a man believes," he finds himself confronted with two important questions: (1) Which is the true Church? (2) How can I discover it?

The answer might be obtained by finding out which Church possesses the marks of unity, sanctity, catholicity and apostolicity, for these are the marks which Christ imprinted upon His Church to distinguish her from all others. It might prove somewhat tedious, however, to examine all of the several hundred Christian denominations to discover if any one of them possesses all these characteristics.

Moreover, there is a shorter way of answering the query, "Which is the true Church?" This shorter way is by discovering first: Which is the Church *founded* by Jesus Christ? If one can discover a Church founded directly and immediately by Christ and authorized to teach in His name, and to which He promised the abiding presence of the Spirit of Truth, then one can be certain that, if the true Church is to be found anywhere on the earth, it must be that institution of which Christ Himself is the Founder.

In maintaining that the facts of history stamp the Catholic Church as the one true Church established by Christ for all mankind, the writer does not wish to convey the impression that the

Church regards all non-Catholics as outside the pale of salvation. Indeed, the broad-mindedness and maternal solicitude of the Church for the salvation of all mankind are nowhere more strikingly apparent than in her teaching that people, even though not in visible communion with Christ's true Church, *may* nevertheless be saved if they act according to the sincere conviction of their own conscience.

No man is guilty in the eyes of God, says the Church, except he who acts contrary to the light of his own conscience. All people who are true to the commands of conscience are related in some way to the Church, and will be rewarded by God for their fidelity. Even though they are objectively wrong, they are in good faith and therefore blameless in the sight of God.

There is a duty, however, resting upon everyone to search for the truth, and thus to enlighten his conscience so that it will honestly reflect the objective realities, instead of the distorted caricatures of the truth which spring from ignorance, prejudice and misunderstanding. The writer asks but one favor of the non-Catholic reader: that he examine the evidence with an *open* mind. If he will do this, the writer is confident that the facts of history will make the same powerful appeal to his mind that they have made to the hundreds of millions of honest men and women who during nineteen hundred years have clung to the Catholic faith as "the pearl that passeth all price."

Turn now to the pages of any reliable history, whether written by Jew, Protestant, Catholic, or nonbeliever, and you will find that there is unanimous agreement among all historians that the Catholic Church at least was founded by Christ. The evidence of the Holy Scriptures, considered simply as historical documents, is too overwhelming to permit any doubt or quibbling on this point. Let us look at the solemn words whereby our divine Savior founded His Church and then clothed it with the power and authority to teach all mankind in His name. The credentials are confined to no one gospel, but are to be found in all four. The words are simple. Their meaning is unmistakable.

It is Christ Himself who is speaking to the Apostles: "As the Father sent Me, I also send you."[1] "All power is given to Me in heaven and in earth. Going therefore, teach ye all nations; baptizing them in the name of the Father and of the Son, and of the

Holy Spirit, teaching them to observe all things whatsoever I have commanded you: and behold I am with you all days, even to the consummation of the world."[2]

These words constitute the evidence of the Church's divinely appointed mission to teach the truths of Christ to all nations. They constitute the charter which the Church is to present to every generation as the imperishable credentials of her delegation as the duly accredited agency to teach in the name and with the authority of Jesus Christ. That the people hearing this teaching are not to regard themselves as free to accept or reject it, is made likewise clear by our divine Master: "Go ye into the whole world, and preach the gospel to every creature. He that believeth and is baptized, will be saved: but he that believeth not, shall be condemned."[3] With equal clarity, St. Luke presents this same insistence of Christ on the duty of the faithful to accept the gospel because of the authority which lies behind it: "He that heareth you, heareth Me, and he that despiseth you, despiseth Me; and he that despiseth Me, despiseth Him that sent Me."[4]

From these clear words of Christ it is evident that our divine Savior did not follow the procedure imagined by many people today: the lackadaisical procedure of merely uttering certain religious and moral truths without establishing any institution to interpret and to transmit them to future generations. The idea that Jesus simply enunciated certain truths, and failed to provide any responsible agency for the transmission of these teachings to all mankind, is not only uncomplimentary to the wisdom of Jesus and to His solicitude for the salvation of all mankind, but it also finds no warrant in Holy Scripture. To have placed upon each individual who was to be born into the world the task of ferreting out for himself from the mists of the historic past the precise teachings of Jesus, and the equally difficult task of interpreting them with unerring accuracy, would have been a procedure which would have foredoomed His enterprise to certain and inevitable failure.

The overwhelming majority of mankind has neither the time nor the ability to accomplish so Herculean a task. It is to be remembered that not only was the printing press not then in existence, but that even the art of writing was the accomplishment of few. Furthermore, there is no evidence that Christ ever

45

wrote a line, or that He commanded any of His disciples to write.

On the contrary, His command to the Apostles was to preach, to teach, in season and out of season. This method renders it possible for the teacher to adapt the presentation of the Master's teachings to the varied capacities of his hearers to understand. It is the only effective method for the transmission of Christ's legacy of truth to mankind; it is the method, as the Scriptures disclose with unmistakable clearness, that Christ actually adopted. The impression so prevalent in non-Catholic circles, that Christ simply uttered certain truths nineteen centuries ago, and then allows every individual to sink or swim in accordance with his ability to ferret out and to interpret for himself the precise meaning of His teachings, finds no support in the pages of Holy Writ.

Hence it is most important that men and women nowadays be brought to realize these fundamental facts of history:

1. Jesus Christ actually founded a Church.

2. He conferred upon that Church that jurisdiction and the power to teach all mankind.

3. The Church which Christ founded and clothed with such power and authority is the Catholic Church.

From the above historical facts there follows with inexorable logic the simple conclusion: The Catholic Church is the one true Church established by Jesus Christ for the salvation of all mankind. Is there any possible escape from this conclusion? While admitting, as all men must admit, that the Catholic Church was founded by Jesus Christ, some have sought to escape from this conclusion by alleging that the Catholic Church in the course of ages ceased to teach the pure truths of Christ, introduced error, and therefore is not today to be regarded as the true Church.

But this can be true only if our Savior broke the promises He made to His Church when He said: "And behold, I am with you all days, even unto the consummation of the world," and "Upon this rock I will build My Church, and the gates of hell shall not prevail against it."[5] If Christ broke those solemn promises, then we can confidently affirm that there is not today anywhere on the face of the earth the true Church of God. That

Christ did not break His pledge is evident from the fact that the Catholic Church is the only institution in Christendom which has come down through nineteen hundred years teaching the world today the same deposit of divine truth which she taught to the Greeks and Romans, the Medes and the Persians, in the first century.

The Church has suffered from kings and emperors, from the days of Nero to those of communist terrorism and persecution in our own; in every land her children have suffered martyrdom for the faith. They have braved the executioner's sword. They have faced the wild lions in the Roman arena. They have withstood the burning fagots at the martyr's stake. Neither have they quailed before the firing squads of our own day.

The Church has witnessed the despoliation of her property by Henry VIII and the captivity of her supreme pontiff by Napoleon Bonaparte; but she has not surrendered, either for king or peasant, one single jot or tittle of those divinely revealed truths which Jesus Christ commanded her to proclaim to all the nations of the world until the crack of doom.

She has withstood the acids of modern unbelief which have eaten so deeply into the traditional fabrics of other faiths; she has refused to surrender to the gilded paganism of the day, and has never lowered her ethical standards to suit the demands of a pleasure-loving world. She has refused to make compromise with Caesar by surrendering any of her sovereignty in the spiritual domain to the heightened nationalism and secularism of the day: she preaches "Jesus Christ . . . yesterday and today, yes, and forever."[6] This perpetuity of the Church, this survival through all the ages without the surrender of any of her truths and without ever ceasing to carry her divine deposit of doctrine to all the nations of the world, is the striking evidence that Christ has kept His promise to be with her all days. The Catholic Church today is as truly the Church of Christ as when she first came from the hands of her Divine Founder nineteen centuries ago in Judea. This is shown in four charts that follow.

Chart I (page 48), *The Voice of History*, shows that the Catholic Church is the only Church in the world today which traces her origin back to Christ. It shows that she alone was founded by Christ, while all other Churches were established by

47

CHART I

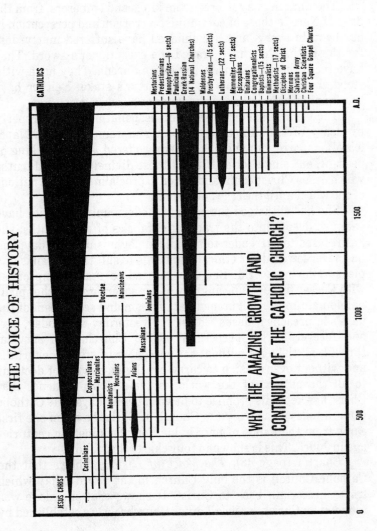

THE VOICE OF HISTORY

CATHOLICS

JESUS CHRIST

Cerinthians
Corporatians
Marcionites
Montanists — Novatians
Arians
Massalians
Docetae
Manicheons
Jovinians

Nestorians
Predestinarians
Monophysites—(6 sects)
Paulicans
Greek-Russian (14 National Churches)
Waldenses
Presbyterians—(15 sects)
Lutherans—(22 sects)
Mennonites—(12 sects)
Episcopalians
Unitarians
Congregationalists
Baptists—(15 sects)
Universalists
Methodists—(17 sects)
Disciples of Christ
Mormons
Salvation Army
Christian Scientists
Four Square Gospel Church

WHY THE AMAZING GROWTH AND
CONTINUITY OF THE CATHOLIC CHURCH?

0   500   1000   1500   A.D.

48

men. It brings this into such clear relief that even he who runs may see that the Catholic Church, with Christ for her founder and protector through all the centuries, is the one true Church of Christ on earth.

The vertical lines indicate the centuries of the Christian era. The horizontal lines represent some of the larger and more important of the many hundreds of religious denominations that have risen during the past nineteen centuries. Those lines indicate the duration of the various sects by beginning at the respective dates of origin and ceasing when they disappeared. The width of the line shows the approximate size of the denomination.

Protestantism, it is to be noted, first appears upon the earth in the sixteenth century, in contrast to the Catholic Church, which had been in existence at that time for fifteen hundred years, having been founded by Jesus Christ in Jerusalem in the year 33 A.D.

While the term "Protestantism" had its origin at the Diet of Spires in Germany in 1529, the first manifestation of the movement occurred when Martin Luther nailed his theses to the doors of the church at Wittenberg on October 31, 1517. All the other Protestant denominations were started by various human founders since that time. Contrast the divine origin of the Catholic Church with the human origins of all the Protestant churches.

Chart II (page 50), *Christ or Luther?*, contrasts the divine origin of the Catholic Church and the human origin of Protestantism. It shows that the problem of deciding which is the true Church boils down to the question: Whom are you to believe — Martin Luther, the founder of Protestantism, or Jesus Christ, the divine founder of the Catholic Church? That is the whole problem in a nutshell.

Chart III (page 51), *A Gap of Fifteen Centuries*, focuses attention upon the *telltale* gap of fifteen centuries that yawns between the foundation of Christ's Church in the year 33 to the establishment of Lutheranism, the first form of Protestantism, in 1524. Why is that gap significant? Because it brings out so clearly and so simply the fact that a Church which did not see the light of day for fifteen or more centuries after Christ had as-

CHART II

CHRIST OR LUTHER?

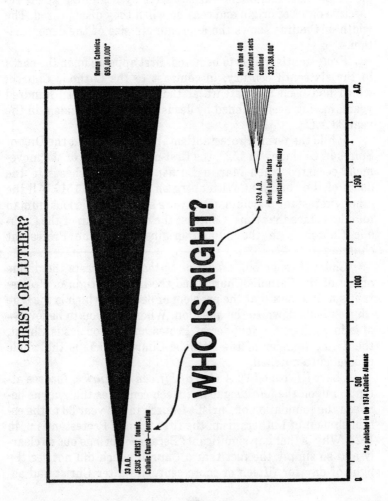

WHO IS RIGHT?

33 A.D.
JESUS CHRIST founds
Catholic Church—Jerusalem

1524 A.D.
Martin Luther starts
Protestantism—Germany

Roman Catholics
659,000,000*

More than 400
Protestant sects
combined
323,288,000*

*As published in the 1974 Catholic Almanac

A.D.

0   500   1000   1500

CHART III

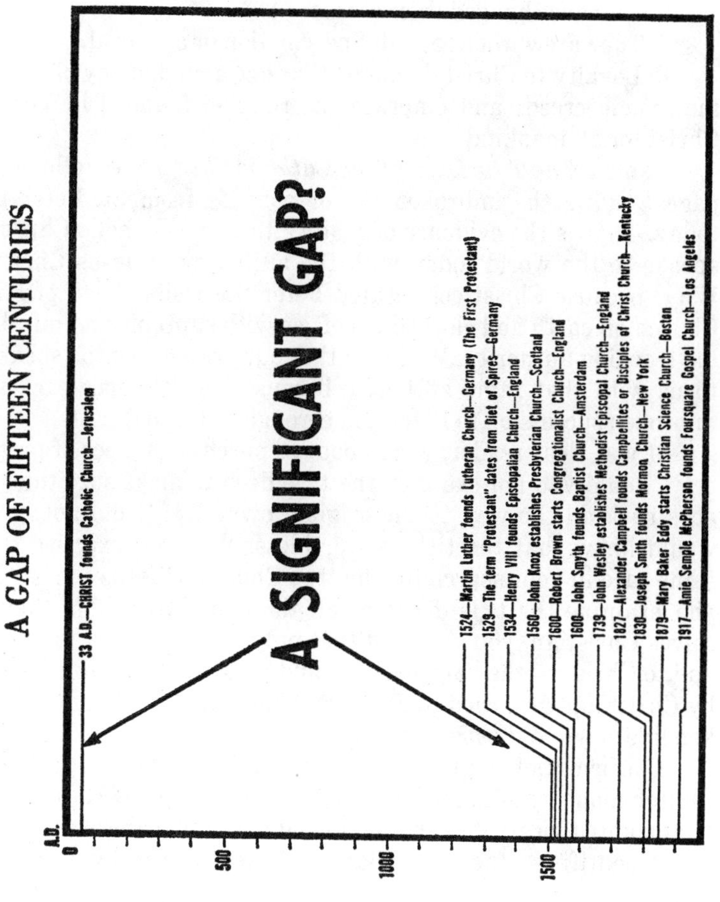

A GAP OF FIFTEEN CENTURIES

A SIGNIFICANT GAP?

33 A.D.—CHRIST founds Catholic Church—Jerusalem

1524—Martin Luther founds Lutheran Church—Germany (The First Protestant)
1529—The term "Protestant" dates from Diet of Spires—Germany
1534—Henry VIII founds Episcopalian Church—England
1560—John Knox establishes Presbyterian Church—Scotland
1600—Robert Brown starts Congregationalist Church—England
1600—John Smyth founds Baptist Church—Amsterdam
1739—John Wesley establishes Methodist Episcopal Church—England
1827—Alexander Campbell founds Campbellites or Disciples of Christ Church—Kentucky
1830—Joseph Smith founds Mormon Church—New York
1879—Mary Baker Eddy starts Christian Science Church—Boston
1917—Amie Semple McPherson founds Foursquare Gospel Church—Los Angeles

A.D.
0
500
1000
1500

cended into heaven cannot possibly claim to have Christ for its founder. This even a blind man can see.

These four charts bring out more clearly and more vividly than a volume of a thousand pages the following important historical facts:

1. The Catholic Church alone has Jesus Christ for her founder.

2. She had been carrying on her divinely appointed work of teaching the religion of Christ to mankind for fifteen centuries before Protestantism saw light of day.

3. All forms of Protestantism are man-made.

4. All have changed their creeds.

5. They are without any divine sanction or approval.

6. Loyalty to Christ demands that one abandon any of these man-made creeds and embrace the religion founded by Jesus Christ for all mankind.

Table I. *The Title Deed of the Catholic Church* (see following pages) shows the unbroken list of pontiffs from St. Peter to today. That is the evidence of history that the Catholic Church speaks to the world today with the authority of Jesus Christ. Why? because Christ constituted Peter the visible head of His Church on earth and clothed his office with supreme and infallible teaching authority. We know that our present pontiff speaks to us with that same authority because his title goes back in unbroken succession to Peter and through Peter to Christ.

If you, dear reader, were about to purchase a piece of property, would you not examine the title deed to make sure that it goes back all the way to the original owner? If it did not, you would know that the title is worthless. Why not exercise the same care in your search for the true Church of Jesus Christ? If you examine the title deeds of all the churches calling themselves Christian, you will find that only one goes back to Peter and to Christ — the holy, catholic and apostolic Church founded by Christ and governed by Peter and his successors in an unbroken line down to the present day.

Confirmation of the all-important fact that the Catholic Church alone was founded by Christ and governed by His divinely appointed vicars on earth is proved not only by her unbroken list of pontiffs — the unassailable title deed of her divine origin

— but also by the fact that she alone has retained *all* the teachings of Christ and of the Apostles. Her doctrinal code today is that of the Apostolic Church of the first century. This identity of doctrine and of practice places upon the Church's title deed the telltale fingerprints of Christ and the Apostles.

These fingerprints show that her doctrines are not the work of innovators, heresiarchs, or so-called reformers who, fifteen to nineteen centuries later, substituted their own private opinions for the ancient faith of the Apostles. Those fingerprints stamp the Church with the seal of divine origin and divine authorization.

Conscious that there has been a continuous line of pontiffs from St. Peter to the present day, the Church gladly avails herself of the findings of historical research to make any necessary revisions in the list of popes. The *fact* of Apostolic succession is not at stake in such revisions: they merely reflect the well-known truth that accurate records of the distant past are much more difficult to secure than those of recent or contemporary events.

THE TITLE DEED OF THE CATHOLIC CHURCH

Unbroken List of Pontiffs from Peter to Today

Christ to Peter: "Thou art Peter; and upon this rock I will build My Church, and the gates of hell shall not prevail against it" (Matthew 16:18).

St. Peter of Bethsaida in Galilee, Prince of the Apostles, who received from Jesus Christ the supreme pontifical power to be transmitted to his successors, resided first at Antioch, then at Rome for twenty-five years where he was martyred in the year 67 of the common reckoning.

TABLE I

Name of Pontiff	End of Pontificate, A.D.
St. Peter	67
St. Linus	76

Of the 263 popes, from St. Peter to John Paul II, 77 are honored as saints, 8, as blesseds—a distinguished list of men, linking the Church with Christ, and constituting the title deed of the one true Church of Jesus Christ on earth.

The original church of SS. Peter and Paul dates back to the days of the martyrs (work on today's St. Peter's Basilica began in 1450). The church of St. John Lateran, Rome, 1600 years old in 1925, was the "pope's church" from the time freedom of worship was granted to Christians—or 1200 years before the advent of Protestantism.

There are many teachings of the Apostolic Church which are no longer found in the creeds of our separated brethren. We shall cite a few of the basic teachings of Christ and the Apostles showing the identity of such doctrines with the Catholic faith and the departure from those truths by Protestant sects.

The Holy Eucharist — Apostolic Church

Jesus and the Apostles taught that the Holy Eucharist contains the body and blood of Christ: "Take ye, and eat; this is My body . . . drink ye all of this, for this is My blood."[7] "The chalice of benediction which we bless, is it not the communion of the blood of Christ; and the bread which we break, is it not the participation of the body of the Lord?"[8]

The Holy Eucharist — Catholic Church

The Catholic Church holds fast to the clear teaching of Christ and the Apostles that the Holy Eucharist contains the body and blood of Jesus under the appearance of bread and wine.

The Holy Eucharist — Protestant Churches

Protestant Churches, with the exception of branches of the Episcopal and Lutheran Churches, reject the doctrine of the Real Presence as idolatrous. They regard the partaking of communion as the receiving of a mere memorial or symbol of Christ's body.

Power of Pardoning — Apostolic Church

Christ conferred upon the Apostles the power to forgive sins: "Whose sins you shall forgive, they are forgiven."[9] St. Paul mirrors the faith of the Apostolic Church when he writes: "God hath given to us the ministry of reconciliation."[10]

61

Power of Pardoning — Catholic Church

As the inheritors of the power and authority of the Apostles, the bishops and priests of the Catholic Church exercise the ministry of reconciliation, forgiving penitent sinners in the name of Jesus Christ.

Power of Pardoning — Protestant Churches

Protestant Churches reject the sacrament of Confession and deny that God delegated to man the power of pardoning sinners in His name.

Marriage Bond Unbreakable — Apostolic Church

Christ taught that the bond of Christian marriage is unbreakable and forbade divorce, saying: "What therefore God hath joined together, let no man put asunder."[11] "Whosoever shall put away his wife and marry another committeth adultery against her. And if the wife shall put away her husband and be married to another, she committeth adultery."[12]

Marriage Bond Unbreakable — Catholic Church

In compliance with Christ's command, the Catholic Church proclaims the indissoluble character of Christian marriage and forbids divorce.

Marriage Bond Unbreakable — Protestant Churches

Protestant denominations have departed from Christ's teaching and remarry persons who have been divorced for the most trivial reasons.

Anointing of the Sick — Apostolic Church

Mirroring the faith of the Apostolic Church, St. James says: "Is any man sick among you, let him bring in the priests of the Church, and let them pray over him, anointing him with oil in the name of the Lord."[13]

Anointing of the Sick — Catholic Church

In conformity with the injunction of St. James, priests of the Catholic Church pray over the sick and anoint them with oil in the name of the Lord, thus administering the ancient sacrament of the Anointing of the Sick.

Anointing of the Sick — Protestant Churches

Few Protestant Churches observe the practice of anointing the sick, notwithstanding the clear injunction of the Apostle.

Confirmation — Apostolic Church

The Apostles, Peter and John, confirmed the newly baptized in Samaria. They "prayed for them that they might receive the Holy Spirit: for He was not yet come upon any of them, but they were only baptized in the name of the Lord Jesus. Then they laid their hands on them, and they received the Holy Spirit."[14]

Confirmation — Catholic Church

As a successor of the Apostles, every Catholic bishop likewise prays over baptized persons and imposes hands upon them in the sacrament of Confirmation through which they receive the Holy Spirit.

Confirmation — Protestant Churches

With the exception of Episcopalians, Methodists and some Lutherans — and even they do not recognize it as a sacrament — Protestant Churches in this country do not impose hands upon the baptized.

Primacy of Peter — Apostolic Church

Christ made Peter the head of the Apostles and conferred upon him the power of ruling His Church: "Thou art Peter; and upon this rock I will build My Church. . . . I will give to thee the keys of the kingdom of heaven."[15] "Confirm thy brethren."[16]

Primacy of Peter — Catholic Church

In conformity to our Savior's teaching, the Catholic Church gives the primacy of honor and jurisdiction to Peter and to his successors.

Primacy of Peter — Protestant Churches

Protestant Churches practically deny the supremacy of Peter over the other Apostles and do not acknowledge the authority of his successors.

Infallible Teaching Authority — Apostolic Church

Christ conferred upon Peter and the other Apostles the power of teaching His doctrines with inerrancy. The Apostles exercised this power and the Apostolic Church recognized and perpetuated it. "When you have received from us the word of God, you received it not as the word of men, but (as it is indeed) the word of God."[17] "It hath seemed good to the Holy Spirit and to us," say the assembled Apostles, "to lay no further burden upon you than these necessary things."[18] "Though an angel from heaven preach a gospel to you beside that which we have preached to you, let him be anathema."[19]

Infallible Teaching Authority — Catholic Church

Perpetuating the faith of the Apostolic Church, the Catholic Church alone proclaims the teachings of Christ with infallible authority. United with the Holy See, her ministers preach with authority and the faithful receive with implicit confidence what the Church teaches because of the promise of Christ to be with her "all days," protecting her from error and falsehood.

Infallible Teaching Authority — Protestant Churches

No Protestant Church teaches with infallible authority or even claims to possess it. Protestant ministers proclaim no authoritative doctrines, but advance their opinions, reflecting their own interpretation of the Bible. Their listeners claim the same right as their ministers to interpret the Scriptures according to their own private judgment. Hence the confusion and ceaseless differences among them.

In contrast with the unbroken continuity of the Catholic Church stretching down through nineteen hundred years, preserving her unity of faith inviolate under one supreme spiritual head, are the various sects which arose in the course of the centuries. They are conspicuous for the lateness of their arrival upon the stage of Christendom, for their impermanence and instability, and for the divisions and disintegrations which have gone steadily on within their own ranks. The heretical sects which sprang up in the early centuries, such as the Novatians, Macedonians and Pelagians, have disappeared from the earth, leaving only their names and the memory of their errors to posterity. As the branch of the tree that is cut from the trunk, and is thus deprived of life-giving sap, speedily withers and dies, so these sects, when separated from the Mother Church, were deprived of the life-giving graces flowing through her sacramental veins to all the members of her organic body.

It was the realization of this truth that brought that gifted scholar, John Henry Newman of Oxford University, England, into the fold of Christ. While engaged in his great historical investigation of the Monophysites and other heretical sects in the early ages, the startling question suddenly burst upon him: "Am I not after all in the same relative position to the Church of Christ as the Monophysites of the fifth century?" As he surveyed the innumerable divisions within Protestantism, the query persisted: "What is the difference in the position of all the Protestant sects which cut themselves off from the historic center of unity in the sixteenth century and the heretical sects which did so in the fifth?" The question gripped him, and would not let him rest.

In his classic *Apologia Pro Vita Sua* he describes his sudden realization of the analogous position of Protestants of the sixteenth century and of his own day to the heretical sects of the fifth century. "There was an awful similitude," he writes, "more awful, because so silent and unimpassioned, between the dead records of the past and the feverish chronicle of the present. . . . My stronghold was antiquity; now here, in the middle of the fifth century, I found as it seemed to me, Christendom of the sixteenth and nineteenth centuries reflected. I saw my face in the mirror," he adds with horror and incredulity, "and I was a Monophysite."

The penetrating realization of the implications of that historical analogy that now loomed up vividly before him, stubborn and ineradicable, proved to be the turning point in his life. Not without a terrific struggle, however, did he surrender. With all the might of his powerful intellect he struggled valiantly to establish some logical justification for Anglicanism as a sect or branch distinct from Rome; but all his continued research into the records of history served only to convince him beyond all possibility of doubt that the Catholic Church alone was founded by Christ, and that she alone retained in their fullness the teachings of the Apostles. The conclusion which follows with irresistible logic, that the Catholic Church is the one true Church of

Christ on earth, brought this gifted scholar, as it has brought many other brilliant minds both before and since his day, into the fold of Christ.

In the twentieth century, as in the fifth, when a branch is torn from the trunk of a tree, it withers and dies. The constant divisions and ceaseless disintegration which have been going on within Protestantism since it separated from the Mother Church is after all but a form of institutional withering and creedal death. There is not a single one of the founders of a Protestant creed who, if he returned to earth today, would recognize either his creed or his progeny.

Table II (page 68) presents the date, place and the name of the founders of the leading Protestant denominations, as recorded by non-Catholic authorities, chiefly the United States Religious Census. Study that table carefully. It shows that the first form of Protestantism did not see the light of day until the sixteenth century — fifteen hundred years after Christ had founded the Catholic Church. In 1524 Martin Luther established the Lutheran Church. Ten years later Henry VIII set up the Anglican Church in England. Amsterdam was the scene of the founding of the Baptist Church by John Smyth in 1600. John and Charles Wesley established the Methodist Episcopal Church in England in 1739. Admittedly all these denominations are of human origin; all of them rejected one or more of the fundamental doctrines of historic Christianity and introduced new tenets of their own devising.

Whom is the earnest searcher after truth to believe — Jesus Christ, the Son of God on the one hand, or Martin Luther, Henry VIII, John Smyth, or John Wesley on the other? The whole question — Which is the true church? — boils down in the last analysis to the question: Am I to believe Jesus Christ in preference to Martin Luther, Henry VIII, John Smyth, or John Wesley? Is not the authority of Jesus Christ greater than that of any of these men and of the other human individuals who set up creeds of their own in contradiction to the plain teachings of Jesus Christ? If the authority of Jesus Christ is greater, then there is no escape from the conclusion that the Church which He Himself founded is to be accepted by all men as the one and only true Church of Christ on earth.

TABLE II*

DATE, ORIGIN, FOUNDERS OF VARIOUS CHURCHES

Name	Year	Founder(s)	Origin
Catholic	33	Jesus Christ	Jerusalem
Lutheran	1524	Martin Luther	Germany
Episcopalian	1534	Henry VIII	England
Presbyterian	1560	John Knox	Scotland
Baptist	1600	John Smyth	Amsterdam
Congregational	1600	Robert Brown	England
Methodist Episcopal	1739	John & Charles Wesley	England
United Brethren	1800	Philip Otterbein & Martin Boehm	Maryland
Disciples of Christ	1827	Thomas & Alexander Campbell	Kentucky
Mormon	1830	Joseph Smith	New York
Salvation Army	1865	William Booth	London
Christian Science	1879	Mary Baker Eddy	Boston
Four-Square Gospel	1917	Aimee-Semple McPherson	Los Angeles

*Information for Table II was obtained from the following sources: (1) the New Testament; (2) S.S. Schumacker in *History of All Denominations;* (3) Macaulay and other English historians; and (4) Religious Bodies: 1936 U.S. Religious Census.

Note that the authority cited for the date and place of origin and the name of the founder in regard to nearly every Protestant denomination is the impartial United States Religious Census. The authorities cited for the other two — namely, the Lutheran and the Episcopalian Churches — are eminent Protestant historians.

The speed with which these dissenting denominations split and disintegrated among themselves is evident from the fact that in America today there are more than three hundred denominations, all disagreeing with one another. Indeed, the larger denominations have undergone a ceaseless division within their own groups. Thus the United States Religious Census for 1936 reports no fewer than twenty different divisions within the Lutheran denomination, no fewer than seventeen within the Methodist, and ten within the Presbyterian denomination. Within the Baptist there are thirty different divisions — grim evidence of the internal dissension that has been ceaselessly at work within the bosom of Protestantism.

Among the divisions listed in the Baptist Church are: Northern Baptist Convention, Southern Baptist Convention, Negro Baptists, American Baptist Association, Christian Unity Baptist Association, Colored Primitive Baptists, Duck River and Kindred Associations of Baptists (Baptist Church of Christ), Free Will Baptists, General Baptists, General Six Principle Baptists, Independent Baptist Church of America, National Baptist Evangelical Life and Soul Saving, National Assembly of the United States of America, Primitive Baptists, Regular Baptists, General Association of Regular Baptist Churches in the United States of America, Separate Baptists, Seventh Day Baptists, Seventh Day Baptists (German, 1728), Two-Seed-in-the-Spirit Predestinarian Baptists, United American Free Will Baptist Church (Colored), United Baptists.

Bewildering as is this multitudinous splitting within the Baptist denomination, it does not, however, tell the whole story. There are branches and offshoots from this denomination, as there are from the other denominations, wherein the name of the original Church has been sloughed off, and in consequence they are no longer listed as divisions of the same. This fact is illustrated in the listing of the United States Religious Census of the various religious denominations. Thus, immediately following the list of the previously enumerated divisions of the Baptist denomination, there is listed the following: "Brethren, German Baptist (Dunkers)." Herein it is evident that the German Baptist body commonly called Dunkers is officially listed as Brethren, though it has actually stemmed from the Baptist parent trunk.

This instance of fission or splitting with the loss of the parent name has occurred times without number in the major religious denominations.

Is this the "one fold" and the "one faith" in which Jesus wished all His followers to be united, and for which He prayed so fervently shortly before his death upon Calvary's cross?

No. On the contrary, it is the confirmation which the twentieth century offers of the persistence of that spirit of internal strife and dissension which characterized the activities of the reformers in the sixteenth century. That this spirit alarmed even the reformers themselves is evident from the following passage in a letter Calvin wrote to Melanchthon:

"It is of great importance that the divisions which subsist among us should not be known to future ages; for nothing can be more ridiculous than that we who have been compelled to make a separation from the whole world, should have agreed so ill among ourselves from the beginning of the Reformation."[20] It is the persistence of this spirit of internal discord and dissension which split Protestantism into so many hundred warring sects that caused the Rev. Peter Ainslie, a Disciples of Christ minister at Baltimore, to characterize this multiplicity of sects as "the scandal of Christendom."

"Disunity in the name of Christ," comments *Time*[21] magazine, "is a scandal and a shame." Pointing out how easily Protestants switch from one denomination to another, *Time* continues: "If U.S. Protestants think of themselves as Presbyterians or Methodists, they tend more and more to pick their churches because they are within walking distance, or because their friends go there, or because they like the preacher — all too few care passionately about doctrinal differences between the limestone church with stained glass, the spired white clapboard and the Georgian brick. Typical is a Hollywood man whose parents were Lutherans and then Methodists; he became a Presbyterian 'because the bass soloist's position was open.'"

Time thinks that one element in the "homogenization of U.S. Protestantism is the decline of ethnic differences between Americans; many a church used to be kept alive by the national loyalties of first-generation citizens and the parental loyalties of their children. Another element is the pressure on Protestantism of an expanding Roman Catholic Church, which is currently growing *more than twice as fast* as the leading Protestant denominations."

Chart IV (page 72), *Growth of Churches in U.S.A.*, shows how the Catholic Church has outstripped all in the marvelous rapidity of her climb to her present position of numerical superiority. In 1785 there were but about 23,000 white Catholics ministered to by 34 priests, according to Bishop Carroll, then prefect apostolic. They thus constituted considerably less than one percent of the population.

From a little colony of immigrants they have increased by leaps and bounds until today they constitute by far the largest religious body in the United States. Their rapid rise to numerical ascendancy in spite of discrimination, opposition and slander offers a striking parallel to the marvelous growth of the early Christians from an impoverished and persecuted minority to the dominant religious body in the United States.

The beloved disciple of Christ, St. John, put his discerning finger upon the salient reason why the Catholic Church has withstood the fall of empires and the invasion of the barbarians which caused even the mighty empire of Rome to collapse; why she has withstood the religious upheaval of the sixteenth century which shook Christendom to its very foundation; and why she is able to withstand today the acids of modern unbelief and the enervating influence of a gilded paganism, when back in the first century he explained with prophetic foresight: "For whatsoever is *born of God*, overcometh the world: and this is the victory which overcometh the world, our faith." Because the Catholic Church was founded directly and immediately by Jesus Christ and because He has remained with her through the ages, protecting her from error, the Church remains today as she has been throughout the past nineteen hundred years, the one true Church of Jesus Christ on earth.

Discussion Aids

What is the acid test of the true Church? Can anyone find it? Why do not all find it? Give a text from each gospel showing that

CHART IV

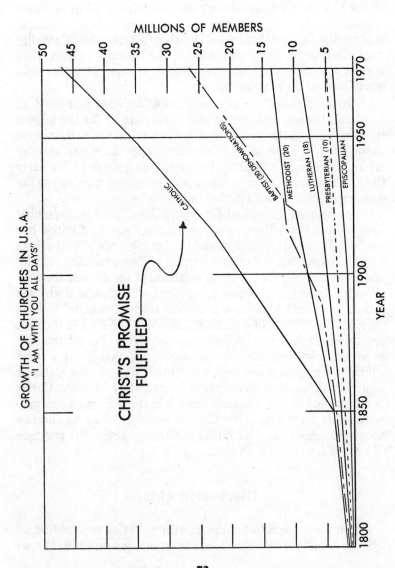

MILLIONS OF MEMBERS

GROWTH OF CHURCHES IN U.S.A.
"I AM WITH YOU ALL DAYS"

CHRIST'S PROMISE
FULFILLED

CATHOLIC

BAPTIST (30 DENOMINATIONS)

METHODIST (20)

LUTHERAN (18)

PRESBYTERIAN (10)

EPISCOPALIAN

YEAR

Christ's foundation was a Church teaching with authority. How do you know that that Church was the present Roman Catholic Church? What three fundamental facts of history become evident from study of development of Church? Cite examples from history showing that Christ has kept His promise that His Church should endure. What discovery on his part brought Newman into the Church? Analyze the fact that more than 200 dissenting denominations (called Christian) have resulted from Luther's schism. What conclusion may be logically drawn as to direct and immediate founding of the Church by Christ?

Practices

Say often the prayer, "I do believe, Lord: help my unbelief" (Mark 1:23).

Read the first twelve chapters of the Acts observing the early Church at work. The prayers at the foot of the altar after Mass are said for the intention of the Holy Father for the welfare of the Church. Be more zealous in joining in them.

Invite non-Catholic friends to go to church with you.

NOTES (Chapter 3)

1. Jn. 20:21
2. Mt. 28:18-20
3. Mk. 16:15-16
4. Lk. 10:16
5. Mt. 16:18
6. Heb. 13:8
7. Mt. 26:26-28
8. I Cor. 10:16
9. Jn. 20:23
10. II Cor. 5:18
11. Mt. 19:6

12. Mk. 10:11-12
13. Jas. 5:14
14. Acts 8:15-17
15. Mt. 16:17-19
16. Lk. 22:32
17. Thes. 2:13
18. Acts 15:28
19. Gal. 1:8
20. Epist. 141
21. *Time*, May 6, 1961

CHAPTER 4

The Marvelous Spread of the Church

I

A Proof of Her Divine Character

While consisting of human beings and having many laws and regulations that are of human origin, the Church as an institution commissioned to teach the truths revealed by Christ to humanity is divine in her origin. Established by Jesus Christ, she speaks to the world concerning His teachings with the authority of her divine Founder.

What is the evidence of her divine origin? In the preceding chapters we have presented various lines of evidence, such as, the four marks of the Church, and her divine origin and commission to teach all nations in the name of Christ. We now appeal to the indisputable fact of her marvelous propagation throughout the world. History knows no parallel. In the story of her origin and growth there is visible to every unjaundiced eye the finger of God.

The more light that is cast upon the conditions surrounding her birth and the obstacles to her growth by the calm white searchlight of historic research, the more vivid and spectacular becomes the dramatic story of her rise and conquest of the world. The more clearly we discern the true character and magnitude of the obstacles, the more strongly are we convinced that they were insurmountable by human ingenuity alone. Only by constant supernatural assistance and unfailing succor from on high could a band of men, most of whom were untutored fishermen, go forth and literally change the face of the earth by effecting the mightiest moral revolution that the world has ever seen.

It is a story that has in it all the rich color of romance and the thrill of adventure and achievement. There is the somber pathos of indescribable human suffering; there is the quickening touch of unparalleled bravery and indomitable courage. There is the tingling thrill of superhuman courage that rose to the loftiest heights of heroic moral grandeur. In the long annals of recorded human history, the story of the daring and the heroism of the early Christians stands out as the one story that has never ceased to move the hearts and thrill the souls of succeeding generations of men. It not only moves and thrills them, but it compels them at the end to exclaim as with a single voice: *"This is not the work of man, but of God!"* Amidst all the minutiae of human phenomena there is discerned the finger of God as clearly and as luminously as the sun shining in the noonday sky.

Let us go back to the very beginning of the sublime story. The opening scene is set in the land of Judea, in the thirty-third year of our Lord. In a world that was plunged in the darkness of polytheism and pagan idolatry, the inhabitants of Judea had for centuries held aloft the torch of monotheism: the worship of the one true God. Through the centuries they had been awaiting the coming of the long-heralded Messiah, who was to restore them to their former glory and to a lofty pinnacle of national greatness and world empire.

These people claimed an old history, dating back 2,000 years; they spoke a rude and unspoiled language of the olden times; they had a religion repulsive for its austerity, whose ceremonies were despised. It was the land of Judea — a fossil land — a mock and a jibe among the nations. In Judea men spoke with contempt of its rudest part, Galilee. On the sandy beach of the sea of Galilee, beneath towering mountains, stood One, who gathered about Him twelve poor fishermen of this little secluded lake, and unto them He said: "All power is given to Me in heaven and in earth. Going, therefore, teach ye all nations; baptizing them in the name of the Father, and of the Son, and of the Holy Spirit, teaching them to observe all things whatsoever I have commanded you: and behold I am with you all days, even to the consummation of the world."[1]

In these words Christ commissioned twelve Galileans, most

of them fishermen, to go and teach whom? Not a few individuals or groups of individuals or even a few nations, but all nations. Teach them what? A few maxims or a few rules? No. They were to teach them "all things whatsoever I have commanded you." The more carefully one studies the character of this command, the more clearly does he realize that this is the most gigantic, the most colossal, the most stupendous task ever placed upon the frail shoulders of man.

Twelve obscure Galileans were commanded to go out and change the face of the world. Without the backing of powerful armies, or the might of human learning, or the force of persuasive eloquence, they were charged to effect the mightiest, the most radical, and the most far-reaching revolution in thought and conduct which the human race has ever known. Well might they have quailed under such a charge. Well, indeed, might they have faltered and demurred!

To understand more clearly the character of that tremendous change which they were charged to effect, let us now turn our eyes upon that world into which they were sent. With the single exception of the Jewish people, polytheism held supreme sway among the nations. Imperial Rome had reached the zenith of her military power and martial glory: in the course of eight centuries, she had grown from a little stone fort on the Palatine Hill into a world empire. She had become the mistress of the seas, the conqueror of the world, the eternal city.

Her empires stretched from the Atlantic on the west to the Euphrates on the east. From the banks of the Danube and the Rhine to the Cataracts of the Nile, her will was the supreme law. Gaul, Spain and Britain, as well as the vast Oriental empires of Egypt, Assyria and Parthia, besides a hundred minor kingdoms, fell before the irresistible might of Roman arms. The Eagles of Rome became the one symbol of universal dominion. All the golden streams of the world's commerce flowed now to one political center, bearing Romeward with equal thoroughness all the confluents of art, literature and luxury. The glorious dreams of Alexander the Great were translated into realities when Roman *Conquistadori* sat at Antioch, Alexandria, Carthage, Saragossa, Lyons and York. Rome had now become the greatest empire that the world had ever known.

Scarcely had the crash of empires falling beneath the victorious arms of Rome died away, scarcely had Rome's task of enslaving the universal world become complete, when there is set up in her own bosom a process that begins to spell her doom. Victorious over all foes from without, the fatal chains of her enslavement are being forged at her own domestic hearth. The cancer of vice and immorality is slowly but surely gnawing into her very heart, sapping her vitality, weakening her moral fiber, and sending its noxious poisons through her whole body politic. The home, the foundation stone of all national greatness, has been undermined by the dread evil of divorce: the waters of the stream of social life have been corrupted at their very source by the domestic evils of abortion, infanticide and conjugal infidelity.

Over that teeming city of three million people vice, immorality, debauchery, licentiousness, swept like a devastating plague, leaving ruin and destruction in their wake; the most shameful Bacchanalian orgies were performed even in the name of the pagan gods. From Rome the cancer of immorality spread quickly throughout the empire. The nation, which for eight centuries had stood as impervious as a wall of adamant against the onslaughts of every foe, fell at last beneath the weight of her own corruption. As water can rise no higher than its source, so the power of a nation can rise no higher than its source — its national conscience or the plane of its moral life.

Into a world, then, plunged into the darkness of pagan idolatry, half-buried in the swamp of moral foulness, shameful licentiousness and bestial immorality, the Master sent these twelve Galileans to preach a doctrine of angelic purity, virginal chastity and self-control. For domestic infidelity and promiscuity there is to be substituted the indissoluble bond of matrimony; for the uncurbed indulgence and license of the passions there are to be substituted restraint and self-control. This was flying in the very teeth of the deep-rooted raging passion of lust.

Unlike Mahomet, who preached greater sensual indulgence, these Galilean fishermen preached less — demanding that the pagans give up their deep-rooted and inveterate passions. To a world steeped in the mire of gross sensuality and carnal indulgence, nothing could be stranger doctrine than this. Humanly

77

speaking, therefore, the *austerity* of the teachings of the Apostles, of their demands for mortification, self-sacrifice and self-denial, reacted unfavorably against their ready acceptance by the sensual, carnal-minded pagans of the Graeco-Roman empire.

On top of this stumbling block there was the additional one arising from the fact that the pagan worship of idols had been made the national cultus or the state religion: it had become woven into the warp and woof of Roman law. The practice of the Christian religion therefore was a civil offense. In the minds of the Romans every misfortune became attributable to the Christians; for it was their failure to propitiate the pagan gods that prompted the deities thus to show their anger. If the Tiber overflowed its banks, the cry immediately arose: *"Christiani ad leones!"* — "The Christians to the lions!" Forthwith hundreds would be carried to the Roman amphitheatre to become the prey of hungry lions. Almost inconceivable was the brutal torture inflicted upon the Christians. Sometimes their tongues were cut off, their eyes burnt out, while many of them were coated with pitch and tar and burned alive as torches to illumine the gladiatorial contests in the Roman amphitheatre. Even women and little children were not exempt from such frightful tortures.

Some of you may perhaps recall the story of Agatha, a little girl of Sicily. Born of rich and noble parents, she was justly famed for her virtue and her beauty. Quintianus was governor of Sicily at the time the Roman Emperor Decius launched his violent persecution against the Christians. Learning through spies and informers that Agatha was a believer in "Christ and Him crucified," Quintianus summoned her from Palermo to Catania, where he was then sojourning. Agatha knew full well the meaning of the summons and the terrible fate which lurked beneath it if she remained true to the religion of Christ.

Undaunted, the youthful Agatha set out on her journey, exclaiming, "Oh, Jesus Christ, all that I am is Thine; preserve me and steel me to resist the threats of this tyrant!"

When Quintanius beheld her, he was struck by her beauty and innocence. So instead of ordering her to offer incense to the idols, the lustful governor commanded her to renounce her faith in Christ by committing a sensual immoral action.

She refused, saying: "Christ is my life and my salvation."

When imprisonment failed to break her will of iron, Quintianus again summoned her before him.

"If thou wilt do what I command," said he, "and thus renounce this God of the Christians, I will give thee not only thy life and liberty, but everything that the heart of a little girl craves."

But all to no purpose. That frail young girl, beautiful and fair as the angels that minister before the great white throne of the eternal King, stood before Quintianus and his court and challenged the power of mighty Rome and the allurement of pagan vice to shake her faith in the Crucified and her unflinching adherence to His laws.

At last, in a rage of passion, Quintianus ordered her breasts to be cut from her body. Finding her still unyielding, he commanded her to be rolled naked upon pointed postherds and sharp rocks, which pierced deep into her tender flesh. As the warm lifeblood slowly ebbed from a hundred deep wounds in her body, crimsoning the rocky ground, this brave little Christian girl, with one last desperate effort, turned her face, still illumined by the trace of a gentle smile toward the heavens and with her arms upraised cried out, "Jesus, now I am all Thine!"

With these words upon her dying lips, her head fell back on the ground while her soul, too precious for the sordid world of pagan vice, winged its way back into the outstretched arms and the tender bosom of her God and Savior, Jesus Christ. With the beautiful white robe of her baptismal innocence still unsullied, she returned to her heavenly home to receive from the hands of her Master, Jesus Christ, the glorious crown of martyrdom. To this day, during volcanic eruptions of Mt. Etna, the people of Catania have sought protection in the veneration of her veil.

This incident of the brave little girl, whom we honor on our altars as St. Agatha, is mentioned only because it is typical of hundreds of others who defied the power of mighty Rome and braved death in many forms rather than give up their faith in Christ and Him crucified. Emperor after emperor, from the imperial throne of the mighty Caesars, hurled forth their anathemas against this new religion. "It must be wiped," they declared, "from the very face of the earth." All the tortures which the marvelous ingenuity of imperial Rome could devise, all the tortures which pagan cruelty and barbarian brutality could prompt, were marshaled against the Christians.

They were seized in their homes at night and during the day while they were at work. Even down into the dark recesses of the catacombs, under the hills of the Eternal City, the powerful hand of the persecutor reached to bring them from the celebration of the holy mysteries, to be torn apart by wild beasts in the Roman amphitheatre or to be burned alive before jeering, howling mobs. In the frantic effort of the pagan emperors to stamp out this religion so many Christians were sacrificed that it is said that the streets of Rome ran with blood, and the waters of the Tiber along the shores of the city were dyed a crimson hue. Ten separate persecutions exhausted their force and savage brutality in the desperate effort to destroy forever the menace of the Christian faith.

Discussion Aids

Review briefly the divine foundation of the Church as evidenced by the four marks and the divine commission (Matthew 28:12-20).

Discuss the monotheistic belief of the Jews as the focal point in the preparation of the Twelve for conquering the world.

What did Christ add to complete the preparation of the Apostles? Contrast the results that were being felt among pagan nations from polytheistic belief. How did the austerity of the Christian teaching constitute a stumbling block to the spread of this teaching? Discuss the pagan state requirement of the worship of idols as an additional impediment. Relate the story of St. Agatha. Discuss such a martyrdom, repeated in hundreds of other cases, as an instrument in the hands of God for overcoming the world.

Practices

Fight the false gods of love of riches and of power in your own life.

80

Be willing to make sacrifices for your Faith.

Keep yourself in union with God especially by night and morning prayer.

II

Calumnies Against the Christian Religion

Not only did imperial Rome use the grosser weapons of brute force and savage violence, but with characteristic cunning, she employed the more subtle weapons of slander and calumny. The most absurd reports were circulated broadside against the Christians: they were charged with coming together at secret places in the night, and butchering an infant and then eating its bloody members. This was the manner in which the pagans perverted the Christian doctrine of Holy Communion. The Christians were represented as stupid, credulous fanatics, whose chief object of worship was an ass's head nailed to a cross. Archaeologists exploring among the ruins of ancient Rome, discovered a graffito or scratching upon the walls of the Palatine Hill, which reveals in a vivid and graphic manner the ridicule and calumny heaped upon the Christians. The cartoon, which is now in the Kircherian Museum in Rome, depicts a man with the head of an ass fastened to a cross, while nearby stands a Christian in prayer. Down below the drawing (page 82) are inscribed in Greek the words: "Alexamenes worships his God."

We are surprised when, during those waves of religious bigotry which periodically sweep over this country, especially at election times, we find the sacred and beautiful doctrines of our Church violently distorted and misrepresented. Our schools, convents, hospitals, homes for the friendless and houses of the Good Shepherd for the care and regeneration of the unfortunate ones in human society — even these beneficient institutions with which the Church has blessed society and furthered the cause of civilization — are attacked and misrepresented as houses of corruption and dens of iniquity. Even the gentle Sisters, ministering angels to suffering humanity, are not spared from the vile, black hand of the defamer.

It is, however, nothing new. Back in the fourth century we find the pagan emperor, Maximinus Daza, in his attempt to discredit the new religion in the eyes of the Roman Empire, placarding the walls and buildings of Rome with vicious cartoons and calumnies, and having these libels circulated among the masses and taught to the children in the schools. They had their Maximinus Daza in the fourth century as we had our notorious and unspeakably vile *Menace* in the twentieth.

Combined with attacks of calumny and libel were the onslaughts of pagan philosophers. The attempt was made to undermine the foundation of the Christian faith by showing that the belief in the Resurrection rested upon the hallucination of Magdalene. The Apostles were represented as ignorant fishermen, victims of a great deception. Celsus, who has been aptly styled "the Ingersoll of the second century," attempted to explain away the miracles as the result of magic; but that which has been termed "the most ample and thoroughgoing treatise which has ever been written against Christianity" came from the pen of the

GRAFFITO OF THE CRUCIFIXION
(From Marucchi's Elements d'Archéologie,
Desclée De Brouwer et Cie)

pagan philosopher Porphyry. His attempt to overthrow Christianity by showing the mythical character of its doctrines fills fifteen large volumes. St. Paul especially is attacked as an unstable, rude, insincere rhetorician. In short, all the dialectical acumen and force of pagan philosophy were leveled at the rational bases of the Christian faith in a last desperate effort to undermine it.

When to the gigantic and apparently insurmountable obstacles of Roman persecution and indescribable cruelty is added the appalling weakness of the very agency chosen to overcome them, our wonder that the Christian religion ever survived at all becomes unbounded. What were the means used to overcome the gross sensuality and licentious profligacy in which the whole pagan world was steeped? What was the wisdom selected to vanquish the proud philosophy of haughty Greece and Rome? What was the power chosen to lower at last the standard of the eagles which betokened the universal sway of the imperial city — the power that was to conquer her who had conquered the world and won for her the proud title of "the Eternal City, the Mistress of the World"?

Was it a group of great scholars whose learning would cause all to bow their minds in ready acceptance of their teachings? Was it a brand of brilliant, silver-tongued orators whose persuasive eloquence would move and sway and thrill the minds and hearts of men as so much plastic putty in the potter's hand? Was it a great and mighty host of warriors who were to compel for the first time the hitherto invincible legions of warlike Rome to bow their heads in the bitterness of defeat?

No! It was, for the most part, a band of simple, obscure Jewish fishermen. Without learning, without human eloquence, without a single soldier, without human power, they are sent out to conquer the world! Could anything appear more impossible, more ridiculous, more bordering on insanity? Even with the prestige of human learning, the moving force of impassioned eloquence and the might of great battalions of soldiery, the task would still have been a gigantic one. But with none of these, who, humanly speaking, would not say that it was foredoomed to inevitable failure?

This conviction is further deepened when we realize that the

Apostles and disciples were not only untutored fishermen, but were drawn from the Jewish race — the most despised race on the face of the earth. To the proud Roman and the cultured Greek, the Jew was an object of obloquy and loathing. Everywhere he was reviled. He was the social outcast, the pariah among the nations of the earth.

Among the Jews there was one section that was looked down upon with particular contempt, even by the Jews themselves. This was the tribe of people living in Galilee, the rudest part. Yet, strange as it may appear to human eyes, Christ chose His Apostles for the most part from the most despised section of this despised race — the scorned Galileans, a mock and a jibe even among the Jews and far worse among the other nations of the earth. Could any choice appear blinder, more out of sorts with every instinct of human expediency? Could Christ have chosen, if He had tried, any agency that could have been weaker, feebler, or more conspicuously unsuited according to every standard of human calculation, to accomplish the most difficult of all undertakings ever committed to mortal hands? Judged by every earthly standard, it would seem not. Measured by every worldly criterion, Christ seemed to have exhausted every possibility of choosing the weakest, the most ineffective and the most appallingly feeble instrument to encompass the achievement which provokes to this day the ceaseless wonder and the undying admiration of the world.

Yet when the Pentecostal fire had descended upon them, this band of untutored Jewish fishermen went out into the dark night of heathen idolatry and the maelstrom of pagan debauchery and literally changed the face of the earth. The mighty empire of the Romans is parceled out among them for their conquest. Beginning at the very heart of the Jewish world, the Prince of the Apostles preaches in Jerusalem and by his first sermon converts three thousand souls, some of whom had doubtless but a short time ago assisted in the crucifixion of Christ. Then St. Peter journeys to Antioch and finally to Rome, where he establishes his see and gains the glorious crown of martyrdom.

Through Europe into Asia penetrates the great Apostle of the Gentiles, burning with zeal for souls. Into Syria and Greece goes Andrew. Into Ephesus and Asia Minor goes John. Even to the far-away Indies, according to tradition, journeys Thomas, planting the mustard seed of the Kingdom and holding aloft the glowing torch of the gospel of Christ that was destined to burn forever. The voice of these Apostolic fishermen was heard on the plains of Arabia and in Scythia, reaching to the Indus, the Ganges, and into Spain, penetrating to the very Pillars of Hercules. Everywhere was heard the preaching of Christ and Him crucified. Well indeed was St. Paul able to exclaim in the words of the prophet: "Their sound hath gone forth to all the earth, and their words unto the ends of the whole world."[2]

They went forth on their mission speaking in foreign tongues and in accents strangely new. Without flinching they met the stubborn opposition of the rabbi, the polish and subtlety of the cultured Greek philosopher, the blind fury and cruel persecutions of imperial Rome, and they overcame them all. For the words of their Master were still ringing in their ears: "If they have persecuted Me, they will also persecute you."[3] "But have confidence, I have overcome the world."[4]

The success which attended the labors of the Apostles is the most phenomenal in all history: during their own lifetime they witnessed the birth of the Christian Church in practically every land in the civilized world. Despite the furious storms of persecution seeking to extinguish it, the gospel of Christ spread like wild-fire among the nations until it became a great glowing flame in the heavens, banishing the darkness of pagan night and ushering in the dawn of a new day. There in the heavens it shone as a mighty beacon light to guide the tottering footsteps of a redeemed humanity in the new and enlarged horizon of human life. With such striking rapidity was the evangelization of the pagan world effected that Tertullian, a convert to the new religion, living in the second century, was able to address these words to the Roman emperor: "We are but of yesterday, and we fill all that is yours: your cities, your islands, your military posts; your boroughs, your council chambers and your camps; the palace, the senate, the forum; your temples alone we leave you."

The story of the conquest of the pagan world by a band of illiterate Galilean fishermen reads like a page from a mighty drama. "First, the Jewish synagogue," says Bernard J. Otten, "still stained with the blood of the God-man, measured its strength with the weakness of the Galilean fishermen, but succumbed in the conflict. Then the world-embracing power of Rome threw down the gauntlet, wholly determined to crush the infant Church. Three hundred years that contest lasted; many thousands of followers of the crucified Nazarene sealed their Faith with a martyr's death. But when the one-sided conflict ceased, the blood-stained sword had fallen from the mailed hand of pagan Rome and the successor of St. Peter sat upon the throne of the Caesars. The sign of the redemption once raised upon Calvary's heights arose over the seven hills of Rome, proclaiming to the world that an empire had been founded which would proclaim its sway over all nations, not by the power of the sword, but by the omnipotence of God's own word. The temples of idols yielded their place to the one true God. The gospel of peace brought sunshine into the lives of men that had but known the darkness of death; churches and schools and charitable institutions arose everywhere as so many manifestations of the spirit of God, which had gone forth to renew the face of the earth."[5] "The purest among the strong, and the strongest among the pure," says Richter, "Christ lifted with His wounded hands, empires from their hinges and changed the stream of centuries."

This changing of the stream of ages, this subjugation of the pagan world, this conquest of the unconquerable Rome, stands out as the mightiest moral and social revolution which the world has ever known. But every effect demands an adequate cause. To say that such a stupendous achievement could have been accomplished through the unaided efforts of a handful of Galilean fishermen is to deny the evidence offered by all the laws of history and human experience. As we have already seen, the human agency chosen was the weakest and the most unsuited that could possibly have been selected. Fishermen of the most despised stratum of the universally despised Jewish race, without learning, without eloquence, without military power, overcoming the proud philosophers of Greece, victorious over the might of Roman arms!

Christ chose these men because of their very *lack* of all human capacities necessary to gain the victory. If Christ had chosen profound philosophers or silver-tongued orators of moving eloquence or mighty generals with innumerable soldiers to propagate His religion, men would have justly exclaimed: "Lo, there is no miracle here! This religion has spread by human power." To prevent just such a possibility Christ chose the agency which, humanly speaking, was so unsuited that men would be compelled to exclaim: "Lo, this is not the work of men, but of God!"

In the vast yawning gulf that stretches between the means used and the effect accomplished, the power of God shines forth most luminously. According to every human calculation the religion of the crucified Christ should have gone down in the most ignominious of failures. Its conquest of the world, in spite of the lack of practically every means needed to attain that end, stamps upon its brow the unmistakable imprint of the divine. The same keynote is struck by St. Paul when he exclaims: "The foolish things of the world hath God chosen that He might confound the wise; and the weak things of the world hath God chosen that He might confound the strong. And the base things of the world, and the things that are contemptible, hath God chosen, and things that are not, that He might bring to naught things that are: That no flesh should glory in His sight."[6]

Alexander the Great conquered nations by wading through a sea of blood. In later times Napoleon Bonaparte changed the map of Europe at the price of uncounted soldiery of France. The Apostles conquered the world, however, without taking a drop of innocent blood, but by the willing shedding of their own blood. It has no parallel, therefore, in all the achievements of the world. It was a victory wrought not by human hands, but by the power of God.

In many respects the propagation of the Catholic religion, which is historical Christianity, was a miracle more marvelous and wonderful than the raising of the dead to life. The latter affected but a single person, while the former operated upon millions of souls. From whatever angle the great drama be viewed, the student of history, with an eye to the facts and with a vision unjaundiced by prejudice, is compelled to cry out: *This religion must be born not of man but of God*. It has triumphed where, according to all the laws of history, it should have failed. It bears upon its brow the indelible imprint of the divine. In the moving drama of its birth and propagation there is evidenced to all men, as clear as the sun in the noonday heavens, the guiding finger of the Most High!"

The marvelous spread of the Catholic religion in the first four centuries has its counterpart in the millions of converts flocking to the Church in our day.

Many of the most brilliant minds in America have thought themselves into the Catholic Church. That line we trace from Orestes A. Brownson, a profound philosopher, to Bishop Frederick J. Kinsman, one of the most scholarly of all Anglican divines, down to Professor Carlton J. Hayes, the outstanding historian of Columbia University. The reasons which brought this galaxy of brilliant scholars, as well as the millions of converts into the Church, can all, as G. K. Chesterton pointed out, be reduced to the one reason: *Catholicism is true.*

"The other day," wrote Professor William Lyon Phelps of Yale University, "I read as a piece of news that in 50 years science will have destroyed religion, so that there will be nothing left of it except a memory. Meanwhile conversions to the Roman Catholic Church continue in such quantity and quality as to excite the attention of all who are interested in what is called the trend of modern thought. I recommend to those who wonder 'how any intelligent man can become a Roman Catholic' a little book called *Restoration,* written by Ross J. S. Hoffman, a professor of history in New York University, who tells us how he went from nothing to everything."

The noted author, John L. Stoddard, thus summarizes what his conversion has brought to him: "The Catholic Church has given me order for confusion, certainty for doubt, sunlight for darkness, substance for shadow." Therein is reflected the experience of all converts. Thus does the Catholic religion in the twentieth century continue to grow and expand as it did in the early centuries, demonstrating the abiding presence of the Paraclete, the Spirit of Truth, within her.

Discussion Aids

Analyze methods of pagan propaganda against Christianity. Give examples. Have the methods changed? Discuss means used against pagan propaganda. Tell something of the missionary journeys of some of the Apostles. How is their success to be explained? Name some of the social and moral revolutions in the world's history. Does any one of them compare with the revolution accomplished by these early Christian missionaries? Discuss the propagation of the Catholic religion today.

Practices

Bring to the meeting a piece of anti-Catholic propaganda and compare the method with that of earlier propagandists of the same kind. Analyze it objectively.

Pray for your enemies and for the enemies of the Church.

Don't lose your temper when your convictions are attacked. Defend them with dignity.

NOTES (Chapter 4)

1. Mt. 28:18-20
2. Rom. 10:18
3. Jn. 15:20
4. *Ibid.*, 16:33
5. B.J. Otten, *The Reason Why*, pp. 190-191 (B. Herder, St. Louis, 1912)
6. I Cor. 1:27-29

PART II

The Church:
An Infallible Teacher
The Basis of the Church's Teaching Authority

CHAPTER 5

What Think You of Christ?
A Study of the Divinity of Christ

The gradual discarding of many of the traditional doctrines of historic Christianity has now reached such a stage, that the central fact of the Christian religion, namely, the divinity of Christ, is no longer held by millions of our fellow countrymen who still profess to be Christians. Far from being confined to the laity, the waning belief in this fundamental dogma of the Christian religion would seem to be even more marked among the ministers. Thus Professor Shirley Case of the Divinity School of Chicago University, in a work on *Jesus Through the Centuries*, pictures Christ as a mere man whose moral code, while suitable for the simple pastoral life of the Palestine of His day, stands in need of radical overhauling to make it fit the complex social and industrial life of our modern day.

It has become the fashion to speak of Jesus as a social reformer, comparable to Socrates or to Gandhi; but there is a conspicuous shying away from the traditional view of the revelation of Jesus as supreme, final and unique. This modern vogue is reflected in the letters of two writers appearing in *The Christian Century*.[1] One is from a Christian Association secretary who says: "Because I look at life as a growing process, and the universe characterized by change, I have come to the position where I assert that the nature of religion is growth. The notion that the Christian revelation is final, that Christ is the absolute, the complete, in my mind has far-reaching consequences for ill that we are just beginning to realize."

The second is from a university instructor who writes: "We can, and by all the logic of an unfinished universe, will, either accidentally or by the pains of growing effort, come upon philosophies of life which far transcend that of Jesus, and possibly patterns of living that will be inconsistent with that taught by Jesus."

That such views are not simply those of a few isolated individuals, but are typical of those prevailing in many Protestant denominations, is clearly shown in the study of Professor George Herbert Betts, *The Beliefs of 700 Ministers*. By comparing the beliefs of 500 ministers concerning Christ and those of 200 theological students about to enter the ministry, Professor Betts finds that the following conception of Jesus is becoming increasingly common among ministers:

"He was conceived and born as other men are; he was not wholly free in his earthly life from moral wrong; he neither raised others from the dead nor himself rose from the dead in physical form; in his earthly life he was subject to the limitations of knowledge and science which applied to his day; man's redemption does not rest alone on his suffering and death; he will not appear in a second visible coming upon earth."[2]

Thus, on the basis of the above study, only 44 percent of the newer recruits to the ministry believe that "Jesus is equal in power, knowledge and authority with God," as compared with 76 percent of the older ministers. Only 42 percent of the younger preachers believe "that after Jesus was dead and buried he actually rose from the dead, leaving the tomb empty," as contrasted with 84 percent of the older ministers. Such is the trend toward the sloughing off of the supernatural and the divine from the Christian religion which is so marked in the Protestant denominations in America today. The study clearly shows that the fundamental truths of historic Christianity, especially the divinity of Christ and the finality of His moral code, are being questioned or rejected by not a few non-Catholics.

This condition is observed not with glee but with profound regret. It means that instead of having allies in the battle against the growing forces of naturalism, rationalism and agnosticism, the Catholic Church will have to bear the increasing brunt of the attack.

In the face of this general breakdown of faith in the traditional tenets of Christianity, the Catholic Church stands today as she has stood throughout nineteen centuries, unfaltering and unswerving in her adherence to the plain teaching of Jesus Christ. With her there is no compromise with the time-spirit, no trimming of sails to suit every new wind that blows. She preaches "Jesus Christ, yesterday and today; and the same forever." She adopts as her own, the reply of Peter to the query addressed to the Apostles by the Savior, when seeing many of the Jews leave Him rather than accept His teaching that He would give them His flesh to eat and His blood to drink, He turned to the Apostles themselves, asking, "Will you also go away?" Peter answered in behalf of all the Apostles, "Lord, to whom shall we go? Thou hast the words of eternal life."[3]

With vast millions of so-called Christians deserting the Master by denying His plain teachings concerning His own divine character, the Church takes her stand by the side of her first pontiff, the chief of the Apostles, and says: "Lord, to whom shall we go? Thou hast the words of eternal life."

Of all the teachings of Christ, none are more important or have such far-reaching consequences as those concerning His divinity. If Christ be not God, but a mere man, then the religion which He founded has no divine authority behind it, no finality to its moral code, no uniqueness to its teachings, no mark which differentiates it essentially and generically from Hinduism, Mohammedanism, Confucianism, or the other religions of the world. In short, the authority of the Christian religion stands or falls with the divine character of its Founder. The tremendous implications of this mighty truth are thus pointed out by Robert Browning:

I say the acknowledgment of God in Christ
Accepted by thy reason, solves for thee
All questions in the world and out of it.

What now is the evidence concerning Christ's divinity? I shall not ask the reader to believe in the deity of Jesus simply because the Catholic Church teaches the truth. I shall ask him to examine the plain teachings of the Savior on this point, as recorded in the gospels. For the purpose of this study, it will not be necessary to regard the gospels as divinely inspired documents but simply as truthful narratives. Surely one who calls himself a Christian will grant that the Evangelists did not invent the character of Jesus but that they recorded the truthful story of His life and teachings.

For the sake of brevity we shall pass over the evidence which implies the deity of Jesus, such as the passages wherein He speaks not as an ambassador but in His own name and by His own authority. We shall come at once to the direct and explicit teaching of the Master that He is in literal truth the Son of God, consubstantial with the Father in heaven.

The first scene occurs at Caesarea Philippi. Christ asks the disciples. "Whom do men say that the Son of man is? But they said: Some John the Baptist, and other some Elias, and others Jeremias, or one of the prophets."[4] Not satisfied with their responses, Christ asks the disciples: "But whom do *you* say that I am?" It is at this time that Peter makes his memorable profession of faith in Christ's divinity, saying: "Thou art Christ, the Son of the living God."

Does the Savior tell Peter that he is mistaken, that he has been carried away by his enthusiasm, and that he attributes to his Leader a divine nature which the latter does not really possess? If Peter were mistaken, it would have been the duty not only of Christ but of any honest man to correct Peter and to remove a false impression under which he was laboring. Does

Christ tell Peter he is mistaken? On the contrary, the Master confirms the truth of Peter's statement by assuring him that his answer was divinely revealed unto him, and by rewarding him in a striking manner for his profession of faith:

"And Jesus answering, said to him: Blessed art thou, Simon Bar-Jona: because flesh and blood hath not revealed it to thee, but My Father who is in heaven. And I say to thee: That thou art Peter, and upon this rock I will build My church and the gates of hell shall not prevail against it. And I will give to thee the keys of the kingdom of heaven. And whatsoever thou shalt bind upon earth, it shall be bound also in heaven: and whatsoever thou shalt loose on earth, it shall be loosed also in heaven."

Here then is a dramatic scene in which the Master with the skill of a great teacher carefully prepares the background which makes Peter's unequivocal profession of faith in Christ's divinity stand out like a flash of lightning against a darkened sky. It is obvious that this Sonship of Christ is not used here in the vague sense, in which all good Christians are sons of God by grace and adoption. It is clear that Christ is infinitely more than that namely, the Son of God by nature, that is, consubstantial with God. For this reason Christ is declared by St. John to be "the *only begotten* of the Father, full of grace and truth."[5]

Not less lucid, nor less dramatic, than the scene of the profession of Christ's divinity which occurred at Caesarea Philippi was that which had its setting before the Sanhedrin, the Supreme Court of the Hebrews in which not Peter but Christ Himself is the speaker. The Master is charged with the crime of claiming divine honors, that is, with claiming to be the Son of God. Among the Jews this offense was punished with death.

Caiphas the high priest addressed Christ in the solemn words: "I adjure Thee by the living God, that Thou tell us if Thou be Christ, the Son of God."[6] Jesus knew full well that if He answered in the affirmative, He would be signing His own death warrant. Does He seek to escape the impending doom by giving an equivocal or misleading reply? Does He seek to escape by the simple expedient of denying His own divinity?

On the contrary, without a moment's hesitation, without the slightest equivocation, He answers simply and clearly: "Thou hast said it." This is the Hebrew manner of saying: "Thou hast spoken the truth: I am in very deed." Immediately upon hearing this reply, Caiphas rent his garments, saying: "He hath blasphemed; what further need have we of witnesses? Behold, now you have heard the blasphemy; what think you?" But they answering, said: "He is guilty of death." The fact that the Sanhedrin accused Christ of *blasphemy* showed that they regarded Him as claiming *true* Sonship, and not merely the Messiaship. The false claim to the latter would have been mere prevarication and not blasphemy.

In literal truth, therefore, it can be said that Christ went to His death upon Calvary's gibbet rather than deny or even equivocate concerning His own divine character. How is it possible then for any person, much less a Christian, who regards the gospels even as historical documents, to doubt or to deny the plain teaching of Jesus Christ concerning His own divinity?

The Master not only declared that He was divine but He confirmed it with signs and miracles, especially the miracle of His resurrection. Thus on more than one occasion He appealed to the Jews to believe His works if they would not believe His words. "The works themselves which I do, give testimony of Me, that the Father hath sent Me."[7] And again He says to them: "Believe you not that I am in the Father, and the Father in Me? Otherwise believe for the very works' sake."[8]

St. Peter merely followed the example of his Master in appealing to the wonderful works of the latter as the convincing evidence of His Messiaship and of His divine Sonship. Thus on the first Christian Pentecost morning, when the Apostles are starting out on their sublime mission of winning the world for Christ, St. Peter thus addresses the Jews: "Ye men of Israel hear these words: Jesus of Nazareth, a man *approved of God among you, by miracles, and wonders and signs, which God did by Him,* in the midst of you, as you know."[9]

The effect made not only upon the disciples but also upon the multitudes who witnessed the miracles wrought by Jesus is reflected in the words of Nicodemus: "We know that Thou art come a teacher from God; for no man can do these signs which Thou doest, unless God be with him."[10] Indeed St. John says explicitly that he had recorded the miracles of Jesus for the express purpose of enabling his readers to believe in the deity of

Christ. "Many other signs," he says, "also did Jesus in the sight of His disciples, which are not written in this book. But these are written *that you may believe that Jesus is the Christ, the Son of God;* and that believing you may have life in His name."[11]

Even if there remained any traces of uncertainty in the minds of any of the disciples as to the deity of Jesus after witnessing the numerous miracles He had wrought, surely those vestiges must have been dispelled by the stupendous miracle of the Resurrection. This occurrence, confirmed by such an abundance of testimony, including that of the Apostles who spoke with the Master after His Resurrection, would seem to have removed the last vestiges of uncertainty from the minds of the disciples as to the divine Sonship of Jesus. Even the centurion who had assisted in the crucifixion of the Master felt compelled by the signs and wonders occurring at the time of the Savior's death to cry out his belief in the divinity of Jesus. "Now the centurion," says St. Matthew, "and they that were with him watching Jesus, having seen the earthquake, and the things that were done, were sore afraid, saying: Indeed this was the Son of God."[12]

In the light of all the evidence thus far presented, which indeed is but a fragment of the great mass filling the gospels, it would not seem to be too much to say that if Christ be not divine, then the New Testament considered not only as an inspired document but even simply as an historical work, falls to the ground and with it the whole superstructure of traditional Christianity reposing upon it. The only way to escape from belief in the divine Sonship of Jesus is by impugning the historical truthfulness of the gospel — a procedure for which there is no scientific justification.

In a desperate effort to escape the compelling evidence of the testimony of the Scriptures as to the divine Sonship of Jesus, certain so-called higher critics and modernists in general contend that the early Church did not have any definite teaching on this point. For the first three centuries, they claim, the Church did not know her own mind, or rather had not as yet made it up, concerning the personality of Christ. Her members were permitted to look upon Christ as a sort of inferior deity, who was above all men but lower than the Father, and therefore not strictly divine. This dogma, they allege, reflects the results of three centuries of evolution, not reaching its crystallized form until the Council of Nicea in 325, when belief in Christ's absolute divinity became a necessary condition for membership in the Church.

If this view were true, it would constitute one of the insoluble riddles of the world; for the Apostles and disciples not only considered Christ as God, but many of them died as martyrs for that belief. Would it not be passing strange if they did not communicate to their converts the central article of the faith for which they were willing to suffer not only tortures and imprisonment but death itself? Let us, however, pass over this theoretical consideration of its extreme improbability and look at the facts themselves.

The teachings of the early Church can best be perceived from the profession of faith required by converts to her fold; from the very first it was the custom to require such a profession before the converts were admitted to baptism. To secure uniformity, a set formula was adopted which reflected the most fundamental articles of the faith then taught by the Church. The formula in general use during the first three centuries has been preserved for us, at least in part, by Tertullian,[13] by St. Justin[14] and by St. Irenaeus,[15] all of whom lived and wrote in the second century. Even hostile critics now generally admit that this formula traces its origin to a period not later than the first century, and that it was common to the Church both in the East and in the West.

In this formula, belief in the divinity of Christ is thus explicitly set forth as a necessary condition for entrance into the fold: "I believe in God the Father Almighty, and in Jesus Christ, His only Son, our Lord, who was born by the Holy Spirit of the Virgin Mary." It is identical with the corresponding article of the Apostles' Creed which we Christians of the twentieth century recite, thus professing the same faith as our co-religionists of the first and second centuries. Eighteen hundred years have not altered either our faith in the divine Sonship of Jesus or its external expression.

The writings of the Fathers of the early Church abound in references to this central article of their faith. St. Clement of Rome, St. Ignatius of Antioch, and St. Justin Martyr lay special stress upon it. In his Apology to the Roman Emperor, written toward the end of the second century, Athenagoras of Athens writes: "Not only is the Father God, but also the Son and the Holy Spirit. In these three divine Persons there is unity of Godhead, and in this unity of Godhead there is distinction of Persons."[16] St. Irenaeus of Lyons writes at about the same time: "If Christ forgives sins, if Christ is mediator between God and man, this is because He is really a *divine* Person."[17]

It was to the universal belief of the early Christians in this great truth that St. Polycarp in the middle of the second century bore witness when, bound to the stake to be burned alive, he cried out: "For all things, O God, do I praise and bless Thee, together with the eternal and heavenly Jesus Christ, Thy well-beloved Son, with whom to Thee and the Holy Spirit be glory, both now and forever. Amen."

The same great truth was emphasized by St. Hippolytus of Rome, by Tertullian of Carthage, by Origen and Clement of Alexandria, by St. Methodius of Tyre and by Melito of Sardis. Indeed every writer of the period who referred to the matter, and whose writings have been preserved, taught the same doctrine.

That the mind of the infant Church was very definitely made up on the matter is evident likewise from her manner of dealing with heretics who presumed to deny the true and absolute divinity of Jesus Christ. Thus when Cerinthus toward the end of the first century proclaimed that Jesus was only the son of Mary and Joseph, and not of God, and that He was not, therefore, true God, the whole Church rose up in protest against his heresy and shunned him as an apostate.[18] The same vigorous condemnation was sounded when the Gnostics, and later on the Arians, assigned to the Savior a middle place between the highest angels and the supreme God, and thus reduced Christ to a sort of inferior deity. Without hesitation the Church promptly branded them as heretics who had departed from the faith delivered to them by the Apostles.

So universal was the belief in the divine Sonship of Jesus among the members of the early Church that they looked upon this as the distinguishing mark of the true Christian. The modern non-Catholic writer, Liddon, accurately mirrors the faith of the Church in the first three centuries when he testifies that "the truth of Christ's absolute Godhead was beyond doubt the very central feature of the teaching of the ante-Nicene Church, even when Church teachers had not yet elaborated the accurate statement of its relationship to other truths around it."

The Christians of the first three centuries not only believed in the divinity of Jesus but they translated their belief into action by worshiping Him as God. This fact stands out with special clearness from the charges of polytheism and even of idolatry brought against them by their enemies. Thus Celsus, a scoffing pagan philosopher of the third century, contended that the Christians had no right to criticize the polytheism of the pagan world since their own worship of Christ was essentially polytheistic. "The Christians," he declared, "worshiped no God; no, not even a demon, but only a dead man.[19] . . . If they do not wish to worship the pagan gods," he said, "why should they not rather pay their devotions to some of their own prophets than to a man who had been crucified by the Jews?"[20]

Origen, the greatest of the early Christian writers, defended the Christians from the attacks of Celsus. This he did, not by denying the charge that they worshiped Christ but by showing that the Savior was worthy of such adoration because He was God. "The gods of the pagans," he answers Celsus, "were unworthy of worship; the Jewish prophets had no claim to it; on the other hand, Christ was worshiped not as a mere man, but as the Son of God, as God Himself. If Celsus," he continues, "had understood the meaning of this, 'I and the Father are one,' or what the Son of God says in His prayer, 'As I and Thou art one,' he would never have imagined that we worship any but the God who is over all, for Christ says, 'The Father is in Me, and I in Him.' "[21]

The evidence of the belief of the early Church in the divinity of Jesus would be sadly incomplete, however, if we did not consider the testimony of the Christian martyrs. They speak to us not merely with words but with the far greater eloquence of their sufferings and their deaths. Gladly did some permit their bodies to be coated with pitch and tar and to be burned alive to illumine the gladiatorial contests of the Romans. Others surrendered themselves to be torn limb from limb by the wild lions in the sand-covered arena. Still others placed their heads upon the swordsman's block, while their companions were nailed in ignominy to the cross. These tortures and others, more excruciating still, they suffered cheerfully and with joy, rather than save their lives and gain the promised preferments by denying their God and Savior, Jesus Christ.

They speak to us with voices that thunder in our inner ear. Their heroic deaths cry out in protest against the mockery of the twentieth-century "modernists" who would relegate the divine Founder of the Christian religion to the status of a mere man. Their life's blood has placed upon their faith the seal of a conviction which neither time nor eternity can break. Instead of growing weaker with the lapse of centuries, their voices grow in volume and in strength so that he must needs be deaf indeed who does not heed their thunderings: "We suffered and died for no mere man, but for our God and Savior, Jesus Christ!" In their accents the attentive ear can discern the echoing of the voices of the Apostles and of Christ Himself.

In order to realize what it meant for the martyrs to profess their belief in Christ as true God and seal that faith with their life's blood, it will be helpful to read the account of their ordeals as handed down by an eyewitness. Many such accounts have been preserved. The following one which even hostile critics admit to be genuine will serve as a sample. Before the tribunals of the prefect Calvisianus there had been brought Euplius, a deacon of the Church at Catania, on the charge of being a Christian. According to the usual custom, the prefect endeavored to persuade the prisoner to renounce Christ and offer sacrifice to the pagan gods, promising him freedom for so doing. Perceiving that his entreaties were in vain, he ordered the prisoner to be stretched upon the rack. An eyewitness thus narrates what followed:

"And while being racked, Euplius said: 'I thank Thee, O Christ, guard Thou me, who for Thee am suffering thus.' The prefect interrupted him, saying: 'Cease, Euplius, from this folly. Adore the gods, and thou shalt be set at liberty.' Euplius answered: 'I adore Christ; I utterly hate the demons. Do what thou wilt; I am a Christian.' Add yet other tortures: 'I am a Christian.' After he had been tortured a long while, the executioners were bidden to hold their hands. Then the prefect said: 'Unhappy man, adore the gods. Pay worship to Mars, Apollo and Aesculapius.' Euplius replied: 'I worship the Father and the Son and the Holy Spirit. I adore the Holy Trinity, beside whom there is no God. Perish the gods who did not make heaven and earth, and all that is in them. I am a Christian.'

"The prefect again said: 'Offer sacrifice, if thou wouldst be set at liberty.' But Euplius answered: 'I sacrifice myself only to Christ my God: more than this I cannot do. Thy efforts are to no purpose; I am a Christian.' Then orders were given that he should be tortured again; and whilst every bone was wrenched from its socket, he cried out: "Thanks to Thee, O Christ. Help me, O Christ! For Thee do I suffer thus, O Christ.' When finally all his strength had left him and his voice was gone, he still repeated these same exclamations with his lips only."[22]

In the dying words of Euplius there is echoed the confession of faith in Christ's divinity that came from the lips not of hundreds but of thousands of martyrs: with their last breath, they breathed the name of their Lord and Master, Jesus Christ. That long line of martyrs, consisting of men, women and children, who withstood the allurements of the prefects and the refined cruelties of the executioners, who poured out their treasures and their life's blood for their Savior, reveal to us the faith of the infant Church with a clarity and a certainty that far transcend the power of mere words to express. Their profession of faith is written in the deathless language of immortal deed.

The writer would like to rest the case here. There is, however, a school of thought in which Jesus is spoken of as a great social reformer, a noble, ethical personality, but not divine, which demands at least brief consideration.

This school of writers, of which Renan stands as an early symbol and in which an increasing number of Protestant ministers are now to be found, depicts Jesus as wiser than Socrates, a greater lawgiver than Solon, a nobler ethical personality than Plato or Spinoza. They speak in superlative terms of His mercy and sympathy; they exalt His humility and mildness; they marvel at His keen insights into human nature; they style Him the noblest and the best of all mankind. They stop just short of crossing the gap separating the human from the divine — carefully refraining from calling Him God.

The following description of Christ by Rev. Dr. Herbert Parrish, an Episcopalian clergyman of note, is typical of the manner in which modernists in general and an increasing number of Protestant ministers speak of Jesus as a beautiful personality while they studiously withhold from Him the crowning glory of divinity: "Man stands at the apex of the visible creation amid the vast eternities of time and space. Before him rises the significant figure of the Christ. No human life compares with the bright and beautiful history of this young Galilean teacher. Greater than Confucius or the Buddha, more persuasive than the dreams of Plato or the arguments of Aristotle, his words have had more effect upon history than the marching of the armies of Alexander or the conquests of Caesar. The famous men in the records of the race pale beside him.

"Leaving aside the slender story of his miraculous birth and the discordant accounts of his resurrection, by which he was accounted an equal to the demigods of the pagan mysteries of the Mediterranean littoral of his day, and paying no heed to the creeds, decrees, conciliar decisions, hairsplitting definitions of theologians, by which it was attempted to reach an exact account of his relation to the divine essence, as a result of which he has become in many minds a kind of second God, it is of the highest value to consider merely his human character and the records of his teaching. . . . Hence, as a man he is the wonder and admiration of the world."[23]

It will be noted that Dr. Parrish is most anxious to efface from the character of Jesus all the lineaments of the divine, while elevating Him to the highest ethical plane as a man or even as a superman of the Nietzsche type. But one wonders: What about the repeated declarations of Christ to be one with the Father, to be divine? What about His profession of His divine Sonship before Caiphas — a profession that sent Him to Calvary's gibbet? Dr. Parrish has a facile solution of these "astounding egoisms" of His character. Jesus suffered from a mental complex! The cause of His strange hallucination is now laid bare and all mystery fades away.

Thus says Dr. Parrish: "His teaching was profound and penetrating. In the moral and spiritual sphere he is admittedly without a rival. Whatever traditional sources he may have used,

102

he gave a colorful simplicity and an added touch to age-long wisdom. The modern critic may conclude that he had what the psychoanalysts would call a complex in that he was convinced that his interior life was illuminated by the divine indwelling and the egoisms attributed to him are of the astounding sort. He was one with the Father. But there is no reason to think that the mind of Jesus received its illumination in any way different from that of other men. As in the cases of the inventors, discoverers, artists and musicians cited, the nights of prayer and meditation, the long preparation invited to the clear mind of a supreme genius an influx of supernal light."[24]

Here, indeed, are some fine antics of juggling. On the one hand, Christ is a great moral and spiritual teacher — admittedly without a rival. On the other hand, this Christ who says He is one with the Father, who tells us He "shall come in his majesty, and all the angels with him, then shall he sit upon the seat of his majesty: and all nations shall be gathered together before him,"[25] is the victim of megalomania, suffering delusions of grandeur, and His testimony is, therefore, thoroughly unreliable. Is this not a capital illustration of a man blowing hot and cold at the same time? Is it not a clear case of a person contradicting with one breath that which was uttered with the previous one? Within the limits of a single paragraph, Christ is depicted as the greatest moral and spiritual teacher in the world. Then suddenly the mask falls. Christ is disclosed to us as suffering from a mental complex, experiencing egoisms "of the most astounding sort," which render His utterances so many hallucinations, the expressions of a diseased mind.

The writer must confess his total inability to reconcile these two mutually contradictory portraits of Jesus. How different from the conclusion of Dr. Parrish was that reached by that other erstwhile skeptic, Thomas, who doubted the testimony of the other Apostles that Christ had appeared to them during his absence. When later the Master appeared in their midst, "the doors being shut," He said to the doubting Thomas: "Put in thy finger hither, and see My hands; and bring hither thy hand, and put it into My side, and be not faithless, but believing." Then it was that the last vestige of doubt was dispelled from the mind of Thomas, who says simply: "My Lord and my God."[26]

Hence, of all the positions which one may take in regard to the character of Jesus, this position of the modernists as expressed by Dr. Parrish is, in the judgment of the writer, the most illogical and untenable. Why? For the simple reason that *if Jesus is simply a good and truthful man, He must be God,* for Jesus claims to be one with the Father, claims to be divine. He goes to His death upon Calvary for His insistence upon this fact; He teaches His disciples this fact. He sends them out to teach the world this truth, and to be willing to die Himself rather than deny it.

Now if Christ be not divine He is either a willful deceiver or the victim of hallucinations which blight His whole character and personality. If He is the unconscious victim of delusions, then He is equally untrustworthy as an ethical teacher or guide. In either event, His whole character and personality wither away, and He becomes totally unworthy of the encomiums heaped upon Him in such profusion by the rationalists and modernists above described. Not only that, but He would be the greatest enemy of God, usurping the sole right of the latter to the adoration of mankind. Yes, even more than that, since Christ wrought miracles in comfirmation of His claim to be divine, if He be not God, then there is no God in heaven!

Hence the relentless logic of the Catholic Church, scorning such pathetic compromises as the modernists have fallen into, proclaims that *Christ is either God or a deceiver.* To thoughtful minds there can be no third alternative. To her mind, truth above all other considerations is paramount. That is why today she holds fast to the truth of the divinity of Christ, undisturbed by the defections of the fainthearted all around her. She realizes that it is the divine character of Christ that gives authority to His religious teachings and validity to His moral code. She realizes, furthermore, that it is not a matter of indifference to the Savior as to whether men acknowledge Him as true God, or deny Him before the Sanhedrins of the twentieth century. For in her memory are enshrined the clear words of the divine Savior: "Every one therefore that shall confess Me before men, I will also confess him before My Father who is in heaven. But he that shall deny Me before men, I will also deny him before My Father who is in heaven."[27]

Christ remains the most potent influence in the life of the world. As Richter has said so beautifully of Him, "The purest among the strong and the strongest among the pure, Christ lifted with His wounded hands empires from their hinges and changed the stream of centuries." Even the sensual Rousseau perceives the lineaments of the divine in the character of Christ as depicted in the gospels, and gives expression to his conviction in the following striking lines:

"I confess to you that the majesty of the Scriptures strikes me with admiration, as the purity of the gospels has its influence on my heart. Peruse the works of our philosophers, with all their pomp of diction; how mean, how contemptible they are, compared with the Scriptures! Is it possible that a book, at once so simple and sublime, should be merely the work of man? Is it possible that the sacred personage whose history it contains should be Himself a mere man? Do we find that He assumed the tone of an enthusiast or ambitious sectary? What sweetness, what purity in His manners! What an affecting gracefulness in His delivery! What sublimity in His maxims! What profound wisdom in His discourses! What presence of mind in His replies! How great the command over His passions! Where is the man, where is the philosopher who could so live and so die, without weakness, without ostentation? . . . Yes, if the life and death of Socrates were those of a sage, the life and death of Jesus were those of a God."[28]

To the query which Christ addressed to the Pharisees nineteen centuries ago — "What think you of Christ? Whose Son is he?" — the Church replies in the twentieth century in the words uttered by Peter in the first: "Thou art Christ, the Son of the living God."

Discussion Aids

What is the central fact of Christianity? Give a few examples of non-Catholic attitude towards this fact. Give main conclusions to be drawn from Professor Betts's study. Examine the evidence for Christ's divinity from:

1. Gospel testimony.

a. Caesarea Philippi (Matthew 27).

b. Christ before the Sanhedrin (Matthew 28). Analyze the charge of blasphemy.

2. Miracles.

a. Christ's own claims (John 5:36; 14:11-12).

b. The Resurrection.

When did the dogma of Christ's divinity crystallize? Name several ante-Nicene witnesses from among the Fathers of the Church. Who were some of the early heretics on the doctrine? Reproduce substance of Origen's argument against Celsus. How is the testimony of the martyrs to the doctrine of the divinity of Christ convincing? Analyze the juggling of the modernists, using Rev. Dr. Herbert Parrish as an example. Defend the contention that Christ was either God or a deceiver. Close the case by quoting Peter's words at Caesarea Philippi.

Practices

Make Karl Adam's *The Son of God* part of your library. Read it thoughtfully.

Salute Christ in the Holy Eucharist, especially at the time of the elevation, saying with St. Thomas, "My Lord and my God!"

Prepare yourself to defend the central fact of Christianity, the divinity of Christ, by reading and meditation.

NOTES (Chapter 5)

1. Elliott Phillips, "Convictions and the Open Mind," p. 731 in *The Christian Century*, June 8, 1932

2. *The Beliefs of 700 Ministers*, p. 35 (Abingdon Press, N.Y., 1920)

3. Jn. 6:68

4. Mt. 16:13-14

5. Jn. 1:14

6. Mt. 26:63

7. Jn. 5:36

8. *Ibid.,* 14:11-12
9. Acts 2:22
10. Jn. 3:2
11. *Ibid.,* 20:30
12. Mt. 27:54
13. *De Praescript,* c. 36
14. *Apol.,* I, 61, 1
15. *Adv. Haer.,* 1, 10
16. C. 20
17. *Adv. Haer.,* III, 9, 2
18. St. Irenaeus, *Adv. Haer.,* V
19. Origen, *Contra Celsum,* VII, 68
20. *Ibid.,* VII, 53
21. *Ibid.,* VIII, 12
22. Ruinart, *Acta Mart.,* p. 439 (Vatican Library)
23. *A New God for America,* p. 213 (Century Co., N.Y., 1928)
24. Op. cit., p. 214
25. Mt. 25:31
26. Jn. 20:28
27. Mt. 10:32-33
28. *Emile,* Book 4

CHAPTER 6

The Infallibility of the Pope

A Divine Safeguard Against Error

There is probably no other dogma of the Catholic religion which is so frequently misunderstood, and which occasions so much opposition on the part of our non-Catholic friends, as that which proclaims the infallible teaching authority of the Church as centered in the person of her supreme head, the pope, the ruler of Christ's Church on earth. Let me invite our non-Catholic readers to consider this question in a calm, friendly manner. I am confident they will find that what they really wage war against is not papal infallibility as held by the Catholic Church, but a caricature of that teaching which exists only in their minds.

To establish the truthfulness and the reasonableness of this teaching of our holy faith, I shall appeal not to the authority of the Church, but to the words of our Lord and Savior, Jesus Christ, and to the court of our common understanding.

First, let us consider what papal infallibility does *not* mean. Contrary to the idea of many people, infallibility does not mean that the pope is inspired. The Apostles and Evangelists received this gift, and their writings are accepted as the revealed Word of God. But the Church does not teach that the pope is inspired, or that he receives a divine revelation properly so-called.

Thus the Vatican Council declares: "For the Holy Spirit was not promised to the successors of Peter in order that they might spread abroad new doctrine which He reveals, but that, under His assistance, they might guard inviolably, and with fidelity explain, the revelation or deposit of faith handed down by the Apostles."

Secondly, infallibility does not signify that the pope is impeccable or incapable of moral wrong. Many people are in the habit of pointing to some one pontiff, whose character is not entirely free from blemishes, and saying: "See, there is a pope who was guilty of a misdeed. That proves that he was not infallible, and, therefore, that none of the popes is." The answer is simple. The objection does not come within speaking distance of the meaning of infallibility. Why? Because infallibility does not mean sinlessness or freedom from all human weaknesses or shortcomings.

As a matter of fact, the popes have been, with few exceptions, men of virtuous lives. Twenty-nine out of the first thirty pontiffs died as martyrs for the faith. Out of the total who have sat upon the Chair of Peter, seventy-seven are invoked upon our altars as saints of God because of their eminent holiness. Only about half a dozen have been charged with serious moral lapses. This is a strikingly small proportion when it is remembered that one out of the twelve chosen by Christ Himself was unworthy — Judas Iscariot.

Even if a great majority of the pontiffs, however, should have led vicious lives, this circumstance would not have impaired the prerogative of infallibility. This was bestowed upon the office they occupied, not for the protection of their morals, but for the guidance of their judgment in their religious teaching. Thus, for example, a judge is clothed by the laws of our country with certain legal power and authority. If in his private life he were guilty of some moral indiscretions, this circumstance would not rob his decisions of their validity. His authority in court is not dependent upon the character of his private life; it is conferred upon him by virtue of the office he holds.

So likewise the prerogative of infallibility is conferred upon the office of the papacy, and is dependent in no way upon the private life of the incumbent. Like the legal authority of a judge, it is conferred upon the office for the welfare of society for which such an office was established.

As a matter of fact, the pontiff proclaims the frailties which he has in common with all humanity. Each morning, at the beginning of Mass, he says at the foot of the altar in all humility: "I confess to Almighty God ... and to His saints, that I have sinned exceedingly in thought, word and deed." Likewise, at the Offertory of the Mass, he prays: "Receive, O Holy Father, almighty, everlasting God, this oblation which I, Thy unworthy servant, offer for my innumerable sins, offenses and negligences."

Despite the eminence of his office, the pope does not pretend to be exempt from either the frailties or the temptations which constitute the common lot of all humanity. Not for a moment does he claim an utter sinlessness of life because of the mark of infallibility inhering in the office he holds.

In view of these facts, is it not strange that ministers of the Christian gospel should seek to discredit the dogma of papal infallibility by telling their congregations that there have been sinful popes? In what manner are the interests of the Prince of Truth advanced by deliberately misrepresenting the teachings of the Catholic Church on this point? Surely Protestantism is not strengthened, nor is Catholicism weakened, by the artifice of building a sham opponent, a man of straw, and then with much gust demolishing it.

Thirdly, infallibility does not mean that the pope is free from the possibility of error in discussing questions of natural science, such as physics, geology, astronomy, or medicine — matters which involve in no way the deposit of revealed truth. Neither does the inerrability of the pontiff extend to purely political questions, such as the form of government a nation ought to adopt, or the candidates for whom Catholic citizens ought to vote. It does not, therefore, restrict the freedom of the scientists nor trespass upon the civil authority of the state.

Fourthly, infallibility does not signify that the pontiff is immune from liability to error in any domain when he speaks merely as a private teacher. In this capacity he is liable to err even in matters of faith and morals. Thus if a pope, like Benedict XIV, were to write a treatise on canon law, his work would be subject to criticism in the same manner as that of any other scholar of the Church.

What, then, does infallibility really mean? Simply this: When the pope in his official capacity, with the fullness of his authority, as successor of St. Peter and head of the Church on earth, proclaims a doctrine of faith or morals binding on the whole Church, he is preserved from error. It is to be noted that three conditions are required:

1. The pope must speak *ex cathedra*, i.e., from the Chair of Peter, in his official capacity.

2. The decision must be binding on the whole Church.

3. It must be on a matter of faith or morals.

The pope has no authority to invent a new doctrine. He is not the author of revelation, but only its interpreter and expounder. He has no more authority to break a divine law or to distort an iota of Scripture than you or I; his function is to hand down unchanged the deposit of divine truth to all generations of men.

His office in the interpretation of Holy Scripture is fundamentally the same as that of the supreme court of the United States in the interpretation of the constitution. When a difference of opinion arises as to the construction of a constitutional provision, the question is referred in the last resort to the supreme court at Washington. When the chief justice with his associates pronounces judgment upon it, that decision is accepted by all parties as final and irrevocable by any other court.

Every citizen of our country praises the wisdom of the founding fathers in arranging this tribunal for the peaceful adjudication of disputes concerning the meaning of the constitution, which the fathers foresaw would inevitably arise. Without such a court the constitution would soon be torn into shreds by conflicting interests. Anarchy, secession and civil war would speedily displace the political union of so many states having diverse racial complexions and different economic interests.

That the Union has been preserved is traceable to the existence of the supreme court. Indeed, historians are agreed that the one Civil War which has occurred in our national existence would have been avoided if our domestic quarrel had been submitted to the supreme court instead of having been left to the arbitration of the sword.

The same basic arrangement which has preserved the unity of our states has safeguarded the unity of the Catholic Church. Without the supreme court of the papacy to appeal to, the Catholic Church would long ago have been torn into a thousand warring factions. One has but to observe the innumerable divisions which have rent the body of Protestantism, during the few centuries of its existence, to perceive the chaos and anarchy that would have developed during the nineteen hundred years of the Church's existence, if she were without the divinely established tribunal of papal infallibility as a court of last appeal. The marvelous unity of the Church which has provoked the admiration of the world is the happy consequence of the work of her supreme and infallible court which has been functioning with unbroken continuity for nineteen centuries.

The analogy between the function of the supreme court in the interpretation of the constitution and that of the pope in the interpretation of Holy Scripture can scarcely fail to make a profound appeal to every citizen of our country regardless of religious belief. A non-Catholic lawyer, to whom the writer pointed out this similarity, commented as follows: "Yes, indeed, the analogy is striking. But there is a difference worth noting. It is this: While recognizing that the decision of the supreme court is binding and without appeal, we do not admit it to be infallible. It may still be wrong. Whereas, you Catholics maintain that the decision of the pope is not only binding but also infallible. In that respect, the comparison limps."

Let me now address to my dear non-Catholic reader the words I then addressed to my legal friend: The difference you point out is true. But it is to be noted that making the decision of the supreme court final and irrevocable demands in theory that it should be infallible. For its decision should not bind unless it be unvaryingly the voice of truth and justice. Otherwise there is the possibility of binding the parties under the penalty of imprisonment to accept a false and unjust decision. The pronouncement has, therefore, all the practical consequences of infallibility. Strict logic would require that a decision that has all the sanctions of infallibility should actually be infallible.

Now it is to be admitted that while the supreme court has the sanctions for an infallible decision, it does not, nevertheless, really possess infallibility. Why? Simply because the founding fathers, who conferred its powers upon it, did not themselves possess infallibility and were not able, therefore, to give the supreme court the actual inerrancy which its decisions, binding, final and without appeal, would logically require.

But Jesus Christ is the Founder of the Catholic Church and of the supreme tribunal of papal infallibility. In giving to the court the power making its decision binding and without appeal, He gave it that which the authoritativeness and the irrevocability of its decisions really demand — actual infallibility.

Unlike the founding fathers, He possessed infallibility and was able, therefore, to confer it upon the highest tribunal in His Church. Yes, more than that, He was in duty bound to confer it. Otherwise He would be responsible for a court whose decision is binding in conscience upon all its members, and yet in that decision there would be the possibility of falsehood and injustice.

"Upon reflection," said my legal friend, "I must admit that I can see no possibility of escape from the logic of that conclusion."

From the binding and irrevocable character of the decisions of the pope speaking in his official capacity, infallibility follows therefore as a logical necessity.

Let us now see if the voice of reason is confirmed by the handwriting of history. Let us see if such inerrancy was, as a matter of historical fact, conferred by Christ upon Peter, the first pontiff of His Church.

The scene occurs at Caesarea Philippi. Peter has just made his memorable profession of faith in Christ's divinity, saying: "Thou art Christ, the Son of the living God." The Master rewarded Peter in the following words: "Blessed art thou, Simon Bar-Jona: because flesh and blood hath not revealed it to thee, but My Father who is in heaven, and I say to thee: That thou art Peter; and upon this rock I will build My Church, and the gates of hell shall not prevail against it. And I will give to thee the keys of the kingdom of heaven. And whatsoever thou shalt bind upon earth, it shall be bound also in heaven, and whatsoever thou shalt loose upon earth, it shall be loosed also in heaven."[1]

This solemn promise to confer upon Peter the primacy among the Apostles and the authority to teach and rule the Church is couched in distinctly Aramaic phraseology, abounding in characteristic Jewish metaphors and idioms. When translated into English the passage loses some of its force. Thus the work "kepha" is used for both "Peter" and "rock" in the language used by our Lord. What Christ said to Peter then was: "Thou art Rock [kepha] and upon this rock [kepha] I will build my Church."

The expression "gates of hell" signifies the powers of death or evil. The conferring of keys is a common Jewish metaphor indicating the bestowal of authority. Down to the present day the key remains the symbol of jurisdiction. When a distinguished visitor arrives in one of our large cities, the officials sometimes confer upon him a large key as the symbol of his authority to rule the city for the day. Translating the rich imagery and symbolism of the Aramaic language used by our Savior into current English, Christ said in effect to Peter:

"You are the solid foundation upon which I will build my Church; I assure you that the powers of death and evil shall not prevail against it. I give you the authority to rule the Church, to bind and to loosen; to decide what is right and wrong, lawful and unlawful; and your decisions are ratified by God Himself."

On the memorable occasion of the Last Supper, Christ said to Peter: "Simon, Simon, behold Satan hath desired to have you, that he may sift you as wheat: But I have prayed for *thee*, that *thy* faith fail not: and thou, being once converted, confirm thy brethren."[2] Here again the Savior assures Peter that the powers of evil shall not prevail against him and authorizes him to guide and strengthen his brethren in the faith.

After His Resurrection when Christ had secured from Peter the pledge of his love and loyalty, He said to him: "Feed My lambs. . . . Feed My sheep."[3] In these words our Lord authorizes Peter to feed with the nourishing food of truth not only the lay members of the fold, but the elders in the flock, the disciples and the Apostles as well.

The conferring of infallible teaching authority, centering in Peter the visible head of the Church, is likewise evident from the words Christ addressed to all the Apostles: "All power is given to Me in Heaven and in earth. Going, therefore, teach ye all nations, baptizing them in the name of the Father, and of the Son, and of the Holy Spirit, teaching them to observe all things whatsoever I have commanded you: and behold *I am with you* all days, even to the consummation of the world."[4]

The expression, "I am with you," occurs some ninety times

114

in the Old and New Testaments, and always signifies that special divine assistance will be given to guarantee the success of the mission assigned. Christ is truth; where Christ is, error cannot coexist. It is the definite assurance to the infant Church that in teaching mankind the religion of Christ, the Church will not lead the world astray by teaching falsehood. Christ says to the Apostles in effect: "I, the eternal truth, will abide with you, will speak and teach through you, and give you My unfailing guidance and assistance."

In the same explicit way Christ promises to send the Holy Spirit, the Spirit of Truth, upon the Apostles: "And I will ask the Father, and He shall give you another Paraclete, that He may abide with you forever. The Spirit of Truth, whom the world cannot receive, because it seeth Him not, nor knoweth Him, because He shall abide with you, and shall be in you. . . . But the Paraclete, the Holy Spirit whom the Father will send in My name, He will teach you all things and bring all things to your mind, whatsoever I shall have said to you."[5]

In these words Christ assures the infant Church of the abiding presence of the Spirit of Truth guiding her in her teaching mission. This assurance of the Church's unfailing fidelity to the teachings of her divine Founder is the evidence of what we call the infallibility of the Church as focused in her supreme head, the pope, the successor of Peter.

Many other utterances of Christ guaranteeing His unfailing guidance to His Church and her leader in the divinely appointed task of teaching all nations might be cited. The ones already presented, however, are ample evidence to carry conviction to the open mind.

A few questions now remain to be considered. First, a university professor once said to me after I had presented the above evidence: "Father, I grant that the Scripture evidence is abundantly sufficient to show that Christ guaranteed to Peter and his fellow Apostles a guidance that would safeguard them from error in their teaching. But isn't there quite a gap from Peter to Pope Paul VI? What evidence is there that Paul VI enjoys in the twentieth century the immunity from error given to Peter in the first?"

Let me address to my dear non-Catholic reader the words I

addressed to my professorial friend: The mission which Christ gave to Peter and his fellow Apostles was that of teaching all nations and all mankind. It was to endure until the last soul shall be gathered into the arms of its Creator. But Peter and his associates were mortal men, destined to pass away with their generation while their mission was to continue with their successors. This is clearly disclosed by the words of Christ: "Behold I am *with you all days even to the consummation of the world.*" Since the Apostles were not to live until the end of the world, Christ promised to be with them in the person of their successors unto the end of time.

The logic of this conclusion can be denied only by those who believe that Christ was interested in saving only the souls of those who lived in His day, and was totally indifferent about all posterity. This, no Christian would maintain. Therefore, Christ must have provided for the certain transmission of His teachings to mankind through all the centuries. This is possible only through a teaching authority that is divinely safeguarded from error. Hence the pope today and all his successors will enjoy the same infallible teaching authority which was conferred upon the first pope, Peter the fisherman.

Second, a non-Catholic bishop in a sermon against papal infallibility recently said: "For my part, I have an infallible Bible and this is the only infallibility I require." While plausible at first view, such a statement cannot stand the test of scrutiny.

Let me address myself in the following kindly manner to this bishop as the representative of all who share such a view: "Either, my dear friend, you are infallibly certain that your particular interpretation of the Bible is the correct one or you are not. If you maintain that you are infallibly certain, then you claim for yourself — and you cannot very well deny the same for every other reader of the Bible — a personal infallibility which you deny only to the pope and which we claim only for him. According to this view each of the hundreds of millions of readers of the Bible becomes a pope, while the only one who is not a pope is the pope himself. You avoid admitting the infallibility of the pope by multiplying infallibility by the number of readers of the Bible.

"If you do not claim to be infallibly certain that your interpretation of the whole Bible is correct, then of what value is it to have an infallible Bible without an infallible interpreter? In either case your statement crumbles. The plain fact is that *an infallible Bible without an infallible living interpreter is futile.* Infallibility never gets from the printed pages to the one place it is needed: the mind of the reader. The myriad divisions within Protestantism offer ample evidence of the truth of this statement."

This fact is well stated by a non-Catholic writer, W. H. Mallock, in his *Is Life Worth Living?* [6] "Any supernatural religion," he says, "that renounces its claim to this [infallibility], it is clear, can profess to be a semi-revelation only. It is a hybrid thing, partly natural and partly supernatural, and it thus practically has all the qualities of a religion that is wholly natural. Insofar as it professes to be revealed, it of course professes to be infallible; but if the revealed part be in the first place hard to distinguish, and in the second place hard to understand; if it may mean many things, and many of these things contradictory, it might as well never have been made at all. To make it in any sense an infallible revelation, or in other words a revelation at all to *us*, we need a power to interpret the testament that shall have equal authority with that testament itself."

Indeed, the question might well be asked of those who deny the establishment by Christ of an infallible teaching authority to safeguard the unity of His Church: Do you not indict the intelligence of our divine Lord when you deny to Him the foresight shown by the founders of the Republic in providing for a supreme authority to interpret the constitution and thus safeguard the permanence of the Union? Is it reasonable to suppose that divine Omniscience would fail to provide as effectively for the preservation of the unity of the Church as the founders did for the unity of the Republic?

Third, a last question remains. Is not the doctrine of papal infallibility an undue infringement upon the freedom of the intellect? Is not a Catholic hampered in his search for scientific truth by a blind degrading obedience to the arrogant claims of an infallible Church? Here a distinction is necessary: there is a legitimate freedom and an illegitimate one. The first is the freedom of believing the truth; the second is the freedom of believing

Catholic Church Alone

Christ Founds His Church on Peter in 33 A.D.

"Thou art Peter; and upon this rock I will build My Church ... And I will give to thee the keys of the kingdom of heaven."

Matthew 16:17-19

Unbroken succession of Popes from St. Peter to present Pope.

Catholic Church in continous existence from days of Christ, embraces all nations, and has largest membership.

Founded by Christ and authorized to teach and preach in His Name. He gave her the title deed to the deposit of divine revelation to teach it to all nations. She alone has valid title deed to all Christian truth.

Has Received Valid Title Deed
Telltale Gap of Fifteen Centuries

FROM CHRIST TO THE FIRST PROTESTANT
CHURCH SHOWS LACK OF ANY VALID TITLE

Martin Luther Founds Protestantism in 1524

SPLITTING OF PROTESTANTISM
INTO MORE THAN 400 SECTS

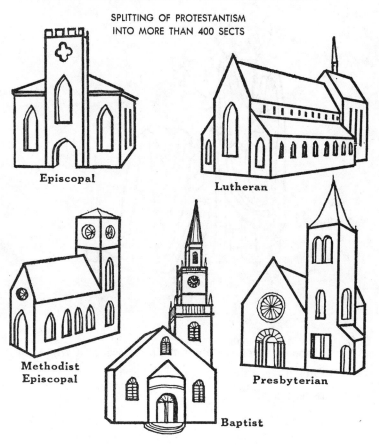

Episcopal

Lutheran

Methodist
Episcopal

Baptist

Presbyterian

Christ Guarantees
Catholic Church

"Thou art Peter; and upon this rock I will build My Church, and the gates of hell shall not prevail against it . . . ."

Matthew 16:18

Permanence of His Church

Founded Upon A Rock

Catholic Church, founded upon rock of Peter, governed by his successors, has more than double the membership of the 400 Protestant sects. Catholic faith is identical with that of Christ and Apostles, unchanged and unchanging.

error, which is in reality an abuse of the mind and constitutes a form of intellectual anarchy.

No one has the right to believe error any more than one has the right to do wrong. The freedom of believing that four plus four are twenty-seven is enjoyed only by inmates of an insane asylum. There is an inalienable obligation binding every rational person to believe the truth. This is the only obligation which the doctrine of infallibility imposes. It is not a limitation of intellectual liberty but an augmentation of it; for the acceptance of truth always enlarges the domain of the intellect. "You shall know the truth," said Christ, "and the truth shall make you free."[7]

A Catholic does not give a blind degrading obedience to a fallible teacher who might ask him to accept without question any preposterous statement. The Church does not possess the authority to invent new doctrines but only to interpret those divinely revealed. Thus the able and scholarly encyclicals of the last four pontiffs are not, strictly speaking, infallible, since they do not absolutely define a dogma of faith. When a dogma is defined for the universal Church, this does not mean that it is invented, but merely that an article of the faith always held implicitly is now set forth in explicit terms.

This doctrine does not restrain a Catholic from the free prosecution of scientific truth, nor prevent him from acceptance of any fact clearly demonstrated by science. Truth can never contradict truth: nor can one truth ever serve as an obstacle to the acceptance of other truth, but only as a stimulus. Infallibility, as Cardinal Newman points out, "is a supply for a need, and it does not go beyond the need. Its object is, and its effect also, not to enfeeble the freedom or vigor of human thought, but to resist and control its extravagances."[8]

While visiting with the writer, Dr. Frederick J. Kinsman, formerly Episcopalian bishop of Delaware and one of the greatest scholars in his Church, repeated to an audience of University students what he had previously written in his *Salve Mater*[9]: "My attitude toward the Church is one of entire submission. 'Crucifixion of the intellect,' some object. I should call it 'resurrection, 'but so long as I experience the fact, I shall not quarrel about the word. My chief consciousness as a Catholic is a new freedom. Cardinal Gibbons, in a little address to me, said that in spite of 'exterior hardships,' which he knew I must encounter, he hoped that I might enjoy 'interior sunshine.' That I think expresses what has been given."

What the compass is to the sailor tossed about in his frail bark by a tempestuous sea in the dark of night, infallibility is to the wayfarer searching for religious truth amidst the error that envelopes him as a mist on every side. It is his certain guide to the harbor of truth: it is the safeguard which a beneficent Father has provided for the unerring transmission of revealed truth to His children in all the centuries of time. Papal infallibility is, therefore, not only entirely reasonable, but it is an absolutely necessary safeguard for the transmission of truth without the admixture of error to all the generations of men.

Discussion Aids

Is the pope inspired? Is the pope incapable of sin? Have many popes been holy men? Give some figures. Does the prerogative of infallibility depend on holiness of life? Distinguish between the office and the man. Is the pope free from the possibility of error on scientific questions? Political questions? As a private teacher (even in matters of faith and morals)? When, then, is the pope infallible? Name the three necessary conditions of infallibility. Does the prerogative enable the pope to invent *new* doctrines? Just what is his function in the matter of infallibility? Draw an analogy between infallibility and the decisions of the supreme court. Show where the analogy (like every other analogy) limps. As evidence of Christ's intentions as to Peter's headship, study carefully and discuss (1) Christ's appointment of Peter as head (Matthew 16); (2) Christ's promise of guidance to Peter (Luke 22:31-32); Christ's authorization of Peter (John 21:15-17). For Peter's infallible teaching power, examine Matthew 28:18-20. For the abiding power of the Holy Spirit examine John 14:16-17. Answer the objection that there is a gap between Peter and Paul VI. How do you answer the statement that the Bible is infallible and sufficient of itself? Why is an infallible teaching power eminently logical? Answer the charge that infallibility is an infringement on intellectual freedom. Quote Newman and Kinsman on infallibility.

Practices

Join fervently in the prayers that are said at the foot of the altar after Mass, which are said for the intentions of the Holy Father.

Read carefully and meditate on the gospel story of Peter's great confession at Caesarea Philippi.

Pray often to St. Peter for prosperity of the Church's teaching.

NOTES (Chapter 6)

1. Mt. 16:17-19
2. Lk. 22:31-32
3. Jn. 21:15-17
4. Mt. 28:18-20
5. Jn. 14:16-17, 26
6. *Is Life Worth Living?*, p. 267 (Belford, Clark & Co., Chicago, 1879)
7. Jn. 8:32
8. *Apologia*, p. 253 (Longmans, Green & Co., 1905)
9. F.J. Kinsman, *Salve Mater*, p. 13 (Longmans, Green & Co., N.Y.)

CHAPTER 7

The Church:
The Interpreter of the Bible

Why the Bible Alone Is Not a Safe Guide in Religion

"The Catholic Church is hostile to the Bible. In the past, she withheld it from the laity by forbidding its translation into the vernacular. By keeping the Bible in Latin, she confined it chiefly to the clergy. She did not want the common people to read it for fear they might begin to think for themselves and thus free themselves from the domination of the clergy. It was the Reformers who put the Bible in the hands of the people. Even today the Catholic Church discourages her members from reading the Bible for themselves, for fear that they might take their religion from the Scriptures instead of from the Church."

Such are some of the charges most frequently brought against the Church by our non-Catholic friends. They were voiced with redoubled frequency during 1946, when Lutherans were celebrating the four-hundredth anniversary of the death of Martin Luther, the founder of their Church. Priding themselves on being Bible Christians, taking their religion directly from the Scriptures, Protestants view with deep-seated disapproval the policy of a Church which, they allege, emphasizes its own authority and minimizes that of the written word of God.

They wonder at the docility of Catholics who submit to an arrangement which centralizes practically all authority in an institution and thus affords them little, if any, opportunity for direct examination of the teachings of Jesus Christ as recorded in the Scriptures. Where is that independent reasoning, that thinking for onself, which is characteristic of our American democracy and of which our citizens are so proud?

What now are the facts? Briefly these: Far from being hostile to the Bible, the Catholic Church is its true mother. She determined which are the books of religion from the many writings circulated as inspired in the early Christian ages and assembled them all within the covers of a single book. She shielded it from destruction by the hordes of barbarian invaders that poured into Europe and translated it into many languages long before Protestantism saw the light of day. If she regarded the Bible as her enemy, she had plenty of opportunity to destroy it centuries before Protestantism came into existence.

The simple fact is the Catholic Church loves the Bible, reveres it as the inspired word of God, gives to it a loyalty and an intelligent obedience greater than any other religious body in the world. She gives to it not merely a lip service, but a loyalty which withstood alike the pressure of Henry VIII and of Napoleon Bonaparte, the mightiest monarchs of their day, who sought to coerce the Church into sanctioning divorces forbidden by Holy Writ — a loyalty of which history knows no parallel.

It is simply amazing to discover how few of our non-Catholic friends have ever stopped to inquire: Where did we get our Bible? Who assembled its various parts? Who determined what books were inspired by God and which were not? Who vouches for it as the authoritative and inspired word of God? The answer to all these queries is: the Catholic Church. The chances are that if they stopped to inquire into the origin of the Bible, into the institution which framed its canon, and mothered it for eleven centuries before the first Protestant was born, they would not long remain Protestants.

Many are heard to speak of the Bible as if they thought it were simply a single book. In reality it is a whole library, a vast collection of 73 different books, 46 belonging to the old Testament and 27 to the New. These books were not written at the same time or in one era: from Genesis, the first book of the Old Testament, to the Apocalypse of St. John, the last book of the New Testament, there stretches a period of approximately 1500 years.

Thus if we were to stand by the bier of Moses and read the

Scriptures then in existence, we would be limited to the first five books of the Old Testament. Even the books of the New Testament did not appear at the same time, but at varying intervals over almost three quarters of a century. It was the Catholic Church which gathered up all these books, placed them within the covers of a single volume, and thus gave to the world what is known today as the Bible.

The chart (page 128), *The Making of the New Testament*, shows when the various parts were written and when they were first assembled within the covers of a single volume. The chart brings into clear relief the following important facts:

1. The New Testament was written in its entirety by Catholics.

2. St. Peter, the first pope of the Catholic Church, is the author of two of its epistles.

3. The Catholic Church determined the canon or list of books to constitute the New Testament.

4. The declaration of the Catholic Church that the books of the New Testament are all inspired by God constitutes the *sole* authority for the universal belief of both Catholics and Protestants in their inspired character.

5. The Catholic Church existed before the New Testament.

6. The Catholic Church is the mother of the New Testament.

If she had not scrutinized carefully the writings of her children, rejecting some and approving others as worthy of inclusion in the canon of the New Testament, there would be no New Testament today.

If she had not declared the books composing the New Testament to be the *inspired* word of God, we would not know it.

The only authority which non-Catholics have for the inspiration of the Scriptures is the authority of the Catholic Church. If the latter be rejected, there remain no logical grounds for retention of the cardinal tenet of all Protestants — the inspired character of Scripture.

With the possible exception of St. John, none of the Apostles ever saw all the writings which now make up the New Testament.

If the Church had not preserved the Bible, shielded it from the attacks of barbarians, copying it in her monasteries through-

THE MAKING OF THE NEW TESTAMENT
The Catholic Church — Mother of the Bible

A.D. 1

| Life of Christ | 30 } 33 } | PUBLIC MINISTRY OF CHRIST |

NOTE CAREFULLY

Catholic Church existed before New Testament . . . was preaching Christ's teachings for 9 years before a word of the New Testament was written . . . and for 67 years before it was completed. The Church is not the child of the Bible, but its mother.

33 ....

← 42—MATTHEW'S GOSPEL WRITTEN

Christ Founds Catholic Church

42 ....

← 52—MARK'S GOSPEL WRITTEN

53 ....

← 63—LUKE'S GOSPEL WRITTEN

New Testament Not Completed Until End of First Century

EPISTLES WRITTEN

← 97—JOHN'S GOSPEL WRITTEN

100 ....

New Testament Not Yet Formed

393—COUNCIL OF HIPPO ....

Canon or List of New Testament Books Determined

Catholic Church determined which books are inspired and are to compose New Testament. Canon first fixed by Council of Hippo, 393, later confirmed by Council of Carthage, 397.

397—COUNCIL OF CARTHAGE ....

New Testament Not Yet Printed

1450—PRINTING INVENTED ....

First Printed in 1450

626 Catholic editions printed in all languages, 17 editions in Germany before Luther's translation; 9 editions before Luther was born.

1552—LUTHER'S TRANSLATION ....

Douay-Rheims

English translation — Douay-Rheims — official Catholic edition — 1582.

1582—DOUAY-RHEIMS ....

King James

Authorized Protestant — King James — English edition appeared in 1611 — nearly 16 centuries after Christ.

1611—KING JAMES VERSION ....

Revised Catholic (U.S.A.)

Catholic scholars in U.S.A. bring out revised edition in 1941.

1941—REVISED CATHOLIC EDITION ....
(U.S.A.)

Knox (U.K.)

Vernacular version by Msgr. Ronald A. Knox, commissioned by English Catholic hierarchy.

1955—KNOX TRANSLATION ....

R.S.V. (U.S.A.)

American Protestant update of King James translation approved for a Catholic edition.

1965—REVISED STANDARD VERSION ....

Jerusalem (U.K.-France)

Cooperative translation by English Catholic and Protestant scholars of French Catholic Bible.

1966—JERUSALEM BIBLE ....

N.A.B.-Confraternity (U.S.A.)

Complete vernacular revision by Confraternity of Christian Doctrine of Catholic edition.

1970—NEW AMERICAN BIBLE ....

Common Bible

New "ecumenical" edition of Revised Standard of U.S. National Council of Churches, designed for use by Catholics, Protestants, Jews.

1973—R.S.V. COMMON BIBLE ....

out the long centuries before the art of printing was invented, the modern world would be without the Bible.

The chart shows that the Catholic Church, founded by Jesus Christ, was teaching and preaching the word of God for nine years before a word of the New Testament was written and for sixty-seven years before it was completed. The truths enunciated by her divine Founder were deep in her heart and fresh in her memory; she was busily engaged in imparting these orally to mankind.

Christ wrote nothing; neither did He command the Apostles to write. He commissioned them to teach His doctrines to all mankind. "Go ye into the whole world," He said, "and preach the gospel to every creature." The Apostles fulfilled the command of Christ by their oral preaching.

Peter, Matthew, John, James and Jude, supplemented their preaching by writing. It is well to remember, however, that the Church was a *going concern,* a functioning institution, teaching, preaching, administering the sacraments, saving souls, before the New Testament saw the light of day.

She is not the child of the Bible, as many non-Catholics imagine, but its mother. She derives neither her existence nor her teaching authority from the New Testament. She had both before the New Testament was born: she secured her being, her teachings, her authority directly from Jesus Christ.

If all the books of the Bible and all the copies thereof were blotted out, she would still be in possession of all the truths of Christ and could still continue to preach them as she did before a single word of the New Testament was written; for those truths are deep in her mind, heart and memory, in her liturgical and sacramental life, in the traditions, written and unwritten, which go directly back to Christ.

Did not the Church, however, discourage the reading of the Bible? The exact opposite is the truth. From the early centuries of the Christian era to the present day, the Church has persistently and tirelessly promoted the reading and study of the Bible by both clergy and laity. Quotations from the early Fathers to this effect could be presented almost without end. Thus, referring to the Bible, St. Jerome declares: "God gave it to you for you to read."[1] Long before this, St. Polycarp said to the Philippians:

"I trust that you are well read in Holy Scripture and that naught is hid from you."[2] Tertullian, writing in the second century, declares: "Look into God's revelations, examine our Sacred Books, for we do not keep them in hiding."[3]

Great emphasis was placed upon the public reading of the Scriptures in church during the early centuries. Thus, St. Irenaeus takes it for granted that every earnest man "diligently reads the Scriptures in company with the priests in the church with whom lies apostolic doctrine."[4] That the custom of reading the Scriptures was widespread is evident from repeated references to the practice in Conciliar declarations and in the writings of the Fathers.

Was not the Bible practically unknown, however, in the Middle Ages when the Church was dominant? Luther's widely quoted statement that before his time "the Bible lay under the bench forgotten in the dust" has contributed to the spreading of this impression among people who take their history from one book, without making any effort to discover the views of contemporary writers. The truth is that Luther's assertion is contradicted by the facts as reported by non-Catholic historians without number. Thus the German historian, Michael, after a lifetime of painstaking research, concludes that the Bible was "the most widely circulated book in the Middle Ages, and had a great influence on the life of the nations."[5]

Kropatscheck flatly contradicts Luther's assertion. "It is no longer possible to hold," he declares, "as the old polemics did, that the Bible was a sealed book to both theologians and laity. The more we study the Middle Ages, the more does this fable tend to dissolve into thin air."[6] Rev. S. R. Maitland, librarian to the Archbishop of Canterbury, conducted extensive research into the state of religion from the ninth to the thirteenth century in England and published his results in London in 1844. He acknowledges that to his surprise he found no single instance in which the Bible had been kept from the people.[7]

"There is," writes Dr. Cutts, "a good deal of popular misapprehension about the way in which the Bible was regarded in the Middle Ages. Some people think that it was very little read, even by the clergy; whereas the fact is that the sermons of the medieval preachers are more full of Scriptural quotations and allusions than any sermons in these days; and the writers on other subjects are so full of Scriptural allusion, that it is evident their minds were saturated with Scriptural diction."[8]

Living at a time when the printing press was not yet invented and when manuscripts were rare and costly, the laity learned much Scripture by listening to sermons and by studying the sculpture, paintings, frescoes and mosaics which filled their churches. What a panoramic view of both the Old and New Testament could be had by a parishioner of St. Mark's in Venice in the thirteenth century can be glimpsed by the visitor there today. The writer spent several days in studying the portrayal of the events, characters, parables and teachings of the Scriptures depicted in the mosaics, sculptures and paintings with which this venerable Cathedral abounds, and came away far from exhausting the treasure-trove. As Ruskin points out: "The walls of the church became the poor man's Bible, and a picture was more easily read than a chapter."[9]

Was not Luther, however, the first to translate the Bible into the vernacular? No. Luther's translation of the New Testament was not published until 1522 and his version of the Old Testament did not appear until 1534. From 1466 to 1522, Catholics had already published 14 complete editions of the Bible in High German at Augsburg, Basle, Strassburg and Nuremburg, and five in Low German at Cologne, Delf, Halberstadt and Lubeck.[10] During the period of seventy years, from 1450 to 1520, Catholics had published 156 Latin and six Hebrew editions of the Bible, besides issuing complete translations in French (10), Italian (11), Bohemian (2), Flemish (1), Limousine (1), and Russian (1).[11]

In the Congressional Library at Washington there is on exhibition a copy of the "Mazarin Bible" printed by Gutenburg, the inventor of the printing press, thirty years before Luther was born. There is likewise at the University of Notre Dame a copy of the Bible printed in German in 1483, the very year of Luther's birth. It is true that Catholics objected to Luther's translation, but only because it was faulty and unreliable. As Emser wrote at the time: "He has in many places confused, stultified and perverted the old trustworthy text of the Christian Church to its great disadvantage, and also poisoned it with heretical glosses and prefaces. . . . He almost everywhere forces the Scriptures on the question of faith and works, even when neither faith nor works are thought of."[12] Emser pointed out as many as 1,400 inaccuracies, while Bunsen, a Protestant scholar, tabulated 3,000.

Is it not true, however, that the monks of the Middle Ages chained the Bibles in their libraries and churches to keep them from being circulated among the common people? This is another widespread misrepresentation calculated to discredit the Church's fostering care of the Bible. The Bible was chained in various churches, not for the purpose mentioned, but for the very opposite: to prevent theft, and thus render it accessible to the greatest number possible. A telephone directory is usually chained in a public booth, but not to keep it *from* the people, but to keep it *for* the people. So, likewise, with the chained Bible.

The first mention of chained Bibles is found in 1040 in the catalogue of St. Peter's Monastery of Weissenburg, Alsace, which refers to four psalters chained in the monastery church. Indeed, throughout the Middle Ages it was considered a pious work to bequeath Bibles and psalters to be chained in church for common use. The Reformers followed the custom of having chained Bibles in their churches, and the practice continued for more than three centuries.

Is it not a fact, however, that the Catholic Church today discourages her members from reading the Bible for themselves? On the contrary, she encourages them to read the Bible frequently, even daily. Leo XIII, in his encyclical on the Bible, declares: "The solicitude of the Apostolic Office naturally urges, and even compels us, not only to desire that this great source of Catholic revelation should be made safely and abundantly accessible to the flock of Jesus Christ, but also not to suffer any attempt to defile or corrupt it."

Pope Benedict XV, in his encyclical on St. Jerome, addresses to all Catholics the words which St. Jerome wrote to Demetrias: "Love the Bible and wisdom will love you; love it and it will preserve you; honor it and it will embrace you." The pontiff adds: "No one can fail to see what profit and sweet tranquillity must result in well-disposed souls from a devout reading of the Bible. Whoever comes to it in piety, faith and humility, and with a determination to make progress in it, will assuredly find therein and will eat 'the Bread that cometh down from heaven.' "

Even to this day the Church requires all her clergy, busy as they are with varied duties, to spend approximately one hour in the daily recitation of the Divine Office. About three-fourths of this is Scripture, and the rest is chiefly commentaries by the early Fathers upon the gospels.

Are not Catholics, however, guilty of reasoning in a circle when they prove the Church by the Bible, and then turn right around and prove the Bible by the Church? This is a widespread impression among our Protestant neighbors: no less a writer than Dr. Douglas C. Macintosh of Yale Divinity School trots out this old charge anew. It is traceable to a failure to understand the Church's real teaching in the matter. If the Church began by proclaiming the Scriptures, she would indeed be guilty of the fallacy of the vicious circle. The Church does not begin, however, by presupposing that the books of the New Testament are in any way inspired.

She goes to them just as she would go to any historical document. She examines them carefully, scrutinizes them in the light of contemporary evidence from other sources, and finds them as a result of proper corroboration to be authentic historical documents. She allows the words of Christ and His Apostles as recorded in the Scriptures to tell their own story of the foundation of a Church and its authorization to teach in the name of Christ Himself. Now this document, whose authenticity and historicity have been proven by the same methods which would be used in the case of any secular document, is found to declare that the Church which Christ established is not only empowered to teach the faithful the truths of religion but is promised by Christ the unfailing assistance of the Holy Spirit in safeguarding it from error and falsehood in the discharge of its divinely appointed teaching mission.

The Church then proceeds to declare by virtue of the teaching authority conferred upon her by Christ, as recorded in the historical document, called the New Testament, that the latter is inspired. Up until that last moment the Scriptures were appealed to simply as historical documents: it is only now, after the teaching authority of the Church has been established by the historical words of Christ, that she terms the Scriptures inspired. Hence it will be seen that at all stages of the journey the procedure of the Church is rigorously logical. Thus the authority of both the Church and the Bible depends ultimately upon the divine Founder of the Christian religion, Jesus Christ.

The Bible may be said to be the Church's charter, the fundamental bill of rights. "For," as Father Hugh Pope, O.P., of Oxford has pointed out, "if you question the Church's claims, she refers you to the Bible as an historical fact — not as historically true, for that is a wholly different matter. If you tell the Church that you find it hard to accept the Bible as historically true, she will tell you to settle that question for yourself. But, she will add, once you accept the Bible — at any rate in its main features — once you accept the 'fact' of prophecy and its culmination in Jesus, the carpenter of Nazareth, who claimed to be, and proved Himself to be, the Son of God, made man for our salvation, then you must also accept me as His divinely appointed means for preserving and interpreting His teaching for the world to the end of time, as being 'the body of Christ, the pillar and the ground of truth.' "

Father Hugh Pope likewise points out that "if you quarrel with the Church's teaching, she will refer you to the Bible as its guarantee. But if you protest that you cannot discover there all the doctrines which she sets forth, the Church will not send you to the Bible for these doctrines — though for some of them she could do so if she liked; she will send you indeed to the Bible, not to discover there the particular doctrines in question, but the fundamental doctrine of the Church's authority to teach at all. And if you prove obstinate and urge that you, or competent scholars, have as much right as any theologians of the Church to discover what really are the teachings of the Bible, the Church will gently remind you that the theologians are not the Church but the Church's children; that when they, for example, teach the doctrine of Christ's Resurrection in the very same flesh in which He 'walked on earth,' they do not do so simply because they think it is true or in accordance with the Scripture, but because they are the children of that Church which was actually present at, and witnessed those scenes, and has handed them down through the subsequent ages."[13]

Is not the Bible alone, however, a safe guide in matters of religious faith? "Where the Bible speaks, we speak, and where the Bible is silent, we are silent," is the motto frequently quoted by Protestants in support of their claim that the Bible alone is a sufficient rule of faith. Let us ask our non-Catholic friends to examine this rule of faith to see if it would give them the safety and sureness they have a right to expect in religious faith. A competent guide for the Christian religion should possess these three qualifications:

1. It must be within the reach of every inquirer after truth.
2. It must be clear and intelligible to all.
3. It must present all the truths of the Christian religion. Now the Bible alone possesses none of these.

First, the Scriptures were not accessible to the *primitive Christians*, for the simple reason that they were not all written until many years after the establishment of Christianity. Thus, St. Luke did not write his gospel until about twenty years after the death of Christ. St. John's gospel did not appear until toward the close of the first century. For many years after the epistles were written, the knowledge of them was largely confined to the particular churches or groups of converts to whom they were addressed. It was not until the Council of Hippo in 393 that the Church gathered these gospels and epistles, scattered about in different churches, and placed them within the covers of a single book, giving the Bible to the world. During the first four centuries, the golden age of the Christian religion, when many of its most perfect members lived and died, the Bible was not yet extant as a guide for their religious faith.

The printing press was not invented until about 1440. Hence from the *fourth to the fifteenth century* it was physically impossible to provide each member with a copy of the Bible. Even at the present time, as in all previous ages and climes, there are millions who are unable to read, millions to whom the Bible remains a sealed book.

Secondly, the Bible is not a clear and intelligible guide to all. There are many passages in the Bible which are difficult and obscure, not only to the ordinary person, but to the highly trained scholar as well. St. Peter himself tells us that in the epistles of St. Paul there are "certain things hard to be understood, which the unlearned and the unstable wrest, as they do also the other Scriptures, to their own destruction."[14] Consequently, he tells us elsewhere "that no prophecy of Scripture is made by private interpretation."[15]

St. Luke narrates in the Acts of the Apostles that a certain man was riding in his chariot, reading the Book of Isaiah. Upon being asked by St. Philip whether he understood the meaning of the prophecy, he replied: "How can I understand unless some man show me?" In these modest words is reflected the experience of practically all readers of the Bible. True, in the first years of his separation from the Church, Luther declared that the Bible could be interpreted by everyone, "even by the humble miller's maid, nay a child of nine." Later on, however, when the Anabaptists, the Zwinglians and others contradicted his views, the Bible became "a heresy book," most obscure and difficult to understand. He lived to see numerous heretical sects rise up and spread through Christendom, all claiming to be based upon the Bible.

Thus, in 1525 he sadly deplored the religious anarchy to which his own principle of the private interpretation of Scripture had given rise: "There are as many sects and beliefs as there are heads. This fellow will have nothing to do with Baptism: another denies the Sacrament; a third believes that there is another world between this and the Last Day. Some teach that Christ is not God; some say this, some say that. There is no rustic so rude but that, if he dreams or fancies anything, it must be the whisper of the Holy Spirit, and he himself a prophet."[16] The hundreds of sects, with their divisions and subdivisions, which the Religious Census of the United States Government lists in our own country, offer grim evidence of the ceaseless dissension and havoc which the principle of the private interpretation of Scripture has wrought in our own day.

Thirdly, the Bible does not contain all the teachings of the Christian religion, nor does it formulate all the duties of its members. Take, for example, the matter of Sunday observance, the attendance at divine services and the abstention from unnecessary servile work on that day, a matter upon which our Protestant neighbors have for many years laid great emphasis. Let me address myself to my dear non-Catholic reader:

You believe that the Bible alone is a safe guide in religious matters. You also believe that one of the fundamental duties enjoined upon you by your Christian faith is that of Sunday observance. But where does the Bible speak of such an obligation? I have read the Bible from the first verse of Genesis to the last verse of Revelations, and have found no reference to the duty of sanctifying the Sunday. The day mentioned in the Bible is not the Sunday, the first day of the week but the Saturday, the last day of the week.

It was the Apostolic Church which, acting by virtue of that authority conferred upon her by Christ, changed the observance to the Sunday in honor of the day on which Christ rose from the dead, and to signify that now we are no longer under the Old Law of the Jews, but under the New Law of Christ. In observing the Sunday as you do, is it not apparent that you are really acknowledging the insufficiency of the Bible alone as a rule of faith and religious conduct, and proclaiming the need of a divinely established teaching authority which in theory you deny?

There are certain truths which Christ and the Apostles taught which are not recorded in the Scriptures but which are embodied in the life, practice and ministry of the Church, in her written and unwritten traditions, which supplement the Biblical record. In other words, the Church in her worship and religious and moral observances, was a *going concern* before a word of the New Testament was written.

St. John ends his gospel by telling us that "there are also many other things which Jesus did which are not written in this book." St. Paul emphasizes the importance of holding fast to the teachings transmitted not only by writing but also by word of mouth. "Therefore, brethren," he exhorts, "stand fast; and hold the traditions which you have learned, whether by word or by our epistle."[17] From all of which it must be abundantly clear that the Bible alone is not a safe and competent guide because it is not now and has never been accessible to all, because it is not clear and intelligible to all, and because it does not contain all the truths of the Christian religion.

The simple fact is that the Bible, like all dead letters, calls for a living interpreter. The founding fathers of our republic did not leave the constitution to be interpreted by every individual according to his whims. That would have spelled speedy destruction to the unity of the infant republic. They wisely constituted the supreme court to be the living, authoritative interpreter of the constitution. When Victor Berger, a congressman from Milwaukee, was arrested and brought into court, charged with treasonable utterances during World War I, he pleaded his constitutional right of freedom of speech.[18]

"But," said the court in effect, "you are not the authorized interpreter of that document. The supreme court has decreed that that passage of the constitution may never be so construed as to countenance treason to the government. Freedom of speech is always limited by the duty to refrain from inciting citizens to rebellion against the government."

Just as the supreme court is the authorized living interpreter of the constitution, so the Catholic Church is the living authoritative interpreter of the Bible. She has been the preserver and custodian of the Bible through the centuries, and she interprets it for us in the name and with the authority of Jesus Christ. Christ never wrote a word, never commanded His Apostles or disciples to write. He taught and commissioned His Apostles to teach and assured them of His abiding presence with them.

His commission to them is as clear-cut as it is impressive. "All power is given to Me," said He, "in heaven and on earth. Going, therefore, teach ye all nations, baptizing them in the name of the Father and of the Son, and of the Holy Spirit, teaching them to observe all things whatsoever I have commanded you: and behold I am with you all days even to the consummation of the world."[19]

That the Apostles understood their mission was to preach the truths of Christ to all the world, and to ordain successors to carry on this work to the end of time, is evident from the words of St. Paul: "Whosoever shall call upon the name of the Lord shall be saved. How then shall they call on Him in whom they have not believed? Or how shall they believe Him of whom they have not heard? And how shall they hear without a preacher? And how shall they preach unless they be sent? . . . Faith then cometh by hearing. . . . 'But I say: Have they not heard? Yes, verily, their sound hath gone forth into all the earth, and their words unto the ends of the whole world."[20]

Students of religious statistics estimate that more than half of the people in the U.S.A. have no functional affiliation with any form of the Christian faith, rarely if ever attending services. Must it not be evident to the thoughtful reader of these lines, whether he be Protestant or Catholic, that the estrangement of such a vast number of our countrymen is traceable in large measure to the division, dissension and anarchy, which the principle of making each individual supreme and a Court of Last Appeal in the interpretation of Scripture has brought into the world?

Scandalized at the spectacle of several hundred warring sects, all disagreeing among themselves as to the meaning of various passages in the Bible, millions of people begin to wonder if any of them has retained all the truths of Christ and can minister to them in the name and with the authority of Christ.

In sharp contrast with the sorry spectacle of Protestantism with its hundreds of warring sects and creeds, agreeing with one another only in their disagreement with all others, there is the Catholic Church with its vast membership — more than twice the total of all the sects of Protestantism combined — speaking every tongue and in every land under the heavens, all united in the strong bonds of a common faith. It offers the greatest spectacle of religious unity which the world affords. To what is this unity due? Aside from that grace and protection from on high which has never failed her, it is due chiefly to the fact that all its members recognize the Church as the authorized living interpreter of Scripture, founded by Christ to teach the world all the truths which Christ commanded, in the name and with the authority of her divine Founder, Jesus Christ Himself.

May we not invite our fellow countrymen of other faiths to return to the holy Catholic Apostolic Church, the historic center of unity and the mother from whom they have strayed, to aid us in stemming the forces of indifferentism and irreligion in America today? It is only thus that we who call ourselves Christians and claim to be followers of the crucified Christ will fulfill the plea which St. Paul wrote from his prison at Rome to his little band of converts at Ephesus and through them to the Christians of all succeeding ages: "I therefore, a prisoner in the Lord, beseech you ... to keep the unity of the spirit in the bond of peace. One body and one spirit; as you are called in one hope of your calling. One Lord, one *faith*, and one baptism."[21]

Discussion Aids

Why is the Church rightly called the mother of the Bible? How many books are contained in the Old Testament? In the New Testament? Were they all written at the same time? Discuss. Were Catholics in the early Church encouraged to read the Scriptures? What evidence have we that Bible reading was encouraged in the Middle Ages? When did Luther's translation of the New Testament into the vernacular appear? His translation of the Old Testament? How many translations of the Bible into the German vernacular had been made before Luther's translation? Into what other languages had the Bible been translated by 1520? Why do Catholics object to Luther's translation? Explain "chained Bibles." Explain the charge of "vicious circle" reasoning. Explain in what way the Bible may be called the Church's charter. Point out the weakness in the claim that the Bible is the sole rule of faith. Discuss fully according to the three qualifications: (1) availability to all; (2) clearness to all; and (3) as containing all teaching of Christian religion. Explain fully why the Bible must have a living interpreter.

Practices

Remember that Pope Leo XIII granted the faithful an indulgence for reading the Scriptures fifteen minutes a day.

NOTES (Chapter 7)

1. On Isaiah, 22:6, Migne, *Pat. Lat.*, Tom. XXIV
2. Ad Philipp XII, *Apostolic Fathers*, p. 86 (Appleton, N.Y., 1884)

3. Apol. XXXI, Migne, *Pat. Lat.*, Tom. I

4. *Adv. Haer.*, Migne, *Pat. Graec.*, Tom. VII

5. *Geschichte der Deutschen Volkes*, III, p. 223

6. *Das Scrift-princip der Luth.*, Kirche, p. 163

7. *The Dark Ages* (London, 1844)

8. *Turning Points of English History*, p. 200

9. *The Stones of Venice*, II, III

10. Janssen, *History of the German People*, XIV, p. 388

11. Falk, *Die Bibel Am Ausganges des Mittelalters*

12. Janssen, *History of the German People*, XIV, p. 425

13. *The Catholic Church and the Bible*, pp. 29-30 (Macmillan Co., N.Y., 1928)

14. II Pt. 3:16

15. *Ibid.*, 1:20

16. Grisar, *Luther*, IV, pp. 386-407 (B. Herder, St. Louis, 1917)

17. II Thes. 2:15

18. *The Chicago Tribune*, Jan. 10, 1919

19. Mt. 28:18

20. Rom. 10:14-18

21. Eph. 4:1-5

PART III

The Sacraments

Channels of Divine Grace

CHAPTER 8

The Sacraments in General

How Christ Applies the Fruits of Redemption to Souls

When Christ came upon earth to redeem mankind He taught men directly, and personally extended to them blessings and graces for both soul and body. But how were the fruits of the Redemption to reach the countless generations as yet unborn? To solve this problem Christ founded a Church which He commissioned to transmit His doctrines to all ages. He likewise established the sacraments which serve as so many channels through which the graces and blessings of the Redemption reach the soul of each individual recipient.

The administration of the sacraments was entrusted to the Church to which Christ gave complete jurisdiction over the deposit of divine truth and over the means of sanctification. In a very true sense the Church may be said to be the extension of the

Incarnation and the application of its fruits to the needs of individual human souls. "Let a man so account of us," said St. Paul, "as of the ministers of Christ, and the dispensers of the mysteries of God."[1]

Like her divine Founder, the Church has a twofold nature, human and divine, visible and invisible. We, too, are not disembodied spirits but are a composite of the physical and the spiritual. The senses are the gateways to the soul. Naturally we expect the life of the Church to reflect our twofold nature and to minister to the invisible spiritual element through the agency of the visible and physical. This is precisely what the Church does for us through her sacramental system. A sacrament is an outward sign of inward grace. Far from being a mere meaningless ritual, it is a beautiful manifestation, a clear signifying in an external manner of a grace which God confers upon the soul.

The sacraments and the holy Sacrifice of the Mass are the chief channels through which the fruits of the Redemption, the blessings and graces of God, are applied to individual souls. If one should travel in the western part of our country, such as Southern California, where irrigation is extensively employed for the cultivation of orange groves, he will see how necessary it is to have not only a vast reservoir of water but also canals to carry the life-giving water to each tree. No matter how vast a quantity of water is contained in the reservoir, if there be no canals to carry the water to the roots of each tree, it will soon die.

Christ by His suffering and death gained vast spiritual riches for us; they may be said to constitute a huge spiritual reservoir. It is necessary that some means be devised to tap the reservoir and carry its riches to our souls. The sacraments are such means: channels of divine grace to the souls of men.

Three elements are necessary to constitute a sacrament. It must be (1) an outward sign, (2) instituted by Christ, (3) to give grace. Thus in baptism the outward sign is the washing with water by pouring, sprinkling or immersing, accompanied by the words, "I baptize thee in the name of the Father and of the Son and of the Holy Spirit." This indicates in an external manner the internal cleansing of the immortal soul from original as well as actual sin.

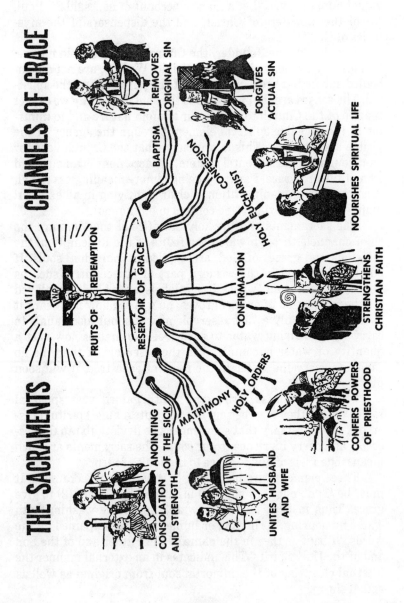

THE SACRAMENTS

CHANNELS OF GRACE

FRUITS OF REDEMPTION

RESERVOIR OF GRACE

BAPTISM — REMOVES ORIGINAL SIN

CONFESSION — FORGIVES ACTUAL SIN

HOLY EUCHARIST — NOURISHES SPIRITUAL LIFE

CONFIRMATION — STRENGTHENS CHRISTIAN FAITH

HOLY ORDERS — CONFERS POWERS OF PRIESTHOOD

MATRIMONY — UNITES HUSBAND AND WIFE

ANOINTING OF THE SICK — CONSOLATION AND STRENGTH

144

Secondly, it was instituted by Christ who gave to His Church the commission to go into the whole world to teach and to baptize in the name of the blessed Trinity. Thirdly, baptism produces sanctifying grace in the soul, cleansing it from sin, and making the person henceforth a child of God and an heir of heaven.[2] The Church could not institute a sacrament, for only Christ can give grace.

While Christ instituted the seven sacraments, He did not indicate, save in a most general way, the matter and form of certain sacraments, such as Confirmation, Holy Orders, and Anointing of the Sick: He permitted the Church to determine them with precision. Thus the sacraments of the Greek Orthodox Church are entirely valid, although they use a different form of Confirmation, employ the deprecatory form of absolution, and say, "May this same God through me a sinner forgive you all, both now and forever," while we in the Western Church use the declarative form: "I absolve thee from thy sins in the name of the Father and of the Son and of the Holy Spirit." In conferring Holy Orders our bishops place both hands upon the head of the person to be ordained, while in the Greek Orthodox Church the bishop places his right hand only. These slight differences of form do not affect the substance of the sacraments nor, therefore, their validity.

As will be shown in detail when explaining each sacrament, the Scriptures refer to all of them but do not present a developed theology of the sacraments: this was left to the Church to work out in succeeding ages. Here we come to a point of far-reaching difference between the Catholic and Protestant conception of the source and rule of faith. The Protestant who expects to find in the Bible his entire religious faith with all its formulations and developments will look in vain for the theology of the sacraments.

A Catholic, however, accepts not only the Bible but also the written and unwritten traditions of the Apostolic era, the active ministry of the Apostles and their successors as reflected in the manner of worship, life and practices of the Church founded by Christ, propagated by the Apostles, and safeguarded by the abiding presence of the Holy Spirit, the Spirit of Truth. There are many truths presented only in germinal form in the Scriptures. But by virtue of the authority conferred by Christ upon His Church to preach and to teach in His name, she draws out in explicit form and unfolds in greater detail the implications of doctrines contained only in germinal form in the Bible.

Thus there is, as Cardinal Newman has pointed out, a development of doctrine within the Church. It is not an evolution, in the sense that it advances from one species of doctrine to an altogether different one. It is, as St. Vincent of Lerins indicated in the fifth century, more like the growth and development that occurs in a human being. His personal identity remains, but he advances in the maturity of his thought and in the deeper comprehension of many things which were previously but dimly discerned. Such a development of doctrine has occurred as regards the sacraments.

Thus the terms *matter* and *form* were not applied to the sacraments until the thirteenth century, although the idea conveyed by these words is found in holy Scripture and in the writings of St. Augustine in the fourth century. These philosophical terms were borrowed from Aristotle, and their use was sanctioned by the Councils of Constance in 1414, Florence in 1439, and Trent in 1547.

They do not imply, however, as some non-Catholics imagine, that the sacraments are material, corporeal things. "What they mean is that just as bodies are composed of two constituents, the one indeterminate and the other determining, so too in the sacraments two elements, the one indeterminate and the other determining, can be distinguished; and these may rightly be called 'matter' and 'form.' "[3] Thus in Baptism, the washing with water is the matter, while the words, "I baptize thee in the name of the Father and of the Son and of the Holy Spirit," which signify why the water is being used and what it symbolizes, are the form.

The Reformers not only reduced the number of the sacraments but also denied their objective efficacy. Thus, Luther characterized the sacraments as "mere tokens of the divine promise that sins were to be forgiven by faith." Calvin referred to them as "mere messengers announcing to men God's deeds of kindness," while Zwingli styled them "mere signs of Christian profession."[4] The erroneous views of the Reformers led naturally

146

and logically to their denial of the objective efficacy of the sacraments.

If justification is effected not by good works but by faith alone, and if justification consists in a merely extrinsic application of the merits of Christ without effecting any interior change in the soul, then the sacraments have no other purpose than simply to stimulate faith, and are really not channels of divine grace to human souls. They become "mere tokens," empty signs, not effective channels of grace. This view of the Reformers represented a radical departure from the faith of the universal Christian Church from the days of Christ down to their own time.

What is the evidence, however, that there are seven sacraments? Do not most Protestant denominations hold there are but two sacraments, namely, Baptism and the Lord's Supper? The fact is that Luther was the first to break with the traditional teaching of the Christian Church when he reduced the number to three: Baptism, Penance and the Lord's Supper. Later, under the influence of Calvin, he reduced the number to two, ruling out Penance.[5]

Though mentioning all the sacraments more or less explicitly, the New Testament never presents a list of them such as one would find in a manual of systematic theology. From the days of the Apostles the Church made use of these means of grace and sanctification, though she did not at once make an inventory of them. The early Fathers mention all the seven sacraments in the course of their instructions to the catechumens and the faithful, but without presenting any systematic treatment of the precise meaning of a sacrament.

A further striking confirmation of the widespread character of this belief in the early Church is found in the fact that it has been the unbroken faith of the Greek Orthodox Church down to the present day. Thus in 1576 Jeremias, the Patriarch of Jerusalem, indignantly spurned the invitation of the Lutherans of Wittenberg to unite with them, because of their heretical denial of the seven sacraments. The Synod of Constantinople in 1638 excommunicated Lukaris of Constantinople for his Lutheran doctrine of two sacraments and declared that Christ had instituted seven sacraments.

The simple fact is that while the sacraments were established by Christ, their theology has been worked out by the Church. "After all," points out Abbe Broglie, "the doctrine has been the same during all ages, because all our sacramental rites have always been used with faith in their efficacy. But the systematic and philosophic form has progressed. The proposition that there are seven Sacraments of the New Law, which alone produce grace, now a dogma of faith, could not have appeared evident in the eleventh century on account of a lack of precision in language. The Church advances in her knowledge of the truth; she advances slowly and prudently, yet she does advance; each century adds more precision, more completeness in her knowledge. The condition of this progress is the assistance of the Holy Spirit, directing human thought, and repressing its errors."[6]

Now let us take up the charge that the sacraments smack of magic. We call that magic when an inadequate and insufficient cause is expected to produce a higher effect, when that which is material is expected to produce a spiritual or divine effect. Thus if a person were to take a rock and rub it against a carpet and expect it to make the carpet speak, that would be magic.

Nothing remotely resembling such a notion is implied in the nature of the sacraments. Their efficacy does not depend upon the person who administers them nor upon any humanly devised formulas which coerce God to act in a certain manner. Instead they depend solely upon Jesus Christ who established them as channels through which His grace flows unto us.

Thus St. Augustine says: "Baptism does not depend on the merits of those by whom it is administered, nor on the merits of those to whom it is administered, but in its own sanctity and truth, *on account of Him by whom it has been instituted.*" What the saintly Bishop of Hippo says of the source whence baptism derives its efficacy is true likewise of all the other sacraments.

"In the sacraments," as Father Hugh Pope, O.P., points out, "the *effective cause* is the Passion of Christ, the instrumental causes are the matter and form, or the outward signs used in the sacraments themselves as applied by properly constituted ministers whom Christ employs for the making of the sacraments and their distribution to the people."[7]

The effects do not transcend their cause, for Christ our Redeemer is the source from which the graces flow to us through

148

the sacraments as channels. Those who make the charge of magic completely misunderstand the Catholic doctrine concerning sacraments. They fail likewise to understand that the Catholic Church condemns magic as a grievous sin, a superstition which reason and common sense as well as religion condemn.

Is it not evident then to every fair-minded person, regardless of religious faith, that the sacraments have absolutely nothing whatsoever to do with magic? What then must we say of those individuals who recklessly slander hundreds of millions of Catholics throughout the world by attributing to them a belief in magic, when as a matter of fact they expressly repudiate it in all its forms and actually condemn it as a mortal sin? We leave it to almighty God, the just judge, who alone knows whether they are malicious or are simply the victims of misinformation and misguidance, to pronounce sentence upon them.

The charge that the sacramental system and other practices of primitive Christianity were borrowed from pagan cults has been ably refuted by such non-Catholics as Anrich, Cumont, Kenedy, Jones and Schweitzer, and by such Catholic scholars as Lagrange, Jacquier, Mangenot, Prat and Venard. The pet fallacy of certain students of comparative religion who appear anxious to show that Christianity is largely a development from various pagan cults is to jump from a few vague similarities to the conclusion that there has been a genetic or blood relationship. "All practices suggested by the religious instinct have a certain analogy between them," as Father Prat points out, "but it would be an unpardonable fallacy to transform these similitudes into proofs of interdependence."[8]

The simple fact is that the early Christians manifested a detestation and horror of the idolatry and superstitious practices of the pagans. They not only refused to participate in their worship but permitted themselves to be martyred rather than to cast a few grains of incense on the fire before their pagan idols.

Enough has been said to show that the sacraments are not mere meaningless ritual, but are beautiful signs which signify in an external manner the effect produced in the soul, and are thus aids to intelligent devotion. They are the great channels through which the grace of God flows to humanity and is applied to the soul of the individual recipient.

Through her divinely established sacramental system the Church is enabled to minister effectively to the spiritual needs of man all the way from the cradle to the grave. She comes to him at all the great crises in his life with sacraments designed to strengthen him with the particular grace needed to cope successfully with every emergency.

Thus shortly after the individual is born, the Church brings him as a tender babe to the baptismal font, and pours over his brow the cleansing waters of Baptism, washing away the stain of original sin and making him a child of God and an heir of heaven. Then, when the budding petals of reason unfold, how carefully she prepares the child for his first Holy Communion. With the Bread of Angels she nourishes and strengthens his spiritual life; with the sacrament of Confirmation she invigorates him and makes him a valiant soldier in the army of Christ, ready to do and die.

When the tempests of youthful passion have left him fallen and bruised amidst the thorns of life's highway, how tenderly she lifts him up and leads him to the tribunal of forgiveness where she breathes into his ear the words of pardon and of courage to rise and try again. When he stands at the dawn of young manhood with the new emotion of conjugal love seeking to find expression in a union that will last until death, the Church brings him and his bride before God's altar and unites them in the indissoluble bond of Christian marriage.

Then when life's fitful fever is over and God sends His angels to lower upon his eyes the curtain of death, how valiantly the priest stands at his bedside to strengthen him with the last anointing and to fortify him for his long journey into eternity with the Holy Viaticum of the body and blood of Jesus Christ. Thus does the Church stand at the side of her children at all the great crises and turning points in their lives with a sacrament specially instituted by Christ to supply the particular grace and strength needed to win the victory.

Discussion Aids

Discuss fully the nature of the sacraments. Illustrate. What three things are necessary? Discuss. Did Christ institute all the sacraments? Did He indicate the matter and form of all of them? Who has the right to define the matter and form of the sacraments where these are not indicated by Christ? Does the Bible give a developed theology of the sacraments? Explain how the Church has the right to develop this theology. Explain what is meant by "development of doctrine." What treatment was given the sacraments by the Reformers? Does the Bible name seven sacraments? How do we know that there are seven? Refute the charge that the sacraments smack of magic. (Have a theologian explain the meaning of the Latin *ex opere operato* in connection with the sacraments.) How do you explain any similarity between pagan cults and Christian worship? Summarize the teaching of the Church on the sacraments.

Practices

Receive the sacraments of Penance and Holy Eucharist with ever-increasing devotion, rereading this chapter from time to time as a preparation.

Visit our Lord in the Blessed Sacrament often, in reparation for the work of the Reformers.

Be able to explain the nature of all the sacraments to a non-Catholic.

NOTES (Chapter 8)

1. I Cor. 4:1
2. Jn. 3:5
3. Wilhelm-Scannell, *Manual of Theology,* II, p. 361 (Kegan Paul, Trench, Trubnes & Co., London, 1898)
4. B.L. Conway, *The Question Box,* p. 230 (Paulist Press, N.Y.)
5. Grisar, *Luther,* II, p. 27
6. *Conferences sur la Vie Surnaturelle,* p. 307
7. *Six Sacraments,* p. 24, ed. by C. Lattery (B. Herder, St. Louis, 1930)
8. *Theology of St. Paul,* II, p. 386 (Benziger Bros., N.Y., 1926)

CHAPTER 9

Baptism

Christ instituted Baptism and commissioned the Apostles to baptize. "Going, therefore," said Christ to the Apostles, "teach ye all nations, baptizing them in the name of the Father, and of the Son, and of the Holy Spirit."[1] Similar is the testimony of St. Mark: "And he said to them, Go ye into all the world and preach the gospel to every creature: He that believeth and is baptized shall be saved: he that believeth not shall be condemned."[2]

In obedience to this command, the Apostles and disciples went out into the countries of the then known world, preaching the gospel and baptizing. Thus on Pentecost, the very day the Holy Spirit came down upon the Apostles in the form of tongues of fire, St. Peter preached to a vast multitude and baptized them in the faith of Christ. "They therefore that received his word, were baptized," St. Luke tells us in the Acts of the Apostles, "and there were added in that day about three thousand souls."[3]

Baptism washes away the stain of original sin and also any actual sins that may be present and makes the person a child of God and an heir to heaven. Original sin is the shadow or state of sin in which we are born as a result of the transgression of our first parents. "Wherefore," says St. Paul, "as by one man sin entered into this world, and by sin death, and so death passed unto all men, in whom all have sinned."[4] Through a singular miracle of divine grace, the Blessed Virgin Mary was exempted from the stain of original sin. This is what is meant by the doctrine of the

Immaculate Conception, which many non-Catholics confuse with the miraculous conception of Christ in the womb of the Virgin Mother.

Baptism constitutes the gateway into the Church of Christ. Without it no other sacrament can be validly received. It is the sacrament which makes a person a Christian and gives him a right to the supernatural kingdom of heaven, to which he has no title by the mere fact of his natural birth. Baptism therefore is a spiritual rebirth or regeneration of the soul.

Thus St. Paul declares: "But when the goodness and kindness of God our Savior appeared . . . he saved us by the laver of regeneration and renovation of the Holy Spirit, whom he hath poured forth abundantly upon us, through Jesus Christ our Savior, that being justified by His grace, we may be heirs, according to the hope of life everlasting."[5]

The importance and necessity of baptism are stressed by our Blessed Lord Himself in the words addressed to Nicodemus: "Amen, amen, I say to thee, unless a man be born again of water and the Holy Spirit he cannot enter into the kingdom of God."[6] These words embrace the whole human race. They explain the solicitude of the Church that Baptism be not unduly deferred even in the case of infants, and why she authorizes any person having the use of reason to baptize when no priest is available and the individual might otherwise die without the sacrament.

Baptism may be validly administered in any of three different *ways*, namely, by *immersion*, or plunging the person into the water; by *infusion*, or pouring the water; and by *aspersion*, or sprinkling. The common method during the first twelve centuries was by immersion; but the other two methods were likewise used from the earliest times. Thus Tertullian, writing in the second century, describes Baptism as "a sprinkling with any kind of water."[7] St. Augustine declares that Baptism is efficacious if the water "merely sprinkles the child ever so slightly."[8] St. Thomas Aquinas tells us that immersion was the common method in the thirteenth century, but is careful to add: "Baptism can also be conferred by sprinkling and pouring."[9]

It seems most improbable that the three thousand converts received after St. Peter's discourse on Pentecost Sunday were immersed, when one considers both their number and the scarcity of water in Jerusalem. It seems likewise improbable that immersion could have been used in the Baptism of the jailer and his family in the prison at Philippi and of the persons in the home of Cornelius.[10] Monsignor A. S. Barnes in his painstaking work, *The Early Church in the Light of the Monuments*, reports that the baptisteries erected in the early centuries of the Christian era in the ceremony of St. Priscilla, in the Coemeterium Ostrianum, and of Pontianus bear unmistakable witness to the existence of Baptism by infusion in the infant Church.

The simple fact is that Christ nowhere specified the precise manner in which water was to be applied, but left that detail, as He has left many others, to the discretion of His Church. While acknowledging the validity of Baptism administered in any of these three ways, the Church now follows the uniform custom of infusion because she finds it the most convenient and practical method.

There are three *kinds* of Baptism, namely, of water, of desire and of blood. Baptism of desire is that which occurs when an individual wishes to receive the sacrament, but because of circumstances is unable to receive Baptism of water. Such is the teaching of the early Fathers of the Church. A striking instance of this belief is the funeral sermon preached by St. Ambrose, Bishop of Milan, in 392 over the emperor Valentinian II who died while still a catechumen. "I hear you express grief," says the bishop, "that he did not receive the sacrament of Baptism. Tell me, what else is there in us, except the will and petition? But he had long desired to be initiated before he came to Italy, and expressed his intention to be baptized by me as soon as possible. . . . Has he not, therefore, the grace which he desired? Surely he received it because he asked it."[11]

Such, too, is the testimony of St. Augustine: "I find that not only suffering for the name of Christ can supply the defect of Baptism, but even faith and conversion of heart, if there be no time for celebrating the sacrament."[12]

The Church with her all-embracing love for human souls and her ceaseless solicitude that no single individual be lost, teaches that many persons, perhaps millions, who are unaware of the command of Christ to be baptized, but who strive to lead good lives and who wish to obey God, may receive Baptism by desire. Even heathens in distant lands where the gospel of Christ has scarcely penetrated, who wish to do God's will in all things may be said to receive this form of Baptism.

The general intention to do the will of God includes the implicit desire to receive Baptism, since this is one of God's holy commands. The implicit desire of Baptism is defined as "a state of mind in which a man would ardently long for Baptism, if he knew that it was necessary for salvation."[13] This does not imply, of course, any lessening of emphasis upon the stern necessity of all who know of Christ's explicit command to receive Baptism of water. It is simply an application of the uniform teaching of the Church that God never punishes any person except insofar as he acts contrary to the light that has been given him.

The third kind of Baptism is that of blood. Martyrdom for Christ was regarded by the infant Church as equivalent to Baptism of water. Thus St. Augustine reflects the teaching of the early Fathers when he writes: "To all those who die confessing Christ, even though they have not received the laver of regeneration, martyrdom will prove as effective for the remission of sins, as if they were washed at the baptismal font."[14]

While there is no explicit mention of the baptizing of infants in the New Testament, it is highly probable that there were some babes among the families of Lydia, Stephanas, and of the jailer at Philippi, where in each instance St. Paul baptized the whole family. The writings of the immediate successors of the Apostles remove all doubt concerning the Apostolic practice of baptizing infants. Thus St. Irenaeus, a disciple of Polycarp, who was a disciple of St. John the Evangelist, writes: "Christ came to save all who through Him are born again unto God; infants and children, boys and youths, and aged persons.[15]

Origen (182-255) declares infant Baptism an Apostolic institution, necessary to wash from their souls the stain of original sin. St. Cyprian and the Third Council of Carthage in 253 decreed that the Baptism of children need not be deferred until the eighth day after birth, as some maintained, but might be administered as soon as possible. St. Augustine reports that this is but the echo of the teachings of the Apostles.

If infants should die suddenly, however, before being baptized, it is the common teaching of theologians under the leadership of St. Thomas Aquinas, that such children will receive a measure of happiness that is proportionate to their nature. It is sufficient to know that the souls of unbaptized innocent children will receive not only justice and mercy, but love and generosity, "pressed down, shaken together, and running over" from God, the Giver of every good and perfect gift.

Nurses, physicians, and all who minister to newborn babes in hospitals should see that any infant born of Catholic parents, if in immediate danger of death, is baptized. All that is required is that the person baptizing should have the intention to baptize according to the mind of Christ and His Church and, while pouring water on the head of the child, say: "I baptize thee in the name of the Father and of the Son and of the Holy Spirit."

It is customary to administer *conditional* Baptism to converts about whose previous Baptism there is the slightest doubt. Thus validity may be wanting either through failure to baptize in the proper manner or through lack of the proper intention on the part of the person baptizing. Because of the necessity of Baptism for the valid reception of any of the other sacraments, the Church instructs her ministers to baptize conditionally where any doubt persists after due inquiry has been made. Conditional Baptism means simply that Baptism is intended to be administered only on the condition that the person has never been validly baptized. If the person has already been validly baptized, then not the sacrament but simply the ceremonies are repeated.

The person who acts as sponsor or godparent at Baptism should regard the baptized as his spiritual child and should see that he is properly instructed in the obligations of the Christian life and encouraged to fulfill them with faithfulness and perseverance unto the end.

Is it not evident, from what has been said, that the sacraments are among the greatest gifts of God to man? They are the channels through which the graces and blessings of the Redemption are applied to the souls of men. Baptism is the sacrament whereby the individual is reborn in Christ, and becomes a child of God and an heir of heaven. Before the eyes of a world whose sensitivity to the spiritual is apt to be dulled by daily contact with the merely physical, the Church blazons anew the commission given to her by her divine Founder when He said: "Going, therefore, teach ye all nations, baptizing them in the name of the Father and of the Son and of the Holy Spirit."

Discussion Aids

What two texts especially show Christ's teaching on Baptism? What event related in Acts 2:41 shows that Baptism was a sacrament of the early Church? Define Baptism. May one receive the other sacraments without first having received Baptism? Explain. Name three methods of valid administration of Baptism. Which method was commonly used during the first twelve centuries? Cite authorities. What method is now most commonly used? Define and discuss Baptism of water, of desire, of blood. Discuss infant Baptism. Was it practiced in the early Church? What is necessary for anyone, Christian or non-Christian, to administer lay Baptism? Explain conditional Baptism.

Practices

Learn how to baptize and be ready to assume the responsibility in case of necessity.

When you are sponsor for a child in Baptism, know your obligations and live up to them.

Renew your baptismal vows when you have an opportunity to do so.

NOTES (Chapter 9)

1. Mt. 28:19
2. Mk. 16:15-16
3. Acts 2:41
4. Rom. 5:12
5. Ti. 3:4-7
6. Jn. 3:5
7. *De Bapt.*, Ch. 6, Migne, *Pat. Lat.*, Tom. I

8. In Joan, 80:3, Migne, *Pat. Lat.*, Tom. XXXV
9. *Summa Theol.*, III, q. 66, art. 7
10. Acts 10:48
11. *De Obitu Valent*, p. 51
12. *De Bapt.*, IV, 22, *Pat. Lat.*, Tom. XLIII
13. Oswald, *Die Lehre von Den Sakramenten*, p. 212
14. *De Civ. Dei.*, XIII, 2, Migne, *Pat. Lat.*, Tom. XLI
15. *Adv. Haer.*, Lib. II, Ch. 22

CHAPTER 10

Confirmation

Confirmation is a sacrament in which through the imposition of the bishop's hands, anointing and prayer, baptized persons are strengthened in their faith and receive the gifts of the Holy Spirit that they may live upright Christian lives.

The sacrament is commonly called *Confirmation* because it *confirms* or strengthens the soul by divine grace. It is sometimes called *the laying on of hands* because the bishop extends his hands over those whom he confirms and prays that they may receive the Holy Spirit.

There is no explicit mention in the New Testament of its institution by Christ. But there are numerous references to its administration by the Apostles. The deacon Philip had preached the gospel in Samaria and had received a number of converts into the Church. He baptized but did not confirm them. What happened then? St. Luke tells us in the Acts of the Apostles: "When the Apostles who were in Jerusalem had heard that Samaria had received the word of God they sent unto them Peter and John, who, when they were come, prayed for them that they might receive the Holy Spirit; for He was not yet come upon any of them, but they were only baptized in the name of the Lord Jesus. Then they laid their hands on them, and they received the Holy Spirit."

Here it is expressly stated that Confirmation is distinct from Baptism and produces a different effect. St. Luke likewise relates that the disciples at Ephesus "were baptized in the name of the Lord Jesus, and when Paul had imposed his hands upon them the Holy Spirit came upon them and they spoke tongues and prophesied."[1] In his Epistle to the Hebrews St. Paul lists Confirmation, or the laying on of hands, together with Baptism and Penance, among the fundamental truths of Christianity.[2]

The Fathers of the Church proclaim the same doctrine as the Apostles, and uniformly teach that Confirmation is a sacrament divinely instituted to strengthen the Christian in his faith. Thus Tertullian writes in the second century: "The flesh is *anointed*, that the soul may be consecrated; the flesh is marked, that the soul may be fortified; the flesh is overshadowed *by the imposition of the hands*, that the soul may be enlightened with the Spirit."[3]

St. Cyprian, speaking in the third century, declares that the sacrament of Confirmation which was conferred by the Apostles on the baptized Samarians is likewise administered to the Christians of his day. "Because they had received," he says, "the legitimate baptism ... what was wanting, that was done by Peter and John, that prayer being made for them and hands imposed, the Holy Spirit should be invoked and poured forth upon them. Which now also is done amongst us, so that they who are baptized in the Church are presented to the bishops of the Church, and by our prayer and imposition of hands they receive the Holy Spirit and are perfected with the seal of the Lord."[4]

St. Jerome likewise bears witness to the universal practice of administering Confirmation. "Do you know," he writes against the sect of Luciferians of this time, "that it is the practice of the churches that the imposition of hands should be performed over baptized persons and the Holy Spirit thus invoked? Do you ask where it is written? In the Acts of the Apostles; but were there no Scriptural authority at hand, the consent of the whole world in this regard would have the force of law."[5]

Our last witness from the early Fathers will be St. Cyril of Jerusalem, who compares Confirmation with the Eucharist: "You were anointed with oil, being made sharers and partners of Christ. And see well that you regard it not as mere ointment; for, as the bread of the Eucharist, after the invocation of the Holy Spirit, is no longer mere bread but the Body of Christ, so likewise this holy ointment is no longer common ointment after the invocation, but the gift of Christ and of the Holy Spirit, being rendered efficient by His Divinity.

"You were anointed on the forehead, that you might be delivered from the shame which the first transgressor always experienced, and that you might contemplate the glory of God with an unveiled countenance. . . . As Christ, after His Baptism and the descent of the Holy Spirit upon Him, going forth overcame the adversary, so you likewise, after holy Baptism and the mysterious unction, clothed with the panoply of the Holy Spirit, stand against the adverse power and subdue it, saying, I can do all things in Christ, who strengtheneth me.' "[6]

Confirmation is still administered in the Oriental schismatic churches. Some of these churches have been separated from the Catholic Church since the fourth century. The fact that they still confer Confirmation, despite their long estrangement from Rome, offers convincing evidence of the apostolic antiquity of this sacrament.

Confirmation is administered by the bishop, and consists in the imposition of hands and the anointing with chrism, a mixture of olive oil and balm, blessed by the bishop on Holy Thursdays. In anointing the forehead with chrism the bishop says: "I sign thee with the sign of the cross, and I confirm thee with the chrism of salvation, in the name of the Father, and of the Son, and of the Holy Spirit."

The imposition of hands symbolizes the descent of the Holy Spirit. Oil was used in ancient times to rub the muscles and limbs of wrestlers and athletes to render them more supple. Balm is used to preserve dead bodies from corruption. Thus the anointing with chrism signifies that the persons confirmed receive the strength to fight as valiant soldiers of Christ and the grace to preserve the supernatural life of the soul from decay. After the anointing the bishop gives the person a slight blow on the cheek to remind him that now he must be ready to suffer persecution and even death itself for the faith of Christ. The bishop then says: "Peace be with thee." It is a reminder that true peace of mind comes from a good conscience and obedience to that divine Captain under whose banner he has sworn to fight.

Confirmation is not necessary for salvation like Baptism,

but all Christians should receive the sacrament if at all possible. "It ought not to be omitted by anyone," says the Council of Trent, "in a matter so full of holiness through which the divine gifts are so liberally bestowed, the greatest care should be taken to avoid all neglect."

The bishop is the ordinary minister of this sacrament. The Holy See has authorized pastors to confer Confirmation upon parishioners in danger of death that they might not be deprived of the graces of this sacrament.

Discussion Aids

Define Confirmation. What is this sacrament often called? Why? Was Confirmation administered in the early Church? Give examples (Acts 8:14-17; 19:6). Name some of the early Fathers who bear witness to the administration of Confirmation. Read aloud from the text their testimony. How is Confirmation administered? Who is the ordinary minister of the sacrament? Are priests ever empowered by the Pope to administer Confirmation?

Practices

Do not neglect to be confirmed yourself and encourage others to receive this sacrament.

Meditate on the value of Confirmation, the sacrament of Catholic Action, by which you are strengthened to share in the apostolate of the hierarchy.

Practice devotion to the Holy Spirit.

NOTES (Chapter 10)

1. Acts 19:6
2. Heb. 6:1-3
3. *De Resur. Car.*, Migne, *Pat. Lat.*, Tom. I

4. Epist. 73, Migne, *Pat. Lat.*, Tom. IV
5. *Dial Advs. Lucifer*, Migne, *Pat. Lat.*, Tom. XXIII
6. Cat. 21, Mys. 3 De S. Chrism, Migne, *Pat. Graec.*, Tom. XXXIII

CHAPTER 11

Can Priests Forgive Sins?

An Answer to a Repeated Question

When Dr. John Rathbone Oliver, an Episcopalian writer and psychiatrist of note, was an undergraduate student at Harvard, his grandfather who was a devout Baptist, became greatly disturbed over John's "Romish practices." One evening he undertook to lecture him on the evil of "auricular confession." Dr. Oliver thus reports the lecture:

" 'I don't see why your mother lets you do such things,' " he said, "for he thought of me still as a wayward boy. 'And I never realized what it might lead to when she insisted on being baptized in the Episcopal Church. I can't imagine what your church is coming to anyhow. Confession! Nonsense! Poppycock! But I'll tell you one thing, my boy, no mortal man shall ever come between my soul and my God!"

Commenting on his grandfather's prejudice against Confession, Dr. Oliver says: "Forty years ago this was the general attitude of the average devout Protestant toward what Catholics call the Sacrament of Penance. My dear old grandfather could not see that 'A Man' — 'The Man' — God in Man incarnate — had not only come between him and his God — but had made Himself the Way by which the world had been brought back to God — had become the main channel of Man's approach to the Everlasting Father."[1]

The writer has presented this incident because it illustrates the common reaction of Protestants and of non-Catholics in general toward the Catholic teaching concerning the power of her priests to forgive sins. While there is a shift in the attitude of some of the leading Protestant divines today, there is no doubt that the great masses of people outside the Catholic Church still look upon Confession with misgiving and suspicion, viewing it as an invention of priestcraft and as an unnecessary intrusion between the individual and his God.

We propose to show that this widespread prejudice of non-Catholics against Confession is based upon a common misunderstanding of its real nature, and is directly traceable to misrepresentations and caricatures, whose circulation among the general public was so greatly increased during the presidential campaign of John F. Kennedy in 1960. We shall show, moreover, that the doctrine is not only reasonable and free from any just censure or offense, but that it is the certain teaching of our Savior Jesus Christ, and that it is, in fact, among the most helpful and comforting of all His gifts to weak and sinful humanity. In establishing this truth, we shall appeal not to the authoritative pronouncements of the Church but to the words of Christ Himself and to the court of our common understanding.

What, then, is the evidence that priests have the power to forgive sins? Let us begin our answer to this question by asking: What was the dominant purpose of Christ's ministry on earth? Was it not to rescue mankind from the effects of their own sinfulness, and to provide suitable means by which they might advance in spiritual perfection and attain everlasting life? The pages of the gospel are replete with instances showing the mercy and compassion of Christ upon suffering and sinful humanity.

He restores sight to the blind, hearing to the deaf, speech to the dumb, and vigor to the paralyzed limb. The evangelist Matthew sums it up when he says simply: "And all that were sick, he healed."[2] While He poured out His benefactions upon the sick of body, He was even more intent upon the healing of the ills of the soul. This primary purpose of Christ's ministry is indicated in His very name. "Thou shalt call his name Jesus," says the angel, "for he shall save his people from their sins."[3]

Among the most touching scenes in the Master's earthly ministry are those which reveal His compassion for weak and sinful humanity, fallen by the wayside, but contrite and willing to rise again. Readers will recall how on one occasion the Jews brought to Jesus a woman taken in adultery, and inquired if she should not be stoned to death according to the Law of Moses.

Jesus said to them: "He that is without sin among you, let him first cast a stone at her." Then he wrote on the ground. Tradition tells us that he wrote in the dust the secret sins of those who stood about. And one by one they went away. Then Jesus said to the woman who alone remained: "Woman, where are they that accused thee? Hath no man condemned thee?" She answered, "No man, Lord." And Jesus said: "Neither will I condemn thee. Go, and now sin no more."[4]

Not less dramatic than the pardoning of the woman taken in adultery is the scene that occurred when Jesus was dining at the home of Simon, the Pharisee, in Bethania. Mary Magdalen, a woman of the streets, looked down upon by the proud Pharisees, enters. With her tears she washes the feet of Jesus, anoints them with ointment from an alabaster box, and wipes them with her hair. The Pharisees, scandalized that Christ has permitted her to so much as touch Him, do not wish to be contaminated by her presence. Fain would they have cast her out. Simon is saying: "This man, if he were a prophet, would know surely who and what manner of woman this is that toucheth him, that she is a sinner."[5]

Does Jesus follow the thought of the Pharisees and drive her away from Him with looks of scorn and words of condemnation? No, indeed! For that scarlet woman of the streets Jesus has nothing but mercy and words of infinite tenderness. To the proud Pharisees He says, "Many sins are forgiven her, because she hath loved much." Then turning to the weeping Magdalen, He speaks these sweet and comforting words which breathe the spirit of infinite mercy: "Thy sins are forgiven thee. . . . Go in peace."[6]

Bent and bowed under the weight of sin, blinded by tears of repentance, that was not Mary Magdalen alone to whom Christ spoke. It was to all womanhood and all mankind in the centuries still struggling in the womb of time. Mary was but the symbol of the race. Into the ears of men and women everywhere, bent and broken under the weight of mortal sin, blinded by tears of repentance, Christ breathes again those tender words of mercy and forgiveness: "Thy sins are forgiven thee. . . . Go, and now sin no more."

Surely these pictures of the gentle Savior pardoning the woman taken in adultery, forgiving the sinful Magdalen, with a prayer for the forgiveness of His murderers on his dying lips, must come to the minds of sinners like the breath of eternal spring. To souls sinking into the slough of despair these words come as the stars that shine in the blackened vault of a moonless sky. No matter if the soul is covered with sins of lust, or gluttony, or envy, or hatred, or all of them together, Christ still stands ready to wash them all away. "If your sins be as scarlet, they shall be made as white as snow: and if they be as red as crimson, they shall be white as wool."[7] "The bruised reed he shall not break, and smoking flax he shall not quench."[8]

So tender and considerate was Jesus toward sinners that the Pharisees complained to the disciples, saying: "Why doth your master eat with publicans and sinners? But Jesus hearing it, said: They that are in health need not a physician, but they that are ill. Go then and learn what this meaneth, I will have mercy and not sacrifice. For I am not come to call the just, but sinners."[9]

There we have in the Master's own words the purpose of His mission on earth — to call the wayward sinners back to Him. To illustrate this truth still more vividly to them, Christ then narrated three parables. The first was the beautiful parable of the Good Shepherd, who leaves the ninety-nine sheep in the desert and searches for the one that is lost until he finds it. Then carrying it home upon his shoulders, he calls together his friends and neighbors, saying: "Rejoice with me because I have found my sheep that was lost." Then the Master shows the application of the parable, saying, "I say to you, that even so there shall be joy in heaven upon one sinner that doth penance, more than upon ninety-nine just who need not penance."[10]

The second parable illustrating this truth is about the woman, who having ten groats, loses one. Immediately she lights the candle and sweeps the house and searches diligently until she finds it. Then she calls together her friends and neighbors, saying: "Rejoice with me, because I have found the groat which I had lost." The third parable is perhaps the most beautiful and touching that ever fell from the Master's lips. It is the story of the Prodigal Son and familiar to all.

With such masterly artistry does it play upon the varied emotions that it seems to strike all the notes on the diapason of the human heart. It reaches its climax when the father seeing in the distance his prodigal son returning, runs to him, embraces him and forgives him. He orders the servants to kill the fatted calf, and wishes all to rejoice with him "because this my son was dead, and is come to life again: was lost and is found."[11] That was the picture which the Master drew of Himself in the long ago: that is still the picture of Him today.

Is there any fair-minded person who in the face of these clear teachings of Jesus Christ can doubt that the primary purpose of His mission on earth was to reconcile sinners to their God? Is it conceivable that He would not confer upon the Church which He founded the power and authority to continue the mission which He Himself had come upon earth to achieve? Was Christ interested only in reconciling the sinners of His day, or was He interested in restoring all mankind to the friendship of God? If His divine mission was to all mankind and not merely to the people of His day, then it follows that there must have been provided means whereby people, living after Christ in His visible form had left the earth, could still be cleansed from their sins.

This dictate of our common intelligence finds its complete verification in the action of our blessed Lord as recorded in the gospels; for Christ conferred upon the Apostles the selfsame power of pardoning which He Himself possessed. To demonstrate that He Himself possessed this power, He worked a physical miracle. Thus He said to the man sick of the palsy: "Thy sins are forgiven thee."

Some of the scribes professed to be scandalized at Christ's claim to exercise such power, saying: "He blasphemeth. Who can forgive sins, but God only?" Whereupon Christ said to them: "Which is easier, to say to the man sick of the palsy: Thy sins are forgiven thee; or to say: Arise, take up thy bed and walk? But that you may know that the Son of man hath power on earth to forgive sins, (he saith to the sick of the palsy) I say to thee: Arise, take up thy bed, and go into thy house."[12]

Now this same power of pardoning, Christ promised to Peter and the other Apostles when He said: "Amen I say to you, whatsoever you shall bind upon earth, shall be bound also in heaven: and whatsoever you shall loose upon earth, shall be loosed also in heaven."[13] Even more specific, and in a manner more impressive than this was the action of Christ after His Resurrection in solemnly conferring upon His Apostles this power of pardoning: "As the Father hath sent Me, I also send you. When He had said this, He breathed on them; and He said to them: Receive ye the Holy Spirit. Whose sins you shall forgive, they are forgiven them: and whose sins you shall retain, they are retained."[14]

In these words Christ reiterates in plain, literal language what He had previously stated to them in the figurative terms of *binding* and *loosing*. It is to be noted that Christ prefaces the conferring of this power upon the Apostles by declaring the identity of their mission with His own: "As the Father hath sent Me, I also send you." He says to them in effect: As I came into the world to reconcile sinners to their God, so likewise are you called upon to fulfill this same mission.

It is to be observed also that Christ gave them power not merely to announce that sins were forgiven but actually to forgive them — "whose sins *you* shall forgive, they are forgiven them." If the authority of the Apostles were restricted to the declaration, "God pardons you," they would then require a special revelation in each case to make the pronouncement valid. Furthermore, the power conferred is a *judicial* one. They are not told to forgive or to retain indiscriminately but judicially, according as the sinner deserves. This obviously requires the specific acknowledgment or confession of sin. Lastly, it is to be noted that their authority is not restricted to any particular kind of sins, but extends to all without exception.

Would it be possible to express in a clearer or more unmistakable manner the conferring upon the Apostles of this power of pardoning than in the plain language and in the solemn manner used by Christ? The divine Master, it would seem, wished to eliminate for all time the possibility of any misconstruction of His meaning by reiterating in the plainest and most literal terms what He had already stated to them in the beautiful and rich metaphor of the Aramaic tongue. How is it possible for any Christian who professes to believe in the truth of Christ's teachings to escape the conclusion that He conferred upon His Church the selfsame power of forgiving sins which He Himself possessed?

There are many people who admit that the Apostles received this power but deny that it was transmitted to their successors. This view, which would confine the solicitude of Christ to the people of His generation, is flatly contradicted by the statement of Christ showing that He conferred authority upon the Apostles, not in their private capacity as individuals, but in their *official* capacity as officers of a moral corporation, His Church, which was to continue till the end of time. Thus He said to the Apostles: "Go ye, therefore, and teach all nations.... And behold I am with you *all* days even to the consummation of the world."[15]

As the Apostles and disciples were all to pass away, it is evident that the authority they possessed was to be transmitted to their successors in office; otherwise Christ's Church would have perished with His Apostles. There is the same need today of reconciling sinners to God that there was in the days of Christ and the Apostles. The Catholic Church, founded by Christ, will continue her divinely appointed ministry of reconciling sinners until the last soul shall have been gathered into the arms of its Maker.

Let us now consider some of the common objections to this sacrament. A non-Catholic friend voiced a difficulty experienced by many outside of the fold when he said to the writer: "I believe that God alone can forgive sins. You priests are not divine. You are entirely human like the rest of us. You have your shortcomings and weaknesses. You have no more power of forgiving sins than I have. In fact, I have as much power to forgive a sin or crime as you or any other human being." Let me now address in a kindly manner to our dear non-Catholic reader, the words I then addressed to my friend:

"Can you pardon a criminal from the state penitentiary at Joliet just the same as the governor of Illinois?" I asked.

"No," replied my friend, "I'll admit I can't do that."

"But aren't you a man," I persisted, "and isn't the governor a man, the same as you? And didn't you say that you had as much power to forgive a misdeed as any other man?"

"Yes," replied my friend, "but I make a distinction. The governor simply as a *man* does not have the power to pardon. It is only because he occupies the *office* of the governor of Illinois that he has such authority."

"Then you admit," I pointed out, "the same basic distinction which the Church makes between a priest simply as a human being and as one who exercises power solely by virtue of the office which he holds. I, in my private personal capacity as Mr. Smith or Mr. Jones, have no more power than you or any other man. But I, in my *official* capacity as an ambassador of almighty God, acting in His name and by His authority, exercise a power which far transcends that of a human being and is in truth, the very power of God Himself."

This distinction between a man in his private capacity, simply as a human being, and in his official position as an ambassador, is woven into the warp and woof of our American government. Thus, a prominent man is sent as the ambassador of the United States to the court of St. James in London. When he acts within the limits of his duly accredited jurisdiction as our ambassador, and signs documents affecting the relations of England and the United States, is there behind his signature the feeble strength of but one elderly man? On the contrary, there is behind his signature the power and strength and the sovereign authority of over 200 million citizens of our country. Why? Because he acts as our ambassador, in our name and by our authority.

It is this very distinction that the Apostle St. Paul pointed out in his Epistle to the Corinthians when he explained to them the beneficent arrangement of divine Providence for the reconciliation of sinners. "God," he says, "hath reconciled us to Himself through Christ, *and hath given to us the ministry of reconciliation.* . . . For Christ, therefore, we are *ambassadors:* God, as it were exhorting *through* us."[16]

St. Paul publicly proclaimed his unworthiness and frailty. He had persecuted the Church of God, and there was given to him a "sting of the flesh, an angel of Satan" to buffet him. Yet he recognized that Christ chose not angels, but weak and sinful men to be His ministers. Every priest receives his priestly power from a bishop, who traces his power back through an unbroken succession of bishops to one of the Apostles, and back ultimately to Christ Himself. That is why a priest as a duly accredited ambassador of God exercises the tremendous power of forgiving sin, a power that comes from God as its ultimate Source.

In delegating priests to act as ministers of reconciliation, Christ is but following the general policy, so clearly recorded in the gospels, of using men as His ambassadors to administer all the sacraments and to preach and to teach in His name. Thus He commissioned the Apostles to teach in His name, saying: "Go ye, therefore, and teach all nations." Similar was His commission to them to baptize: "Teach ye all nations; baptizing them in the name of the Father, and of the Son, and of the Holy Spirit."[17]

Is it not passing strange that Christians who frankly admit that Christ chose men to be the heralds of His gospel and the ministers of Baptism and the other sacraments should yet seek to exclude from them the one sacrament of reconciliation? Surely the fair-minded reader must see that in so doing they are going directly against the plain teaching not only of St. Paul but of Jesus Christ Himself.

Another difficulty experienced by many non-Catholics arises from their custom of confessing their sins to God privately, and from their belief that such a confession is sufficient to secure forgiveness. Thus a university student whom I was instructing in the faith said to me: "Father, I have been in the habit of including in the prayers I address to God an acknowledgment of my shortcomings. I beg almighty God to forgive me. I have been taught to believe that God pardons me directly and immediately without the intermediary agency of any minister or priest. Surely God has the power to forgive me. How do you know but what He does forgive me in answer to my prayers — without benefit of clergy?"

Let me now address to our dear non-Catholic reader the explanation I submitted to my young friend: It is true that God can forgive a person directly and immediately. It is not for us to place limits either to the power or the mercy of an omnipotent and all-merciful Father. It seems evident, however, that we ought to seek forgiveness through the means which He has revealed to us as the ordinary channel by which His pardon is extended to us, and not to demand that He act in accordance with our private whims and caprice.

Have you the right to dictate the manner in which God must pardon you? Or has He the right to specify the manner in which His clemency will be extended to you? Surely, God has that right, and He has exercised it through the revelation made by His divine Son as to the ordinary means by which that forgiveness is extended to mankind. That channel, as the gospels record, is the Sacrament of Penance in which sins are confessed to the duly appointed ambassadors of God.

Of course if a person is dying and no priest is available, then the person may confess directly to God, and by eliciting an act of perfect sorrow, receive forgiveness directly from Him. God does not ask the impossible from any person. It is a dictate of reason, as well as the teaching of the Church, that under such unusual circumstances God not only may, but actually does, forgive the penitent in the extraordinary method just described. Indeed, whenever an act of perfect contrition is elicited, the sins are forgiven directly and immediately by God, though there remains the obligation of submitting them to the tribunal of Penance.

There would be, however, neither purpose nor meaning to the action of our divine Lord in solemnly delegating the power of forgiving sins to His Apostles and their successors, if people could ordinarily confess to God in secret and receive pardon directly from Him. No one would care to reveal his shortcomings to another human being, if he could go directly to God and completely disregard the ambassadors accredited by Christ here as the ministers of reconciliation. The solemn conferring upon them of the power of binding and of loosing, of retaining and of forgiving, would be hollow mockery of the most foolish and deceptive character.

This objection in reality is by no means new. St. Augustine encountered it back in the fourth century. "Let no one," remarks the illustrious Bishop of Hippo, "say to himself, I do penance to God *in private;* I do it before God. Is it, then, in vain that Christ has said: 'Whatsoever ye shall loose on earth shall be loosed in heaven?' Is it in vain that the keys have been given to the Church? Do we make void the gospel, void the words of Christ?"[18]

173

In these words St. Augustine points out that the question for us is not how God is *able* to act but how He *has actually chosen* to act. God *could* have chosen other means for the reconciliation of sinners, just as He could have created a world different from the present one: but it is our concern to discover how God has actually chosen to reconcile sinners and then to avail ourselves with gratitude of this wonderful gift to weak and sinful humanity.

Christ did not allow the remission of sin to rest solely upon the shifting sands of subjective disposition and the whimsicalities of private emotion. On the contrary, He established a definite objective agency for the certain accomplishment of this all-important end. There is a comfort, an ease, and an assurance of certain pardon which is given by the Sacrament of Confession which no private confession to God could possibly afford. If you were to ask a Catholic what are the happiest moments in his life, he would tell that among them are the moments immediately after Confession when his conscience enjoys perfect peace because there has been lifted from his soul the burden of mortal sin.

A last objection. Some contend that the confession of sins to a priest was not practiced in the infant Church but is merely a development of many centuries later, being an invention of priestcraft to enable the clergy to keep the laity in subjection. The answer is simple. In conferring this power of forgiving sins upon the Apostles, Christ intended that it should be utilized; otherwise it would be meaningless. That it was utilized, is clearly recorded by St. Luke in the Acts of the Apostles where he tells us: "Many of them who believed came confessing and declaring their deeds," to the Apostles.[19]

Why did they confess their sins unless they were instructed by the Apostles to do so? It was this teaching of Christ and of the Apostles to which St. John bears witness when he says: "If we confess our sins, He is faithful and just to forgive us our sins and to cleanse us from all iniquity."[20]

The significance of these texts of Scripture becomes all the more evident from the writings of the Fathers of the early Church: from the first to the last they insist upon sacramental confession as a divine institution. Let me cite just a few out of an imposing list of such witnesses. In the fourth century, St. Ambrose rebukes the Novatians who "professed to show reverence for the Lord by reserving to Him alone the power of forgiving sins. Greater wrong could not be done than that which they do in seeking to rescind His commands and fling back the office He bestowed. . . . The Church obeys Him in both respects, by binding sin and by loosing it; for the Lord willed that for both the power should be equal."[21] Further, this power belongs to the priesthood: "It seemed impossible that sins should be forgiven through penance; Christ granted this (power) to the Apostles and from the Apostles it has been transmitted to . . . priests."[22]

A last witness. Writing also in the fourth century, St. Basil compares the confession of sins to priests to the revealing of the secret infirmities of the body to the physician in order to secure a remedy. "In the confession of sins," he says, "the same method must be observed as in laying open the infirmities of the body; for as these are not rashly communicated to every one, but to those only who understand by what method they may be cured, so the confession of sins must be made to such persons as have the power to apply a remedy."[23]

Later on he tells us who those persons are. "Necessarily, our sins must be confessed to those to whom has been committed the dispensation of the mysteries of God. Thus, also, are they found to have acted who did penance of old. . . . It is written in the Acts, they confessed to the Apostles, by whom also they were baptized."[24]

In testifying to the universal practice of auricular confession in the early Church, St. Augustine, St. Ambrose and St. Basil but echo the voice of all the Fathers of both the East and the West. Thus the practice continued unbroken from the days of Christ down to the Protestant Reformation in the sixteenth century. Indeed, it will be a matter of surprise for most non-Catholics to know that Martin Luther bore witness to both the practice and the utility of Confession, declaring that "auricular confession, as now in vogue, is useful, nay, necessary: nor would I have it abolished, since it is the remedy of afflicted conscience."[25]

In conclusion then, Confession is not the invention of priest-craft, nor the work of bishops or popes, but the institution of

Jesus Christ. It is the sacrament which enables the Church to carry on the essential mission of Christ — to call not the just, but sinners, to repentance." It is the living testimony of Christ's undying love for mankind. When we read of the tender mercy and compassion shown by Christ toward the thief on the cross, toward His very murderers, we find ourselves wishing that we could have been privileged to have lived in His day to receive from His hand a benediction and from His lips such soothing words of pardon.

Then we recollect: Christ still lives in His Church! The centuries have not foreshortened His hand nor stilled His voice. When the hand of His divinely appointed ambassador in the tribunal of Confession is raised in absolution over us, with the eyes of faith we see again the hand of Christ that was raised in benediction over the sinful woman, prostrate in the dust of the street in Jerusalem, while we hear again an echo of that same divine voice that whispered to her, "Thy sins are forgiven thee. . . . Go, and now sin no more."

Discussion Aids

What was the primary purpose of Christ's ministry? Give two instances in which Christ forgave sins. What was His attitude towards repentant sinners? In what three parables does He reveal this attitude? Where in the gospels does Christ promise to His Apostles the power to forgive sins? When did He fulfill this promise? How do we know that the successors of the Apostles also have this power? Distinguish between a man and his office, giving examples. What does St. Paul call God's ministers? Did Christ appoint men as His ambassadors to carry on His work? Why not, then, for Penance? Explain why Catholics confess to a priest. What does St. Augustine say of the objection that is made to confessing to a priest?

Practices

Practice frequent Confession in an effort to weed out your serious faults.

Pray earnestly for your confessor after every Confession.

Take a non-Catholic into the church and show and explain to him the confessional.

NOTES (Chapter 11)

1. J.R. Oliver, "Psychiatry and the Confessional," p. 60 in *Scribner's*, July 1930
2. Mt. 8:16
3. *Ibid.*, 1:21
4. Jn. 8:11
5. Lk. 7:39
6. *Ibid.*, 7:48-50
7. Is. 1:18
8. *Ibid.*, 42:3
9. Mt. 9:11-13
10. Lk. 15:7
11. *Ibid.*, 15:24
12. Mk. 2:9-11
13. Mt. 18:18
14. Jn. 20:21-23
15. Mt. 28:20
16. II Cor. 5:18-20
17. Mt. 28:19
18. *Sermon*, cccxcii, Migne, *Pat. Lat.*, Tom. XXXIX
19. Acts 19:18
20. I Jn. 1:9
21. *De Poenit*, I, ii, 6
22. Op. cit., II, ii, 12
23. *In Reg. Brev.*, quaest, ccxix, T. II, p. 492
24. *Ibid.*, cclxxxviii, p. 516
25. "Ibid. de Capt. Babyl. cap de Poenit," in Martin Luther's *First Principles of the Reformation* (John Murray, London, 1883)

CHAPTER 12

Does Confession Make Sinning Easy?

A Glimpse into the 'Secret' Confessional

In the smoking compartment of a Pullman car, five men were seeking to lessen the tedium of traveling by puffing away at their cigarettes and pipes and discussing the topics of the day. They had elected the next president, solved the ills of the long-suffering farmer and pointed the way to permanent peace. After solving with easy dispatch such large problems of the world, like Alexander the Great they were beginning to sigh — or was it yawn? — because there were no more worlds to conquer. Suddenly during the lull, one of the group seeking to rescue the conversation from approaching death, brought up the topic of religion.

"Have you ever noticed," he queried, "that you don't ever find Catholic priests going to the county poor farms? Do you know the real reason why? I'll tell you," he continued. "They have a nice system of priestly graft. They have what they call a 'confessional' where Catholics come to have their sins forgiven at so much per. The price the priests charge for pardoning depends upon the seriousness of the sins and the number of them. It's a pretty soft racket for the priests, I'll say."

This incident was recently narrated to me by a non-Catholic gentleman who was present at the time and who is now receiving instructions in the Catholic faith. In the statement just quoted, there is disclosed in all its artless nakedness a conception of Confession that prevails among vast numbers of people outside the Catholic Church. It poisons their minds against the Church and her priesthood and precludes the possibility of their making any investigation into the claims of the Church to be the institution established by Jesus Christ to teach all mankind the divinely revealed truths of religion and to guide them along the paths of justice and truth and love that lead to God.

Vast numbers of our separated brethren, probably the majority of them, have heard this charge whispered about the confessional. After I had spoken to a motley throng in the courthouse square of a town in North Carolina, a listener asked: "Why do Catholics pay priests for forgiving their sins?"

Curious to know how many of them labored under that illusion, I inquired: "How many of you have been told that priests charge money for forgiving sins?" Whereupon virtually every man and woman in the crowd held up their hands. Not only had they heard such a charge but they also believed it to be true.

Indeed, a non-Catholic acquaintance once informed me that he was assured of the truth of this charge by his own minister — one who ascends the Christian pulpit as the herald of the Prince of Truth! Catholics only smile at the absurdity of such a statement and marvel at the credulity of people who put any stock in it. What are we going to say to our dear non-Catholic friends in answer to this charge? We make our own the expressive words of Uncle Abe Martin: "It's all right, only it ain't so."

Not only does a priest make no charge for administering the sacrament of forgiveness, but so strict is the law of the Church, he may not accept in connection with this sacrament any offering or gift which might appear in any way as a payment for the pardon.

Another objection to Confession frequently encountered among non-Catholics is that it is a needless prying into private matters, embarrassing the penitent with the fear that his secret sins may be made public. This difficulty, like the preceding one, could exist only in the minds of people who have never had any experience in the reception of this sacrament. The simple facts are: No name is ever mentioned in Confession. The confessor must observe with scrupulous fidelity the same laws of propriety which bind every other human being. The sins are confessed briefly, without irrelevant details, in an entirely impersonal and objective manner. The penitent is free to go to Confession to any priest he chooses.

He is assured not only of complete privacy but of the most absolute and inviolable secrecy. Kneeling in a part of the confessional partitioned off from the chamber wherein the confessor sits, his voice penetrates through a small grated aperture into the ear of the ambassador of God. Under no circumstances whatsoever, not even to save his own life, may a confessor reveal the tiniest venial sin breathed into his ear in Confession. All history is eloquent with the story of the deathless fidelity with which this trust has been observed. Cheerfully have priests gone to their death rather than violate the seal of Confession.

In the fourteenth century, for example, King Wenceslaus of Bohemia, insanely jealous of the Queen and curious to know what she mentioned in Confession, summoned before him her confessor, Father John Nepomucene.

"What is it," said the Emperor, "that the Queen confesses to you? Reveal it to me and I shall give you riches. Refuse and I shall cast you into the dungeon."

"Not for you nor for all the kingdom of Bohemia," replied the saintly priest, "will I reveal that which has been disclosed only to the ambassador of God."

Whereupon the Emperor had him cast into the dungeon. Then seeking to shake his iron will, his body was stretched on a rack, and burning torches were placed against his flesh. In spite of the excruciating torture, no sound escaped his lips save the words, "Jesus" and "Mary." Seeing that he was obdurate and unmoved by any instrument of torture his savage cruelty could devise, the Emperor had him bound hand and foot and on Ascension Even, the sixteenth of May, 1383, he was hurled from the bridge at Prague into the dark waters of the Moldau River — a martyr to the seal of the confessional.

When in 1719, after the lapse of over three centuries, his grave in the Prague cathedral was opened, his flesh had disappeared. But one member, though shriveled, remained incorrupt. That was his tongue — in its silence still giving glory to God and testifying with its mute eloquence to the unbroken seal of the sacrament.

The martyrdom which St. John Nepomucene suffered illustrates what every priest in Christendom would willingly undergo rather than reveal the tiniest venial sin mentioned in Confession. It is no exaggeration to say that in all the scope of human life, there is no secrecy so absolute, impenetrable and inviolable as that which is protected by the seal of the confessional.

The objection, however, which is even more widespread among non-Catholics, and which apparently weighs more heavily with them than either of the ones just mentioned, is of a different character. A non-Catholic inquirer stated the difficulty which many, if not the majority of people outside the Church, experience in regard to Confession in the following way:

"Non-Catholics in general," he said, "feel that the securing of pardon for sins simply by telling them to a priest, places too much stress and value upon the external and mechanical aspects of repentance, and too little upon true internal sorrow for sin, wherein alone genuine repentance consists. The mere mechanical enumeration of sins to a priest gives no assurance of contrition or purpose of amendment. The way it works out in practice is that by making the forgiveness of sins so easy to obtain, confession rather encourages moral laxity. An individual, tempted to commit some sin, instead of being deterred is rather encouraged to go ahead and commit the misdeed, knowing that whatever its gravity be, he will be pardoned merely by mentioning it under the protecting anonymity of the confessional. Instead of a barrier to sin," he concluded, "confession with its emphasis upon external formalism thus serves as an indirect encouragement or incentive to commit sin."

Like all other objections to Confession, this one is based upon a failure to understand the real nature of the Sacrament of Confession and of the dispositions requisite for its valid reception. If the picture drawn by our non-Catholic friend were an accurate one, we could not quarrel with the conclusion he reaches: the fact is, however, that he has described the outward shell but has overlooked the very heart of the sacrament. Let me now address in a kindly way to our non-Catholic reader the explanation I submitted to my friend who voiced the difficulty just mentioned.

If the forgiveness of sins were dependent upon the mere

mechanical enumeration of them to a priest, then confession would justly be open to the charge of formalism and externalism in the worst sense and would be properly indicted for its neglect of the internal dispositions of mind and heart and will, wherein all hope of reform must be. But the fact is that the Church teaches in the clearest and most unmistakable manner that *there can be no forgiveness of sin unless there is sorrow for sin and purpose of amendment* by the penitent. Thus she declares that if a person confessed his sins to all the priests, bishops and cardinals in Christendom, and even to the Holy Father himself, and even if they all pronounced the words of absolution over him, there would be *no* real forgiveness if he did not have internal sorrow for sin and the resolve to avoid sin in the future.

More important even than the examination of conscience is the arousal of contrition and purpose of amendment. Thus the Council of Trent, in enumerating the qualities necessary for a good confession, cites sorrow for sin as holding first place and as including the purpose of amendment. "Contrition," says the Council of Trent, "which holds the first place among the acts of the penitent is sorrow of heart and detestation for sin committed, with the resolve to sin no more."[1]

Hence to state that the sinner receives pardon merely by "telling his sins to a priest," is to misrepresent the essential nature of the sacrament. If an individual while telling his sins in confession had the intention of repeating them just as soon as the occasion offered, not only would he not be pardoned but he would be guilty of another sin — that of making mockery of the sacrament. Likewise, if a person has stolen the property of another, and refuses to restore it to its rightful owner, no priest would absolve him. Why? Because he lacks the disposition necessary for forgiveness, namely, the firm purpose of amendment, which would include in this case the intention to restore the stolen property.

Where funds have been stolen and retained for a considerable time, not only must the original amount be returned but the interest which would ordinarily accrue on it must likewise be added to the amount restored. This applies not only to tangible goods but also to intangible ones, such as a person's good name and reputation. Thus if an individual has robbed another of his

182

good name by telling lies about his character, he is bound to promise to repair the damage done to his neighbor, even though it causes embarrassment to himself, in order to secure forgiveness.

From this it is apparent that the Sacrament of Penance is no mere glossing over of sin, no mere placing of a white mantle of forgiveness on a person, whose heart and will and soul are black with the corruption of unrepented sin. On the contrary, the sacrament requires that the renovation must be from within, that the mind and heart and soul must be detached from the sin and attached to God in love and loyalty. In other words, Confession *strikes at the very* root of the evil by penetrating beyond the outward surface into the very heart and will and soul of man wherein lie the roots of good and evil.

Hence it is morally impossible for any individual to remain an habitual addict of any vice, if he will come often and make a good confession. Why? Because the repeated arousal of the strong determination of the will to avoid the sinful practice in the future is bound eventually, aided by God's grace, to break the links in the chain of any sinful habit. It is to be noted that sincere purpose of amendment requires the prudent avoidance of the occasions: persons, places, or things which past experience shows, have led one into sin.

What more is there that any human being can do to free himself from habits of sin than is required by the Sacrament of Confession? To the native strength of the will is added the grace given by God in the sacrament and the additional strength and encouragement that comes from the consciousness that one is starting with a clean slate instead of one already disfigured by so many past transgressions that an additional one would not make much difference. Indeed, *it is no exaggeration then to say that Confession is the most powerful and effective agency for the moral reformation of humanity that exists in the world today.*

Sermons, lectures, exhortations, books are all too general. Confession alone comes to close grips with the reins of conduct in each individual, and pulls the reins so strongly that no individual can be insensitive to its tugging nor mistake the direction of its guidance. In public sermons, to employ a military phrase, the fire is at random, it may hit or miss; but in the confessional it is a dead shot — right to the heart of the penitent.

No wonder it was, then, that after over fifty years of ministering to the moral and spiritual needs of men, seeking to uplift them by sermons, by writing books, and by building schools for their religious education, Cardinal Gibbons, toward the close of his long and eventful life, voiced his deep conviction on the matter in the following memorable words: "My experience is that the confessional is the most powerful lever ever erected by a merciful God for raising men from the mire of sin." To this judgment of the distinguished Cardinal, so beloved by his fellow citizens of every faith, probably every priest who has had even a modicum of experience in the care of souls would heartily subscribe.

This is the conviction not only of those who have had actual experience of the sacrament, such as priests and penitents, but it is also the conclusion reached by those outside the Church who have made careful observations on the effects of the confessional upon the lives of those who frequent it. Thus Voltaire, who was no friend of Christianity, found himself forced to declare "that there is not perhaps a more useful institution than confession."[3] Similarly Rousseau, who was not less hostile to the Church, declared: "How many restitutions and reparations does not confession cause among Catholics!"[3]

In Germany, the great philosopher, Leibnitz, though a non-Catholic, paid tribute to the usefulness of the confessional to the welfare of society. "This whole work of sacramental penance," he writes, "is indeed worthy of the divine wisdom and if aught else in the Christian dispensation is meritorious of praise, surely it is this wondrous institution. For the necessity of confessing one's sins deters a man from committing them, and hope is given to him who may have fallen again after expiation.

"The pious and prudent confessor is in very deed a great instrument in the hands of God for man's regeneration. For the kindly advice of God's priest helps man to control his passions, to know the lurking places of sin, to avoid the occasions of evil doing, to restore ill-gotten goods, to have hope after depression and doubt, to have peace after affliction, in a word, to remove or at least lessen all evil, and if there is no pleasure on earth like unto a faithful friend, what must be the esteem a man must have for him, who is in very deed a friend in the hour of his direst need?"[4]

In Great Britain, Dr. Martensen, a distinguished Protestant theologian, pays tribute to the confessional not only because it ministers directly to the social welfare by insisting upon truth, honesty and justice, and upon restitution when the latter is violated, but also because it ministers directly to the hunger of the individual soul for personal spiritual regeneration. "Absolution," he says, "in the name of the Father and of the Son and of the Holy Spirit, derived from the full power of binding and loosing which the Church has inherited from the Apostles is not unconditional, but depends on the same condition on which the gospel itself adjudges the forgiveness of sins, namely, change of heart and faith. . . .

"It cannot easily be denied that confession meets a deep need of human nature. There is a great psychological truth in the saying of Pascal, that a man often attains for the first time a true sense of sin, and a true staidness in his good purpose, when he confesses his sins to his fellowman, as well as to God. Catholicism has often been commended because by confession it affords an opportunity of depositing the confession of his sins in the breast of another man, where it remains kept under the seal of the most sacred secrecy, and whence the consolation of the forgiveness of sins is given him in the very name of the Lord."[5]

In our own country there was probably no voice in all of Protestantism which was listened to with such eagerness and respect by so vast a number of our fellow countrymen as that of the Rev. Dr. Harry E. Fosdick, then pastor of the Riverside Baptist Church of New York. Speaking before more than 1000 ministers at the annual meeting of the Greater New York Federation of Churches, Dr. Fosdick strongly urged the restoration of the confessional to Protestant churches.

"We Protestants are losing more," he said, "than we have any business to lose by not coming in closer contact with the individual. When a Catholic would take his mental troubles to his priest, the Protestant would go to a psychoanalyst or like specialist, and the church would gain nothing in experience. . . . The confessional, which Protestanism threw out the door, is coming back through the window, in utterly new forms, to be sure, with new methods and with an entirely new intellectual explanation appropriate to the Protestant churches, but motivated by a real determination to help meet the inward problems of individuals.

"Clergymen are giving different names to this form of activity, such as 'trouble clinics,' 'personal conferences on spiritual problems,' 'the Protestant confessional.' The name makes little difference. What does matter is the renewed awareness in the churches that they are in danger of surrendering to the psycho-analyst that vast field of human need where the confession of sin and spiritual misery is met with sympathetic and intelligent treatment. To be sure, a wise minister will work with a psychiatrist, not without one, but if the churches substitute any other kind of success for the successful handling of the spiritual aspects of individual problems, they will be vacating their most obvious function."[6]

It is to be noted that Dr. Fosdick urges the restoration of the confessional on the grounds that it ministers to the psychological needs of people oppressed with a consciousness of sin. In other words, confession does for the masses the work for which the wealthy pay large fees to the psychoanalyst and the psychiatrist. There can be no doubt that the confessional is of distinct value in promoting the mental health of people.

It is a principle of modern psychology that a source of disturbance to one's peace of mind, if not removed by the process of rationalization, that is, by realizing that worry won't help matters, or that the item is being stretched to assume undue importance, or by some other therapeutic means, tends to form a central focus which gradually spreads to other areas of one's mental life and thus creates various types of mental disorders. Such is the fertile breeding ground of many of the phobias, tics, and complexes which upset the delicate balance of one's mental life, and cause one to appear "queer."

Now one of the sources of worry common probably to the vast majority of mankind is traceable to their consciousness of doing at times what they know is morally wrong, and then experiencing the gnawings of remorse. If the canker of remorse bites continuously at the individual's peace of mind because of the persistence of the sense of guilt, not only the individual's happiness is likely to be seriously disturbed but the very health of his mind is apt to be affected.

What is probably the most effective means, verified by the findings of modern psychology as well as by the experience of the race, for the removal of such worries as are undermining one's mental health? The simple means of disclosure, unbosoming oneself to one's friend, revealing the sin — the cause of the worry — to the priest in the secrecy of the confessional.

When the sin is confessed, the sense of guilt is washed away, and peace of mind returns. It is like opening the door of a closet, in which mildew has accumulated in the darkness. When the fresh air and the bright sunshine stream in, the parasitic denizens which thrive only in the darkness, speedily vanish. So when the door of the mind is opened, and the distorted fancies and exaggerated worries are exposed to the sunlight of reason and the wholesome counsel of friends, they too have a marked tendency to disappear. This purging of the mind of the worries that prey upon it and endanger its even functioning is called "catharsis" by psychologists. While comparatively few may be familiar with its scientific name, practically every adult human being has experienced it and knows how necessary it is for his peace of mind.

Every confessor can recall numerous instances where the relief experienced by the penitent has been indeed remarkable. Penitents at times enter the confessional, so visibly disturbed in mind that their voices quaver and break, sighs of anguish escape them, and tears even course down their faces. After their confession is completed, and they receive the absolution of God's ambassador, and hear from him words of counsel and encouragement to rise and strive again with renewed courage and faith in God's abiding help, they leave the confessional enjoying a calmness, a peace of mind, and a courage that has transformed them into new men and new women.

Familiar as such occurrences are to priests and to members of the Catholic laity, it is interesting to note that even non-Catholics have observed the visible effects of Confession upon people tortured with the guilt of grievous sin. Thus Dr. John Rathbone Oliver, an Episcopalian novelist and a psychiatrist of distinction, who was kneeling in a Catholic church one Saturday afternoon when confessions were being heard, narrates the following striking instance of such a transformation:

"A few weeks ago, I was kneeling at the back of such a church. In front of me there knelt a girl of perhaps sixteen or less. She was tense — tormented, apparently. She twisted about; she could not keep still. The glimpse that I caught of her showed me the face of a person in great mental distress. I could not take my eyes from her. She seemed anxiety personified. A few moments later, she got up, and went into the confessional. I also got up from my knees, and walked up to the high altar to kneel before the Blessed Sacrament. Time passed quickly there. Then someone pushed by me — and knelt down on the altar steps, just a few feet away. It was the same girl. But I have never seen such a change in any human being.

"All her tenseness was gone; the lines of worry had been smoothed from her face. No signs of mental torment now, no anxiety, only perfect relaxation, peace — and, apparently, a great happiness — for her lips were parted in a smile. If I, as a psychiatrist, could have done for that girl in three hours what had been accomplished in fifteen minutes, I should have thought myself a clever physician indeed.

"I watched her make the sign of the cross, from forehead to breast, from shoulder to shoulder, with a hand that was steady, coordinated, efficient, exact. Then she folded her arms on her breast, and lifted her face to the Tabernacle. That face still bore traces of dried tears; but the eyes were bright — unclouded. I left her there, with a prayer of thanksgiving, left her there at peace with man — and, if I may say so without irreverence — at home with her God.

" 'All magic — all superstition — all emotional self-hypnosis,' my materialistic friends may say. Well, let them say so as often as they please. I shall begin to listen to them when their own particular type of magic and hypnosis gets the same results."[7]

In recent years, not only religious leaders but professional psychologists have come to recognize more clearly and with increasing appreciation the wholesome and healing influence which the confessional exercises upon the mental health of the hundreds of millions of people who find in it relief and encouragement. In a volume on *Mental Hygiene* by Groves and Blanchard, which Dr. J. Howard Beard, the former head of the department of health at the University of Illinois, informs me is considered a classic on this subject, the noted authors, though non-Catholics themselves, pay the following high tribute to the therapeutic value of the Catholic confessional:

"The Roman Catholic Church's provision for oral confession to the priest has a moral and therapeutic value which Protestant Churches generally lack. The psychiatrist is frequently called upon to act the role of priest, listening to revelations of guilt that the patient dare not share with any one except when protected by the professional code of secrecy, and assuring the patient that the guilt need not longer be carried as a hidden burden. Protestantism needs to develop a better method of dealing with personal guilt than public confession of general sinfulness. There is a craving to *particularize* the guilt to get definitely rid of the burden, and this impulse at present is adequately recognized *only* by the Roman Catholic Confession."[8]

While the mere disclosure of sin to a sympathetic friend has a therapeutic value, Confession in the Catholic Church has a far greater and more beneficial effect because it not only permits the confession of sins but also gives to the penitent that which he craves above all else — God's *pardon*. It is this latter element which far more than the former restores peace to the soul.

Why should he worry, when because of his sorrow and purpose of amendment he has received through the ambassador of God the pardon of the Most High? There is a craving, it is true, to confess one's guilt. But the far deeper and more insistent craving is for the *remission* of the guilt. This is the real reason why the confessional exercises such a marvelous influence upon the mental health of penitents.

Every Catholic will view with sympathy the desire of Dr. Fosdick and other leaders of Protestantism to restore the confessional to their churches. But he cannot fail to perceive that the confessional will yield but a small fraction of its rich therapeutic value until they likewise restore the doctrine upon which the confessional is founded, namely, the actual forgiveness of the sins confessed to the properly accredited ambassador of Almighty God.

It was the important truth which that discerning scholar, Dr. John Rathbone Oliver, perceived and expressed with admirable lucidity in an article on psychiatry and the confessional.[9] He is apparently in the Anglo-Saxon wing of the Episcopal church, for he includes himself in the Catholic body. Commenting on the marked trend among Protestant leaders to restore the confessional because of its therapeutic value, he says:

"Our Protestant brothers are doing something of the same kind. But it is an utter misunderstanding of the situation to imagine that the Protestant can ever undo the damage of the 'outlawing of the confessional.' It is possible that a Presbyterian or a Methodist pastor might set up in his church a so-called 'confessional box'; he might sit on one side of it behind the grating, and might listen to the outpourings of the sins and troubles of some members of his congregation. No doubt the person who there poured out his soul, might be benefited by the procedure; might get helpful advice and go away feeling happier. But all the confessional boxes in the world could not bring back to the Protestant bodies the one thing that really matters — the one thing that is more important than confession, than all the confessional boxes in the world — the thing that we Catholics call 'absolution.'

"It is the 'absolution' that gives to the confessional its great power to help and to heal. It is the Sacrament of Penance, in which by the 'power that our Lord Jesus Christ has left upon earth to absolve all sinners who truly repent and believe in Him,' the priest, acting in Christ's name and by His authority, 'absolves from sin' — in which he, as it were, pours upon the head of the penitent the precious blood that was shed upon the cross, in the one perfect sacrifice, oblation and satisfaction for the sins of the whole world. And where there is no priesthood, there is no absolving priest; where there is no absolving priest there is no absolute blotting out of all past sin, no complete restoration to God's grace and to complete forgiveness. To the Catholic, every Confession and absolution is a fresh start. He begins his Christian life all over again. All past guilt is wiped out. And fresh grace is given him to start on the road of life once more."

It is to be noted, then, that over and above the benefit which Confession gives to mankind in restoring their tranquillity and peace of mind by the assurance of their forgiveness by God — a peace of mind which all the money in the world could not buy — it provides human society with a benefit still greater. It brings about the *actual regeneration* of the human character and serves as the most effective agency for moral reform in the world. It does not allow its values to remain in the realm of mere feelings. It insists that these subjective dispositions be translated into action.

It requires that the individual prove the sincerity of his resolves by a better moral life. It demands that the individual translate his aspirations for nobility of character into deeds of honesty, justice and charity in all the relations of man to man. It demands not mere velleities but positive volitions. It demands deeds, not words; actual reform, not mere promises.

Hence, Confession is to be regarded not as a mere device to assuage disturbed feelings, or to relieve the mind oppressed with a sense of guilt — valuable as is its contribution in this regard — but as a powerful lever that actually lifts man prostrate in the mire of vice, and sets him to walk, with head erect, upon the paths of justice and mercy and truth. The Sacrament of Confession reflects not only the mercy of the divine Master, Jesus Christ, who came "to call not the just but sinners to repentance," but His justice as well.

Rightly, then, does the sacrament demand that the penitent struggle manfully and courageously to keep the promises he makes in Confession — to avoid sin and to rise to a higher and nobler life. Because the sacrament works in the secrecy of the human soul, where no eye but God's is a witness of its stirrings, this world will never fully know the powerful leverage for moral regeneration which the sacrament exercises upon the lives of the hundreds of millions of people who come to it for renewed hope and courage.

But if it were given to us to penetrate the veil that hides from our eyes the secret springs of human conduct, we are convinced that we would find that the sacrament's insistence upon the avoidance of the occasions of sin is a deterrent against crime more powerful and efficacious than all the policemen in the world. Not only is Confession a bulwark against the relapse into vice but it is a most powerful incentive to a life of virtue.

The Sacrament of Confession is not only the perpetuation of the voice of Christ assuring the sinful woman prostrate in the dust of the street in Jerusalem that her sins are forgiven, but it is also an extension of that divine hand which raised her up, and set her unsteady feet to tread henceforth the shining path of virtue, while the voice whispered the sweet command: "Go, and now sin no more."

Discussion Aids

How is the charge that a money payment is exacted for absolution to be answered? The charge that confessors reveal the sins of penitents? Relate the story of King Wenceslaus and St. John Nepomucene. How answer the charge that Confession is an encouragement to sin? What two conditions *must* a penitent fulfill before his sins can be forgiven? Explain sorrow for sin and purpose of amendment fully, giving examples. Quote Cardinal Gibbons, Voltaire, Rousseau, Dr. Fosdick, and Leibnitz on Confession. Give the psychologist's and the psychiatrist's view on Confession. Speak of Confession as an agency in the improvement of human society.

Practices

Let your demeanor before and after Confession show that you realize the seriousness of what you are doing.

In explaining Confession dwell especially on the necessity of true contrition and purpose of amendment.

Try to influence a negligent Catholic to go to Confession.

NOTES (Chapter 12)

1. *Sess.* XIV, c. 4
2. *Remarques sur l'Oympe*
3. *Emile*

192

4. *Systema Theologicum*, p. 270
5. *Christian Dogmatics*, p. 443ff
6. *Literary Digest*, Dec. 17, 1927, p. 2
7. *Scribner's*, July 1930, p. 66
8. *Mental Hygiene*, p. 316 (Henry Holt & Co., N.Y., 1930)
9. Scribner's, *July 1930*

CHAPTER 13

Indulgences: What Are They?

Light on a Much Misunderstood Question

Some time ago Professor L. M. Larson, the distinguished former head of the Department of History at the University of Illinois, called upon this writer and thus stated the object of his visit: "Father," he said, "I am writing a history of England. I have encountered so many different and conflicting statements of historians as to the nature of an indulgence that I have come to you, as a representative of the Catholic Church, to find out what an indulgence really is. I want to know the authentic teaching of the Catholic Church on this subject so that I can present the doctrine truthfully and accurately to my readers instead of merely repeating the confusing statements of second-hand authorities who have never understood what the Church really means by an indulgence."

It is because many other writers have been less careful than Professor Larson, and have taken their idea of indulgences from the caricatures drawn by misinformed or prejudiced authors that there prevail among our non-Catholic fellow citizens to this very day many grotesque misconceptions as to the meaning of an indulgence. Many consider it a pardon of past sin, others regard it as a license to commit future sin. Some think of it as an exemption from a law or duty which binds other Christians. In some histories it is even depicted as a sort of magical lever that lifts a soul from purgatory.

Coloring all these notions is the idea that "whatever the

kind of indulgence, it may be purchased at a stipulated price. They are all for sale, and the lust for money is at the root of the whole business." The term "indulgences" has thus come to stand in the minds of our separated brethren as the symbol of mercenary fraud and corruption in the Church of Rome. It is regarded as the match that kindled the flames of Luther's revolt against the most repugnant elements of the superstition and humbuggery of the Roman system.

May I ask our dear non-Catholic friends to follow the example of Professor Larson, whose insistence upon going to the original sources to find the real facts in the matter, has enabled him to achieve world eminence in his field? In so doing they will get an insight into the true meaning of an indulgence. They will then see that what they fight against is not the Catholic doctrine of indulgences but the grotesque caricatures drawn either by the misinformed or by the Church's antagonists.

I do not hesitate to say that if an indulgence were really the mercenary fraud commonly imagined by non-Catholics, I too would rebel against it with vehemence not less than theirs. It is only because I know the authentic teaching of the Church on this subject that I see in indulgences an incentive not to evil but to deeds of virtue and holiness. Here again I would ask of our non-Catholic readers but one favor — an *open* mind. In return, I give the assurance that instead of playing the role of an attorney, glossing over all the hostile evidence and playing up only that which is favorable, I shall essay the role of the historian recording with impartial hand the abuses as well as wholesome fruits of the practice of indulgences.

What is the real meaning of an indulgence? It is simply the remission of the *temporal punishment* due to sin after the sin itself has been forgiven. The one phrase in the above definition that may not be entirely clear to our non-Catholic reader is "temporal punishment." To understand that, one must first understand that according to the Catholic Church every grievous sin has attached to it a twofold penalty — an eternal punishment which is suffered either in this world, or in purgatory, or partly in both.

The guilt with its eternal punishment is always forgiven in a good confession. The temporal punishment may or may not be

195

remitted in confession, depending upon the quality of contrition. If it is not forgiven, it may be remitted: (1) through the propitiatory efficacy of deeds of penance and virtue, and (2) through the gaining of indulgences attached by the Church to certain works of charity and piety.

Basic in this whole conception is the idea that even after the eternal punishment due to mortal sin is remitted, there may still remain temporal punishment. While this idea does not seem to be familiar at the present time to those outside the Catholic Church, it is nevertheless rooted in the Scriptures. Thus Moses, even though he was forgiven his transgressions by God, was nevertheless punished by not being permitted to enter the Promised Land, being allowed to view it only from the distance of Mt. Nebo.

David was forgiven for his double crime of murder and adultery, but was compelled to suffer a temporal punishment in the death of the offspring of this adulterous union. "The Lord also hath taken away thy sin: thou shalt not die," said the prophet Nathan. "Nevertheless, because thou hast given occasion to the enemies of the Lord to blaspheme, for this thing, the child that is born to thee, shall surely die."[1] Here is a clear instance of a temporal punishment remaining after the eternal guilt has been remitted. To satisfy the requirement of God's justice for such temporal punishment, and thereby to remit it, is the function of indulgences.

Let me endeavor then to make still clearer to my dear non-Catholic readers the meaning of temporal punishment, so essential to the understanding of indulgences, by the following illustration. Suppose Tom Smith is guilty of stealing a hundred dollars from the home of his neighbor, John Brown. The culprit is arrested and the judge pronounces him guilty and sentences him to prison for a year by way of punishment.

While in prison Mr. Smith comes to realize the grievous injustice he inflicted upon his neighbor by his theft, and is thoroughly repentant. He writes to Mr. Brown, humbly asks his forgiveness and assures him that as soon as he earns a hundred dollars after he is out of prison, he will repay him. Touched by the evident sincerity of the prisoner's contrition and purpose of amendment, Mr. Brown asks the governor to pardon him. Upon investigation the governor finds that the prisoner has served four months of his sentence and has a record of good behavior during this period. Because of this fact and because of the circumstances mentioned by Mr. Brown, the governor remits the remaining eight months of imprisonment and releases the prisoner on parole.

The sentence to serve a year's imprisonment may be said to represent the temporal punishment due to sin even after the sinner has repented and the formal guilt of the sin has been remitted. The remission of the remaining eight months of the sentence may be said to represent an indulgence. The illustration also serves to show the wholesome effect that the temporal punishment is likely to have upon the penitent sinner.

Granting then the fact of a temporal punishment, what is the evidence that the Church possesses the power to remit it? This is to be found in the authority vested by Christ in His Church when He said to Peter: "I will give to thee the keys of the kingdom of heaven. And whatsoever thou shalt bind upon the earth, it shall be bound also in heaven: and whatsoever thou shalt loose on earth, it shall be loosed also in heaven."[2] From these words of Christ it is clear that no limit was placed upon the power of the Church to loose from any and all bonds of sin — from the temporal as well as from the eternal punishment. Indulgences constitute, therefore, a supplement to the sacrament of penance, removing every obstacle that separates the creature from the friendship of his God.

Indulgences are of two kinds: *partial* or *plenary*. A partial indulgence remits a portion of the temporal punishment, while a plenary one remits all of it.

Indulgences are gained only by the living. They may not be applied to the souls of other living persons; but, unless the contrary is stated, they may be applied to the souls in purgatory. To understand the possibility of such a transfer of indulgences, it is necessary first to understand these three teachings of Christ and of His Church:

(1) *The Communion of Saints.* This means that the members of Christ's Church, whether on earth, in heaven, or in purgatory, are all members of Christ's mystical body and are all capable of assisting one another by their prayers and good works. "We

being many," says St. Paul, "are one body in Christ, and every one members one of another."[3]

(2) *The Principle of Vicarious Satisfaction.* To every good action of the just man there is attached a twofold value: merit and satisfaction or atonement. Merit is personal and cannot be transferred. Satisfaction, however, can be applied to others. This truth St. Paul thus communicates to the Colossians: "Who now rejoice in my sufferings for you, and fill up those things that are wanting of the sufferings of Christ, in my flesh, for His body, which is the Church."[4] Moreover, all Christians admit that we have been redeemed through the atoning sufferings and death of Christ. This principle of vicarious atonement lies, therefore, at the very heart of the Christian faith.

(3) *The Spiritual Treasury of the Church.* Since Christ suffered far more than was necessary to redeem us, and since there resulted from His death a fund of infinite satisfaction, it follows that there has been created a vast and inexhaustible treasury which the Church may draw upon in payment of temporal punishment. This spiritual treasury has been increased by the superabundant satisfaction of the Blessed Virgin and of the saints. "All the saints," says St. Thomas, "intended that whatever they did or suffered for God's sake should be profitable not only to themselves but to the whole Church."[5]

The existence of an infinite treasury of merits in the Church was formally set forth by Pope Clement VI in 1343. "Upon the altar of the Cross," says the Pope,[6] "Christ shed of His blood not merely a drop, though this would have sufficed, by reason of the union with the Word, to redeem the whole human race, but a copious torrent — thereby laying up an infinite treasure for mankind. This treasure He neither wrapped up in a napkin nor hid in a field, but entrusted to Blessed Peter, the key-bearer, and his successors, that they might for just and reasonable causes distribute it to the faithful in full or in partial remission of the temporal punishment due to sin." Hence when Luther asserted that "the treasures of the Church from which the pope grants indulgences are not the merits of Christ and the saints," the statement was promptly condemned by Leo X.

For without such a spiritual treasury for the Church to draw upon in payment of temporal punishment still due by her children, indulgence would be both ineffective and meaningless. It is part of the authority committed by Christ to Peter and his successors to specify to what extent, and under what conditions, the funds of this common treasury shall be made available to the individual members.

As the concept of a common spiritual treasury consisting of the inexhaustible merits of Christ and the superabundant satisfaction of the saints, while essential to the understanding of indulgences, is unfamiliar to those outside the fold, it may be helpful to show how deeply imbedded in the Christian faith was this doctrine, centuries before the birth of Protestantism. Back in the thirteenth century, St. Thomas bears witness to the universal belief of Christians in the existence of such treasury and in its availability to remit temporal punishment.

"All this treasure," says St. Thomas, "is at the dispensation of the chief rulers of the Church, inasmuch as our Lord gave the Keys of the Church to Peter. When then the utility or necessity of the Church requires it, the chief ruler of the Church can draw from this infinite store of merits to communicate to any one who through charity is a member of the Church, as much as he deems to be opportune, whether it be such as will suffice for the total remission of his punishment, or up to a certain portion of the whole: in such wise, namely, that the Passion of Christ (through whom alone the merits of the others have efficacy) and the other saints may be imparted to him just as if he himself had suffered what was necessary for the remission of his sin — as happens when one person satisfies for another."[7]

These then are the three basic truths, the communion of saints, the principle of vicarious atonement, and the common treasury of the Church, upon which the doctrine of the applicability of indulgences to the souls of the faithful departed as well as to the living rests. The authority to grant indulgences, as has been indicated, flows from the power of the keys, the unlimited power of binding and of loosing, conferred by Christ upon St. Peter and his successors.

There is an important difference, however, in the application of indulgences to the living and to the dead. The living are subjects of the Church's immediate jurisdiction; the deceased are not. To the former she grants an indulgence as an exercise of her judicial authority. To the latter she makes an indulgence available by way of suffrage. That is, she petitions God, under whose sole jurisdiction the deceased are, to accept the works of satisfaction and in consideration thereof to mitigate the sufferings of the souls in purgatory.

Can we say, therefore, that an indulgence gained by the living for any individual in purgatory will be applied with infallible certainty to that particular soul? While we piously believe that the individual soul will be benefited to some degree, we cannot say with certainty that it will be applied in its entirety to that particular soul. That lies within the jurisdiction of Almighty God, and we rest content with the knowledge that the case is in the hands of a Father who is both infinitely just and infinitely merciful.

It is well, too, to remember that there are some veils that cannot be penetrated this side of eternity. The effort to do so usually results in fine-spun speculations and subtleties, which do not carry conviction and which are usually less satisfactory than the humble acknowledgement that we simply do not know. The answer to this question is one of the many then that we leave with content to the wisdom of our heavenly Father.

"Is not an indulgence," queried a non-Catholic acquaintance, "a mere glossing over of sin, a lazy man's method of getting his punishment remitted instead of the normal time-honored method of repentance and amendment? I do not see any need for indulgences," he continued, "as long as Christ has pointed to repentance as the way back to His love and friendship. 'Much is forgiven her because she hath loved much. Go now and sin no more.' This was the burden of Christ's message to mankind. It seems to me that indulgences are morally unwholesome because they lessen the need for such interior repentance and amendment."

Such is the common view of our non-Catholic friends. It overlooks, however, an essential condition for the gaining of an indulgence. The latter is not a glossing over of sin. It does not touch upon the *guilt* of sin in any way. In fact, an indulgence cannot be gained unless the guilt of mortal sin has been first removed by the sacrament of penance, of which true interior contrition and purpose of amendment are indispensable requi-

200

sites. Therefore an indulgence can be gained only by a person who is already in the friendship and love of God.

Instead of lessening the need for genuine repentance and amendment, indulgences emphasize their imperative necessity. For without such repentance there can be no indulgences, and no forgiveness of sin, either by the Church through the Sacrament of Penance or directly by God. No person or institution in the world insists more strongly upon the inescapable necessity of genuine and not feigned repentance for the obtaining of forgiveness of sin than the Catholic Church.

The picture, then, of a man wallowing in the mire of sin and gaining an indulgence through the offering of an alms to spare himself the trouble of repentance and amendment, does not reflect the teaching of the Catholic Church. Such a picture exists only in the imagination of some of our separated brethren and is traceable to the widespread misrepresentation of the nature of an indulgence.

Suffice it to say here that the doctrine of indulgences while perhaps not explicit in the holy Scripture is at least implicit therein. It is likewise in accordance with reason. Far from being subversive of true repentance and purpose of amendment, it stimulates the arousal of these subjective dispositions by stressing their necessity for the gaining of an indulgence.

The official teaching of the Church on the subject is thus expressed by the Council of Trent: "Since the power of conferring Indulgences was granted by Christ to the Church, and she has, even in the most ancient times, used this kind of power, delivered unto her of God; the Sacred Holy Synod teaches and enjoins that the use of Indulgences, for the Christian people most salutary and approved of by the authority of the Sacred Councils, is to be retained in the Church; and it condemns, with anathema, those who either assert they are useless, or who deny that there is in the Church the power of granting them."[8]

Note how moderate and restrained is the official statement of the Church's teachings. It simply affirms two truths, namely, that the Church has the power to grant indulgences, and that their use is salutary. Thus it is evident that the Church does not thrust them upon any of her children. If one will appraise the doctrine of indulgences, not as caricatured by her enemies but as actually taught by the Church, he will come, I think, to the two following conclusions:

1. Indulgences constitute a powerful incentive to deeds of virtue, piety and charity, quickening man in his love of God and in his service to his fellowman.

2. Indulgences are a beautiful dispensation of Divine Providence emphasizing the social solidarity of our race and binding us all together as members of the mystical body of Christ by the golden ties of love and prayer.

We do not struggle as lonely wayfarers, climbing slowly up life's rough mountainside, with no one to cheer or help us when we falter on the way. We travel as pilgrims in a goodly company, and as soldiers in a mighty army, with the hands of angels stretched down to help us when we stumble, with the prayers of the faithful pleading for us before the Throne of the Most High, and with the sacrifices and good deeds of our brothers-in-arms to hearten us when we weary on the way. The gaining of indulgences is, therefore, but an integral part of that consoling doctrine of the communion of saints, the sweet reasonableness of which is so beautifully portrayed in the words of Tennyson:

More things are wrought by prayer
Than this world dreams of. Wherefore, let thy voice
Rise like a fountain for me night and day,
For what are men better than sheep or goats
That nourish a blind life within the brain,
If knowing God they lift not hands of prayer
Both for themselves and those who call them friends?
For so the whole round earth is every way
Bound by gold chains about the feet of God.[9]

Discussion Aids

Define an indulgence. What twofold penalty is attached to every grievous sin? Make very clear what you mean by "temporal punishment." Which penalty is always removed by a good confession? Which penalty may or may not be so removed? If temporal punishment is not removed by confession how may it be removed? What temporal punishment was suffered by Moses? By David? How do you know that the Church has the power to remit temporal punishment? What two kinds of indulgences are there? Is a transfer of indulgence sometimes possible? Explain (1) The Communion of Saints; (2) Vicarious Satisfaction; (3) The Spiritual Treasury of the Church. Explain the difference in the application of indulgences to the living and to the dead. Explain what is necessary for the gaining of an indulgence. Explain how the gaining of indulgences for one another is a part of the doctrine of the Communion of Saints.

Practices

Direct your intention every day to gaining as many indulgences as you can.

Read the Scriptures for fifteen minutes daily; you thereby gain an indulgence.

Make the Sign of the Cross with holy water; you thereby gain an indulgence.

NOTES (Chapter 13)

1. II Kgs. 12:13-14
2. Mt. 16:19
3. Rom. 12:5
4. Col. 1:24
5. *Quodlib*, II, q. vii, art. 16
6. *Unigenitues Dei Filius*, issued Jan. 25, 1343
7. See note 5
8. *Sess. XXV*
9. *Morte D'Arthur*

CHAPTER 14

The Real Presence: Fact or Fiction?
How Christ Answered an Ever-Recurring Question of Today

"Do you not have to be born a Catholic to be able to believe that Jesus Christ is really and substantially present in Holy Communion?" queried a doctor during a discussion. "It seems to me," he added, "that it is so hard to believe that Christ is really present beneath the appearance of a Eucharistic wafer, that I cannot imagine a person believing such a doctrine unless it were inculcated into his mind as a little child and he were thus brought up in such a belief from the days when his reasoning powers were just beginning to unfold." The doctor stated thus frankly a view of many non-Catholics concerning belief in the real presence of Christ in the Holy Eucharist. By way of reply, let us simply ask our separated friends to examine the evidence in the matter for themselves.

The traditional policy of the Catholic Church is to ask her children to accept a doctrine only when there is sufficient and compelling evidence of its truthfulness. Is the doctrine of the real presence of Christ in the Holy Eucharist an exception to this general rule? Does she secure its acceptance, as the doctor implied, only by foisting it upon the uncritical minds of little children when they are unable to reason for themselves?

Belief in the real presence does not rest upon the reasoning or the decision of any priest, bishop, pontiff, or council, but upon the words of Jesus Christ Himself. Is the presentation of the doctrine by our divine Savior vague and equivocal, or is it clear and unmistakable? While all the teachings of Christ are set forth in clear and simple terms, I think it can be safely affirmed that nowhere in the Scriptures is there to be found a presentation of a doctrine with greater clarity or with more painstaking effort to remove all uncertainty than that which characterizes the divine Master's exposition of the Holy Eucharist, as recorded in the sixth chapter of St. John's gospel and in the gospel narrative of the Last Supper. The student of pedagogy will find in it a model of skillful exposition of subject matter and a revelation of keen insight into the successive stages of the learning process. The exposition may be divided into four stages:

The first is the stage of preparation. Like the wise teacher that He was, Christ first prepared the minds of His hearers for the suitable reception of the great teaching He was about to impart to them. Accordingly He allowed a multitude to follow Him into a mountain to the northeast of the Sea of Galilee. There He worked the tremendous miracle of multiplying five barley loaves and two fishes to such an extent that His disciples were able to feed the multitude of five thousand men together with their wives and children. After they had partaken, the disciples gathered up twelve baskets of the fragments.

One can well imagine the profound impression made upon the people by this manifestation of supernatural power. Actions constitute the universal Esperanto, the one language understood by all mankind. In this unmistakable language did the Master present the credentials of His divine power and authority. In no spirit of mere obstentation did the Savior work this miracle; it was for the special purpose of convincing the people of His divine power and thereby preparing their minds for the reception of the great doctrine of the Holy Eucharist.

Shortly after the miracle of the multiplication of the loaves and fishes, Christ performs another one, that of walking upon the Sea of Galilee, and entering the boat of the Apostles which was then "twenty or thirty furlongs" from the shore. These two miracles served admirably to prepare the minds of the people for the sublime doctrine He was about to present to them.

The second is the stage of promise. Jesus utilizes the two previous miracles to inculcate the necessity of belief in Him. Thus when the Jews asked: "What shall we do, that we may work the works of God?" Jesus answered: "This is the work of God, that you believe in Him whom He hath sent."[1]

In leading up to the promise that Jesus is about to make to them, He refers by way of contrast to the manna which their fathers received during their journey across the desert. "I am the bread of life," He says. "Your fathers did eat manna in the desert, and are dead. This is the bread which cometh down from heaven; that if any man eats of it he may not die. I am the living bread which came down from heaven. If any man eat of this bread, he shall live forever." Now note how after pointing out the superiority of the bread which He is about to give them over the manna rained down from heaven upon their fathers, Christ proceeds at once to tell them what that bread is: "And the bread," He says, "that I will give, is My flesh, for the life of the world."[2]

Did the Jews understand Christ to speak figuratively or literally when He made this great promise? That they understood Jesus to speak literally is unmistakably evident from their immediate response: "The Jews therefore strove among themselves, saying: How can this man give us His flesh to eat?"

Now, if Christ wished to be understood in a figurative manner, it would have been His duty not only as the Son of God, but even as an honest teacher, to correct the Jews and say to them: "You misunderstand me. You think that I am referring to my flesh, whereas I am speaking figuratively and am referring only to a symbol." Is that actually what Christ does? Let St. John make answer: "Then Jesus said to them: Amen, amen, I say unto you: Except you eat the flesh of the Son of Man, and drink His blood, you shall not have life in you."[3]

It is to be observed that Jesus now speaks more emphatically than ever. The use of the double expletive, "Amen, amen," indicates that the words which follow are of especial moment. Instead of softening His statement, He increases its vigor to the extent of declaring their deliberate refusal to accept His great gift will rob them of eternal life.

Then without pause, Christ restates His teaching in the plainest and simplest terms, so that it would seem almost impossible for even the most dull-witted auditor in the crowd to fail to perceive His meaning. Thus He says: "He that eateth My flesh, and drinketh My blood, hath everlasting life: and I will raise him up on the last day. For My flesh is meat indeed, and My blood is drink indeed. He that eateth My flesh, and drinketh My blood, abideth in Me, and I in him."

It will be noted that in each of the four consecutive sentences, Jesus uses the double phrase "to eat My flesh and drink My blood." Even to the extent of what might seem to some as wearisome repetition, the Master exhausts all the possibility of human language in making His meaning unmistakably clear; He evidently wishes to place it forever beyond dispute.

Jesus follows the exposition of the gift He is soon to bestow upon them by revealing His loving purpose, saying that he who does this "abideth in Me and I in him." It is a pledge of the intimate union of the soul of the creature with its God. Then the Master reminds them of His divine power and authority, saying: "As the living Father hath sent Me, and I live by the Father; so he that eateth Me, the same also shall live by Me."

Human nature does not always bend its stiff neck, however, to accept the yoke of a doctrine, no matter how sweet and light, and no matter how overwhelming the authority from which it emanates. This doctrine involves a mystery. In spite of all the clarity with which it had been presented, in spite even of the divine authority of the Teacher, it staggered some who apparently did not wish to accept any doctrine which they could not understand from center to circumference.

St. John discloses that some of the disciples demurred at the acceptance of the doctrine just presented by the Master. "Many therefore of His disciples," he says, "hearing it, said: This saying is hard, and who can hear it?" A little later he reports: "After this many of His disciples went back; and walked no more with Him."

When Jesus heard them say that it was a hard doctrine, did He offer to soften it by stripping it of its mystery, pulling it from the infinite reaches of the supernatural to the realm of the merely natural, and bringing it in its entirety within the compass of their finite intelligence? When He saw the disciples whom He loved, and for whose salvation He had become incarnate, leaving Him, did He call to them: "Come back and I will alter the doctrine; I will promise to give you not really My flesh and blood but only a symbol, a reminder of Me; I will take from it all the elements of supernatural mystery and eliminate all necessity of your making an act of faith in the truth I am proclaiming to you"?

Not thus did Jesus speak; not thus did He act. Instead, He turned to His own chosen twelve with the words: "Will you also go away?" He was willing to allow His own Apostles to leave Him rather than soften or modify in any way the great teaching and the great promise which He had just presented to them. Peter answered with the memorable words, instinct with unwavering faith: "Lord, to whom shall we go? Thou hast the words of eternal life." Thus concludes the stage of the promise.

The third stage is the fulfillment of the promise: the institution of the Holy Eucharist. The Savior waits for about a year, until there arrives an occasion which is most suitable for the realization of His promise: it is the occasion of His last supper with them, the night before He died. The Master gathers His Apostles about Him to receive His last will and testament; the occasion is one of unusual solemnity.

The circumstances, touching and memorable, constitute an impressive frame for the epochal words of the Savior. Let St. Matthew describe the scene which then occurred: "And while they were at supper, Jesus took bread, and blessed and broke and gave to His disciples and said: Take ye and eat. This is My body. And taking the chalice, He gave thanks and gave to them, saying: Drink ye all of this; for this is My blood of the new testament, which shall be shed for many unto remission of sins."[4]

Notice how literally Christ fulfills His promise to them. Note how admirably the words of institution dovetailed into the words of promise and form the concluding link in a carefully arranged chain. Observe how clearly and simply Christ speaks: This is My body; this is My blood. What words could be plainer? What more could even an Omnipotent Being have done to have insured the utmost clarity in presenting His doctrine? It would seem that Christ had exhausted every means of setting forth His teaching in the clearest and most unmistakable terms.

The question now arises: How did the Apostles understand Jesus to speak? They who were within the sound of His voice, they who understood and spoke the same language as the Master, surely they are better calculated to understand the meaning of Christ's words to them than critics who are separated by a chasm of nineteen hundred years, and who do not understand the language with the intimacy and the accuracy of those to whom it was their vernacular — their familiar daily means of communication.

To answer this question we have but to ascertain how the Apostles applied His teaching in their ministry. This may be said to be the fourth and final stage — the translation of a teaching into actual practice. Did the Apostles bless and distribute merely bread and wine, or did they administer what they believed to be the body and blood of Jesus Christ under the appearance of bread and wine? If they professed to distribute merely a symbol or reminder of the Savior's flesh and blood, then the Catholic interpretation falls to the ground. If on the other hand, the Apostles proclaimed that they were dispensing the body and blood of the Savior, and were doing so at His express command, then every fair-minded person will surely be compelled to acknowledge that the Catholic interpretation is that of the Apostles and of Christ, and alone is tenable.

Let St. Paul answer for the Apostles. About eight years after St. Matthew wrote his gospel, St. Paul wrote a letter to the Christian community at Corinth, in which he reminds them: "The chalice of benediction which we bless, is it not the communion of the blood of Christ? And the bread which we break, is it not the partaking of the body of the Lord? ... For, I have received of the Lord that which also I delivered to you, that the Lord Jesus, on the night in which he was betrayed, took bread, and giving thanks, broke it, and said: Take and eat: this is My body which shall be delivered for you. This do for the commemoration of Me. In like manner also the chalice, after the supper, saying: This cup is the new Covenant in My blood. This do ye, as often as ye shall drink, for the commemoration of Me. For, as often as ye shall eat this bread, and drink the cup, ye shall show the death of the Lord until He come. Therefore, whoever shall eat this bread, or drink the chalice of the Lord unworthily, *shall be guilty of the body and of the blood of the Lord.* But let a man prove himself; and so let him eat of that bread and drink of the chalice. For, he who eateth and drinketh unworthily, eateth and drinketh judgment to himself, *not discerning the body of the Lord.*"[5]

In these words, St. Paul expressed clearly and unequivocally the faith of the Apostles and of the infant Church in the real presence of Christ in the Holy Eucharist. Mark how he charges the person who receives the sacrament unworthily with the guilt "of the body and blood of the Lord." But how could a person be guilty of so heinous a crime, if he had merely eaten a little bread and drunk a little wine? Surely one cannot be charged with the crime of homicide if he does violence merely to the picture or statue of a man, and does not touch the man himself. St. Paul's solemn admonition therefore would be utterly meaningless if the person receiving the sacrament did not really receive the body and blood of Christ.

"Plain and simple reason," observes Cardinal Wiseman, "seems to tell us that the presence of Christ's body is necessary for an offense committed against it. A man cannot be 'guilty of majesty,' unless the majesty exists in the object against which his crime is committed. In like manner, an offender against the Blessed Eucharist cannot be described as guilty of Christ's Body and Blood, if these be not in the Sacrament."[6]

The interpretation of St. Paul but reflects the unanimous teaching of the Fathers and Doctors of the early Church. Space will permit the testimony of but one of the Fathers, St. Cyril of Jerusalem, who wrote in the fourth century as follows: "As a life-giving Sacrament we possess the sacred Flesh of Christ and His Precious Blood under the appearances of bread and wine."[7] "What seems to be bread is not bread, but Christ's Body; what seems to be wine is not wine, but Christ's Blood."[8]

A further guide to the belief of the early Church is found in the method of administering this sacrament. The custom of receiving Holy Communion while fasting dates from the early centuries of the Christian era. Upon administering the sacred Host the celebrant said: "The Body of the Lord," and the communicant answered: "Amen." Receiving the Host into his hands he placed It at once in his mouth. The deacon then offered the chalice, saying: "The Blood of the Lord." The communicant drank from it after having replied: "Amen." The faithful were instructed to exercise the greatest care lest any of the sacred

210

species fall to the ground because it was the body of the Savior.

It was the common practice to bring the sacred Host to the sick and to prisoners. If persecution made the task too dangerous for deacons, even children would be permitted to discharge the sacred mission rather than allow Christians to die without receiving their heavenly Food. It was while on such an errand that the little boy, Tarcisius, was set upon by persecutors of the Christians and beaten to death.

Upon the tomb of the martyred youth, Pope St. Damasus inscribed the epitaph: "He preferred to yield his soul in death than to betray the heavenly members (of Christ) to raving dogs." Do men and even little children risk injury and even death itself to protect a mere piece of bread? To ask the question is to answer it. In the inscription upon the tomb of St. Tarcisius the belief of the infant Church in the real presence of Christ in the Holy Eucharist shines forth more luminously than in a ton of theoretical arguments.

Such was the faith not only of the Apostles and of the early Church, but such remains to this day after the lapse of nineteen centuries the faith of all branches of Christianity save only Protestantism, which appeared upon the scene only in the sixteenth century. For the Greek Church which seceded from the Catholic Church about a thousand years ago, the present Russian Church, the schismatic Copts, Armenians, Syrians, Chaldeans and in fact all the Oriental sects, even though no longer in communion with the see of Rome, still hold fast to the teaching of Christ and the belief of His Apostles in the real presence of the body and blood, soul and divinity of our Lord in the Holy Eucharist.

"Why do you give Communion to the laity," asked an inquirer recently, "under the form of bread alone and not under the form of wine as well?" The fact is, contrary to the assumption underlying the above question, that Christ is present whole and entire, both under the form of bread and under the form of wine. Christ clearly taught this when He said: "If any man eat of this bread, he shall live forever."[9]

St. Paul plainly taught the same truth when he wrote to the Corinthians: "Whosoever shall eat this bread *or* drink the chalice of the Lord unworthily shall be guilty of the body and blood of

211

the Lord."[10] While it was the common custom for the first twelve centuries to give Communion under both kinds, the concurrent practice of administering the Holy Eucharist under either kind had likewise the approval of the Church.

The present law of giving Communion to the laity under the form of bread dates from the Council of Constance in 1414, which condemned the contention of the Hussites of Bohemia that the cup was necessary. The Council of Trent confirming the law, declared: "Laymen and clerics when not celebrating are not obliged by any divine precept to receive the Sacraments of the Eucharist under both kinds, neither can it by any means be doubted, without injury to faith, that Communion under either kind is sufficient for them unto salvation."[11]

Long before the present law was enacted, the custom of receiving under the form of bread alone had become widespread for practical reasons. The reasons as enumerated by the Council of Trent were: the danger of spilling the Precious Blood, the difficulty of reserving the Sacrament under the species of wine, and the danger to health from partaking of a chalice touched by infected lips. As the question involves merely discipline, the Church exercises her right as the guardian of the sacraments to adapt her methods of administering them to the changing condition of the times.

Let me now prescind from the detailed intricacies of textural analysis and interpretation and address in a kindly manner to my dear non-Catholic reader the following simple analogy, which seems to me to go to the heart of the matter. A father who has a large farm with barns, cattle, machinery, and all the equipment of a well-organized farm, has often promised his children to bequeath it all to them upon his death. "It will be," he says, "a manifestation of the love I bear for you, my children. I will leave you better provided for than I was when starting out as a young man."

A fatal illness falls upon the father. The doctor assures him that he has but a few hours more to live. Accordingly the father calls his children to his bedside. "I want to make known to you," he says, "my last will and testament." The children recall his oft-repeated promise to give to them his farm with all its equipment. At this point, however, the father reaches behind his pillow and draws therefrom a picture of his farm. "This," he says, "is what I leave to you — a picture of my farm. It will be a symbol, a reminder of me."

Can you not imagine the expressions of amazement on the faces of the children as they listen to such strange words from their father's lips? Would they not say: "Surely, father must be suffering from hallucinations, his mind must be in a delirium. Otherwise, he would not utter as his farewell to us, words which make a hollow mockery out of all that he has spoken to us. If he were in his right mind, surely he would not taunt and mock us by bequeathing to us not the reality which he promised, but merely an empty symbol of it — a hollow worthless shell."

Do not those who say that in the Lord's Supper, Christ gave us not what He promised, not His real body and blood but merely a symbol of it, merely a piece of bread and a little wine to remind us of Him, do they not attribute to Christ the same preposterous mockery which characterized the conduct of the dying farmer? Do they not reduce the Savior to the status of an archdeceiver? Yes, worse than that. They portray Him as lifting up the hearts and hopes of His hearers by promising them the greatest possible gift, insisting upon their believing His promise, and then dashing to the ground all their fond expectations and crushing their trust in Him by making a cruel jest of it all.

Such a conception would undermine not only the moral character of Jesus but also the possibility of believing in the religion of which He was the Founder. The consideration goes to show how belief in the real presence is intimately linked up with the veracity of Jesus and His whole moral character as well as with the validity and trustworthiness of the religion which He commanded mankind to accept in His name and on His authority.

Is it not evident, therefore, to every fair-minded reader who faces the facts honestly and squarely, that the Scriptures show that Christ taught the doctrine of the real presence clearly and unmistakably? Is it not evident that the Catholic in accepting this doctrine is simply manifesting his faith in the veracity and teaching authority of Jesus Christ? Why then is it that the majority of non-Catholic Christians do not accept the doctrine despite the clarity with which it is taught by the Savior?

In the writer's judgment one of the important reasons is because the divinity of Christ and His authority as an infallible teacher are no longer held by vast sections of Protestantism. Another is because it involves a mystery and is beyond the capacity of the human mind fully to comprehend. And mysteries and the supernatural are unpalatable to many non-Catholics today. A further reason is because environment and rearing have closed their minds against such a doctrine and they have never taken the pains to investigate for themselves.

The question, however, that is most difficult to answer is: How can people who call themselves Christians and still profess to believe in the divinity of Christ, deny that which Jesus Christ taught in the clearest terms, namely, the doctrine of the real presence? It is easy enough to understand how the agnostic, though mistaken, can deny the doctrine because of his denial of the divinity of Christ. But how a Christian who professes to believe in the teaching authority of Christ can deny His plain teaching concerning the real presence is indeed difficult to understand.

For 1500 years all Christendom was united in the literal understanding of the Savior's words. In the sixteenth century it became the fashion to give new and arbitrary interpretations to passages in the Scriptures in accordance with one's private whim and fancy. The amount of religious anarchy and confusion which was brought about by this practice is evident from the fact that within seventy-five years over 200 different interpretations were given to the clear, simple words of Christ: "This is My body." At Ingolstadt in 1577 Christopher Rasperger wrote a whole book entitled, "Two Hundred Interpretations of the Words: 'This Is My Body.'" It shows how hard pressed the founders of the new sects were to defend their arbitrary interpretations.

Till his death Luther defended the literal interpretation against such innovators as Zwingli, Carlstadt and Oecolampadius, though with characteristic ill logic, he warred against the sacrifice of the Mass. Indeed he confesses that he was tempted to deny the real presence in order "to give a great smack in the face of Popery," but the words of Christ in the Scriptures and the voice of antiquity were too overwhelming in its favor.

Thus in a letter to the Christians of Strasburg, written in 1524, he acknowledged that the plain natural meaning of the words was so clear and forceful as to admit of no escape. "I am caught," he wrote, "I cannot escape, the test is too forcible."[12]

It is moreover a law of interpretation, universally recognized by scholars, that a passage is always to be construed in its obvious meaning unless there is some good reason for interpreting it figuratively; but the words of Christ "to eat My flesh, and drink My blood," cannot be interpreted figuratively without doing violence to the whole passage. Why? Because this phrase when interpreted figuratively has a meaning which is totally repugnant to the whole context.

Thus, the phrase, "to eat the flesh and drink the blood," when used figuratively among the Jews, as among the Arabs of today, meant to inflict upon a person some serious injury, especially by calumny or by false accusation. To interpret the phrase figuratively then would be to make our Lord promise life everlasting to the culprit for slandering and hating Him, which would reduce the whole passage to utter nonsense.

Unless the words of Christ concerning the Holy Eucharist are taken at their face value and in their plain literal meaning, they become meaningless and incoherent. Yes, worse than that, Christ would be an archdeceiver! For He allowed and encouraged and even insisted upon the disciples understanding Him in a literal manner when, according to the non-Catholic view, He was speaking in a purely figurative manner.

True, the words of Christ involve a mystery, a truth far beyond our capacity fully to understand; but the Trinity and the Incarnation are likewise mysteries. We do not on that account however, assign them to the scrap heap: we believe them on the authority of Christ, the Revealer. The Christian religion would not long survive if every doctrine involving a mystery were to be discarded. Science as well as human life are filled with mysteries. Why should religion be the solitary exception?

May we not believe then that the fair-minded reader, who has followed honestly and squarely the evidence thus far presented will feel compelled both by weight of the evidence and by the laws of logic to agree with the following reasonable conclusions? The Scriptures show that Christ taught the doctrine of the real presence. In accepting that teaching, Catholics are but loyal to Jesus Christ.

To fail to do so, would be to flout the authority of Jesus and to undermine the whole basis of the Christian faith. In a world where sects shrug their shoulders and say: "This is a hard saying and who can hear it?" and proceed to walk away, the Church answers the query, "Will you also go away?" which Christ now addresses to her as He did to the Apostles of old, by making her own the memorable reply of Peter: "Lord, to whom shall we go? Thou hast the words of eternal life."

Discussion Aids

Name two of Christ's miracles that were a preparation for the doctrine of the Holy Eucharist. What promise did Christ make in regard to the Holy Eucharist? Did Christ's followers think that He was using figurative language? How did Christ emphasize the fact that His words were to be taken literally? How was Christ's promise received by the disciples? Who answered for those who received the promise with faith and what did that spokesman say? When did Christ fulfill His promise that he would give Himself to us in the Holy Eucharist? Discuss the details of this fulfillment. Show that the Apostles administered this sacrament as the body and blood of Christ, quoting St. Paul. What was the teaching of the Fathers and Doctors of the early Church? Describe an early method of administering this sacrament. Tell the story of the boy Tarcisius. Why do the laity receive only under the form of bread? How old is this law? What happened to the doctrine of the real presence at the time of the Reformation? How many interpretations of the text "This is My body" had resulted by 1577? Sum up the case for the doctrine of the real presence.

Practices

Receive Christ in the Holy Eucharist as often as you can; daily, if possible.

Make frequent visits to Christ in the Holy Eucharist.

Adopt a special Eucharist devotion — reception of Holy Communion on the first Friday, frequent attendance at Benediction, etc.

NOTES (Chapter 14)

1. Jn. 6:28-29
2. *Ibid.,* 6:48-52
3. *Ibid.,* 6:54
4. Mt. 26:26-29
5. I Cor. 10:16 and 11:23-29
6. *Lectures on the Real Presence,* p. 319 (Duffy & Co., Dublin)
7. In Luc. xxii, 19
8. Cath., iv, 9
9. Jn. 6:51
10. I Cor. 11:27
11. *Sess.* 21, Ch. 1
12. De Wette, II p. 577

CHAPTER 15

The Holy Eucharist and Reason

How Science and Reason Harmonize with Faith

An outstanding characteristic of the present day is the emphasis it places upon the appeal to reason. Of doctrines proposed for the belief of Protestants up until the last half-century or so, the questions were first asked: Is the doctrine based upon the Bible? Has it the authority of the inspired word of God behind it? These were the primary criteria by which former generations of Protestants tested the orthodoxy of articles proposed for their belief. The present generation shows little inclination to test the validity of doctrines in the light of such traditional standards.

Belief in both the inspired character and in the inerrancy of Holy Writ has waned very markedly among our non-Catholic fellow citizens. Private interpretation of Scripture has brought such a conflicting variety of opinions into the world as to cause religious chaos and anarchy, and to leave little taste in the average person for wordy controversies over the meaning of Scriptural texts. Still less is his interest in tradition. In fact, many seem to find it unpalatable to be asked to keep step in religious matters with the Fathers of the early Church. They seem to think that progress implies that they should have outgrown the naive and primitive conceptions of the Christians of the early and medieval Church.

Instead of such former criteria, the present generation asks: Is the doctrine reasonable? Does it harmonize with the scientific knowledge and the enlightened intelligence of the present day?

218

Or does the doctrine ask us to believe something that runs counter to the rational temper of the day simply because it has its roots in the Bible or in ancient traditions?

We have previously shown the doctrine of the real presence of Christ in the Holy Eucharist to be based upon the words of Christ as recorded in the Scriptures and to be backed by the whole weight of Christian tradition. Can we show that this is likewise in harmony with the scientific knowledge and the enlightened intelligence of our day?

"No," say many non-Catholics, "regardless of what the Bible or tradition may say, the doctrine runs directly contrary to reason and to the scientific temper of our day."

Let me ask my dear non-Catholic friend to examine with an open mind the doctrine of the Holy Eucharist, and see for himself if there be anything unreasonable in this cardinal tenet of the Catholic faith. In the first place, let it be frankly acknowledged that the doctrine involves a mystery. Like the doctrine of the Trinity and of the Incarnation, it too transcends the capacity of the human mind fully to understand. It is a truth, however, not against reason but above it: in other words, as far as reason can go in fathoming the truth, it can find no element of contradiction or repugnance.

The doctrine says in brief that when the words of consecration, "This is My body . . . this is My blood," are pronounced, the bread and wine are changed into the body and blood, soul and divinity of our Savior, Jesus Christ. This change is effected by the power of God, exercised through the agency of His ambassador, a duly ordained priest. *How* it is done, we do not know: that it *is* done, we believe on the authority of Christ Himself.

In believing that Almighty God can effect such a change, there is nothing unreasonable: God can create and He can annihilate. This change of one substance into another, called by the Catholic Church *transubstantiation,* involves no power not implicit in the dual power of creation and annihilation; and all Christians admit that Almighty God possesses such dual power.

Moreover, the Christian who reads his New Testament attentively will find in it an instance of a transformation that approaches closely to transubstantiation. Thus St. John tells us that at the wedding feast at Cana in Galilee, Christ miraculously changed the water into wine.[1] What was this but a kind of transubstantiation? Furthermore, the multiplication of five barley loaves and two fish into such a quantity as to enable the disciples to feed five thousand men together with their wives and children is a miracle of the same generic character as that of transubstantiation.

An objection is raised here. "The doctrine of the Holy Eucharist is impossible," wrote a non-Catholic friend, "because it involves a self-contradiction: it implies that the same thing is both bread and not bread at the same time. The Eucharist is claimed to be both bread and flesh at one and the same time: this violates the most fundamental law of reason and of common sense."

Like many other objections to the Catholic faith, this too is traceable to a misunderstanding of what the Church really teaches. The doctrine of the Eucharist implies that after the words of consecration are pronounced, the substance of bread is no longer really bread but has been changed into the substance of Christ's body. What has not been changed are the outward appearances of the bread, that is, its color, size, shape, taste, weight — in short, what is apparent to the senses. The reality of a thing lies, however, not in its accidents, or visible parts, but in the substance which is beneath the surface. How different in appearances in all that pertain to the senses are steam, water, and ice? Yet they all constitute the same substance, the same elements.

In the Eucharist the substance of Christ's body has none of the sensible qualities or appearances of a human body. Consequently it would be incorrect to say: "The body of Christ is long or round, or has a light color." It is not extended in such a way as to occupy space, although it is united to the appearances or sensible qualities of the bread in the Holy Eucharist. It is true that this involves a mystery: it is not against our reason but above it. A striking analogy can be found, however, in the manner in which the human soul, a spiritual substance, is present in the body. The soul, like all other spiritual beings, has no extension; yet it animates the body which occupies space.

Father Dalgairns thus develops the comparison: "This then is what God has done to the body of Jesus in the Blessed Sacrament. It has ceased to be extended, and all at once it is freed from the fetters which bound it to a place. It is not so much that it is in many places at once, as that it is no longer under the ordinary laws of space at all. It pervades the Host like a spirit. It uses, indeed, the locality formerly occupied by the bread, in order to fix itself in a definite place, but it only comes into the domain of space at all indirectly through the species, as the soul only enters into its present relations with space through the body. Who will say that this involves contradiction, or that it is beyond the power of Omnipotence?"[2]

Hence it is obvious that the presence of the body of Christ in the Eucharist is not to be interpreted in so gross a manner as to imagine that the head is in one part of the sacred Host and the limbs in another part. Christ is present, whole and entire, in every particle of the sacred Host. The human soul likewise is confined to no part of the body but is present in every part. The manner in which Christ is present in the Holy Eucharist, although unique, is nevertheless somewhat similar to the manner in which the soul is present in the body. It is incorrect then to think that, by breaking the sacred Host into several parts, the body of Jesus would be mangled, dissevered or mutilated in any way.

While confessing that we are here face-to-face with a mystery, it is well to point out that what substance really is, is likewise a mystery to philosophers and to scientists as well. What are the ultimate constituents of matter, and what is their nature? Such distinguished scientists as Millikan, Pupin, Eddington, and Jeans confess that the answer has so far eluded the most penetrating and persistent investigations of science. A whole new sub-atomic world of marvelous mystery has been discovered; the atom has been broken up into neutron, proton and electron; the whole concept of matter has been revolutionized. Instead of matter consisting of hard, inert pellets, as the man in the street still imagines, science has shown these infinitesimal constitutents of matter to be in a state of tremendous activity.

The atom is viewed as a small solar system. Around its nucleus of positive electricity, called protons, the electrons revolve as the planets do about the sun. The movements, however, apparently follow no fixed path or orbit. While the atom is so small as to be invisible to the naked eye, science has measured the speed of these electrons and tells us that they move in an orbit of less than one-millionth of an inch in diameter — faster than an airplane or a bullet from a revolver.

Thus the average electron revolves around its central nucleus several *thousand million million* times every second, with a velocity of hundreds of miles a second. This amazing orbital speed which is greater than that of the planets or even of the stars, is achieved in spite of the infinitesimally small chamber in which it is imprisoned — namely, less than one-millionth of an inch in diameter.

If this statement, which modern physics assures us has been thoroughly verified, were announced to the people living only half a century ago, would they not have laughed it out of court as ridiculous, absurd and impossible? Would they not have protested that such an occurrence would constitute a miracle, greater even than that of transubstantiation? Would they not have exclaimed like the Jews of old: "This saying is hard, and who can bear it?"

I mention a few of the amazing discoveries of modern physics to show how unwise it is for an individual to play the role of King Canute and set limits to the power of Almighty God, by saying, "Thus far, and no farther can His power go." At the very time when Bishop Barnes, for example, was shocking England by proclaiming that transubstantiation was outmoded by the advances of modern science, physicists were at work in their laboratories changing one chemical element into an altogether different one. They were consigning to the scientific scrap heap the two fundamental laws of the older physics, namely, the laws of the conservation of matter and energy. Thus, Sir James Jeans declared in 1929: "The two fundamental cornerstones of twentieth century physics, the conservation of matter and the conservation of energy, are both abolished."[3]

The theory which has gained general acceptance among physicists, and which completely revolutionizes the traditional conception of matter, is that the whole universe is composed of only two kinds of ultimate bricks, namely, electrons and protons. These are but the names for positive and negative electricity. Furthermore the differences between all the elements is but

222

a difference in the nuclear structure and in the number of electrons within the atomic cell.

Thus Dr. Jacob Kunz, former Professor of Mathematical Physics at the University of Illinois, and an eminent authority in his field, informs me that scientists have already modified the nuclear structure of the atomic cell and have thus produced one element from another. By bombarding the proton in an atom of beryllium with alpha particles, Dr. Kunz states, a rearrangement of the nuclear structure was effected, producing therefrom the altogether different element of hydrogen. This has been done likewise with aluminum, phosphorus, and other elements. The alpha particles travel at an amazing velocity, varying from 12,800 miles a second to the slowest at 8,800 miles a second.

If, then, scientists with merely human ingenuity and human power can effect a kind of transubstantiation, who will be so presumptuous and so rash as to deny that power to Almighty God? Who will say now that there is any contradiction or repugnance implied in the change of one element into another? In the light of the amazing discoveries of modern science, men are much less cocksure in proclaiming that such a thing is impossible than they were even at the beginning of the present century.

Science asks us to believe as literal facts statements which no amount of reasoning could have induced the previous generation to accept. What a world of almost infinite potentialities are locked up in a small particle of matter, awaiting the skillful hand to release them from their thralldom! Consider the energy stored up in a piece of coal smaller than a pea. Jeans states it as a scientific fact that if all the atomic energy locked up in so tiny a piece of coal could be released, it would be sufficient to take the Mauretania, once the largest ship afloat, across the Atlantic and back again! "If the energy in a single pound of coal could be completely utilized, it would be sufficient to keep the whole British nation going for a fortnight, domestic fires, factories, trains, power stations, ships and all."[4]

Indeed the traditional conception of matter has been revolutionized by the discoveries of modern science. "When we compare the universe as it is now supposed to be," observes the distinguished scientist, A. S. Eddington of the University of Cambridge, "with the universe as we had ordinarily preconceived it, the most arresting change is not the rearrangement of space and time by Einstein but the dissolution of all that we regard as most solid into tiny specks floating in void. That gives an abrupt jar to those who think that things are more or less what they seem. The revelation by modern physics of the void within the atom is more disturbing than the revelation by astronomy of the immense void in interstellar space. The atom is as porous as the solar system. If we eliminated all the unfilled space in a man's body and collected his protons and electrons into one mass, *the man would be reduced to a speck just visible with a magnifying glass.*"[5]

This means that the human body which we naively imagine is a solid mass of matter measuring about six feet in height and weighing about 175 pounds consists in sober scientific reality chiefly of gaps, crevices and fields of force, empty save for infinitesimal particles which, if packed all together, would constitute so small a speck of matter as to be invisible to the naked eye. This, I hasten to add, is not a selection from *Alice in Wonderland,* but a page from one of the universally accepted texts in modern physics.

These discoveries of modern science shove back the frontiers of the possible far beyond the horizon glimpsed by any previous generations. They open a doorway to a world of almost limitless possibilities; they show, too, what a truly mysterious thing *substance* really is. Science today regards protons and electrons as the ultimate material of all the universe; but these are only names for positive and negative electricity. And we are forced then to ask, What is electricity? Science gives no answer.

To the scientists and the philosophers of today, the ultimate nature of substance presents as baffling a mystery as it did to their predecessors of previous centuries. The investigations of modern science and the studies of modern philosophers on this problem serve but to reinforce with new emphasis the conclusion of that profound thinker of the nineteenth century, Cardinal Newman, when after a lifetime of study and reflection, he said: "What do I know of substance or matter? Just as much as the greatest philosopher; and that is nothing at all."[6]

I have offered an analogy between the change of elements effected by Almighty God through the words of consecration pronounced by His ambassador, and the kind of transubstantiation effected by the physicist in his laboratory, with a view of showing the rashness of those who would prematurely close the door to such occurrences on the grounds of stark impossibility. May I ask our dear non-Catholic reader to consider one further analogy which I consider not less striking?

During the course of a chemistry lecture in a public high school some years ago, the instructor was stressing the permanence and immutability of the chemical elements which incidentally we have just seen is now thoroughly discarded by the leaders in modern science.

"You can change the form and the appearances of the elements through various combinations," said the instructor, "but you can never change their nature as distinct and immutable elements." Then he digressed from his lecture. "Catholics," he continued, "have a curious doctrine known as the Eucharist. They believe that bread and wine are changed into the body and blood of the Lord. But this is impossible. It is contrary to the laws of chemistry. Bread always remains bread and wine remains wine. They cannot be changed into something different."

On hearing this, a young Catholic girl in the class arose and said: "Professor, I am very much surprised to hear you say that bread and wine cannot be changed into flesh and blood. Especially to hear you say that in the name of chemistry. What becomes of the bread which you eat and the wine which you drink? Are they not changed by the laws of nature into your own flesh and blood? If God can effect that change through the laws of nature, of which He is the Author, why can He not effect that change directly and immediately by His own power?"

The comparison was striking, the reasoning cogent, and the conclusion inescapable. The instructor was big enough to admit it.

"Thanks," he said. "I had never before adverted to the fact that the process of metabolism in the human body is constantly effecting much the same change as you believe takes place at the consecration. I withdraw my comment as unfounded and incorrect."

Surely every Christian will admit that all the potency of the laws of nature comes from God, their Creator. If He causes these laws to effect the transformation of bread and wine into flesh and blood, then no one can deny the logic of the girl's reasoning that He can do directly and immediately that which He delegates and empowers His creatures to do. "Nature," as Chaucer has observed, "is but the vicar of the Almighty Lord."[7]

The laws of nature are His ambassadors, proclaiming the presence of an infinite Mind behind the scaffolding and framework of the universe. Without such an Intelligence dovetailing the myriad laws of nature into the harmony of coordinate action for the accomplishment of purposed ends, the cosmos would not be an orderly universe, but a chaos of hopeless anarchy and confusion.

When all is said and done, it is to be acknowledged in the frankest manner that the Holy Eucharist remains a tremendous and impenetrable mystery: this side of the grave it will always remain so. Only in the life to come, when the darkness of the human intellect will be illuminated by the divine light, shall we come to a better understanding of the manner in which Christ is able to hide Himself under the lowly species of the Eucharistic host to be our nourishment and our abiding strength. Yet the fact of its being a mystery should be no barrier to its acceptance by the human mind. Why? Because nature literally abounds in mysteries. They surround us on every side.

What is the manner in which a blade of grass transforms dead inorganic matter into living protoplasm and endows it with the power of reproduction? All the chemists in the world with all their accumulated learning and all their laboratory equipment are unable to duplicate the action which every blade of grass and every leaf on the tree effects every day of their lives. In some mysterious manner they succeed in bridging the enormous chasm that separates the inanimate world from the living, a chasm that no scientist has yet been able to cross.

What is the secret by which such vast stores of atomic energy are locked up within a single grain of sand, defying man's ability to release? Science knows no answer. How is it possible for the electrons within the atom of a particle of dust to travel about in their tiny prison of less than one-millionth of an inch in diameter with a velocity greater than that of an airplane, while the particle of dust itself appears to be perfectly motionless to the human eye? "A baffling mystery," is science's only reply.

Take one of the apparently simplest actions a human being can perform — the raising of one's finger. What is the manner by means of which this mental concept or wish is telegraphed by the mind to the proper physical member, involving the appropriate action of millions of neurons, the opening of certain nervous paths and the closing of others, the stimulation of certain muscles and the inhibition of others, until the proper finger is lifted to just the desired height?

All the psychologists in the world are unable to answer that simple question: like the others, it remains an impenetrable mystery. That man will be able to answer that apparently simple question this side of eternity seems more than unlikely. In short, while we know that actions take place and effects are attained, the answer to the *ultimate how, the precise manner, the detailed process* by which even the simplest actions are performed, remains in almost every case veiled in an opaque mantle of mystery.

The realization that we are surrounded on every side by mysteries which envelop us as the air we breathe, induces an attitude of intellectual humility which prevents a person from brushing aside a doctrine as untenable simply because it involves a mystery. In submitting this consideration to my readers, I would like to make it clear that I make no plea for intellectual obscurantism. I ask merely that the same fundamental consideration which obtains in the scientific viewpoint be not deemed invalid when the truth proposed for belief lies in the field of religion instead of in the domain of science — namely, that assent be not withheld if there be sufficient evidence in its favor simply because knowledge as to the detailed manner in which an effect is achieved cannot be supplied.

The point we make then is that the acceptance of the truth of the Holy Eucharist involves no violence to reason, simply because we do not understand *how* the real presence is achieved. Far from disparaging reason, this procedure not only pays proper deference thereto but asks simply that reason follow in religious matters the same method which obtains in science and

227

in all other fields, where it has enhanced its dignity by the conquest of truths which lay hidden in the arcana of nature, hopelessly veiled from the scrutiny of the senses. In believing, then, in the real presence of Christ in the Holy Eucharist, reason and faith travel hand in hand.

Some superficial critics there are who say that the words of consecration are only words and effect no change in the elements. They fail to see that it is the power behind the words, and not merely the words themselves, which determine their efficacy. Take water, for example. By itself it will not generate light; but put the power and skill of an engineer behind it, and he will harness it and cause it to generate power and light for an entire city or even for whole states. Take a piece of paper. Put on it the signatures of honorable men and it will spell the difference between war and peace, between world slaughter and world friendship.

Take a word. Put the power of a poet behind it and it will make music, beauty and cadence and will sing in the hearts of men. Put the power of an orator behind it and it will thrill vast multitudes. Put the power of a judge behind it and it spells the difference between innocence and guilt, between freedom and jail, between life and death. Put the power of God behind it and it pulls a universe into being out of the yawning abyss of nothingness. Take a piece of bread. Put the power of a human being behind it and it is transformed into his flesh and blood. Put the power of God, expressed in a few words, behind it and it is transformed into the body and blood, soul and divinity of our glorified Lord and Savior, Jesus Christ.

What is determinative, decisive and all important is not so much the word as it is the *power behind the word*. When infinite power and intelligence are put behind a word it becomes the plenipotentiary ambassador of the Most High, clothed with a divine efficacy which transcends the power of man as the radiance of the sun surpasses the flickering light of a candle. God and a word can cause a universe to spring into being. God and a word can bring our great High Priest, Calvary's Victim for the sins of man, Jesus Christ, upon our altar under the lowly species of bread and wine.

A final word about the fruits of this great sacrament. The

Holy Eucharist may be viewed as the extension of the Incarnation, and its application to the needs of the individual soul. Holy Communion effects a closer union of the soul with Christ by love, floods it with sanctifying grace, strengthens it against sin, and serves as a pledge of its glorious resurrection and future union with God by love in the Beatific Vision.

Only the recipient of a worthy Holy Communion can experience that foretaste of heaven and of the intimacy of that union which Christ spoke of when He said: 'He that eateth My flesh, and drinketh My blood, abideth in Me, and I in him." A lover shrinks from the thought of separation and yearns to be united with the object of his love. By means of the Holy Eucharist, Christ pursues us with His love to the far ends of the world.

Some years ago I had this driven home to me in a striking manner. I was sojourning in Cairo, Egypt, on returning from the Holy Land. One evening a white-robed Egyptian boy came to the rectory with the message that an American was dying and calling for a priest. I was delighted to bring the last sacraments to the dying man. It was in a little room above a cheap cafe in the slum section of the city that I found the patient. He had been for many years a soldier of fortune, sailing on a trading vessel in the Indian sea. He was now in the last stages of that fatal malady of Egypt, the black fever. His face was emaciated and wan.

After I had heard his confession and given him Holy Communion, he said: "Father, I have been worried for weeks at the thought of dying here in this out-of-the-way corner of the world, friendless and alone, until I became almost delirious. But now," he continued, with tears in his eyes, "it doesn't matter. For I know I'll meet them all again. For Christ will bring me safely home."

As I was about to leave, he remarked: "Isn't it wonderful, Father, to think that I have received the same Christ here in Africa that I received when I made my first Holy Communion twenty years ago in San Jose in Southern California?"

I went out into the dark crooked streets of the ancient city. There on the hill overlooking the city loomed up the rock-ribbed citadel built by Napoleon in conquering the city. Over in the East rose up under the pale light of the moon the sphinx of Egypt and the pyramids of Ghizeh, erected by the Pharaohs over five thousand years ago. Their vast armies have now been sleeping for fifty centuries beneath the sands of the Sahara. Along the streets loomed up into the night the grotesque figures of the mosques of Mohammed.

The words of the dying man came back to me: San Jose, California, and Cairo, Egypt, stood suddenly side by side! The chasm of the centuries was spanned. The intervening stretch of eight thousand miles across land and sea was annihilated by the power of the divine love that knows no limitations of time or space, "border, nor breed nor race."

Truly indeed is the Holy Eucharist the golden bond by which an Omnipotent Being unites Himself with His children on earth and gives to them a foretaste of that ineffable union through love in the Beatific Vision which St. Paul sought dimly to describe when he said: "Eye hath not seen, nor ear heard, neither hath it entered into the heart of man, what things God hath prepared for them that love Him."[8]

Discussion Aids

Is the doctrine of the Holy Eucharist contrary to reason? Discuss. Is it a self-contradiction? Discuss, using the union of the soul and body as an analogy. Discuss the mystery of substance and the kind of transubstantiation possible to the scientists. If protons and electrons are the ultimate material of the universe and they are only names for positive and negative electricity, a something which is itself a mystery, explain why Catholics may with reason hold the doctrine of transubstantiation. Name some of the mysteries to be found in nature. Can science explain them? Do these mysteries do violence to our reason? Why, then, should the mystery of the real presence? What are the fruits of the Holy Eucharist?

Practices

Learn to see the glory of God in the beauties and wonders of nature. Take a good look at the sky on a clear night.

Make your visits to Christ in the Holy Eucharist a source of increased knowledge of God's love for us.

Make frequent use of the prayer, "I do believe, Lord: help my unbelief" (Mark 9:23).

NOTES (Chapter 15)

1. Jn. 2:1-11
2. *The Holy Communion*, i. 35, 36 (Duffy & Co., Dublin, 1892)
3. *The Universe Around Us*, p. 178 (Macmillan Co., N.Y., 1929)
4. Jeans, *ibid.*, p. 181
5. *The Nature of the Physical Universe*, pp. 1-2 (Macmillan Co.)
6. *Apologia*, p. 375 (Longmans, Green & Co., N.Y., 1905)
7. *Parlement of Foules*, I, p. 379
8. I Cor. 2:9

CHAPTER 16

Frequent Holy Communion: Why?

Divine Nourishment for the Soul

The greatest gift which a loving and merciful God has ever bestowed upon mankind is Jesus Christ; for Christ is God incarnate. His delight was to be with the children of men. That He might be with them always as their changeless Friend, their inspiring Counsellor, and their great High Priest, He instituted the sacrament of the real presence.

In myriad tabernacles scattered among all the countries of the world, the Eucharistic Christ is dwelling among His people. Not only does He dwell among them, but He gives Himself to them for the nourishment of their souls. Jesus Christ, the Son of the Eternal Father, consubstantial with the Father, gives Himself, body and blood, soul and divinity to mortal man in Holy Communion. Through a miracle of divine power, Jesus Christ gives Himself to us for our daily bread.

Here is divine omnipotence emptying itself in the frail bosom of humanity; here is divine love exhausting itself in the heart of man. Stripping Himself of the outward effulgence of the God-head that He might not overawe man with His dazzling splendor, Jesus Christ comes under the lowly appearance of the Eucharistic Host to weak and mortal man. He is our daily bread. Truly, this is God's supreme gift to man. The mind reels and staggers in trying to conceive how even an infinite God could bestow upon mankind a greater gift.

Christ who cleansed the lepers, restored sight to the blind,

232

healed the sick, pardoned sinners and died on Calvary's Cross for the redemption of mankind is present in the Eucharist. When Christ appeared to His Apostles in the upper chamber after His resurrection, the doors and windows were closed. Yet Christ stood suddenly in their midst and spoke to them. In that same glorified body which transcended the properties of matter, Christ is present in the sacrament of His love.

The real presence of Christ in the Eucharist stands, therefore, as an antidote for the vagueness of contemporary thought and as an anchor against the shifting currents of modern uncertainty and doubt. It takes God out of the mists of speculation and brings Him into our very midst to be our Counsellor, our Inspirer and our changeless Friend. In Holy Communion He comes to us as our heavenly manna, the bread of angels and the nutriment for our souls. All who hold steadfast to this central doctrine of historical Christianity will find in it an invincible armor against the assaults of modern unbelief.

One day a messenger, breathless with haste, burst in upon King Louis IX of France with surprising news. "Your Majesty," he cried, "hasten to the church! A great miracle is occurring there. A priest is saying holy Mass, and after the consecration, instead of the host there is visible on the altar Jesus Himself in His human figure. Everybody is marveling at it. Hurry before it disappears."

To the astonishment of the messenger, the saintly monarch calmly replied: "Let them go to see that miracle who have any doubt regarding the real presence of our Lord in the holy sacrament. As for me, even if I saw Jesus on the altar in His visible form, and touched Him with my hand, and heard His voice, I should not be more convinced than I now am, that He is present in the consecrated Host. The word of Christ is sufficient for me. I need no miracle." Such too should be the faith of every believer in Christ.

We now come to the question: What use are we making of the greatest gift within the power of an Omnipotent God to bestow upon mankind — the real presence of Christ in the Holy Eucharist? We can avail ourselves of this divine benefaction by attending holy Mass and offering in union with the priest the Eucharistic Victim in atonement for our sins, by visiting our

Eucharistic King in the tabernacles on our altars, and particularly by receiving our divine Lord in Holy Communion. No devotion is dearer to the Church than that of frequent, even daily, Holy Communion. The late Holy Father, St. Pius X, encouraged all the faithful to receive frequently this heavenly food. It offers the greatest assistance in living an upright and holy life, and constitutes our sure defense against all the temptations which assail us.

The fruits of this sacrament are manifold. It deepens our sense of the reality of God, makes us conscious of His comradeship, enables us to perceive Him as the witness of our every deed, the auditor of our every word, the spectator of the thoughts and aspirations which stir inarticulately in the silent kingdom of the soul.

It thus frees us from the tyranny of the senses with their dependence upon the visible, the tangible, the palpable. It helps us to realize that the most profound realities of life are those which are spiritual and lie beyond the reach of the senses. It enables us to understand what St. Paul meant when he said: "The things which are seen are temporal, but the things which are unseen are eternal." It prompts us to exclaim with the holy souls of every age: "Ah! Christ, impalpable, I grasp Thee; inapprehensible, I clutch Thee."

It delivers us from the narrow prison cell of time and place by making us one in spirit with the choice souls of every generation to whom the presence of God is the most abiding reality in life. It enables us to break through the shell of external circumstance and grasp the kernel of spiritual reality which alone gives meaning and significance to human life. This sharpened perception of spiritual realities, this heightened sense of the presence of God constitutes the essential difference between the religious-minded person and the worldling.

While making a pilgrimage to the Holy Land in 1925, I chanced to pass through Smyrna, Turkey. It was shortly after the Turks had pillaged and burned the Christian section of the city, and put many to the sword. Still standing among the ruins was a convent. Among the nuns was one from Ireland.

"Do you not feel lost," I asked, "in this out-of-the-way corner of the world, so far from your home in Ireland?"

Pointing to the tabernacle, she replied: "Father, wherever the Blessed Sacrament is, there I am at home. For there is my Lord and my God."

How true that is! They are the words which every priest, religious or lay person can utter. How effectively does the Eucharistic Lord dispel the touch of nostalgia from the heart of the missionary arriving in a foreign land. Where our Lord and our God is, there can be no homesickness: He is the essential element in every home.

It is not only to missionaries in distant lands and to Christians under the fire of persecution, however, that the Holy Eucharist brings strength and intrepidity but to all lonely and homesick souls. One day at the University of Illinois, a student said to me:

"Father, when I came here a few weeks ago, I was homesick and lonely. It is so large an institution and it's my first time away from home for any length of time. But after receiving Holy Communion all feelings of loneliness and homesickness vanished."

He little knew that he was but voicing the experience of every student and of every person away from the warmth of the family fireside and the loving atmosphere of home. When Christ comes into our hearts, there we are at home — in any city or in any land.

Everyone who has felt the warm intimacy of the love of Christ in frequent Holy Communion is able to make his own the words of a contemporary poet:

Whoso has felt the Spirit of the Highest
   Cannot confound nor doubt Him nor deny:
Yea with one voice, O world, tho' thou deniest,
   Stand thou on that side, for this am I.[1]

Another fruit of Holy Communion is the strength which it gives to resist temptation and to break any habit of sin previously acquired. There are some who think that frequent Holy Communion should be the exclusive privilege of pious souls far removed from the dangers of sin. Yet the Sacred Congregation of the Council thought otherwise. For in its "Decree on Daily Holy Communion" the Council expressly declares:

"The desire of Jesus Christ and of the Church that all the faithful should daily approach the sacred banquet is directed chiefly to this end, that the faithful, being united to God by means of the sacrament, may thence derive strength to resist their sensual passions, to cleanse themselves from the stains of daily faults, and to avoid those graver sins to which human frailty is liable so that its primary purpose is not that the honor and reverence due to our Lord may be safeguarded, or that the Sacrament may serve as a reward of virtue bestowed on the recipients. Hence the holy Council of Trent calls the Eucharist 'the antidote whereby we are delivered from daily faults and preserved from deadly sins.'"

It is therefore needed most of all by those who are weak and are struggling to break the manacles of a sinful habit. It is the supreme remedy against temptation and the most powerful influence in freeing one from a vicious practice. There is no habit, no matter how strong the links in the chain of its practice, which can long resist the sledge-hammer blows of this sacrament. The manacles of sensuality, intoxication, anger, jealousy, greed, all fall into smithereens before the devastating blows of this divine power.

This truth is illustrated by an incident related by St. Philip Neri. As a result of a long life spent in ministering to the youth of Rome, this holy priest was wont to declare that frequent Holy Communion is not only the most efficacious means of safeguarding virtue but is also the only effective means of breaking the chains of certain habits of sensuality. One day a youth came to his confessional and said:

"Father, I am bound hand and foot by the chain of a sensual habit which I have tried in vain to break. In spite of all my efforts to reform, I find myself falling again and again. I would do anything if I could but free myself from its galling tyranny which is making my life a living hell."

"Do you really wish to break yourself of this habit?" asked St. Philip.

"Father," replied the youth, "give me any penance and see if I will not gladly do it."

"All right, then," said the priest, "I will give you an infallible remedy. You go to daily Holy Communion for a month. If you should be so unfortunate as to experience a single relapse, which may God avert, I ask you to rush immediately to Confession and then to Holy Communion."

This the youth did. At the end of the month he was able to say: "Father, for the first time in years I am able to draw the breath of a free man. Not only has daily Holy Communion freed me from this practice, but it has filled me with such revulsion for that vice that I feel confident I will never again stoop to that degradation."

In the experience of that young man there is mirrored the experience of all mankind, young and old. So true is this that every confessor can say to any penitent groveling in the mire of sensuality, manacled by the chains of an oft-repeated act: "My friend, do you really wish to break this habit? Then if you do, you will go to daily Holy Communion until you have broken this habit. If you are not willing to do this, then you are making a mockery of the purpose of amendment. You are lacking in determination and in sincerity." It is high time for penitents to realize that purpose of amendment means more than a mere moving of the lips. It means the wholehearted utilization of a remedy of demonstrated effectiveness; in short, it means having recourse to daily Holy Communion.

During the persecution of the Roman Emperor Diocletian many Christians paid with their life for their faith in Christ. Among the number seized on one occasion were a father and his young son. Brought before the pagan tribunal, the Emperor commanded the father to offer incense to the gods of imperial Rome or pay the penalty with his life.

"Rather than betray the faith," replied the father, "which has been purchased for me at the cost of the precious blood of Jesus Christ, I will die."

Whereupon he was cast into the arena, and there before the howling savage mob he suffered the gladiator's sword to sever his head from his body, thus sealing with his life's blood his faith in the crucified Christ. As the son, a little boy of twelve, witnessed the cruel death inflicted upon his father, he was overcome with horror. His face grew pale with fear; tears filled his eyes. The Emperor, seeing the terror-stricken condition of the boy, said:

"You surely will not do such a foolish thing as your father. Come, offer incense to the gods of Rome and I will not only spare your life but will give you anything your youthful heart will ask."

The boy had taken a few steps toward the incense pyre when suddenly he stopped spellbound in his tracks. What was that voice he heard echoing in his inner ear? It was the voice of his martyred sire uttering his dying words. Turning about, he walked quickly over to the spot in the arena where the sand was still crimsoned with the warm lifeblood of his father. He stooped and, clenching it in his hand, said:

"But a few moments ago I was weak and about to yield, but now I am strong with the blood of my father. Rather than deny the faith purchased for me by the blood of Jesus Christ and of my own martyred father, I too will die."

With a smile lighting up his youthful countenance, and a prayer on his lips, he placed his head upon the swordsman's block. As the head fell, severed from the body, the blood trickling down in the sand mingled with the warm lifeblood of his father. Devout Christians who stood nearby saw in that union a reflection of that other union that took place beyond the skies, where father and son were clasped in the arms of the Master to receive from His hand the glorious crown of martyrdom.

Those words of the martyred youth in ancient Rome are the words which every communicant can truthfully utter: "A little while ago," he can say, "I was weak and about to yield. But now I am strong with the blood of my Father and my God. Rather than betray Him by the commission of a deliberate mortal sin, I too would be willing to die."

For in Holy Communion we do not merely clench in our hands sand crimsoned with blood, but we receive into our very hearts the body and blood, the soul and divinity of our Lord and Savior, Jesus Christ. We become partakers of a divine life and secure a foretaste of that union with Christ in the beatific vision which constitutes the essential happiness of heaven.

Among the other fruits of Holy Communion are an increase of sanctifying grace, the remission of venial sins, a strengthening of the will, an increased horror of sin and the remission of the temporal punishment due to sin. Even mortal sin is washed from the soul of the person who unmindful of such an offense receives Holy Communion in good faith. This implies that the communicant has sorrow for all his sins and that if the mortal sin should later come to his mind, he will mention it in his next Confession.

The reason for this indirect remission of mortal sin through Holy Communion is to be found in the fact that it infuses sanctifying grace into the soul of the person who does not knowingly place an obstacle in the way. But sanctifying grace not only beautifies the soul, but removes any sin, mortal or venial, that may be there; hence Holy Communion indirectly remits even mortal sin.

Treating of the efficacy of the sacrament in strengthening the will to resist temptation, the Catechism of the Council of Trent says: "In the holy mysteries is, moreover, such efficacy as to *preserve us pure and unhurt from sin and from the assault of temptations*, and prepare the soul, as it were, by a heavenly medicine against the easy approach and infection of virulent and deadly disease. . . . It also restrains and represses the lust of the flesh for, whilst it inflames souls more with the fire of charity, it of necessity extinguishes the ardor of concupiscence."[2]

St. Thomas Aquinas, the prince of the Church's theologians, thus sums up the far-reaching effects of Holy Communion: "The Sacrament of the Body of the Lord puts the demons to flight, defends us against the incentives to vice and to concupiscence, cleanses the soul from sin, assuages the anger of God, enlightens the understanding to know God, inflames the will and the affections with the love of God, fills the memory with spiritual sweetness, confirms the entire man in good, frees us from eternal death, multiplies the merits of a good life, leads us to our everlasting home, and reanimates the body to eternal life."

The person who is strengthened to resist temptation is by that very fact heartened to fight more courageously for virtue, honor, right, manliness. One who knows he is free from sin and whose friendship with his Lord and Maker has been deepened and made more intimate through Holy Communion throws himself into his undertakings with greater courage and abandon.

Knute Rockne, the famed coach of Notre Dame, tells of the deep impression made upon him by witnessing his players arise on the morning of a game and go off to receive Communion. His observant eye could not fail to notice the abandon with which such players threw themselves into the game and fought with the courage of untamed tigers.

Here, in brief, is the way Rockne tells the story: "I used to be deeply impressed at the sight of my players receiving Communion every morning, and finally I made it a point of going to Mass with them on the morning of a game. I realized that it appeared more or less incongruous, when we arrived in town for a game, for the general public to see my boys rushing off to church as soon as they got off the train, while their coach rode to the hotel and took his ease. So, for the sake of appearances, if nothing else, I made it a point to go to church with the boys on the morning of a game.

"One night before a big game in the East, I was nervous and worried about the outcome of the game the next day and was unable to sleep. I tossed and rolled about the bed, and finally decided that I'd get up and dress, then go down to the lobby and sit in a chair alone with my thoughts. It must have been two or three o'clock in the morning when I arrived in the deserted lobby, so I took a chair and tried to get that football game off my mind by engaging some bellboys in conversation.

"Along about five or six o'clock in the morning I started pacing the lobby of the hotel; when suddenly I ran into two of my players hurrying out. I asked them where they were going at such an hour, although I had a good idea.

"Then I retired to a chair in the corner of the lobby where I couldn't be seen, but where I could see everyone who went in or out of the door. Within the next few minutes, my players kept hurrying out of the door in pairs and groups, and finally when they were about all gone, I got over near the door so I could question the next player who came along. In a minute or two, the last members of the squad hurried out of an elevator and made for the door. I stopped them and asked them if they, too, were going to Mass, and they replied that they were. I decided to go along with them.

"Although they probably didn't realize it, these youngsters

were making a powerful impression on me with their piety and devotion, and when I saw all of them walking up to the Communion rail to receive, and realized the several hours' sleep they had sacrificed in order to do this, I understood for the first time what a powerful ally their religion was to those boys in their work on the football field. This was when I really began to see the light; to know what was missing in my life, and, later on, I had the great pleasure of being able to join my boys at the Communion rail."

What are the requirements for daily Communion? In answer to this question, the Sacred Congregation of the Council decreed on December 16, 1905 as follows:

1. Frequent and daily Communion, as a thing most earnestly desired by Christ our Lord and by the Catholic Church, should be open to all the faithful, of whatever rank and condition of life; so that no one who is in the state of grace, and who approaches the holy table with a right and devout disposition, can lawfully be hindered therefrom.

2. A right disposition consists in this: that he who approaches the holy table should do so, not out of routine, or vainglory, or human respect, but for the purpose of pleasing God, of being more closely united with Him by charity, and of seeking this divine remedy for his weaknesses and defects.

From this it is evident that any person who is not certain that he is in the state of mortal sin, and who approaches the holy table for the purpose of nourishing his soul with this heavenly bread, is to be admitted to the sacrament. Mere scruples or doubts are not sufficient to prohibit him. Nothing but the absolute certainty of mortal sin.

Furthermore, it is not necessary for one to go to confession every time one wishes to receive. This would impose some inconvenience on a person and would doubtless deter a number. The Council is explicit in declaring that nothing need keep a person from approaching as often as he wishes, provided only that he is in the state of grace and has the proper disposition. By making daily Holy Communion so easily available, the Church shows her profound solicitude in having the faithful approach with the greatest possible frequency.

Pope Pius XI in his radio address to the National Eucharistic Congress in New Orleans in 1938 said: "May we not discern, however, a promise of better things for the Universal Church in the reflowering among you and among all peoples of Eucharistic love and the daily increase of ardent devotion for the august Sacrament? . . . While we exhort you from our paternal heart to most holy zeal towards the Blessed Sacrament, we fervently pray with you that, strong in youth, your people, who stand forth in wealth and power, may also be a shining example of Catholic faith and Christian virtue."[3]

I do not consider myself worthy to receive Holy Communion often.

This objection is based upon a misconception of the primary purpose of Holy Communion. It is not so much a reward for virtue as an antidote for sin. "If you are not worthy to communicate every day," asks St. Ambrose, "are you more worthy after abstaining a year from Communion?"[4] The very fact that you feel yourself weak and easily drawn into sin is the very reason why you should receive often. The Church bids you to repeat with the priest before Communion the humble acknowledgment: "Lord, I am not worthy." The longer you abstain from this heavenly food the less worthy do you become to receive, since it is, as the Council of Trent points out, "the antidote whereby we are delivered from daily faults and preserved from deadly sins."

Paderewski tells us that when he failed to practice on his piano for a single day, he could notice the difference in his playing. When he remained away two days, his wife could notice the difference; three days, his friends could observe it, and when he remained away four days, the whole audience could notice the difference. So too it is with those who are accustomed to keep not their fingers but their hearts and consciences sensitive to the music of divine grace and the warmth of divine love by daily Holy Communion. Each day's abstention leaves its perceptible effect in dulling the sensitivity of the conscience to the music of divine inspiration and in blunting the delicacy of the love for our Eucharistic Lord.

I am afraid of losing my respect and devotion for Holy Communion by too great familiarity. The reception will become too much of a mechanical routine.

Loss of devotion will result from improper preparation. But

if one prepares devoutly for Holy Communion, frequent reception will deepen the sentiments of reverence and love. Familiarity in the sense of intimacy and union with Christ is not to be deprecated but is the object of all prayer and spiritual exercise. In regard to routine, two kinds are to be distinguished. There is the routine objected to in *Rule 2* of the *Decree on Daily Holy Communion*. This is the *purely mechanical* reception of the Sacrament with an attitude of irreverence or at least of indifference, in short, with an absence of "a right and devout disposition." This attitude is the very opposite of the one engendered by frequent Communion when care is taken to prepare properly for this great act by the arousal of sentiments of reverence and love. "They that eat Me, shall yet hunger; and they that drink Me, shall yet thirst." This saying of Ecclesiasticus reflects the experience of every devout recipient of frequent Communion.

The second kind of routine is that which is synonymous with *habit*. In this sense routine indicates a facility of action which is most desirable in regard to all virtuous deeds. Thus it is eminently desirable to make the daily recitation of one's morning and evening prayers a matter of routine or habit. Hence too it is most desirable to make the devout reception of daily Holy Communion a matter of habitual practice instead of being dependent upon whim or caprice: the whole aim of the spiritual life is to render the performance of virtuous actions a matter of routine or habit.

I don't like going to Communion without Confession and I don't have either the time or the opportunity to go to Confession each day.

The Church teaches that one may receive Holy Communion repeatedly without going to Confession, provided of course one is not conscious of any mortal sin. Why then should you insert an action not required by the pope? The *Decree on Daily Communion* explicitly states that only two conditions are requisite, namely, the "state of grace" and "a right and devout intention." It is not the mark of a good Catholic to be more exacting than the pope. Consequently, one may go to Communion for several weeks, if he desires, on the one Confession.

Frequent Holy Communion is all right for women and children but is somewhat inappropriate for men.

With God there is no double standard of morality or piety, one for women and another for men. Prayer and the sacraments are the means of grace alike for men, women and children. Because men are frequently more exposed to temptation than women, there is a correspondingly greater need for this divine antidote to sin. It is a complete misconception of the purpose for which Christ instituted the Holy Eucharist to think that it was meant chiefly for women and children. It is meant for all and especially for those who are exposed to danger. It is their best fortification.

The martyrs who walked into the arena of the Roman amphitheater to face the gladiator's sword or the savage lions found in the devout reception of the Holy Eucharist the strength which sustained them for their ordeal without faltering. "The strongest among the pure and the purest among the strong," said Jean Paul Richter, "Christ with His wounded hands lifted empires from their hinges and changed the stream of centuries." He who bows his head in the frequent reception of this divine manna becomes the strongest, the most manly and the most courageous among men.

I do not have sufficient time for proper preparation for Holy Communion nor for the thanksgiving afterwards. Hence, I cannot receive often.

True, there should be due preparation. But does this mean the recitation of many prayers, the performance of many devotional exercises? Not at all. The best preparation for Communion is a good life and the sanctifying of one's ordinary daily actions. Moreover, "frequent Communion is the best preparation for Communion," says a Lapide; "one Communion is thanksgiving for another; and the Communion of today is the best preparation for the Communion of tomorrow." "Therefore," says St. Alphonsus Liguori, "if you have not time to prepare yourself, in consequence of some good work or some duty of your state, do not abstain from Communion on that account. Only take care to avoid useless conversations and occupation that is not urgent."

If one is hurried, it will still be possible to make the immediate preparation while going to the church, and to continue the thanksgiving on the way home. There are two axioms which apply here, namely, "Where there is a will, there is a way," and

"Love will find a way." The individual who has once experienced the warmth and intimacy of daily union with Christ in Holy Communion will laugh at the trivial excuses which deter the fainthearted and the indifferent.

Why should I start the practice of daily Communion when I know that I shall not be able to keep it up?

Because a half a loaf is better than none at all. Even if the practice cannot be continued when one leaves school, or moves to a different location, it will nevertheless be a matter of supreme importance to have fortified one's character and deepened one's virtue and piety by having received frequently for even a limited period. The fact is that young people during the plastic days of their youth stand in need of greater spiritual reinforcements than they will after their characters are formed.

During adolescence new passions are awakening within them. Their experience is very limited and offers but little help in restraining the forces striving for the mastery. During this crucial period when youth is sculpturing his character for weal or for woe, it is an immense advantage to form the habit of frequent Communion so that he will have the most powerful ally in the world on his side.

There can be no doubt of the successful outcome if the youth will employ the most effective antidote for the temptations that press round about him on every side. The *habit* of frequent Communion will tide him over the critical years of adolescence and plant so deep in his young soul the seeds of piety and virtue that the afteryears will bring an abundant harvest. Daily Holy Communion for the youth of every school and college in our land is the ideal placed before us by the Sovereign Pontiff. A ministry of over fifty years among the youth of two great universities has crystallized in me the unshakable conviction that the formation of such a habit is the best guarantee of their enduring faith and character and the most valuable contribution we can render to them.

In the chapel of Keble College, Oxford, there hangs the famous masterpiece, "The Light of the World," by Holman Hunt. It depicts the Master standing and knocking at a door upon which vines are growing. The hinges are rusty from long disuse. In His hand He holds a lantern. "Behold!" He is saying, "I stand at the door and knock." When Hunt had finished his painting, he invited his fellow artists to inspect it. They viewed it carefully from this angle and from that. Loud were they in their praise.

"It is a masterpiece of all time," they said.

"But," said one of them, "you have forgotten one thing."

What is that?" asked Hunt.

"You have forgotten to place a knob on the door."

"No," said Hunt, "I have not forgotten it. I have omitted it purposely. For that is the door of the human heart and it opens only from within."

Christ may knock; Christ may plead; but it is only we who can admit Him. Christ is standing today before the door of every human heart, pleading for admittance in the Sacrament of His Love. Will you not open it each day and let Him in?

If Catholics but understood how easy and simple it is to receive Holy Communion frequently, even daily, and how fruitful is this practice, the number of frequent communicants would grow by leaps and bounds. Certainly, weekly reception is most easy. We all are obliged to hear Mass on Sunday. Why not arise at the Communion time and walk up to the railing and receive the Source of all goodness and the Author of all holiness? Why not thus receive the maximum fruit of the Eucharistic Sacrifice?

Will you not, dear reader, put aside all vacillation and hesitancy and do your part through frequent Communion in bringing about that Eucharistic renaissance which means so much for the happiness of the individual and the peace and welfare of the world? Let us show the world once and for all by the eloquence of our actions that we believe with a profound and deathless faith the words of our divine Master, Jesus Christ: "My flesh is meat indeed; and My blood is drink indeed. ... He that eateth My flesh and drinketh My blood hath everlasting life: and I will raise him up on the last day."

Discussion Aids

What is God's greatest gift to man? Why? How is Christ present in the Holy Eucharist? The Holy Eucharist is an antidote for what? Tell the story related about King Louis. What are some of the fruits of the Sacrament? Explain how the Eucharist is a hidden source of strength. How does frequent Holy Communion help one resist temptation to sin? Under what conditions will Holy Communion indirectly cleanse the soul of mortal sin? How does St. Thomas sum up the effects of Holy Communion? What effect did the good example of his players have on Rockne? What are the requirements for frequent or daily Holy Communion? Let five members in turn discuss and refute the excuses often advanced by those who are not frequent communicants.

Practices

Resolve to receive Holy Communion frequently, daily if possible, or at least weekly. Form within your discussion club or your family a daily Mass and Holy Communion league by having at least one member represent the club or family at Mass and Communion each day.

If you cannot actually receive Holy Communion daily, invite God to come to you spiritually.

NOTES (Chapter 16)

1. W.H. Myers, *A Victorian Anthology*, p. 291 (Houghton Mifflin Co., Boston)
2. Part ii, Ch. 4, q. 51
3. *The Register*, Denver, Oct. 23, 1938
4. *De Sacramentis*, lib. V.C. IV

CHAPTER 17

The Priesthood: A Divine Institution

The Priest Is Christ's Ambassador to Men

The Catholic Church differs from Protestant denominations in that it alone possesses an altar and a priesthood. It worships Almighty God not alone by prayer but by sacrifice as well. It offers up in an unbloody manner the Sacrifice of Christ on Calvary. This sacrifice was foreshadowed in the Old Law by the bloody sacrifice of the priesthood of Levi: the offerings of sheep and goats and oxen. The offering of the sacrifice of bread and wine by Melchisedech, King of Salem, and priest of the Most High, typified the clean oblation of which the prophet Malachi spoke:

"From the rising of the sun even until the going down, my name is great among the Gentiles, and in every place there is sacrifice, and there is offered to my name a clean oblation: for my name is great among the Gentiles, saith the Lord of hosts."[1] Such is the divinely inspired prophecy concerning that clean oblation, the holy Sacrifice of the Mass which constitutes the central act of worship in the Church founded by Christ.

Without a priesthood, however, there can be no altar and no sacrifice, as the experience of our separated brethren abundantly demonstrates. There can be preaching and prayer. But that essential element of worship, sacrifice, which bulks so large in the Old Testament, is lost without a priesthood. Did Christ found a Church but make no provision for a priesthood to offer sacrifice? Did He fail to institute a priesthood which would continue in all ages the work He had begun? Did He launch His bark without captain or crew to guide it over the uncharted waters of the centuries yet to come?

That Christ acted in this strange manner would seem to be the belief of our non-Catholic friends: for in their eyes the minister who preaches to them is clothed with no divine power. His authority comes solely from the congregation which employs him. He is like the artist who plays the organ, the secretary who keeps the books, and like them too is dismissible at the will and caprice of the congregation which hires them.

That Christ did not act in the strange manner just described — founding a Church but failing to make any provision for its perpetuation through a definite ministry — has been the constant belief of the Church which He founded. The Church teaches that Christ not only instituted the priesthood but conferred upon it clearly specified powers and authority. It is inconceivable to her that a Divine Being, Jesus Christ, would found a Church to minister to the spiritual needs of mankind in all succeeding ages without establishing a ministry and conferring upon it the power and authority necessary to enable the Church to fulfill her divinely appointed mission. Such is the procedure which both reason and common sense would lead us to expect.

Such is the procedure which the New Testament shows us Christ *actually* followed. It tells us that Christ selected twelve Apostles and constituted them His first priests. Upon them He conferred the power of ordaining others to continue their work. The sacrament by which men are ordained and receive the power and grace to discharge the duties of the priestly office is Holy Orders.

It was instituted by Christ at the Last Supper, when after consecrating the elements of bread and wine into the Holy Eucharist, He said to the Apostles: "Do ye this for a commemoration of Me."[2] The Council of Trent declares: "If anyone says that by these words: 'Do ye this for a commemoration of Me,' Christ did not constitute the Apostles priests, or did not ordain that they and other priests offer His body and blood, let him be anathema."

At the Last Supper, Jesus Christ, the High Priest of the New Law according to the order of Melchisedech, fulfilled the promise which He had previously made to the Apostles that He would give them His flesh to eat and His blood to drink. He instituted as a permanent and official act of worship the Eucharistic Sacrifice which He had just offered. In commanding the Apostles to do what He had just done, He gave them the power which that act entails, namely, the power to *consecrate*. In authorizing them to offer the selfsame Sacrifice which He had instituted, Christ made the Apostles and their successors the sharers of His eternal priesthood.

Christ completed the communication of His priesthood to the Apostles, when a few days later He conferred upon them the other strictly sacerdotal *power of forgiving* sins. On that first Easter Christ appeared to His Apostles and said to them: "As the Father hath sent Me, I also send you." When He had said this, He breathed on them; and He said to them: "Receive ye the Holy Spirit. Whose sins you shall forgive, they are forgiven them; and whose sins you shall retain, they are retained."[3]

The Apostles regarded themselves henceforth as ministers of reconciliation. Thus St. Paul writes to the Corinthians: "God hath reconciled us to Himself through Christ, *and hath given to us the ministry of reconciliation*. . . . For Christ, therefore, we are ambassadors; God, as it were, exhorting through us."[4] In other words God sends Christ to reconcile sinners; Christ sends priests.

The third great power which Christ conferred upon His priests is that of *preaching the gospel* with authority. While this is not so distinctly a sacerdotal power as that of celebrating Mass or of forgiving sins, it is nevertheless a mark of divine delegation which sets them off from the laity. This power of teaching in His name was conferred upon His first priests by Christ when He said to them: "Going, therefore, teach ye all nations . . . teaching them to observe all things, whatsoever I have commanded you. And, behold, I am with you all days, even to the consummation of the world."[5]

The right of the priest to preach the gospel with authority entails upon the laity the correlative obligation of listening to it and of heeding its precepts. Christ sets forth this obligation in the following explicit manner: "He that heareth you heareth Me; and he that despiseth you despiseth Me; and he that despiseth Me despiseth Him that sent Me."[6]

It seems most probable from the evidence afforded by the New Testament that Christ ordained the Apostles priests and empowered them to offer the Eucharistic Sacrifice with no special ceremony but with the simple words: "Do ye this in commemoration of Me." Here, as in the case of some of the other sacraments, Christ after instituting the sacrament left it to His Church to determine the matter and form and the precise manner in which the sacrament was to be conferred upon subsequent recipients.

This was apparently determined shortly after the sacrament was instituted. For St. Luke in the Acts of the Apostles and St. Paul in his epistles mention all the elements of the sacrament, namely, the external symbolic rite of the imposition of hands and prayer, the internal grace thus communicated, and the institution of the sacrament by Christ. Thus St. Luke writes: "These [the seven deacons] they set before the Apostles, and they praying, imposed hands upon them."[7] "Then they, fasting and praying, and imposing their hands upon them [Paul and Barnabas] sent them away."[8]

Paul and Barnabas ordained priests to carry on their ministry among colonies of newly converted Christians, while the two Apostles moved on to new fields. "And when they had ordained to them priests in every church, they commended them to the Lord, in whom they believed."[9] St. Paul warns Timothy that the sacrament of Orders is to be conferred only on those candidates who gave every assurance of fitness for holy priesthood, saying: "Impose not hands lightly upon any man."[10]

Some non-Catholic writers have contended that the distinction between clergy and laity arose solely from the need of maintaining good order in the Church and that the priests were mere officeholders deriving their authority from the congregation. Such a contention, however, is contradicted by the unanimous voice of Christian antiquity. From the earliest days we find express reference in the writings of the Fathers to bishops, priests and deacons, as indeed we do in the Acts of the Apostles and in the epistles of St. Paul.

St. Clement is explicit: "Christ is from God, and the Apostles from Christ. Preaching from city to city and throughout the country, the Apostles appointed their first converts, testing

251

them by the Spirit, to be bishops and deacons for the future Christians."[11] He administers a severe rebuke to the Christians of Corinth for daring "to dismiss from the ministry those who had been placed in office by the Apostles or their successors with the approval of the whole Church."[12]

I have before me the citations of many of the early Fathers showing a clear recognition by the infant Church of the priesthood as a divinely established office, for the reception of which the sacrament of Orders was instituted. Space permits but the following one from St. Gregory of Nyssa[13] who reflects the mind of all the early writers: "The same power of the word," he says, "renders sublime and honorable the priest, who, by the newness of Ordination, has been singled out from the multitude; he who was yesterday one of the people suddenly becomes a commander, a presiding officer, a teacher of righteousness, and the dispenser of hidden mysteries."[14]

The Council of Trent declares that there is in the Catholic Church a divinely established hierarchy of bishops, priests and deacons, and that bishops are superior to priests and possess the power of confirming and ordaining.[15] Since Christ established the priesthood as a permanent institution, He certainly conferred upon some priests, namely, bishops, the power of communicating the priesthood to others. It is evident from the New Testament that the Apostles were bishops, for it depicts them frequently as ordaining, which is the function characteristic of bishops. The episcopate is the fullness of the priesthood.

St. Ignatius of Antioch[16] describes the three orders of bishops, priests and deacons, and points out clearly the divine origin of the episcopate and its superiority over the priesthood. "The college of presbyters," he writes, "adheres to the bishop as the strings to a lyre."[17] "Where the bishop is, there let the multitudes (of believers) be; even as where Jesus Christ is, there is the Catholic Church."[18]

"Why don't priests marry?" is one of the questions most frequently asked by non-Catholics. The celibacy of the clergy is not a precept of the divine or natural law, nor a dogma of the Catholic Church. It is simply a disciplinary regulation of the Western Church, imposed with a view to the more effective discharge of the priestly duties and a closer approximation to the ideal of our great High Priest, Jesus Christ. "He that is without a wife," says St. Paul, "is solicitous for the things that belong to the Lord, how he may please God. But he that is with a wife is solicitous for the things of the world, how he may please his wife; and he is divided."[19]

During the first three centuries there was no law of the Church enforcing celibacy. Clement of Alexandria speaks of married priests and deacons, and the historian Socrates refers to the married episcopate in the Eastern Churches. To this day the secular clergy in the Greek Catholic Church, that is the Church in communion with Rome, are married, though the bishops are celibates. In short, it is not a question of dogma, but solely of ecclesiastical discipline. On this particular point of discipline there exists a difference between the Church of the West and that of the East, though both are united in the acceptance of the dogma proclaiming the divine origin of the priesthood.

Having presented the evidence from Scripture and the writings of the early Fathers as to the divine origin of the priesthood and its essential powers, let us now briefly consider the dignity of the office, and the benefits which accrue to human society from its exercise. The priest is singled out by God who chooses him to be His ambassador to men. The words which Christ addressed to the Apostles after the Last Supper may be applied to all His priests: "You have not chosen Me, but I have chosen you; and have appointed you, that you should go, and should bring forth fruit; and your fruit should remain."[20] It was this same divine teaching which St. Paul reechoed when he declared to the Hebrews: "Neither doth any man take the honor to himself, but he that is called by God, as Aaron was."[21]

The priest is called by God not only into the line of Aaron, into the tribe of Levi, into the family of Samuel, into the priesthood of Melchisedech, but into the discipleship of Jesus Christ. He is made a member of that goodly company of disciples whose sound has gone forth unto the ends of the earth. Throughout nineteen hundred years they have borne the teachings of the divine Master into every race and every land from the frozen snows of the Arctic to the burning sands of the Sahara, and even unto the far-distant shores washed by the waves of the Australasian seas.

253

"Behold!" said Christ, "I am with you all days even to the consummation of the world." With these words echoing in their ears, the Apostles went out into the countries of the then known world, preaching the gospel fearlessly to every creature. They quailed not before the lions in the Roman arena, nor before the pitch and tar with which they were to be burned alive to illumine the gladiatorial contests of the Romans. Why? Because they realized that they were speaking not in their own names but in the name of Jesus Christ. Because they realized that they were His divinely appointed ambassadors, clothed by the Master with plenipotentiary power to speak and teach in His name. That is why St. Paul was able to say with truth: "Let a man so regard us as ministers of Christ and dispensers of the mysteries of God."[22]

A distinctive power of the priestly office is that of pardoning. When the priest raises aloft his right hand and pronounces the words of pardon over the sinner in the tribunal of Confession, the shackles of sin are torn from the soul of the penitent. The priest pardons as effectively as if the words fell from the lips of Christ. It is a power which transcends that of kings and emperors. The power of kings is over the bodies of men. But they stand impotent before the kingdom of the soul. The hand of the priest reaches up beyond the horizon of the sky, and with golden keys unlocks the treasury of God's mercy and forgiveness and applies them to the souls of men.

The priest preserves inviolate the secrecy of the confessional even at the cost of life itself. Under no circumstances does he ever reveal the slightest imperfection breathed into his ear in Confession. The sacrifice which every Catholic priest stands ready to make to preserve this trust inviolate is illustrated by the following historical incident. In 1899 Father Dumoulin, a French priest, was charged with the crime of murder. The sexton had murdered and robbed a wealthy woman. To throw suspicion from himself he dipped the smoking revolver in the victim's blood and placed it in Father Dumoulin's room. Then to seal the lips of the priest, he went to Confession to Father Dumoulin, accusing himself of the murder.

Circumstantial evidence pointed to the priest. Knowing how secure he was behind that sacramental seal, knowing that the priest could not open those lips to reveal the guilty person even to save his own life, the sexton gave testimony convicting the priest. He was given a sentence that was worse than death — life imprisonment at hard labor on Devil's Island under the tropical sun, whither France sends her worst criminals. Suffering the loss of his good name, the ostracism of his friends and a public ignominy that was more painful than death itself, Father Dumoulin, like the good priest he was, remained faithful to his trust.

For twenty-five years he toiled under the burning rays of the tropical sun among the outcasts of mankind, guarding ever the secret in his bosom. In those twenty-five years he saw his mother die of a broken heart, carrying to her grave the blight of her son's imprisonment. Twenty-five years of grinding convict toil had left him with gray hair, a face deeply lined, a body broken and bent, on the brink of the grave.

In a wretched hovel in a slum district in Paris a man lying on a bare cot is calling hysterically for a priest before he dies. As the priest enters, he shouts aloud: "I am guilty of the murder for which Father Dumoulin was condemned. I sealed his lips with Confession and threw the guilt on him." Unwilling to face his God with that foul crime upon his soul, he seeks forgiveness through the very agency of Confession whose inviolable secrecy he had perverted to convict an innocent priest.

What a tardy retribution that could not undo those twenty-five years of mental torture, that could not recall the dead from their graves, nor reveal to them his innocence. And yet that is precisely what every priest in Christendom would willingly undergo rather than reveal the tiniest venial sin breathed into his ear in Confession. Such is the absolute, impenetrable and inviolable secrecy with which a priest guards the contents of every Confession.

The supreme power of the priestly office is the power of consecrating. "No act is greater," says St. Thomas, "than the consecration of the body of Christ."[23] In this essential phase of the sacred ministry, the power of the priest is not surpassed by that of the bishop, the archbishop, the cardinal or the pope. Indeed it is equal to that of Jesus Christ. For in this role the priest speaks with the voice and the authority of God Himself.

When the priest pronounces the tremendous words of consecration, he reaches up into the heavens, brings Christ down from His throne, and places Him upon our altar to be offered up again as the Victim for the sins of man. It is a power greater than that of monarchs and emperors: it is greater than that of saints and angels, greater than that of Seraphim and Cherubim.

Indeed it is greater even than the power of the Virgin Mary. While the Blessed Virgin was the human agency by which Christ became incarnate a single time, the priest brings Christ down from heaven, and renders Him present on our altar as the eternal Victim for the sins of man — not once but a thousand times! The priest speaks and lo! Christ, the eternal and omnipotent God, bows his head in humble obedience to the priest's command.

Of what sublime dignity is the office of the Christian priest who is thus privileged to act as the ambassador and the vice-gerent of Christ on earth! He continues the essential ministry of Christ: he teaches the faithful with the authority of Christ, he pardons the penitent sinner with the power of Christ, he offers up again the same sacrifice of adoration and atonement which Christ offered on Calvary. No wonder that the name which spiritual writers are especially fond of applying to the priest is that of *"alter Christus."* For the priest is and should be *another Christ.*

The priesthood is a sublime ministry, more meet for angels than for weak and sinful men. Truly indeed did Isaiah proclaim with prophetic insight six hundred years before Christ the grandeur of the Christian priesthood in those inspired words: "How beautiful on the mountains are the feet of him that bringeth good tidings and that preacheth peace; of him that showeth forth good, that preacheth salvation, that saith to Sion: Thy God shall reign."[24]

Is it not apparent to every person, regardless of religious affiliation, who has followed this discussion with an open mind, that the Christian priesthood is an institution founded by Jesus Christ whereby men receive the power and authority to preach the gospel, to reconcile sinners and to offer sacrifice to the Most High? When Luther discarded the office of the priesthood, the confessional as a tribunal for the reconciliation of sinners and the altar, with its august sacrifice of the Mass, disappeared. In the churches of our separated brethren there remain but the four bare walls and a pulpit.

While the highest element of worship, the offering of sacrifice, has completely vanished, even the other elements of worship are fast disappearing. Listen to the words addressed by Dr. Edmund S. Conklin to the ministers of our country: "After no small amount of observation, reading and careful inquiry, I am forced to the conclusion that worship as a religious exercise is disappearing from Protestant Churches."[25]

Is it not apparent that this decay of worship in the Churches of our non-Catholic friends is due to their abandonment of the priestly office? Is it not also apparent that the great decline in the Church attendance deplored by ministers throughout the country is traceable to the discarding of the priesthood and the consequent disappearance of sacrifice and worship? More and more such churches are ceasing to be temples for the worship of God and are becoming lecture halls for the discussion of political, social and economic problems. But man does not live by bread alone. In the unfathomable depths of his nature, he strives now, as in the days of Cain and Abel and of Melchisedech, to offer sacrifice and worship to his God and Maker.

In the priesthood of the Catholic Church he will find a divinely established agency, through which that deep and ineradicable hunger of his nature will find adequate satisfaction. In that Church the searcher after truth will find not only preaching and prayers and the singing of hymns, but more than that — altar and priest, worship and sacrifice. For in the memory of the priest within that Church there echo the solemn words addressed by Jesus Christ to His first priests, the Apostles, at the Last Supper: "Do ye this in commemoration of Me." In faithful compliance with that divine command, the priest offers up each day in all the countries of the world the august sacrifice of the Mass, saying in the words of the psalmist: "I will take the chalice of salvation and I will call upon the name of the Lord."

Discussion Aids

What is the Sacrament of Holy Orders? When and by whom

was it first conferred? What great power was given at this first ordination? When was the second great power conferred by Christ? What third power was conferred on the Apostles by Christ? When was it given? Is this third power as distinctively a priestly power as the other two? Quote some scriptural texts showing the use of the Sacrament of Holy Orders in the Apostolic Church. What did the Council of Trent say about the Catholic hierarchy? St. Ignatius of Antioch? Why do not priests marry? Is the law of celibacy a matter of divine law or ecclesiastical discipline? Discuss the power of consecration and the necessity of this power for sacrifice, the essential act of worship.

Practices

Pray daily for *all* priests.

Distinguish between the office and the man. Honor all priests because of the powers God has conferred on them for our salvation.

When a priest visits your home ask for his blessing.

NOTES (Chapter 17)

1. Mal. 1:11
2. Lk. 22:19
3. Jn. 20:21-23
4. II Cor. 5:18-20
5. Mt. 28:19-20
6. Lk. 10:16
7. Acts 6:6
8. *Ibid.*, 13:3
9. *Ibid.*, 14:23
10. I Tm. 5:22
11. Ad Cor. 43:2
12. *Ibid.*, 44:3
13. Born 331 and died about 395
14. *Orat. in Bapt. Christi*, Migne, *Pat. Graec.*, Tom. XLV

15. *Sess.* 23, Canons 6, 7
16. *Ibid.*, 98-117
17. Ad Eph. 4:1, Migne, *Pat. Graec.*, Tom. V
18. Ad Smyr. 8:2, Migne, *Pat. Graec.*, Tom. V
19. I Cor. 7:32-33
20. Jn. 15:16
21. Heb. 5:4
22. I Cor. 4:1
23. St. Thomas, *Summa Theol.*, lib. III in Suppl., q. 40, a4, 5
24. Is. 52:7
25. E.S. Conklin, "The Disappearance of Worship," in *The Christian Century,* July 11, 1934

CHAPTER 18

Anointing of the Sick

A Sacrament Little Understood by Non-Catholics

One of the sacraments which is but little understood by those outside the Catholic Church is the Anointing of the Sick, as the following would indicate. Some years ago I listened to an exposition of the Catholic religion to a large audience in Hyde Park, London, by Mr. Francis Sheed, a leader in the work of the Catholic Evidence Guild in England. After the lecture, questions concerning any phase of the Catholic religion were invited. Whereupon one man in the crowd spoke up:

"I read in the newspaper that a Catholic priest gave Extreme Unction [as the Anointing of the Sick was then called] to a sick lady and that she died after receiving it. How can you justify such cruelty on the part of your priests?"

"What do you think the priest did when he administered Extreme Unction?" inquired Mr. Sheed.

"Well," replied the questioner, "I judged from the fact that it was *extreme* and that the lady died after getting it, that it must have been kind of a pummeling or beating."

While probably few non-Catholics in America would guess Extreme Unction to be any kind of a beating, it is equally probable that exceedingly few of them understand what it really is. Let us then consider the nature of this sacrament, its purpose, and its establishment by Jesus Christ.

The Anointing of the Sick is a sacrament in which the sick by the anointing with holy oil and the prayers of the priest, receive spiritual aid and even physical invigoration when such is conducive to their salvation. This was once called Extreme Unction, because it is administered to persons who are in extreme or grave danger of death, and is usually the last of the holy anointings administered by the Church. The first anointing is received in Baptism, and the second in Confirmation.

The Apostle, St. James, refers to this sacrament: "Is any man sick among you, let him bring in the priests of the Church, and let them pray over him, anointing him with oil in the name of the Lord, and the prayer of faith shall save the sick man and the Lord shall raise him up and if he be in sins, they shall be forgiven him."[1] In these words St. James describes the essential characteristics of a sacrament. The anointing with oil and the prayer of the priest constitute the visible sign which confers upon the soul the sanctifying grace causing the remission of sin.

The Fathers of the early Church make numerous references to this sacrament. Thus Origen (185-255) speaks of it as a complement of penance in his homily on "Leviticus," saying: "There is also a remission of sins through penitence, when the sinner . . . is not ashamed to declare his sin to the priest of the Lord, and to seek a remedy . . . wherein that also is fulfilled which the Apostle James saith: 'But if any be sick among you, let him call in the priests of the Church, and let them impose hands on him, anointing him with oil in the name of the Lord.' "[2]

In his treatise on the priesthood,[3] St. John Chrysostom draws a comparison between the power of priests and that of parents. "Our parents beget us into this life," he writes, "and the priests unto the other. Parents, moreover, can neither ward off bodily death from us, nor repulse impending disease. But priests often heal the soul when it is sick and about to perish, rendering milder the punishment of some and preventing others altogether from falling and doing this not by teaching only, but by the aid of prayer. And not only when they regenerate us (Baptism) do they pardon our sins, but they also have power to forgive sins committed afterwards: For St. James says: 'Is any one sick among you,' " etc. Since the Anointing of the Sick remits sin, it must have been instituted not by the Church but by Christ who alone can confer sanctifying grace.

In a letter written in 416 to Decentius, Bishop of Gubbio,

Pope Innocent I cites the words of St. James to prove that the Anointing of the Sick is a sacrament on a par with Penance and the Eucharist. He further states that while the oil is to be blessed solely by the bishop, the sacrament can be administered by either priests or bishops and that it remits sin.

The Sacramentary of Serapion, Bishop of Thmuis in Egypt, was written in the first quarter of the fourth century. In this liturgical ritual there is found a prayer for the blessing of the oil of the sick, which shows that the sacrament was administered in those early days as in our own for its healing effect upon both soul and body. It reads as follows: "We invoke Thee . . . Father of our Savior Jesus Christ, and we pray that Thou wilt send a healing power of the Only Begotten from heaven upon this oil, that it may become for those anointed . . . a casting out of every disease, an antidote against every demon . . . good grace and the remission of sins, a medicine of life and safety, health and integrity of soul, body and spirit, a perfect strengthening."[4]

In the West the Gelasian Sacramentary (735) and the Gregorian Sacramentary (795) both contain prayers for the blessing of the oil of the sick. They beseech God not only "to heal all the sick person's ills, but also to have mercy on all his iniquities; that he may feel Thy medicine not only in his body but also in his soul." These liturgical rituals of both East and West afford an authentic insight into the teaching and practice of the early Church; for the prayers of the Church constitute an unfailing index of her belief.

It should be noted too that the Greek Church which separated from the Roman Catholic Church in the ninth century is equally insistent upon the sacramental character of the Anointing of the Sick. In its profession of faith, it states: "The seventh Sacrament is [the Anointing of the Sick], prescribed by Christ; for, after He had begun to send His disciples two and two,[5] they anointed and healed many, which unction the Church has since maintained by pious usage, as we learn from the Epistle of St. James: 'Is any man sick among you,' etc. The fruits proper to this Sacrament, as St. James declares, are the remission of sins, health of soul, strength — in fine, of body. But though it does not always produce this last result, it always, at least, restores the soul to a better state by the forgiveness of sins."

All the other Oriental churches, some of which separated from Rome as far back as the fifth century, likewise list the Anointing of the Sick among their seven sacraments. Does not such identity of doctrine, proclaimed for so many centuries by churches widely separated, offer unmistakable evidence of its apostolic origin? Is it not also convincing proof that this sacrament was instituted by no other than by Jesus Christ, the divine Founder of the Christian religion?

The sacrament of the Anointing of the Sick is administered to those who are dangerously ill, by anointing them on the forehead and hands with olive oil, or, if necessary, with another vegetable oil, properly blessed, and saying once only the following words: "Through this holy anointing and His most loving mercy, may the Lord assist you by the grace of the Holy Spirit, so that, when you have been freed from your sins, He may save you and in His goodness raise you up."

In case of necessity, however, it is sufficient that a single anointing be given on the forehead or, because of the particular condition of the sick person, on another more suitable part of the body, the whole formula being pronounced. This sacrament can be repeated if the sick person having once received the anointing, recovers and then again falls sick, or if, in the course of the same illness, the danger becomes more acute.

The chief effects of the sacrament, as enumerated by the Council of Trent, are the conferring of grace, the remission of sins, and the alleviation of the sick. "This effect," declares the Council, "is the grace of the Holy Spirit, whose unction blots out sins, and alleviates and strengthens the soul of the sick person, by exciting in him a great confidence in the divine mercy, sustained by which he bears more lightly the troubles and sufferings of disease, and more easily resists temptations ... and sometimes, when it is expedient for his soul's salvation, recovers bodily health."

Its primary effect is the conferring of the grace of fortitude, its secondary effect is the remission of sin. Being a sacrament of the living, it supposes the recipient to be free from mortal sin but if the sick man be in grievous sins, is unable to confess them, and has only imperfect sorrow for them, it also remits them.

This sacrament should not be deferred until the last moment when the patient is unconscious. It should be administered while the patient is conscious and able to unite his prayers with those of the priest. Its conferring does not necessarily indicate that the person is about to die: it should be remembered that one of its purposes is to assist the patient to recover his health. If we do not hesitate to call in the physician to minister to the needs of the body, why should we hesitate to call in the priest who ministers to the needs of both body and soul? "For surely a spiritual medicine," says Cardinal Gibbons, "which diminishes the terrors of death, comforts the dying Christian, fortifies the soul in its final struggle, and purifies it for its passage from time to eternity, should be gratefully and eagerly made use of especially when prescribed by an inspired Physician."

There is a touching picture which the evangelist, St. John, draws for us of a scene which occurred on the hillsides of Galilee. With His disciples the Master has just come from Judea into Galilee when he is met by a certain ruler. He is a high officer of Herod Antipas, tetrarch of Galilee. His heart is torn with grief, for his son lies at home in Capharnaum at the point of death.

Though not one of the followers of the Savior, he has heard of the wonderful cures He has wrought in Judea and Samaria, healing the sick, restoring sight to the blind, hearing to the deaf, cleansing the leper, curing the halt and the lame. Stranger that he is, his paternal solicitude for his dying son thrusts him into the Master's presence, as he cries out in words of poignant yearning: "Lord, come down before that my son die." How tenderly Jesus turns to him with the consoling words: "Go thy way, thy son liveth."

With the haunting melody of the Master's mercy reverberating in the memory of the race, mankind has for nineteen centuries turned its wistful eyes to the Savior, and at the imminence of death has reechoed the age-old cry of the ruler of ancient Galilee: "Lord, come down before that my son die." For nineteen hundred years the Master has been answering that cry by soothing the feverish brow of the sick and giving strength and courage to the dying in the sacrament of the Anointing of the Sick. It is the divinely established means for conveying the clemency and succor of the Savior to the sick and the dying.

Many years ago I had occasion to assist a pastor in the mining region of Pennsylvania at the Christmas season. After the Mass on Christmas morning a sick call came. I answered it for the elderly pastor. It took me to a little cottage where a father lay dying. For twenty-five years he had labored in the black pits of the mines, and as sometimes happens, the air laden with the fine dust of the coal had coated his lungs so that he was dying from what is known as "miner's consumption."

His face was haggard and drawn with suffering, in his deep-set eyes one saw a look of sadness tinged with latent rebellion against his lot. One heard the merry jingle of sleigh bells outside, the cheery echoing of Christmas carols, spreading their message of Yuletide joy and gladness far and wide. Through the window one saw the people passing by, with their arms loaded with Christmas presents, greeting one another with a "Merry Christmas."

Father," he said, "it doesn't seem that I'm getting a square deal. Others are happy with their Christmas joy, while I'm being pulled down to the grave with this hacking cough in my chest."

I spoke to him as best I could of the mercy and the love of God and of His ability to compensate for the inequalities of happiness here. Then I relied upon the sacraments to accomplish that for which my words were all too feeble. After hearing his confession and giving him the Holy Viaticum, I anointed him with the holy oils and gave him the last blessing. While imparting the blessing, and having him repeat after me the words: "Lord, here burn, here cut, but spare me for eternity," I noticed that a new fervor crept into his voice, and a look of peace and serenity softened the hard lines of his face.

As I was about to go, he clasped my hand with a rugged tenderness.

"Father," he said, pointing to the people outside hurrying to the church, "they are going to see the Christmas crib on the altar, aren't they? But soon I may be able to see the Christ Child Himself."

Only the hand of God extended through the sacrament of the anointing could effect a transformation as touching as it was inspiring. Only the life-giving grace of the sacraments that tap the infinite treasury of the divine exchequer could infuse such a transmuting sweetness into the rebellious souls of men.

The devastating hand of death comes to ravage every fireside and to snuff at last the breath from every mortal. But death is robbed of its sting and the grave of its victory by this consoling sacrament of the Anointing of the Sick, which infuses the divine strength into the dying children of men. It comes with its unfailing reinforcement at the greatest crisis in human life. The sacrament of the Anointing of the Sick is the stretching forth of the hand of God from the regions of the other world across the desert of time and space, seeking to clasp our weary hand in His to guide us gently and sweetly up out of the valley of darkness and death to the beautiful sun-kissed mountain peaks of the everlasting and eternal day.

Discussion Aids

What is the Anointing of the Sick? Where do we find it mentioned in the New Testament? Give the testimony of some of the early Fathers on the Anointing of the Sick; of the Liturgy. When may the Anointing of the Sick not be administered even though there is imminent danger of death? What are the effects of this sacrament?

Practices

Always have on hand the articles necessary for a priest's visit in case of serious illness, and have the table prepared for his call.

If you witness an accident make it your business to summon a priest if the injured person is a Catholic.

NOTES (Chapter 18)

1. Jas. 5:15
2. *Homil.*, 2:43, Migne, *Pat. Graec.*, Tom. XII
3. John Chrysostom, *Lib. 3 de Sacred*, Migne, *Pat Graec.*, Tom. XLVIII

4. *Dictionnaire d'Archaeologie et Liturgie,* v. 1032 (Letouzy et Ane, Paris, 1924)
5. Mk. 6:7-13

PART IV

The Church and Marriage
Guidance in the Quest for Happiness

CHAPTER 19

Courtship and Marriage

Falling in love is an experience which comes to every youth. Usually it comes when youth is at the threshold of young manhood or womanhood: the tender emotions which have been simmering during adolescence flame into raging love when youth singles out from among all young women the sweetheart whom he hopes to win as his partner on the journey through life. Around that experience cluster memories that will bring the fragrance and bloom of spring to the sere and yellow leaf of his autumn. Upon that choice hinge consequences that will stretch to the journey's end — and beyond.

Because that choice is made while the emotions are pounding sledgehammer blows upon his heart, youth stands at this time in particular need of guidance. Emotions tend to disturb the even functioning of the mind. They speak a language of their own — the language of love; but into that language, the voice of reason must creep and make itself heard. Love is proverbially blind: only intelligence can give it eyes.

Happy indeed is the youth who while listening to the soft whisperings of love, still keeps his foot on the ground and keeps at least one ear attuned to the voice of reason. Youth makes love in the parlor, but he must not forget the practicalities of the kitchen. The eyes of youth tend to rest content upon the beauty of the face of his sweetheart, but he must learn to penetrate to the disposition and character with which he must live when the bloom of skin has long since vanished.

We do not seek to throw cold water on love's young dream: we want to see it come true; we wish to see the radiant happiness of sweethearts blossom into the mature love of husband and wife and reach the crowning glory of fatherhood and mother-hood. We want to see the shining castle of their dreams materi-alize into the sanctuary of the Christian home, where love, peace and happiness abide. We want their home to be a little bit of heaven here below, a harbinger of that eternal home where love enraptures the soul with an ecstasy that never dies.

How can youth's dream be realized? By hearkening to the advice and guidance of our Holy Mother, the Church. She speaks to youth with the accents of the divine: no merely theoretical message does she bring, but one laden with the rich experience of the centuries.

She has listened at the altar as millions of young couples plighted their deathless troth; she has listened to the stories of domestic tragedies and has seen eyes heavy with tears; she has fought against the lust of kings in protection of the sanctity of Christian marriage and the permanence of the Christian home. Better than any institution in the world, the Church can guide youth safely along that dangerous path, strewn with a thousand pitfalls, that leads to the threshold of a happy marriage and into the fireside of a Christian home.

Pointing out that marriage is indissoluble except by death, the Church warns young people to be on their guard against the factors which make for separation and divorce. One of the chief causes is that the couple discovers after marriage that they are mismated. When the dreamland of their honeymoon has yielded to the realities of a workaday world, they begin to perceive what a blind man could have pointed out to them before: that they have little in common.

They are uncongenial in temperament and disposition, they differ in moral character and in religious outlook, they vary in culture and in tastes. The delicate bonds which spring from congeniality in these fields and remain intact, even after mere sentiment has largely shot its bolt, are lacking. Association first loses it charm, then its interest: boredom sets in and finally yields to chafing and aversion. The divorce court has new grist for its mills.

Why do not young people perceive these facts before it is too late? Why do so many of them make no honest effort to explore beforehand those important qualities of mind and character without which any union rests only on the quicksands of capricious sentiment?

A young man seeks to court a girl because of the texture and color of her skin, the radiance of her eyes, the contour of her face, and other superficial items; but character, disposition, intelligence, understanding, sympathy and unselfishness are the things which count in making for the happiness of the home and the permanence of the union.

While beauty and good looks are not to be disparaged, the qualities of mind, heart and soul just mentioned are far more valuable. The delicate coloring of the skin changes, the beauty of the complexion vanishes, but character remains. It grows in strength and beauty and unselfishness with the passing years. The man who seeks to build the citadel of his conjugal happiness upon such gossamer threads as complexion and appearance, with scant attention to moral character and disposition, often finds out later that he has neglected the important item of a solid foundation. True happiness is seldom found in a fool's paradise.

The Church urges young people to select their helpmates for life with due regard to the important requisites for a happy and enduring union. She warns them in advance that they will pay a heavy penalty for negligence, for impetuosity, for rashness in this matter. Before she admits candidates to the priesthood, she requires them to spend long years in training and discipline, meditating all the while on the seriousness of the step they contemplate. Yet Holy Orders imposes no obligation of greater duration than that imposed by matrimony. The consequences of both last until death. Why then should not candidates for matrimony bestow at least a small measure of the care and consideration demanded of those who are called to aspire to the sacred ministry?

The simple truth is that all the voices of earth and sky and heaven thunder in the ear of the young person contemplating marriage to make sure of the presence of those qualities of mind and heart and soul which alone can guarantee lasting happiness for his union. While the heart may flutter on the wings of love, he should keep his feet on the solid ground of reality, listen to the voice of reason, and look carefully whither he is about to leap. In every domain of human life, the use of reason yields a rich premium, its neglect a heavy penalty. In no field, however, is the premium richer or the penalty heavier than in the choice of a partner for all the years of one's life.

Prudence suggests that before making so momentous a choice, the advice of parents and of other sensible persons of experience should be sought. Before making an investment of consequence, a prudent person will secure the council of other parties, better informed and more experienced than himself. While such council is by no means infallible, at least it greatly lessens the hazards involved. When a person is about to invest his whole life with its hopes of enduring happiness, why should he not at least consult wise and judicious counsellors about the momentous choice he is contemplating?

The tendency of young people to confide in no one about their engagement, and to keep the whole affair a secret until after the marriage, closes the door to many helpful influences which would at least lessen the danger of an obviously unwise choice. No other decision which a person is ever called upon to make involves consequences of a further-reaching character than that entailed in the selection of a helpmate for life. Does it not follow, therefore, that here above all other places, a young person should exhaust all prudence and the common sense he possesses to see that he does not make a fatal error?

Older persons will recall the words of a ditty, popular a generation ago, but voicing the question in the minds of many in this day as well:

Will some one kindly tell me,
Will some one let me know,
How I picked a lemon in the garden of love
Where I thought only peaches grow.

If the person asking this question afterwards had only consulted sensible friends beforehand, he would have found an abundant answer to the query he asks now — all too late. Life knows no adequate substitute for prudence and practical common sense.

Some of my readers may feel inclined at this point to say: "Yes, what you say is true. Young people should use prudence and reason in choosing a life partner. But are you not insisting at needless length upon so obvious a truism?" The fact is, however, that this truth, so readily admitted in theory, is frequently ignored in practice. Thousands upon thousands of marriages occur each year and end shortly in the divorce courts. Why? Simply because young people insist upon throwing reason overboard, and refuse to consider the factors indispensable for a stable union and enduring happiness.

Why do so many lament afterwards: "If I had only stopped to think! If I had listened to my heart, I would have perceived how blind and how foolish I was! Oh, if I were only free to make the choice over again, I would not be such a fool."

What pastor has not heard this refrain with too tragic frequency? Indeed, it is not too much to say that if young people used prudence and common sense, consulted wise and judicious friends, explored the item of congeniality in matters other than sentiment, made sure of the character, disposition, reliability, and religious outlook of the person involved, the vast majority of unfortunate marriages ending in disaster would have been avoided.

It is one thing to know a truth: it is a different thing to practice it. It is narrated that in his old age St. John preached with great frequency the simple truth, "My little children, love one another." When some of his hearers complained of the tiresome monotony of its continued repetition, the beloved disciple replied in effect: "Little else matters, for if you observe this precept, you will observe the others as well." If St. John were less charitable he would probably have replied: "I will continue to preach this truth until you begin to practice it." The Church never wearies of pointing out to her children the supreme importance of exercising the greatest care in the selection of a partner for life.

One of the dangers which the Church warns against is that of excessive haste. Her law requiring the proclamation of the banns on three Sundays preceding the wedding serves as a brake against too precipitate action. Judges who preside at divorce courts have repeatedly voiced the conviction that a large percentage of the cases appearing before them are traceable to excessive haste. A young man takes a sudden fancy to a girl; it is probably kindled by her complexion, her contour, or the radiance of her eyes. Infatuation, but not love, comes at first sight. A whirlwind courtship ends in a sudden elopement; they awake from the honeymoon to discover they are as different from one another as day is from night. The divorce court will not be idle long.

As a result of their observations, jurists have frequently sounded the tocsin against precipitate speed in rushing into marriage. They have urged the enactment of laws requiring individuals to register their intention to wed, and then to wait for a certain length of time before the marriage could occur. The idea is that in the required interval the ardor of many mismated couples would cool down, and allow them to see each other with the eyes of reason and not merely through the rose-colored lens of inflamed emotions. The garish light of day reveals a multitude of imperfections, glaring and strident, but glossed over by the magic of the moonlight, calling forth dreams of high romance. In the effort to stem the flood of such ill-considered unions, some states have already enacted laws along the lines suggested above.

In a class in sociology at Columbia University the late Professor F. H. Giddings was pointing out the urgent need for some such brake upon the too precipitate speed of couples eager to act in haste, only to repent at leisure. Whereupon a Catholic student explained the Church's law in regard to the proclamation of the banns. The explanation evoked from Professor Giddings the following interesting observation: "Aside entirely from its religious implications, I want to commend highly the social utility of such a law. As a professor of sociology, I am convinced that if such a law were enacted in every state in the Union, it would enable a vast number of mismated couples to discover their uncongeniality before they rushed headlong into the marital contract only to clutter up the docket of the divorce court later on." This law of the Church is therefore a safeguard for marriage, not only in its sacramental character, but also as an institution that plays a vital role in the welfare of human society.

While the Church warns against courtships of undue brevity, she likewise counsels against those of excessive length. No hard and fast rule can be laid down determining the exact length of courtship: in general, it should be of sufficient duration to allow young people to know the character and disposition of each other quite well. This can usually be done in a period ranging from six months to a year.

Being a period of stress and strain in many respects, courtship should not be unduly protracted. Persons who keep company for many years are without the sustaining influence of the Sacrament of Matrimony, and are exposed to much danger. A courtship too long drawn out wears away the glamour and leads many a promising romance to the rocks.

The function of courtship is to enable young people to know one another sufficiently well to embark together on life's voyage. But where no such end is anticipated, courtship has little or no meaning. Courtship may be compared to a porch, over which people walk to reach the door of the home. What would one think of people who entered upon the porch and proceeded to remain there indefinitely, just as though they were unaware that it was not intended as the terminal, but merely as the entrance to the home proper? Similar is the state of those who, having entered upon courtship, forget that it is not the end but merely the means to the end, merely the vestibule leading to the great sacrament.

The following incident is related of the famous American

humorist, Bill Nye. As a young man he called one Sunday afternoon upon his lady friend to take her for a buggy ride. He waited in the parlor for what seemed to him a young eternity — probably a matter of an hour. At last the young lady appeared groomed with meticulous nicety. She had just opened the door, preparatory to descending to the waiting surrey, when her eyes fell upon the lean and patient horse.

"What!" she exclaimed indignantly. "Do you expect me to ride behind such a skinny nag?"

"But, my dear," replied Bill Nye, "when I came here this afternoon that was a fat horse."

Young men at times draw out courtship to such unending length, that the lady would be justified in paralleling the reflection of the American humorist by saying: "When you first began to keep company with me, I was a young girl. Now I am almost a middle-aged woman." The simple fact is that a grievous injustice can be done to the girl by monopolizing her attention for several years, depriving her of many other opportunities, and then when her youthful charm has waned, walking out. It is neither chivalrous nor honorable: neither is it fair nor just. When courtship is being protracted to unseemly length, the father of the girl should inquire of the young man what his intentions are — and incidentally what is the reason for the long delay.

In America we carry to extremes the idea that marriage is an affair that concerns only the two individuals involved. If parents are genuinely interested in the happiness of their daughter, why should they not manifest that solicitude in the honest and effective manner just mentioned? In the countries of Europe parents take a much more active part in assisting their children in forming suitable unions. They view the matter with less sentiment, perhaps, but with much more practical common sense. The time has come in America, with its divorce rate mounting higher than practically any other country in the civilized world, when parents and pastors must take an increasing interest in assisting young people in the successful solution of the most crucial problem life presents to them — the choice of a helpmate for life.

In common with all mankind, young people are engaged in the endless quest for happiness; but happiness is not a private or a solitary affair. Suppose that we say to an individual: "Here is a thousand dollars. Go and buy happiness for yourself alone. You must not seek it, however, in the friendship and love of other people." We would be assigning to him an end, but would be forbidding him the only effective means of achieving it. Why? Because happiness is a social affair: it is found in the esteem and friendship and love of others. Like the moon which shines by reflected light, happiness is found in the reflection of the sympathy, trust and affection of others. Wealth, knowledge and fame are no adequate substitutes for the latter, and hence cannot bring true happiness.

Among the worst miseries of life is that of unrelieved loneliness. To go to one's dwelling at evening, only to find it empty of any person interested in your struggle, rejoicing in your achievements, softening the sting of defeat with the balm of sympathy and understanding, is to live in a darkened chamber whither the sunshine of human comradeship and love scarcely penetrates. As other forms of life, when deprived of the sun's rays wither and die, so human life, robbed of the sunshine of love and sympathy, loses its zest, its enthusiasm and its vigor. Love is the radiance which brightens the world of human life with the sunshine of happiness. Francis William Bourdillon expressed a profound truth when he wrote in lines of simple beauty:

> The night has a thousand eyes,
>   And the day but one
> Yet the light of the bright world dies
>   With the dying sun.
> The mind has a thousand eyes,
>   And the heart but one
> Yet the light of a whole life dies
>   When love is done.

Not long ago a young man, receiving instruction in the Catholic faith, said to the writer: "Father, when the clock in our bank registered four o'clock, I was always at my wit's end to devise ways of passing the two hours till dinner time. After I married and God blessed us with a little babe, I could scarcely wait for the clock to reach four, so anxious was I to get home to be with my wife and child. The Church's emphasis upon the finding of happiness at the fireside of the home is well placed. I had sought happiness before," he continued, "in the forms of entertainment which engage the attention of single men, but now that I have tasted the great joys of conjugal love and fatherhood, I can truthfully say that I am just beginning to live. Until a man has partaken of these two great experiences, he doesn't know the meaning or purpose of human life." In these words every pastor of souls will perceive the refrain whispered in his ear times without number by young men and women who have hearkened to that divine voice calling them to life's great adventure.

Love, courtship and marriage are so often treated in a spirit of levity, and are made the butt of so many jokes, that it is worthwhile to point out that they are part of a divine plan. This is made clear to us by the scene that is disclosed at the very dawn of human existence. After Almighty God had created the universe and all living things thereon, He placed man in the Garden of Paradise, and gave to him dominion over all living creatures.

Sovereign of Paradise that he was, richer than any mortal man in material wealth and in the chaste beauty of nature's virgin landscape, there still remained, in spite of it all, a void and an emptiness that rested like a somber pall upon his lonely heart. Then out of the heavens the voice of Almighty God is heard: "It is not good for man to be alone: let Us make him a help like unto himself."[1]

When Adam gazes upon the face of Eve, his eyes behold a new beauty and a loveliness which nothing in all the vast pageantry of nature can duplicate or rival. The emptiness in his heart vanishes: in its place he feels a new and a strange emotion never felt before. The prosaic coloring of the flowers is suddenly transformed into a gorgeous pageant of poetic beauty; the meaningless chirping of the birds is transmuted into a symphony of moving melody. Life takes on a new meaning, a fresh significance. Now for the first time he sees the beauty and the poetry and the romance of human existence.

Moved by a divine impulse, he plights his deathless troth to Eve. There under the arching vault of the virginal sky, in the morning of life, in the presence of the priesthood of nature, Adam seals his vow with the first kiss of love. With prophetic vision into the unwritten future, God proclaims the law for all mankind: "Wherefore a man shall leave father and mother, and shall cleave to his wife, and they shall be two in one flesh." It is the great mystery of human love which makes two hearts beat as one. It is a sacred flame for it is kindled by a spark from the eternal and uncreated love of God.

"It is not good for man to be alone." How often the words of Almighty God, uttered at the dawn of the race's history, come back to the priest, as he sits for long hours in the tribunal of Confession, listening to the sins of men and women journeying along over life's highway. How vividly he comes to realize the meaning of that divine admonition. No one can realize more clearly than the priest of God, to whom are unbosomed the secrets of hearts, the dangers, pitfalls, and tragedies that beset the path of the lonely traveler.

God created a helpmate like unto himself to be a companion for man, a promoter of his happiness and a protector of his virtue. The Sacrament of Matrimony is, therefore, a great source of mutual consolation, as it is a great safeguard for the virtue of both men and women. That is why the confessor often has occasion to point to the Sacrament of Matrimony as an invaluable spiritual prophylactic and an important aid in the attainment of one's eternal salvation.

Aside entirely, however, from its spiritual succor, matrimony is among the most potent influences in the development of the human personality to its manifold perfections and in the promotion of human happiness. As the bud on the rosebush reaches its full bloom only by opening its petals, shedding its perfumed fragrance on the passing zephyrs and dying to itself in the full-blown blush of its mature beauty, so human character is spiritualized and rendered beautiful and unselfish by losing itself in ministering to others.

Fashioned by the Almighty hand as the complement to man's incomplete nature, woman has been endowed by God with that divine forgetfulness of self that finds its happiness in ministering to the happiness of man. She increases the joy of victory and softens the sting of defeat: she is his inspiration in success and his comforter in the dark hours of adversity. From the time that Eve came to dispel the void and loneliness in the heart of Adam to the time that Mary stood weeping at the foot of the Cross, when the Apostles themselves had fled, down to the present hour when womanhood embodies in richer measure the virtues of chastity and unselfishness, woman has been the crowning glory of God's creative power.

Out of the union of these diverse natures, man with his aggressive strength, woman with her tender sympathy, is born in the Sacrament of Matrimony the Christian home. It is the cornerstone of human society, a sanctuary of conjugal fidelity, before whose tabernacle there burns the vigil light of a deathless love. How carefully the Church rears about that sanctuary its loftiest fortifications and guards it against the invasion of a profane intruder. How the happiest and the holiest of our memories cluster about the fireside of the home!

If some wealthy philanthropist were to promise to bestow upon a young man, upon reaching maturity, the gift of a million dollars, how delighted he would be! Yet Providence stands ready to confer upon every young man on reaching maturity an even greater gift. The reader may feel inclined to say: "Surely, that is an exaggeration, a figure of speech." Let us see. When Joseph Grogan had been working for three years after graduation from college, in spite of his boon companions, his parties and dances, he began to feel the shallowness and emptiness of it all.

It was an echo of that primeval hunger that gnawed at the bosom of his first father, Adam, alone in the Garden of Eden, and that still reverberates in the breasts of all his progeny. Joe felt the need of an incentive to urge him on to greater success, someone to inspire him toward a loftier ideal. One day he revealed his discontent to the priest in Confession. His confessor pointed to the Sacrament of Matrimony as the agency divinely established to fill that void in the hearts of men: Joe saw the sacrament now in a new light.

In this serious quest, he passed over the social butterflies with their painted faces, tempting dress, and languishing eyes. "They're all right," Joe said, "to while away an idle hour with, but they're giddy and empty." They begin to pall after a while because they do not stir the deeper spiritual elements in man's nature. They kindle no noble thoughts nor holy resolves to fire the soul of man to higher things, for it is the subtle *after-echo* that tells the true-value companionship. For a helpmate through life he wanted not mere gossamer, capricious as the changing winds. He wanted something more substantial to weather not merely the gentle zephyrs of spring but the storms of life's winter as well.

At last Joe found her, a lovely Catholic girl, unselfish in disposition, with a moral character that caused him to think only noble thoughts and breathe holy resolves. When the priest joined them in the deathless union of the sacrament at a nuptial Mass, Joe and Mary tasted the sweetest happiness that God grants to man in this vale of tears. Then God blessed their union with that most wonderful of all his gifts, a little angel in human flesh. Joe understood now the romance and the mystery of life; that little babe bound those hearts still more closely together in a blessed trinity of love. Mary was not only his wife now, but the mother of his child as well; he loved her with a love as strong as life itself. In that sanctuary of the home, a tabernacle of holy love, Joe came as near to that celestial paradise as earth can ever go.

Then out of a clear sky, the sombre pall of a critical illness falls upon Mary. For days she hovers between life and death. Dazed, Joe watches at her bedside, night and day, praying with a fervor never known before. A tear steals into his eye as with broken voice he prays: "Spare her, O God, and do anything Thou wilt with me instead." Go to Joe as he stands there and ask him what he would take to part with the gift God had given to him upon receiving the Sacrament of Matrimony.

Would Joe part with her for a million dollars, aye, for the Presidency of the United States? Not for all the gold in Solomon's mines, not for the Presidency of the United States, not for the glitter of kingly thrones would Joe part with her who was all that life meant to him. All these things were but as dross without the love which gave to life its meaning. God hearkened to his prayer, and in granting it, He gave Joe the most precious thing in human life.

That is the gift which Almighty God stands ready to bestow upon every young man who proves himself worthy of the great

Sacrament of Matrimony — the love of a good and virtuous girl. For the flame of love that burns in the bosom of sweethearts is kindled by no human hand but by a spark from the love that is eternal and divine. That is the gift which transformed the ennui of Eden into a garden of happiness for Adam, and which still transmutes for all his progeny the toil of life into a labor of love. It is God's perfect gift to man.

The sophistication of the twentieth century has not rendered superfluous nor out-of-date the warning of the Most High, uttered at the dawn of human history: "It is not good for man to be alone."

Discussion Aids

Why is common sense so important a factor in choosing a life partner? What is to be said in comparing the preparation for Holy Orders and for Matrimony? Should advice of parents and other advisers be sought by those preparing for marriage? Discuss the value of prudence of choice as a preventive of divorce. What danger is averted by the publication of banns? What is to be said of unduly long courtships? With what danger and injustice are they beset? Discuss love, courtship and marriage in the light of the divine plan. Discuss marriage as a mutual consolation, safeguard, and development of personality.

Practices

Make courtship a prayerful affair, commending yourselves to the special protection of the Blessed Mother and St. Joseph.

Talk freely and seriously with parents or other capable advisers early in your friendship with the opposite sex.

NOTES (Chapter 19)

1. Gn. 2:18

CHAPTER 20

Why No Divorce?

The Church Defends the Sanctity of the Family

"Why does the Catholic Church forbid divorce?" is a question frequently asked by our dear non-Catholic fellow citizens. Witnessing the spectacle of one out of about four marriages contracted in the United States ending in the divorce courts, our separated brethren often wonder why the Church has never wavered in her historic stand against divorce. Their wonderment increases when they behold their own ministers officiating at the marriages of persons who have been married two and three times previously.

In order to present the fundamental grounds for the Church's unswerving opposition to divorce it is necessary first of all to point out that the Church regards the union of two Christians, that is, two baptized people, as constituting not only a civil contract but also a sacrament instituted by Christ. This conception immediately removes the marriage of Christians from the exclusive jurisdiction of the civil authority and places it, at least in its religious aspect, under that of Christ and His Church. To the religious authority, therefore, it belongs to declare the conditions under which a sacrament may be validly received.

One word then about the sacramental character of matrimony. In his letter to the Ephesians, St. Paul refers to marriage as "a great sacrament," declaring that he speaks "in Christ and in the Church."[1] St. Augustine, writing in the fourth century, reflects the universal belief of the infant Church, in his insistence upon its sacramental character. "It is certain," he writes, "that not fecundity only, the fruit of which consists of offspring, nor chastity only, whose bond is fidelity, but also that a Sacrament is recommended to believers in wedlock when the Apostle says, 'Husbands, love your wives, even as Christ also loved the Church.' Of this Sacrament the substance undoubtedly is that the man and the woman who are joined together in wedlock, should remain inseparable as long as they live."[2]

Further confirmation of the universal belief of the Christian Church up to the time of the Reformation in the sacramental character of matrimony is found in the creed of the churches of the East, such as those of the Nestorians, Monophysites, Copts and Jacobites. Although separated from the Mother Church since the first five centuries, the rituals of these churches bear witness to their inclusion of matrimony among the seven sacraments. When the professors of Tubingen University in the sixteenth century sought to win the Greek Church to the creed of the Reformers, the Greek patriarch, Jeremias, indignantly scouted their suggestion that his church could ever be won to their doctrine of but two sacraments. Testifying to the unvarying belief of the Oriental Church in the seven sacraments, including matrimony, he terminated their overtures with a scornful refusal. Thus eloquently do the voices of Christian tradition testify to the sacramental character of matrimony. Like all the other sacraments, it too was instituted by Christ.

Let us now proceed to answer the question: Why does the Church forbid divorce? The answer is simple: *because Christ forbade it*. As the institution founded by our divine Savior and commanded to teach His doctrines, the Church could sanction divorce only by being faithless to the command of Christ. To distinguish divorce from mere legal separation, we shall use the term in this discussion in the sense in which it is commonly understood by our non-Catholic friends, as a severance of the marriage bond with the consequent freedom of being able to marry again.

That our Lord forbade divorce is explicitly recorded by three evangelists and is corroborated by St. Paul. When the Pharisees asked Christ: "Is it lawful for a man to put away his wife for every cause?" He answered them: "Have you not read,

283

that He who made man from the beginning, made them male and female? For this cause shall a man leave father and mother, and shall cleave to his wife, and they shall be two in one flesh. Therefore now they are not two, but one flesh. What therefore God hath joined together, let no man put asunder."

When they persisted: "Why then did Moses command to give a bill of divorce, and to put away?" Christ replied: "Because Moses by reason of the hardness of your heart permitted you to put away your wives: but from the beginning it was not so. And I say to you, that whosoever shall put away his wife, except it be for fornication, and shall marry another, committeth adultery; and he that shall marry her that is put away, committeth adultery."[3]

The inference has been drawn by some of our dear non-Catholic friends that when a wife has been guilty of adultery, her husband may not only put her away but may marry another. Such an inference, however, is unfounded; for Christ declares without any limitation: "He that shall marry her that is put away, committeth adultery." This can be true only on the supposition that the previous marriage remained intact, even though the husband has separated from his wife because of her infidelity. Hence, the meaning of Christ's answer to the Pharisees is: In case of infidelity to her marriage vows, a husband may separate from his wife, but if he contracts a new marriage he himself becomes an adulterer.

That such is the correct interpretation of our Savior's teaching is confirmed by St. Mark and St. Luke. St. Mark records it thus: "When his disciples asked him concerning the same thing, He said to them: Whosoever shall put away his wife and marry another, committeth adultery against her. And if the wife shall put away her husband, and be married to another, she committeth adultery."[4] The statement of St. Luke is similarly comprehensive. Addressing the Pharisees, Christ said: "Every one that putteth away his wife, and marrieth another, committeth adultery."[5]

From both these texts, which refer directly to the marriage of separated parties, it is evident that Christ makes no exception whatsoever. In the clearest and most absolute terms He declares that though separation is allowed for the grave reason mentioned, remarriage during the lifetime of the other party is never permitted, but constitutes the sin of adultery. When Christ made the solemn and impressive proclamation, "What therefore God hath joined together, let no man put asunder," He made the marriage bond indissoluble henceforth by any human power.

To this teaching of Christ concerning the indissolubility of the matrimonial bond, St. Paul bears witness. Writing to the Corinthians, he admonishes them that this doctrine is not of his invention but is the teaching of Christ Himself. "To them that are married," he writes, *"not I but the Lord commandeth,* that the wife depart not from her husband. And if she depart, that she remain unmarried, or be reconciled to her husband."[6]

These words of the great Apostle of the Gentiles should be placed conspicuously before the eyes of the American people today; for it must be admitted that large numbers of people, even many calling themselves Christians, no longer regard marriage as indissoluble save by death. They look upon it in much the same light as any other civil contract which is voidable at the option of the contracting parties. While it is easy to understand how such a view could be held by non-Christians, it is difficult to understand how those who profess to adhere to the teachings of Christ can at the same time hold a view explicitly condemned by the Founder of the Christian religion.

Do they not need to have repeated to them today the warning words which St. Paul addressed to the Christian colony at Corinth nineteen centuries ago, "Not I but the Lord commandeth"? The doctrine of the absolute indissolubility of the bond of Christian marriage is not the invention of the Apostles, of the councils or pontiffs of the Church, or of any man, but the plain unmistakable teaching of Jesus Christ Himself. Because the Catholic Church believes in Christ and seeks to honor and reverence Him, she holds today, as she has held throughout the centuries, to His teaching concerning the sanctity and the permanence of Christian marriage. To do otherwise would be to commit treason against her divine Founder.

What about the social benefits and the relief from domestic unhappiness alleged to result from divorce? To persons who believe in the divinity of the Founder of the Christian faith, it must be apparent that no teaching of Christ could be detrimental to the welfare of society or to the enduring happiness of mankind. Like all the other laws of Christ, this one concerning the sanctity and the indissolubility of marriage has for its end the welfare of human society *as a whole*.

There are probably few, if any, laws ever framed, no matter how wholesome and necessary for the general welfare, which have not pinched an individual here and there. Nor need it be denied that particular cases can be cited where the innocent party in a marriage that turns out badly is called upon to make a great and even heroic sacrifice. Let it even be admitted that a complete severance of the marriage bond with the consequent privilege of remarrying would be conducive to the happiness of an individual who is the innocent victim of such a marriage. Does this admission justify divorce? Not at all.

In her solicitude for the happiness of all her children, the Church permits complete separation where circumstances require it. But if an exception were once allowed to Christ's law against divorce, it would be but a short time before the law would be so riddled by exceptions as seriously to cripple the law and thus to impair the attainment of its purpose: the welfare of society as a whole. This is particularly true of a law which seeks to guide into beneficent social channels the tumultuous passions of human nature.

If anyone doubts the truth of this, let him look at the experience of our Protestant brethren. Within the Christian fold, divorce was practically unknown until the Protestant Reformation. Substituting their own opinions for the clear teaching of Christ as transmitted by the three Evangelists, by St. Paul and by the unbroken tradition of fifteen centuries, the founders of the principal Protestant denominations began by permitting divorce on the sole ground of adultery. It was the fatal entering wedge that was destined to pry apart millions of unions which Christ had forbade any man to put asunder. Under the pressure of man's unbridled lust, the grounds for divorce began to be multiplied, until today they are so numerous as to permit people to sever the sacred tie for the slightest and silliest reasons.

Thus on the very day on which I write these lines, the newspapers of the country carry a story sent out by the Associated Press to this effect: In a city in California a woman has filed suit for divorce because her husband "diagrammed the wing formations of the football team he is coaching, on the fluffy biscuits I made for his breakfast." This, she alleged, constituted "mental cruelty"; hence her petition for divorce. If the court follows the precedent in many states of granting divorces for the flimsiest and silliest reasons, the sensitive spouse will have received her divorce before these lines reach the printer's ink. To such a degradation has sunk the sanctity of the most sacred vows ever plighted by husband and wife — the vows of deathless love and loyalty.

Ministers in most of the non-Catholic denominations now unite persons, divorced three, four, or more times, in new marriages with no apparent recollection of the stern warning of the divine Founder of Christianity: "What therefore God hath joined together, let no man put asunder." This is the teaching of Christ concerning the holiness and the permanence of marriage torn into shreds and tatters. The thousand grounds on which divorce is granted have practically annihilated in the churches of our separated brethren the law of Christ concerning the sanctity and the indissolubility of the marriage bond.

The experience of non-Catholic churches in the matter offers, therefore, abundant testimony to the folly of making exceptions to the universal validity of the laws of Christ — especially when they are seeking to hold in leash the passions of men. Inserting the opening wedge of a single exception to Christ's law on marriage is like inserting a slender blade through the dikes restraining the sea from the lowlands of Holland. Under the battering of the tumultuous seas, that slight crevice will expand until soon there will be pouring through the opening a roaring avalanche of ocean that will flood the land and spread death and destruction in its wake. The Church stands as a sentinel upon the dike of the Sacrament of Matrimony, instituted by Christ to promote the happiness and welfare of the race, and to hold in check the passions which, if unleashed, would spread ruin and disaster everywhere.

In this connection it should be pointed out that Martin Luther, the father of the Protestant Reformation, did most to destroy the Christian faith of the people in the unity and permanence of marriage. He began by declaring "marriage is a mere worldly thing."[7] Then he encouraged divorces by announcing from his pulpit that after the example of the Assyrian king, every husband who was not satisfied with his spouse could substitute Esther for Vashti, and put the servant in place of the mistress.[8] Going even further, he sanctioned a plurality of wives. In his sermon, *On the First Book of Moses*, he declared: "It is not forbidden, however, that a man have more than one wife, though I could not today advise it."[9]

Nor did he permit his teaching to remain mere theory: he reduced it to practice. Together with his fellow Reformers, Melancthon, Bucer, Lenning, Corvinus and Wintfert, he authorized Philip, the Landgrave of Hesse, to take a second wife when he was still living with his first, by whom he had already eight children and from whom he had no intention of separating. Here one sees at work at the very birth of Protestantism those forces which have been ceaselessly operative within her numerous divisions, and which under the stress of human passions have so twisted and distorted the great ideal proclaimed by Christ: the union of husband and wife in a marriage indissoluble by any human power.

That the practice of tearing Christian homes asunder through the institution of divorce is directly traceable to the teachings and the example of the Reformers is now frankly acknowledged by our separated brethren. Thus the Protestant Bishop of Maine some years ago made the following candid avowal: "Laxity of opinion and teaching on the sacredness of the marriage bond and on the question of divorce *originated among the Protestants* of Continental Europe in the sixteenth century. It soon began to appear in the legislation of Protestant States on that continent, and nearly at the same time to affect laws of New England. From that time to the present it has proceeded from one degree to another in this country, until especially in New England and in states most directly affected by New England opinions and usages, the Christian conception of the nature and obligations of the marriage bond finds scarcely any recognition in legislation or in the prevailing sentiment of the community."[10]

It should be added, however, that the example has been quickly followed by the Western states. Today the divorce courts of Reno, Nevada, have achieved notoriety throughout the nation for the speed and facility with which they tear asunder for trivial reasons the sacred bond of Christian marriage.

Entirely aside from religious considerations, many careful observers of the growing laxity in regard to the marriage vows are pointing to the unhappy consequences for the individual and for society. Thus H. L. Mencken condemns the agitation for companionate marriage, not on grounds of religion or morality, but because it violates the elementary principles of human psychology. "The trouble with the companionate marriage scheme," he writes, "is that it destroys security and trust. Neither party can ever be quite sure of the other, and hence neither can give the other full confidence. A normal man does not marry a woman thinking of her as a possible enemy; he marries her thinking of her as a perpetual friend. If there be any chance of happiness in the companionate scheme, then all that has been taught about human psychology is false."

In an address at the University of Illinois, Rabbi Stephen S. Wise declared anent the movement to change the laws of marriage to make divorce easier: "What is needed is not a change in the laws of marriage, as reformers are fond of picturing, but a change in the heart and in the morals of the individual who is unwilling to remain true to his conjugal vows, but who is willing to enthrone lust in their place."

Every nation or society that wishes to survive must develop in its individual members a sense of social solidarity and a willingness to sacrifice private interests for the public weal. In time of war the citizen is called upon to defend his country even at the risk of his life. The measure in which an individual is willing to subordinate his own selfish interests for the welfare of his family, his state, his nation, or humanity in general, is largely the measure of his unselfishness and nobility of character.

When a marriage turns out badly and the innocent victim feels tempted to have recourse to divorce and remarriage, Christ calls upon such a one to be willing to sacrifice his own selfish interests for the larger welfare of society as a whole. The divine Master would have him remember that if an exception were made in his case, there could be no drawing of the line, and that consequently the unity and permanence of marriage would in a large measure be destroyed. An individual should recognize that in such circumstances he is called upon to play the role of a self-sacrificing hero and to place the public weal above his private interests. Such a one is no less worthy of the gratitude of his fellow countrymen than is the soldier who defends his country from the attack of the enemy. Nor less worthy of the reward of Almighty God.

Did not Christ and His Blessed Mother set us the example of conforming to the law, even though in their cases there was no real need for the performance of the required actions? Did not Christ as a little babe undergo the rite of circumcision as demanded by the Mosaic law, even though there was no real need for such purification in His case? Did not Mary present herself at the Temple forty days after the birth of Jesus and submit to the rite of purification as required by the Judaic law, even though her virginity was not impaired by motherhood? Thus did Christ and His Blessed Mother set an example to the Christians of all ages by obeying a law instead of claiming, as well they might, that exception be made in their cases.

As this point is crucial and, in the writer's judgment, is the only logical grounds on which one can appeal to the innocent victim of an unfortunate marriage to conform to a law for the common weal, even though it pinches him individually, let us present one final illustration. The law of the secrecy of the confessional forbids the confessor to divulge any sin, even the slightest, mentioned by the penitent in Confession. Yet individual instances can be cited where the revelation of such information would seem to be warranted because of unusual circumstances.

Take the case of a prisoner charged with a serious crime. A priest through his office as confessor knows that another individual has accused himself of that very crime. Might he not say to himself: "By divulging a secret of the confessional to the civil authorities I can free a man unjustly accused of a serious crime, and bring to judgment the real culprit. By so doing I would promote the cause of justice. Therefore in these unusual circumstances the law of the secrecy of the confessional does not bind me." No, indeed. He would be utterly wrong in so concluding.

While it can be frankly admitted that, in that particular

case, justice would be promoted and a single individual would be better off, yet the harm done by undermining the confidence of people in the inviolable seal of the confessional would affect millions. It would in the long run wreak such damage to the public weal and the welfare of humanity in general as to outweigh a million times the benefit accruing to a solitary individual by making his case an exception to the law. It is precisely the same in regard to marriage. If the sworn vows of deathless fidelity plighted by bride and groom are to instill abiding trust, their efficacy must not be crippled by exceptions which would undermine the confidence of mankind in their universal validity and as a consequence in the sacredness and permanence of the marriage bond itself.

In the light of the facts presented in this chapter, the following conclusions seem fully warranted: In the Church's unswerving stand for the sanctity and indissolubility of marriage, our American democracy has its strongest bulwark and support. By preserving the home intact, the Church is not only safeguarding the foundations of orderly government but she is also promoting the highest type of family life. She is protecting the interests of husband, wife and children and their happiness as well.

In teaching her children to subordinate their private interests to the public weal, she is rendering an invaluable contribution to the development of the noblest type of American citizenship. Her family fireside merits the praise of all our citizens who place the welfare of their country and of society as a whole above the satisfaction of their private whims. In the ears of those who would ask the Church to lower her lofty standards in regard to Christian marriage, and would riddle her law of indissolubility with multitudinous exceptions, she would whisper again the words of the great Apostle, St. Paul: "Not I but the Lord commandeth."

Discussion Aids

What authority has the Church to legislate for her members in regard to marriage? How do you know that marriage is a sacrament? Why does the Church forbid divorce? From what scriptural texts do we know that Christ forbade divorce? What was St. Paul's teaching to the Corinthians on the indissolubility of marriage? What relief does the Church grant in individual cases of extreme hardship in marriage? Is separation with remarriage ever permitted? What errors in regard to matrimony were made by the Reformers? What have been the results? Cite some statistics on the increase of divorce. What is to be said of subordinating our selfish interests, even in an unfortunate marriage, to the public welfare? Sum up the case for the indissolubility of marriage.

Practices

Help in organizing discussion clubs for young people on the subject of marriage.

Seek opportunities of placing in the hands of people entering upon marriage pamphlets or books of instruction on matrimony.

Before marriage, or during marriage, pray daily for the success of this "great sacrament" in your case.

NOTES (Chapter 20)

1. Eph. 5:25-32
2. *De Nupt. et Concup.*, i, 10, Migne, *Pat. Lat.*, Tom. XLIV
3. Mt. 19:3-9
4. Mk. 10:10-12
5. Lk. 16:18
6. I Cor. 7:10-11
7. Martin Luther, *Dr. Martin Luther's saemtliche werke*, Vol. XVI, pp. 518-519 (Frankfurt a.m., Zimmer, 1877)
8. *Sermon on Marriage*, Wittenberg, 1522, op. cit., Vol. XX
9. Martin Luther, *Dr. Martin Luther's saemtliche werke*, Vol. XXXIII, p. 324 (Erlander Heyder, 1843)
10. *The Calling of a Christian Woman*, by Rev. Morgan Dix, Appleton, N.Y.

CHAPTER 21

Marriage: Catholic or Mixed?

A Sore Spot in Protestant and Catholic Relations Frankly Discussed

"Why does the Catholic Church forbid her members to marry persons outside her fold? In our country where religious tolerance is so necessary and should be encouraged in every way possible, is not the ruling of your Church on this subject narrow-minded and apt to breed intolerance? It builds up needless barriers between our citizens. It isolates them into clannish groups, and prevents their free assimilation into a unified citizenry, so essential for the well-being of a country such as ours, which is composed of people of every race and of every faith."

Such was the concerned view expressed to the writer by a non-Catholic friend. His words reflect a sentiment common among our separated brethren. In proceeding to answer the criticism, let us first assure our dear non-Catholic readers that we agree heartily with them upon the necessity not merely of tolerance, but even of friendliness and goodwill, throughout the whole vast domain of our common civic relationships. To discriminate against a person in business or politics simply because of a difference in religion or in race is indeed un-American. We Catholics, who have been among the chief victims of such discrimination, will be the last people in the world to defend bigotry in any of its forms. Whether those forms be racial or religious, they are all alike — ugly, un-American, and un-Catholic — and merit our unqualified condemnation.

The idea of tolerance, however, can be pushed too far. It can be intruded into domains where it has no relevance. Thus to the query, "What is the sum of two and three?" no one would expect the teacher to smile as benignly and as friendly upon the response, "ninety-seven," as upon the answer, "five." Why? Because truth has rights which error does not possess. Tolerance does not imply that people cannot hold certain principles to be true and others to be false without being guilty of narrow-mindedness.

Thus Catholics believe that the doctrines taught by Christ and promulgated by the Church which He founded are correct. They believe that all doctrines which contradict anything in the deposit of divine revelation are wrong. But they do not carry their disagreements on matters of religious belief into the altogether disparate field of business or politics, and discriminate in these fields against those with whom they differ on religious grounds. To do so would be intolerance, bigotry and fanaticism; it would go counter to the whole spirit of the Catholic Church and to everything for which she stands.

Having thus cleared the way, we can now come to grips with the real problem: Why does the Church oppose mixed marriages? She does so, not because she is lacking in high esteem for non-Catholics nor because she is indifferent to their happiness. It is precisely because she loves non-Catholics, children of the same heavenly Father as we, and because she is as solicitous for their happiness and welfare as she is for that of her own children, that she bids them to marry those of their own faith and bids Catholics to do likewise. From long experience she knows that marriages between persons sincerely attached to different religious faiths contain elements of danger to the happiness of both parties and to the stability of their union.

The Church speaks in this matter not from the experience of but one generation or of one country, but from many centuries of experience in all the countries of the world. Reason and common sense testify that where there is a difference on one of the most important matters in life, there is a subtle line of cleavage which should not be present in a union that is meant to be the most intimate that human beings can ever contract on this earth — a union of heart, mind and soul, a union of aspirations and of prayer.

Then too it must be remembered that the Church, mindful of the obligation imposed on her by her divine Father of safeguarding the faith of her children and of her children's children, is deeply concerned over their entering for life into an atmosphere likely to damage or at least to chill their faith. It is because such marriages frequently lead to religious indifference on the part of the parents and to the neglect of the religious uprearing of the offspring that the Church forbids them. In her eyes the greatest treasure in life is the deposit of religious truth given to mankind by Jesus Christ; it is the pearl of great price. She would rather suffer death a thousand times than to deny that faith or to betray her trust; no consideration of wealth or social preferment or political influence could ever recompense for the loss of faith in even one of her children.

With this profound faith in the supreme value of the religion of Jesus Christ, and with a keen consciousness of her divinely appointed duty of safeguarding that deposit of truth in all its integrity for all generations of men, is it not natural that she would warn against any and every danger threatening the faith of her children? She would not be a faithful mother if she did not exhaust every ingenuity to remove any condition menacing her children's birthright. Must not our fair-minded citizens of other faiths then be prompted to sentiments of admiration for the Church's ceaseless policy of protecting her children from serious dangers to their faith — a policy which is alone consistent with her belief in its supreme value?

"But if the Catholic religion is the true religion, as a Catholic believes it is, then why should there be any danger of his losing his faith from association in marriage with a non-Catholic? Does this not imply a lack of conviction in the intrinsic strength of the credentials of the Catholic faith? It shows that the Catholic religion needs a hothouse atmosphere, from which blasts from the outside are carefully excluded, to preserve it intact." Such is the objection which some of our non-Catholic readers may feel inclined at this point to interject.

The objection overlooks the fact, however, that men and women are not mere machines for logical reasoning but are flesh and blood, influenced by emotions and feelings as much perhaps as by intellectual considerations. Take a young man, for instance, who has the conviction that the moral law should be obeyed; it is a conviction well grounded in reason. Place him in an environment where temptation assails him on every side: vice clothed in the beguiling garb of beauty intrigues his imagination, stirs his emotions, inflames his passions. He is like a reed shaken by the wind. No person of experience will question the powerful influence of daily environment upon any human being. Because the Church recognizes this fact she strives to safeguard her children from lifelong residence in surroundings uncongenial to their religious faith.

Then, too, owing to the lack of religious instruction in school and in the home, many of her children are not properly grounded in their faith. In consequence, unfavorable criticism, ridicule, social pressure, political discrimination and many other extraneous considerations prompt them to sell their birthright for a mess of pottage.

The influence of the home environment is probably most marked in the case of the children. With the spectacle of a division in religious creed among their own parents, it is indeed difficult to develop a strong, robust faith in the offspring. How natural it is then for the child who has grown up in such a divided home to say: "If my own parents cannot agree as to which is the true religion, how can I?" Even when the non-Catholic father goes to no church and honestly tries to encourage the children to practice the faith of their Catholic mother, he is working against great odds. Example is more powerful than precept. If the latter does not square with example, it is likely to be of little value, as the following incident illustrates.

In a home where the non-Catholic father strove to fulfill the promise he made at the time of his marriage to see that the children were reared in the Catholic faith, there was every outward appearance of success crowning his efforts. On Sunday morning the father prided himself on the regularity with which he called the children and saw that they went to Mass with their mother. He himself remained at home reading the worldling's bible — the Sunday newspaper. In such an environment where the paternal example was at right angles with the precept, the children grew to maturity.

Finally on one Sunday morning when he called his son for

Mass, the latter refused to arise. Astonished, the father said to him:

"Why, what does this mean? Have I not trained you from early youth to attend to your religious duties? Why are you not going today the same as on other Sundays?"

"Father," replied the son, "you have always called me and told me to go, but you have never gone yourself. I am no child any longer. I am a man. And I figure that if you don't have to go, neither do I."

The logic of his contention the father could not deny. Little had he realized that his own example was undermining the foundations of the faith he was seeking by precept alone to build for his child. Thus in every home where there is a division of religious faith, the force of parental example is fashioning slowly but surely its tangled imprint upon the impressionable mind and memory of the children — an imprint they will carry with them to their dying day.

As this point is crucial in securing a correct understanding as to why the Church does not consider a mixed marriage as the ideal, let us present one further illustration. In a large city parish a class of little children had just been prepared to receive their First Holy Communion. The pastor had established the beautiful custom of having the parents kneel at the side of each child and receive their Eucharistic Lord along with their offspring. As he went along the rail, distributing the bread of angels to his young communicants and to their proud parents, he could not wholly close his eyes to the beauty, innocence and happiness radiating from the upturned faces of the little children. Then all of a sudden he came upon one, a little girl of eight, whose reddened eyes and saddened face contrasted sharply with the holy joy mantling the countenances of her schoolmates.

On one side the mother was kneeling. But on the other there was . . . a vacancy. Thinking that some foolish scruple was disturbing her, the priest bent low and said: "Don't worry, my dear child, Jesus will comfort and bless you."

Then after placing upon her tongue the heavenly manna, he whispered: "Come into the sacristy for a moment after the Mass." When later she appeared with her mother, the secret came out.

Appareled in her dress of white, with a wreath of flowers upon her brow, and the smile on her face mirroring the joy in her heart, the little child, just before leaving for Mass, had turned to her father with the words:

"Won't you please come with me, Daddy, and kneel near me when I make my First Communion?"

"I don't believe in such things," the father had replied and walked away.

If he had taken a dagger and plunged it into the heart of his little girl, he could scarcely have broken her heart more completely. Taught by the sisters in school and by her mother that she would receive her Lord and Savior in Holy Communion, the words of her father, not intended to hurt her, had actually stabbed her to the quick.

Example *does* count. The influence of the home is more powerful than any school; for it teaches not by precept alone but by example as well. Parents are designed by God and nature to be the child's most effective teachers. If there is disagreement on the matter of religion between these two teachers, it is difficult to see how the pupil can escape the penalty in the form of religious confusion and bewilderment.

It is true there are those who say: "Difference in religion need not affect the happiness of the family life, nor mar its unity." If all such could have witnessed the crushing effect of the father's words upon his little child, they would realize that they are in a world of speculative theories and not in our actual world of flesh and blood, where the tears flow and hearts ache because a family is cut in twain by the sword of religious differences. Religion does count in the happiness of the family; it is a *bond* that unites or a *sword* that tends at least to separate. It touches the unity of the family at a crucial point. There are exceptions, of course, but they only prove the rule.

"If the Church has a law forbidding mixed marriages, why does she grant so many dispensations therefrom, thus allowing such marriages to take place?" Such is a question often on the lips of our non-Catholic friends. While holding fast to the ideal of a Catholic marriage, the Church understands that the ideal is not capable of realization in every instance and under all circumstances. Her vast army of more than six hundred and fifty million members are scattered out among all the nations of the world.

In daily contact with such neighbors, surrounding us on every hand, the Church realizes that the occasional development of friendships and courtships leading to the marriage of a Catholic with a non-Catholic is, in such an environment, simply inevitable. She does not bury her head in the sand, ignoring unpleasant realities, she faces them honestly and squarely. She applies her laws in the light of actual conditions, having always in mind the welfare and happiness, temporal and eternal, of her children.

When circumstances prevent the attainment of the ideal, then the Church legislates to obtain the next best result. Rather than say to one of her children, who, deeply in love with a non-Catholic, feels that her life's happiness is conditioned upon her marrying him, "You can never, under any circumstances, marry such a person," the Church follows a kindlier and more sympathetic policy. It is a policy which reflects the Church's twin solicitude for the promotion of human happiness and the preservation of the faith of her children. She grants a dispensation to such an individual for sufficient grounds, permitting her to marry a Protestant or a person unbaptized in any faith. This she does, however, only when she has been given assurances of the proper safeguarding of the faith of the Catholic party and of the children.

Since Vatican Council II (1962-65), which gave such great encouragement and impetus to the movement for Christian unity, the Church has made some significant concessions in regard to mixed marriages. While there are variations in details in different dioceses, permission is now generally given by the local bishop to have an interfaith marriage take place in a Catholic church, instead of the rectory as was formerly the case, with the non-Catholic minister assisting.

The priest witnesses the exchange of the nuptial vows, proclaims the couple husband and wife, imparts the nuptial blessing and celebrates the Mass. The minister may then recite appropriate prayers, read passages from Scripture, give a brief exhortation and impart his blessing to the bridal couple. The whole subject of interfaith marriages is under extensive study by the Church and further adjustments to foster the ecumenical movement may result.

Christ founded not many churches, but one Church. Catholics honestly believe that theirs is that Church. On the basis of actual fact and historical truth, the Church's policy is not unreasonable, but on the contrary, is the only one which demands for truth rights which error does not possess. If the Church were to compromise, allow some to be brought up outside her fold, she would be false to her divinely appointed mission of teaching to all mankind the truths taught by Christ. The Church is, therefore, under a *divine* obligation to protect the faith of her children and of her children's children. The Church not only believes in her divine origin and mission, but she has the courage to translate that belief into action.

For the same reason the Church finds herself obligated to require that the marriage be performed by a Catholic priest. To sanction the marriage of one of her children with a non-Catholic before a non-Catholic minister would mean that the Church was implicitly recognizing such a denomination, founded by a mere man, to be of equal validity with the Church established by Jesus Christ. This the Church could do only at the cost of her intellectual integrity.

Moreover, the Catholic Church regards marriage as a sacrament, while most non-Catholic ministers do not. With no wish to hurt the feeling of our dear non-Catholic friends, the Church finds herself compelled by the clear consciousness of her divine origin and of the mission divinely appointed unto her, to give to error no more recognition than her divine Founder gave to it.

To place the churches founded by Martin Luther, John Calvin, John Knox, John Wesley, Mrs. Mary Baker Eddy and Mrs. Aimee Semple MacPherson Hutton on the same plane as the Church founded by Christ, and to clothe them with the same authority, would be for her to commit the sin of apostasy.

Catholics who attempt marriage before a civil officer, such as the justice of the peace, sin mortally and do not contract a valid religious marriage. They do not, however, incur the penalty of excommunication, because they have not committed the sin of apostasy or of treason to the faith. Since the *Ne Temere* decree of Pius X, which went into effect on Easter Sunday, April

19, 1908, a Catholic can be validly married only before a Catholic priest. This legislation applies only to Catholics, as the Church does not legislate for non-Catholics as such. Contrary to a charge frequently made, the Catholic recognizes the validity of the marriage of Protestants, contracted either before their own ministers or before a civil officer.

In conclusion, it can be truthfully said that the Church has never envisaged, and does not now envisage, mixed marriages as occasions for increasing her membership at the expense of non-Catholic faiths. On the contrary she wishes her children to live in peace and friendship with their fellow citizens of every faith. She is anxious to remove every needless source of friction which carries over into the civic relationships of her members with those of other faiths. In her marriage legislation she has at heart the welfare and happiness not only of her own children but of those who are without. Rather than blast forever the dreams of happiness of a non-Catholic by depriving him of all possibility of marrying the girl he loves, the Church permits such a union, provided proper safeguards for the faith are assured.

Does not this maternal attitude reflect an admirable blending of unfaltering loyalty to the truth with a tender solicitude for the happiness of all people, Catholic and non-Catholic alike? Can our fellow Americans justly criticize the Church for her stand on mixed marriage, when she does everything possible, short of betrayal of her divinely appointed trust, to enable the non-Catholic to realize his dreams of conjugal love and happiness? In the Church's attitude on this vexing problem, our fellow citizens of other faiths, who have followed this discussion with open minds and in a spirit of impartiality, will perceive, we are confident, a reflection of the love and loyalty of the Church to her divine Founder and of her love and devotion for all His children.

Discussion Aids

Is the Church intolerant because she does not believe in mixed marriage? Explain why the Church is opposed to mixed marriages, (1) for the sake of the contracting parties; (2) for the sake of their children. Why are dispensations sometimes granted? What are the requirements for such dispensations? Why are these requirements not unreasonable? Can a Catholic be validly married before a civil officer? Is the penalty excommunication? Why not? What does the marriage legislation of 1908 make necessary for Catholics? Does the Church recognize the validity of Protestant marriages contracted before their own ministers or a civil officer? How explain to a Protestant that the law of the Church on mixed marriage is neither "one-sided" nor a "crafty device"? Explain the attitude of the Church as one of brotherly love.

Practices

Help to organize a social movement in your parish to foster acquaintance between Catholic young men and women.

Provide Catholic literature on marriage for your children.

Pray for a happy Catholic marriage.

PART V

The Mass and Other Devotions

An Exposition of the Prayer Life of the Church

CHAPTER 22

The Mass: A Reenactment of Calvary

Christ Is Sacrificed Again

Sacrifice is the offering to God of some tangible object, with the destruction of the object, to acknowledge God's dominion over life and death. The custom of offering sacrifice is as old as humanity: when the curtain is first raised upon the human scene, we find the children of Adam offering oblation to the Most High. Abel offered the firstlings of his flock, while Cain offered of the fruits of the earth. The first act of Noah upon issuing from the Ark, which enabled him and his family to escape from the deluge, was to offer holocausts to the Almighty in thanksgiving for his preservation. It was the custom of the Jewish priests to offer each day two lambs as a sacrifice to God, thus prefiguring the great sacrifice of the New Law in which is daily offered on the altar "the Lamb of God who taketh away the sins of the world."

The sacrifice of the Old Law served as a preparation and a foreshadowing of the sacrifice of the New Law. When this sacrifice was instituted, the former immolations were to cease. The old sacrifices were to be succeeded by a clean victim which would be offered not alone in Jerusalem but in every part of the world. God spoke to the Jews through the mouth of the prophet Malachi:

"I have no pleasure in you, saith the Lord of hosts, and I will not receive a gift of your hand. For, from the rising of the sun, even to the going down, my name is great among the Gentiles, and in every place there is sacrifice, and there is offered to my name a clean oblation, for my name is great among the Gentiles, saith the Lord of hosts."[1] These prophetic words have received their fulfillment in the sacrifice of the Mass in which Christ is offered up in every country of the world as the clean victim for the sins of mankind.

The Mass is the unbloody reenactment of the sacrifice of Calvary. Through the consecration of the bread and wine into the body and blood of Christ, the Mass perpetuates the sacrifice of the Cross by offering to God the same Victim that was immolated on Calvary for the redemption of man. In the Mass the priest speaks not in his own name, but as the ambassador of Jesus Christ, speaking the very words which Christ uttered at the Last Supper. Thus Jesus Christ is both the High Priest and the Victim in the sacrifice of the Mass and in the sacrifice of the Cross, and the ends for which both sacrifices were offered are identical.

The manner in which the sacrifices are offered is alone different: on the Cross Christ really shed His Blood and was really slain; in the Mass, however, there is no real shedding of blood, no real death; but the separate consecration of the bread and of the wine symbolizes the separation of the body and blood of Christ and thus symbolizes His death upon the Cross. The Mass is the renewal and perpetuation of the sacrifice of the Cross in the sense that it offers anew to God the Victim of Calvary and thus commemorates the sacrifice of the Cross, reenacts it symbolically and mystically, and applies the fruits of Christ's death upon the Cross to individual human souls. All the efficacy of the Mass is derived, therefore, from the sacrifice of Calvary.

Christ instituted the Mass at the Last Supper on the night before He died. St. Matthew thus records the institution: "And whilst they were at supper, Jesus took bread, and blessed, and broke; and gave to His disciples, and said: Take ye, and eat. This is My body. And taking the chalice, He gave thanks, and gave to them, saying: Drink ye all of this. For this is My blood of the New Testament, which shall be shed for many unto remission of sins."[2]

Christ commanded the Apostles to reenact this Eucharistic Sacrifice when He said to them after the consecration: "Do ye this for a commemoration of Me."[3]

In compliance with the command of Christ, the adorable sacrifice of the Mass has been daily reenacted in all our churches from the days of the Apostles to the present time and will be continued until the end of the world. Tradition with its myriad tongues proclaims the universal custom of the early Christians of offering up the *Holy Mysteries,* as they called the Eucharistic Sacrifice in those days. Seeking refuge from the persecutions of imperial Rome, the Christians went into the dark catacombs and there over the tomb of martyrs, their spiritual shepherds reenacted the Eucharistic Sacrifice while the faithful joined in the prayers and in the singing of hymns. St. Justin Martyr (160) bears witness to the Apostolic faith when he writes: "The oblation of the flour, which was commanded to be offered up for those cleansed from leprosy was a type of Bread of the Eucharist, which Jesus Christ commanded us to celebrate . . . concerning those Sacrifices which are offered to Him in every place by us Gentiles, that is, the Bread of the Eucharist, and similarly the Cup of the Eucharist."[4]

Tertullian (160-220) thus testifies to the widespread practice of offering the Eucharistic Sacrifice in the second century. He writes: "Will not your fast be more solemn, if you stand at the altar of God? When you receive the body of the Lord, you place in security both the participation in the Sacrifice and the fulfillment of duty."[5]

Writing in the third century, St. Cyprian sets forth the Catholic doctrine on the Mass as clearly as a theologian of the twentieth. He teaches that the Eucharist contains an immolated Victim and is a true and complete sacrifice; that it was instituted by Christ, and is a commemoration of His passion, and is even identical with that Passion. "Christ," he writes, "is the Teacher and Founder of this Sacrifice. . . . Who is more a priest than Jesus Christ, who offered a Sacrifice to God the Father, and offered the very same thing which Melchisedech offered, that is, bread and wine, namely His Body and Blood? . . . For if Jesus Christ, our Lord and God, is Himself the Chief Priest of God the Father, and has first offered Himself a Sacrifice to the Father, and has commanded this to be done in commemoration of Himself, surely that priest discharges the office of Christ who imitates what Christ did; and he then offers a true and full Sacrifice to God the Father in the Church, when he proceeds to offer it according to the manner in which he sees Christ to have offered . . . because we make mention of the Passion in all Sacrifices (for the Lord's Passion is the Sacrifice which we offer), we ought to do nothing else but what He did. For the Sacred Scriptures say, as often as ye eat this bread and drink this cup, ye show forth the Lord's death until He come."[6]

At the Last Supper Christ instituted the Holy Eucharist which is both a sacrament and a sacrifice. As a sacrament its primary purpose is to sanctify our souls, while as a sacrifice its primary purpose is to offer homage and worship to Almighty God. As the sacrament of Holy Communion it is the perpetuation of the Last Supper, while as the sacrifice of the Mass it is the perpetuation of the sacrifice of Calvary.

The sacrifice of the Mass is offered up for the same ends for which Christ died on the Cross, namely, to propitiate Almighty God for the sins of man, to render homage, praise and thanksgiving for His benefits, and to supplicate Him for graces and blessings. We should therefore assist at Mass with the same devotion with which we would have knelt at the foot of the Cross and have offered up the dying Christ as the Victim for the sins of the world; for Christ is offered up on the altar as truly as He was on Calvary's Cross. The Mass is more valuable than any prayer: it is the supreme offering which the creature is able to return to the Creator. As Thomas a Kempis well says: "When a priest celebrates Mass he honors God, he rejoices the angels, he edifies the Church, he helps the living, he obtains rest for the dead, and makes himself a partaker of all that is good."[7]

The Mass is the very heart of Catholic worship. Just as the heart pumps the life-giving blood to every member of the body, vitalizing and nourishing it, so the Mass radiates its abundant graces and merits to all the subordinate devotions of the Church, enriching and invigorating them with its own might and power. As the planets cluster around the sun, from which they receive their light and heat, so do all the various types of prayer and ritual cluster around the sacrifice of the Mass. It is the central act of worship in the Catholic Church and no other devotion can compare with it in spiritual richness and efficacy.

"For sheer beauty, dignity and sublimity," says Father J. M. Cooper, "there is naught in the whole realm of religious literature that can compare with the prayers of the Mass as the outpouring of the human heart's deepest reverence and purest love and warmest pleading to the Father of us all. In their sustained majesty and in their august simplicity they are a worthy setting for the supreme act of Christian worship. And they are the more venerable and beloved by us in that for nearly a millennium and a half they have been consecrated by the untold millions who in all ages and climes and races have professed faith in and loyalty to the Eucharistic Christ."[8]

The Council of Trent thus summarizes the Church's teaching concerning the Mass:

1. There is in the Catholic Church a true Sacrifice, instituted by Jesus Christ — the Sacrifice of His Body and Blood under the appearances of bread and wine.

2. This Sacrifice is identical with the Sacrifice of the Cross, inasmuch as Jesus Christ is Priest and Victim in both; the only difference lies in the manner of offering, which is bloody upon the Cross and bloodless on our altars.

3. It is a propitiatory Sacrifice, atoning for our sins, and the sins of the living and of the dead in Christ, for whom it is offered.

4. Its efficacy is derived from the Sacrifice of the Cross, whose infinite merits it applies to us.

5. Although offered to God alone, it may be celebrated in honor and memory of the saints.

6. The Mass was instituted at the Last Supper when Christ, about to offer Himself on the altar of the Cross by His death for

our redemption wished to endow His Church with a visible Sacrifice, commemorative of His Bloody Sacrifice of the Cross. As High Priest, according to the order of Melchisedech He offered to His Father His own Body and Blood under the appearances of bread and wine, and constituted His Apostles priests of the New Testament to renew this same offering until He came again by the words, "Do this in commemoration of Me."[9]

In the Mass Jesus pleads our cause and becomes our Advocate before the throne of the Eternal Father: "If any man sin," says St. John, "we have an Advocate with the Father, Jesus Christ the just; and He is the propitiation for our sins; and not for ours only, but also for those of the whole world."[10] Reflecting this truth the celebrant recites at the offertory of the Mass the following prayer: "Receive, O holy Father, almighty, eternal God, this immaculate victim which I, Thy unworthy servant, offer to Thee, my living and true God, for my innumerable sins, offenses and negligences, for all here present, and for all the faithful living and dead, that it may avail me and them to life everlasting.[11]

The sacrifice of the Mass is the most effective form of supplication which we humans can offer to the Eternal Father. "For, if the blood of goats and oxen," says St. Paul, "and the ashes of a heifer being sprinkled, sanctify such as are defiled to the cleansing of the flesh, how much more shall the blood of Christ, who, by the Holy Spirit, offered Himself without spot to God, cleanse our conscience from dead works to serve the living God?"[12] If the prayers of Moses and David were so powerful in behalf of God's children, how much more powerful must be the intercession of our Advocate, Jesus Christ?

If the suffering of the martyrs too plead so eloquently for us, how much more eloquent must be the blood of Christ that is shed daily for us upon our altars? What legions of saints and angels can intercede for us before the throne of God so effectively as the divine Son who humbled himself even to the death of the Cross? Verily the Mass is a "throne of grace" to which we should go with confidence, "that we may obtain mercy and find grace in seasonable aid."[13] It is the most priceless of all the treasures which have come to us from the Giver of every good and perfect gift.

Discussion Aids

What is sacrifice? Give a short history of sacrifice in the Old Testament. What Old Testament prophecy is fulfilled in the Sacrifice of the New Law? What is the Mass? Explain how it is the renewal and perpetuation of the Sacrifice of the Cross. When was the Mass instituted? Quote St. Matthew's text on the institution of the Mass; St. Luke's text. Trace the history of the Mass briefly to the present day. What are the four ends of the Mass? How does the Council of Trent summarize the teaching on the Mass? Explain how the Mass is the center of Catholic worship and the most effective form of supplication.

Practices

Include the Mass in your morning offering.

Try to increase your appreciation of this great Sacrifice by occasional meditation.

NOTES (Chapter 22)

1. Mal. 1:10-11
2. Mt. 26:26-29
3. Lk. 22:19
4. *Dial Cum. Tryph.*, 41, Migne, *Pat. Graec.*, Tom. VI
5. *De Oratione*, 19, Migne, *Pat. Lat.*, Tom I
6. Epis. 63, Migne, *Pat. Lat.*, Tom. IV
7. *The Imitation of Christ*, Book 4, Ch. 5
8. Cooper, *Religion Outlines for Colleges*, Vol. 2, p. 189 (Catholic University Press, Washington, D.C.)
9. *Sess.* 22
10. I Jn. 2:1-2
11. *Missale Romanum*
12. Heb. 9:13-14
13. *Ibid.*, 4:16

CHAPTER 23

Why Attend Sunday Mass?

The Spectacle Which Thrills the World

"There is too large an element of compulsion in the Catholic religion. Its members are constrained by multitudinous laws to do this, forbidden to do that. They seldom enjoy any option in the matter. Take their attendance at Mass on Sunday. They are obliged under pain of mortal sin to attend. Why not recognize that children at last grow up? Why not respect the intellectual maturity of the individual and allow him to decide for himself whether he wishes to attend Mass, instead of forcing him by a positive command? Why not make it a matter of option instead of obligation?"

Such a view is frequently expressed by our non-Catholic fellow citizens. While admiring many features of the Church's teachings, many profess to be deterred from entering the fold because they fear their liberty would be too greatly restricted. They wish to engage in religious exercises only when the spirit moves them, only when they feel like doing so. With them the attendance at religious worship is a matter of mood and caprice, not one of principle or law binding them independently of mood or whim.

The practice of making one's religious life hinge upon mood or rest upon the stable foundation of principle and law represents a point of fundamental divergence between the Protestant denominations and the Catholic Church. For the sake of clarity and brevity, we will focus our attention upon the matter of attendance at divine services, though what is said here will be seen to apply all along the line. Let us ask our dear non-Catholic friend to look into the matter with an open mind, and see for himself if the policy of the Church in this regard does not reflect the voice of reason and the voice of God. Let us see whether the teaching of the Church mirrors a spirit of excessive paternalism cramping the freedom of the individual or whether it is a mighty bulwark against the anarchy of riotous individualism and an antidote necessary to safeguard the stability of the religious life from the menace of mood and whim.

General obligations need to be *particularized* and rendered specific if they are to secure universal or widespread observance. The obligation to worship God is universal: it binds all mankind — red, white, black, yellow and brown. Its observance has not been left to the caprice or whim of man; for amid thunder and lightning, Jehovah gave to Moses on Mount Sinai the tablet on which was inscribed the command: "Remember thou keep holy the Sabbath day." Thus did Almighty God particularize a general obligation.

The mandate to worship God was carved not only on tablets of stone but upon the fleshy tablets of the human heart. The tendency to worship springs spontaneously from one of the deepest instincts of our nature; that tribe is yet to be discovered which offers not prayer or sacrifice to the great Supreme Ruler of the universe. Anthropologists and historians investigating the life and customs of ancient races, in all stages varying from barbarism to civilization, have been struck by the universality of the practice of rendering homage to the deity. Pope was thus able to write with scientific accuracy:

"Father of all; in every age,
In every clime adored,
By saint, by savage, and by sage,
Jehovah, Jove, or Lord."

Though the methods of worship and sacrifice differ in a thousand ways, though the deity is called by various names and worshiped under myriad forms, running through all of them is the same fundamental human cry: the cry of the creature to his Creator, the voice acknowledging the absolute dependence of the subject upon his Lord and God. It is this acknowledgment of the creature's complete dependence upon the Creator that constitutes the very heart and soul of all religious worship. Our coming to church, our kneeling down, our prayers, especially our assistance at Mass, are so many ways in which we profess our dependence upon God and acknowledge His sovereign dominion over us.

The worship of God does not rest, however, upon mere custom, no matter how universal or hoary that may be: it is founded upon the very law of nature. By creating us out of nothing, Almighty God possesses sovereign dominion over us by the strongest of all titles, namely, creation. By taking a worthless block of crude, unshapely marble and carving out of it a great statue, "a thing of beauty and a joy forever," a sculptor acquires title to the statue. Why? Because by his toil and genius he gives to it whatever value it possesses. So by the even stronger title of absolute creation has the Creator complete dominion over all His creatures, the work of His hands. The relationship existing between the creature and the Creator, as rooted in the law of nature, is therefore, one of the most complete dependence on the part of the creature upon his Creator, both for his creation and for his conservation in existence. Every human being owes the duty of acknowledging this dependence by acts of worship and adoration. Consequently the duty to worship springs from the law of nature, binds all human beings who have reached the age of reason and has been given explicit formulation in the divine positive law revealed by Almighty God to Moses.

Can not such a duty be fulfilled, however, by giving to God merely interior worship, that is, by adoring Him in our minds only, without any external manifestations of our worship? Thus one might say: "I will stay at home on Sunday morning and worship God in my own mind, without kneeling down or folding my hands or uttering words of prayer, and thus satisfy the natural precept of worshiping." The person who would do only this would fail to give God the complete worship to which He has a right; for God is the Creator of our bodies no less than of our minds and souls. Therefore both the mind and the body should participate in rendering to the Almighty a complete act of worship.

As a matter of fact this dictate of our reason is further confirmed by an interesting sidelight which modern psychology offers. Psychology tells us that the person who never gives external expression to his internal sentiments and feelings will cause them to be choked, stunted and gradually atrophied, while on the other hand, suitable external expression strengthens and intensifies them. Thus the devotions of the Church in which the faithful kneel before the altar in suppliant posture, fold the hands, strike the breast, and utter ardent words of prayer, far from lessening fervor, greatly strengthen and vivify it.

So much, then, for the existence of a general obligation on the part of all mankind to worship God. Now let us examine the specific manner in which that obligation is to be discharged, as revealed to us not by unaided human reason but by the light from on high.

In the Old Law, the strict observance of the Sabbath was prescribed under the severest penalties, even the penalty of death itself. "Observe the day of the Sabbath, to sanctify it, as the Lord thy God hath commanded thee."[1] In thundering tones the prophets condemned violations of the Sabbath, saying: "What is this evil thing that you are doing, profaning the Sabbath day? Did not our fathers do these things and our God brought all this evil upon us, and upon this city? And you bring more wrath upon Israel by violating the Sabbath."[2] The Book of Maccabees records that the arrogant monarch Antiochus who defiled the temple and desecrated its altars, and violated "the sabbaths" and "the solemn days of the fathers," was punished with a loathsome and fatal malady.

When Christ came upon earth He did not nullify this law, but by His own example He confirmed it. He did strip it, however, of some of the accretions of the Pharisees, who considered works of charity and of mercy as unlawful on that day. It was on the Sabbath that Christ cured the sick at the pool of Bethsaida, healed the cripple with the withered hand in the synagogue, and restored health to the man sick with the dropsy. To the Pharisees who appeared scandalized that the master should work a good deed on the Sabbath, He said: "For the Son of Man is Lord even of the Sabbath." "The Sabbath was made for man and not man for the Sabbath." "What man shall there be among you, that hath a sheep: and if the same shall fall into a pit on the Sabbath day, will he not take hold on it and lift it up? How much better is a man than a sheep? Therefore it is lawful to do a good deed on the Sabbath day."[3]

Under the Old Law, the Sabbath or seventh day of the week was observed because on that day God rested from his labors of creation, and on that day He delivered the Jewish people from the galling yoke of their Egyptian bondage. The observance of the Sabbath served, therefore, as a traditional reminder of their miraculous deliverance in accordance with the words of the Almighty: "Remember that thou also didst serve in Egypt and the Lord thy God brought thee out from thence with a strong hand and stretched out arm. Therefore hath He commanded thee that thou shouldst observe the Sabbath day."[4]

The Old Law was but an image or foreshadowing of the Light and Truth that was to come. When that Light came in the personality of Jesus, the old Mosaic law having fulfilled its function of preparing the Jews for the coming of the Messiah was abrogated as regards its ceremonial prescriptions in favor of the new dispensation or law of Christ.

To signalize this transition from the Old to the New Law, the Apostles transferred the observance to the Sunday, the first day of the week. Sunday was chosen because on that day was wrought the greatest miracle of the Christian religion — the resurrection of Christ from the dead. It was on Sunday also that the Holy Spirit descended upon the Apostles and sent them out to preach the gospel to the world. Sunday is, therefore, the birthday of the Christian Church.

How are we to observe the Sunday? The Church by the authority divinely committed to her has given explicit formulation of the obligation contained in the third commandment by telling us in her first precept: "Thou shalt hear Mass on Sunday and holydays of obligation and thou shalt abstain from servile work." The positive part of this precept binds all the faithful who have attained the use of reason to hear Mass on Sunday and holydays under pain of mortal sin. Grave causes such as sickness, lack of a church in the town or within a reasonable distance, or other circumstances which render it very difficult to attend Mass, will excuse a person from guilt in this matter. A person with a good conscience will not magnify little inconveniences into insurmountable obstacles. He will scorn such flimsy excuses as the weather being too hot or too cold, rain or snow, as unworthy of a true follower of Jesus Christ. Realizing that the secrets of the heart are as an open book to Almighty God who knows whether or not the individual can attend if he really wants to, he does not engage in the chicanery of trying to throw dust in the eyes of an omniscient deity by manufacturing weak and flimsy excuses.

The history of the past nineteen hundred years demonstrates the wisdom of the Church's action in rendering this divine command definite and specific and in attaching to it a proper moral sanction. By that I mean, making it bind in conscience under penalty of grievous sin. Not only in our country but throughout Christendom it is Catholics who give to the world a demonstration of the vitality of religion and of unfaltering belief in a God worthy of our reverence and worship, by thronging to Mass at every Catholic church in the world.

Some years ago a Chicago newspaper undertook to find out how many people were attending church on Sunday. Stationing reporters at every church and synagogue in that great city, they counted every person who entered. The results were little short of startling: they discovered that eighty-five percent of all the people attending divine services passed through the portals of a Catholic church. So it is largely throughout our country and throughout Christendom.

Take the campus of the University of Illinois. With students in attendance from most of the cities and towns in the state and from throughout the nation, it represents a fair cross section of our population. Non-Catholic friends who have attended most of the other churches on the campus have estimated that the student attendance at all the churches averages about two thousand. Though we number but about ten percent of the student enrollment at the university, we have in attendance each Sunday about as many as all the other churches and synagogues on the campus put together.

I mention this not in a spirit of boasting, but as an evidence

315

of the wisdom of the Church in lifting this matter out of the domain of unstable whims and moods and rendering it one of stern obligation — of obedience to a divine command. It is an evidence too of the inexhaustible vigor and vitality of the Catholic religion which has always made the worship, the love, and the service of God its primary objective.

In a letter published in *The Daily Illini*, a student told of visiting two of the so-called "liberal churches" on the campus on Homecoming Sunday. "I had expected," she said, "to find a large attendance at such churches in a university community. What I actually found was a picture of desolation — an attendance of thirty-seven at one and forty-nine at the other. What is the matter with students at this university?" was the plaintive query with which she closed. Without uncharitableness the question might better have been: "What is the matter with such churches?"

The answer is: They have abdicated their most important and distinctive function — the worshiping of God, and the instilling of love and deathless devotion to Him in the hearts of their people. Instead of temples for the worship of God, they have become lecture halls for the discussion of problems in sociology, economics, ethics, philosophy, science and politics. The name of God is spoken but rarely and then half apologetically as a curtsy reluctantly given out of deference to ancient religious usage and thought which are now largely passé. At other times the name of God is used in a vague, nebulous manner, as a synonym for Nature or the Cosmos, from which every condemnation uttered by Christ against those who misused the temple in His day might well be paraphrased today: "My house is a house of prayer; but you have made it a lecture hall for the discussion of everything under the sun but religion."

The simple truth is: People may discuss science and art. They may be interested in the coloring of a rose. They may admire a sunset or a waterfall; but they can love only a person and worship only a God. There can be no substitute for a personal God, a heavenly Father, from whom we come and to whose all-embracing arms we shall ultimately return. The golden calf of wealth, the fleshpots of sensual indulgence, the fetish of science — all intrigue for a day but they leave unsatisfied the deepest craving of the human heart for union with its God and Maker. "Our hearts have been made for Thee, O God, and they shall never rest until they rest in Thee!" This cry of Augustine, sounded after running through the whole diapason of the varied sensuality of ancient Rome, reechoes the anguish of humanity today, surfeited with myriad pleasures which excite but never satisfy.

Francis Thompson portrays the relationship between God and man which holds today, and which will hold till the crack of doom, when he depicts the Almighty warning wayward man: "All things betray thee who betrayest Me." There is something in the structure and in the heart of the universe which responds to goodness, truth, beauty and love, with divine compensations but which dooms their opposites to decadence and death.

The Mass is the central act of devotion in the Catholic religion. It is the unbloody renewal of the sacrifice of Calvary. When the priest bends low over the bread and wine and pronounces those tremendous words, the most momentous ever framed by human lips, "This is My body . . . this is My blood," the heaven of heavens opens, and the King and Ruler of the universe, Jesus Christ, comes down upon our altar, to be lifted up as a sacrificial Victim for the sins of the world. If we could but tear away the veil which hides from our eyes the vision of our Lord and Savior, how we would kneel breathless and transfixed in the rapture of a great devotion. It is a moment when the world falls away and we unworthy sinners kneel in the presence of the divine. "I could attend Masses forever," said Cardinal Newman, "and not be tired." That brief hour at Mass should be the happiest and the holiest of all our week.

The attendance at Mass is the mark of a practical Catholic. One who fails to attend is not worthy of the name. While all mortal sins involve great malice, there is attached to this sin a peculiar and unique malice. Other sins like anger or lust are usually the result of a great passion which clouds the reason and shakes the will; but missing Mass is done in cold blood — calmly, deliberately, willfully. The sinner says in effect: "Though you suffered excruciating pain on Calvary's Cross and died thereon for me, yet I will not give you one hour out of the 168 hours you give me every week." It is the action of an ingrate; God punishes it accordingly; it is one of the surest ways of losing one's religion and dying in mortal sin. As the tree inclines, so shall it fall; as it falls, so shall it lie. As a man lives, so shall he die; as he dies, so shall he spend eternity.

Why do people miss Mass? Failure to understand the meaning of Mass, carelessness, laziness, worldliness, and a lack of moral backbone when in non-Catholic surroundings. These are some of the causes; but the chief cause is a sinful life. Habits of sin, secret or public, cry out against attendance at a religious service which scourges them with ceaseless reproach. Why attend Mass when every moment rebukes me for my secret vice? is a question that inevitably arises. This fact is illustrated by the following incident.

A student had ceased to attend Mass and had abandoned the practice of his religion.

"It's all buncombe," he said to some of his fellow students who tried to remonstrate with him. "Priests are in it for what they can get out of it," he said. "It's just a racket, and I want none of it. I don't believe in it any longer."

Some months later he was about to be arrested on a paternity charge. Seizing an auto he sought to escape. Rounding a corner at full speed, the car turned over and pinned him, badly mangled, underneath.

"God," he cried to the state policeman who had just caught up with him. "Get me a priest. I'm dying. I want a priest badly."

With eternity closing in upon him, he threw aside his mask of make-believe and faced the terrible reality.

Blood was flowing from gaping wounds in his neck and forehead. The policeman sped for the nearest Catholic church several miles away. When he returned with a priest, consciousness had almost left the dying man. Glassy eyes, distorted with the wild look of horror that came into his face as he realized he was dying in mortal sin, was all that greeted the priest bending low over him, seeking to hear his confession. "God! God!" he was murmuring half-unconsciously. "It's too late — too late." A few convulsive twitchings of the lips . . . and he was dead.

In the inside pocket of his coat was found a newspaper clipping: it told of a priest who had gone wrong. What a flood of light that frayed clipping threw upon the mental processes he had gone through in those last five months. It requires no expert in psychology to see therein the sop he was trying to throw to his disturbed conscience. Stabbed with the consciousness of a double life, a habit of flagrant sin, he sought to *rationalize* his conduct. That is, he tried to find reasons to justify it. Unwilling to make conduct conform to the moral code of his religious faith, he sought to destroy the latter, saying, "It's all buncombe. It's all a racket."

He reached out for the clipping concerning a single priest as a drowning man grasps for a straw. Because Judas betrayed Christ, because Peter denied Him, because Thomas doubted, religion is all buncombe! Such are the straws for which people with guilty consciences have grasped throughout the ages in the futile effort to stay the waves of remorse flooding their soul and drowning them in a sea of anguish and torture.

This mental quirk is called by psychologists the tendency to rationalize conduct: it had better be called the tendency to irrationalize conduct, for that is what it is. Nature rebels against a dichotomy, a splitting of itself into two warring camps. When a man believes one thing and does the opposite, nature seeks to effect a unity. The logical procedure is to make his conduct conform to his approved moral code. Failing to do this, nature seeks to stop the gnawing of remorse by making belief conform to practice. This subtle treachery of the mind is a mechanism of escape, a symptom of a mind awry. It is a flight from a disagreeable situation into a world of unreality, where folly masquerades in the garb of make-believe and hides under a veneer of artifice.

Woman, it has been said half in humor, uses her intelligence to find reasons to support her intuitions. The sinner, unwilling to reform, uses his intelligence to find reasons to justify his mode of life. The name for this tendency of the mind to rationalize bad conduct is new, but the knowledge of it is old. Shakespeare gives a capital illustration. In the castle at Inverness, Macbeth has just murdered Duncan, the king. His hands are bloody, his face pale with fear, as he meets Lady Macbeth and reports hearing two servants of the king wake in their sleep and speak.

The following dialogue occurs:

Macbeth:
> One cried, *God bless us!* and *Amen*, the other;
> As they had seen me with these hangman's hands.
> Listening their fear, I could not say Amen,
> When they did say, God bless us.

Lady Macbeth: Consider it not so deeply.

Macbeth:
> But wherefore could I not pronounce, Amen?
> I had most need of blessing, and Amen
> Stuck in my throat.

Lady Macbeth: These deeds must not be thought after these ways; so, it will make us mad."[5]

When Shakespeare depicts Lady Macbeth uttering those words, he gives recognition to a universal tendency of the human mind to shrink from the frank acknowledgment of an evil deed, and to endeavor to escape by dressing it up in the garb of virtue. Murder must yield to a sweeter name which breathes the fragrance of innocence. It is a habit as old as Adam, who sought to hide his guilt behind his helpmate, Eve.

The remedy for the habit of missing Mass, for negligence in the practice of one's religion, for alleged lack of faith, is seldom argument. In most cases the remedy is to tear down the skeleton dangling in the family closet, to confess the secret vice, to begin to obey the moral law, to turn to Christ in penitence and prayer. A good conscience and a pure heart are more helpful than clear eyes in seeing God and in sensing the invisible realities of the spiritual world. Face toward the light and the shadows flee behind you.

The precept of hearing Mass obliges one to be present at the very inception of the holy sacrifice. People who display diligence and ingenuity in getting to their other appointments on time and to their trains ten and fifteen minutes in advance will, strangely enough, tramp into the august sacrifice with shocking tardiness. Such tardiness not only distracts and disedifies the entire congregation, but it manifests a lack of reverence for the great supreme Master, who is both the High Priest and Victim of the sublime sacrifice that is being offered at the altar.

Accidents, of course, are always liable to happen. Any one may at some time be late through unavoidable circumstances; for such there is no blame. There is, however, something singularly lacking in reverence for the holy sacrifice in the action of the person who is frequently or almost habitually late. If one but observes, he will note that as a rule, it is the same individuals who Sunday after Sunday come tramping into Mass with such disedifying tardiness. In order to avoid mortal sin a person must be present before the reading of the *Offertorium*, a short versicle read immediately preceding the unveiling of the chalice. The only safe rule for a person to follow is to aim to be present in the church from five to ten minutes before Mass time.

The true Catholic will not be deterred by slight inconveniences from attending Mass; he will exhaust every ingenuity to find a way. Christopher Columbus has given an inspiring example of respect for the sanctity of the Sunday under the most trying circumstances. It illustrates the spirit of unfaltering trust in God which guided him in his voyage across the uncharted waters of unknown seas in quest of a new world. Intensely anxious though he was to reach his journey's end, with a crew mutinying because of the continued failure to sight land, the intrepid explorer nevertheless insisted on anchoring the Santa Maria and the other vessels, and spending the day in prayer out of respect for the sanctity of the Sunday. How richly the Master rewarded his fidelity, all the pages of history record.

Destroy the sanctity of the Sunday and you throw civilization back into the darkness and mire of pagan materialism; you turn back the hands on the clock of progress. In the religious chaos and anarchy following the French Revolution, the irreligious suppressed the observance of the Sunday only to find the revolt of outraged human nature and interests of national progress compelling them to return to this divinely established plan. Though no friend of religion, Rousseau was eloquent in proclaiming that the observance of the Sunday was essential to the welfare of the nation.

The overwhelming majority of Catholics observe this third commandment with admirable fidelity. By the thousands, hundreds of thousands, millions, and even hundreds of millions they come — a vast army wending its way through the bleak countryside as well as in the populous cities. Peasant, artisan, housewife, merchant, scholar, king, there are in that mighty and innumerable throng that comes to bend their heads in worship before their uplifted King and Savior, to assist at that "clean oblation that is offered up among all nations from the rising of the sun even to the going down thereof."

There is no part of the habitable globe where that clean oblation foretold by Malachi is not offered. The traveler witnesses the fulfillment of this prophecy all the way from the little ice-covered chapel in the far stretches of the frozen North where the black-robed Jesuit missionary raises the Eucharistic Lord before the adoring eyes of the Eskimos, down to the burning sands of the Sahara where the white-gowned son of St. Dominic opens the portals of heaven and brings down to the altar the King of kings to listen to the prayers that flow from the strange tongues of the untutored children of Africa. From the mission chapels in the valleys of the Orient to the ones that nestle in the eternal snows of the Matterhorn, from the great crowded cathedrals in the populous cities of Europe to the little adobe chapels that dot the wind-swept plains of Arizona and New Mexico — everywhere there is offered that sublime drama of the Mass, the mystery of mysteries, the unbloody renewal of the Sacrifice of Calvary. In that great hymn of praise that rises up from all the corners of the world there is mingled the soft liquid tongue of the Italian, the Spaniard, and the Frenchman with the sharper notes of the Teuton and the Slav, embracing in its final volume all the tongues of mankind as it swells into a mighty paean of adoration before the throne of the Most High. What a wonderful privilege it is to be a member of this countless host, the Catholic Church, the kingdom of God on earth!

It is the spectacle of this mighty throng of over six hundred and fifty million men, women and children, leaving aside the cares of the world and marching through rain and snow and inclement weather to Mass every Sunday, that constitutes a source of never-ending wonder and of mystery to our separated brethren. In spite of musicals, paid singers, and extensive advertising, their own churches remain largely empty. Why the difference? One is a Church divinely established, dowered with a Pentecostal fire which has never ceased to burn. Conscious of her divinely appointed mission to speak as the voice of God to all mankind, she commands the worship of God and demands the attendance at Sunday Mass of every Catholic.

The other Churches founded by men, conscious of no divine authority, dare not command. They entreat, plead, cajole and entice; but mankind perceives the uncertainty and vacillation in their voices. They respond according to their mood and caprice: the result is empty churches, and the decadence of religious worship among them. Is it not evident then to every fair-minded person, Catholic or non-Catholic, that the policy of the Catholic Church, in removing attendance at divine worship on Sunday from the quicksands of mood and whim and placing it on the solid foundation of principle and law, is wise and just? Indeed her action in so doing is not one of expediency but of principle: it is a compliance with the law of nature, with the voice of reason, and with a divine command.

Discussion Aids

Name a point of fundamental divergence between Protestant denominations and the Catholic Church. What obligation is universal for mankind? What is at the heart of this religious worship? Explain this relationship between Creator and created. Is interior worship sufficient? Why not? Describe Sabbath observance under the Old Law. What did Christ do in regard to the existing Sabbath observance? Why was the seventh day of the week observed as the Sabbath under the Old Law? Why is Sunday observed in the New Law? What does the Church prescribe for keeping Sunday holy? Discuss. What is the Mass? Discuss attendance at Mass as the mark of a practical Catholic. Discuss "rationalizing conduct" as a reason for missing Mass. How is Malachi's prophecy fulfilled?

Practices

Do not let trivial excuses keep you from attending Sunday Mass.

Never be late for Mass.
Assist at Mass with recollection and devotion.

NOTES (Chapter 23)

1. Dt. 5:12
2. II Esd. 13:17-18
3. Mt. 12:11-12
4. Dt. 5:15
5. *Macbeth*, Act 2, Scene 2

CHAPTER 24

The Invocation of Saints

A Consequence of the Communion of Saints

An article of the Apostles' Creed which Christians of most denominations are accustomed to recite with all too little comprehension of its significance is: "I believe in the communion of saints." By these words we express our belief in the teaching of Christ and the Apostles that there exists an intercommunion between all the children of God, whether triumphant in heaven, or waging the battle for their salvation on earth, or suffering the purging penance of purgatory. Christ is the head and we are the members of His mystical body. By virtue of the communion of saints, the blessed in heaven can pray and intercede before the throne of God both for us and for the souls in purgatory. We too can offer our prayers and sacrifices for the relief of the souls in purgatory; they in turn can pray to God for us who are still members of the Church militant on earth.

The invocation of the saints may be said to follow as a consequence of the general doctrine of the communion of saints. The Church's teaching on the invocation of saints is thus defined by the Council of Trent: "The saints, who reign together with Christ, offer up their own prayers to God for men. It is good and useful suppliantly to invoke them, and to have recourse to their prayers, aid and help for obtaining benefits from God, through His Son Jesus Christ, who alone is our Redeemer and Savior. Those persons think impiously who deny that the saints, who enjoy eternal happiness in heaven, are to be invoked; who assert that they do not pray for men; who declare that asking them to pray for each of us in particular is idolatry, repugnant to the word of God, and opposed to the honor of the One Mediator of God and men, Christ Jesus."[1]

The Old and New Testaments clearly teach the principle and the practice of asking the prayers of our brethren. Thus God commanded Abimelech to ask Abraham's prayers: "He shall pray for thee and thou shalt live."[2] God hearkened to the prayers of Moses interceding for the sinful children of Israel in the desert.[3] God said to the friends of Job: "My servant Job shall pray for you; his face I will accept."[4] St. Paul writes: "Now I beseech you, brethren, for the Lord Jesus Christ's sake ... that you strive together with me *in your prayers to God for me.*"[5] To the Thessalonians he writes: "Brethren, pray for us."

Is it reasonable to suppose that a Christian who, while on earth prays for his friends, will cease to remember them or to care for them when he becomes a member of God's family in heaven? Surely his interest instead of waning will increase because he now perceives more clearly the spiritual needs of his friends on earth, and is more capable now as a saint of God of interceding for them. This has been the belief of the Church from the days of the Apostles to the present time. Let St. Jerome (340-420) bear witness to the faith of the early Church:

"If Apostles and martyrs," he writes, "while still in the flesh and still needing to care for themselves, can pray for others, how much more will they pray for others after they have won their crowns, their victories, their triumphs. Moses, one man, obtains God's pardon for six hundred thousand armed men, and Stephen prays for his persecutors. When they are with Christ will they be less powerful? St. Paul says two hundred and seventy-six souls were granted to his prayers, whilst they were in the ship with him. Shall he close his lips after death, and not mutter a syllable for those who throughout the world have believed in his gospel?"[6]

We learn that the angels pray for men from the vision of Zacharias and from the words of the angel Gabriel to Tobias: "When thou didst pray with tears ... I offered thy prayer to the Lord."[7] That they are interested in our struggles and rejoice in our victories is stated by Jesus Christ Himself: "There shall be joy before the angels of God upon one sinner doing penance."[8]

A non-Catholic friend once objected to the practice of praying to the saints in these words: "God is our Creator, and Christ is our Redeemer. In praying to the saints, you Catholics dishonor God and make void the mediatorship of Jesus Christ. You put the creature above the Creator and give to a creature the honor that belongs to God alone." This objection assumes that we pray to the saints *independently* of God and of their relationship to Him. If this assumption were true, the objection would be well founded. But such is not the case. The Church teaches, on the contrary, that God alone is the Source of all blessings and graces, the Giver of every good and perfect gift.

She teaches that whatever *influence* the saints possess comes from God and is traceable to their relationship with Him. Just as the moon borrows her light from the sun, so the saints borrow their light from the Sun of Justice, Jesus Christ, whom St. Paul calls "the one mediator of God and men."[9] Hence when we pray to the saints we ask them to aid us through the merits of Jesus Christ, while we beg Christ to assist us through His own merits. So careful is the Church to make the distinction clear to her children that she ends practically every prayer asking the saints to intercede for us and to succor us with the words "through our Lord and Savior, Jesus Christ."

A second objection to the invocation of the saints runs thus: Granted that there is no dishonor to God in this practice, the question still remains. Why should we pray to them when we can pray directly to God who can hear and answer us? "If it is vain and useless to pray to the saints because God can hear us," says Cardinal Gibbons in answering this objection, "then Jacob was wrong in praying to the angel; the friends of Job were wrong in asking him to pray for them, though God commanded them to invoke Job's intercession; the Jews exiled in Babylon were wrong in asking their brethren in Jerusalem to pray for them; St. Paul was wrong in beseeching his friends to pray for him; then we are all wrong in praying for each other. You deem it useful and pious to ask your pastor to pray for you. Is it not, at least equally useful for me to invoke the prayers of St. Paul, since I am convinced that he can hear me?"[10]

The fact is that our prayers to God do not and of course

should not decrease because of our prayers to the saints. On the contrary a devotion to the Blessed Virgin or to any of the saints tends inevitably to increase our love of God and quicken our loyalty and reverence for Him. Then too it must be remembered that while the Church declares it is necessary for salvation to pray to God, she merely states that it is "good and useful to invoke the saints, and to have recourse to their prayers, help and assistance, in order to obtain benefits from God through Jesus Christ, who alone is our Redeemer and Savior."

The practice of praying to the saints has assisted in keeping more vividly in the minds of the faithful the realities of heaven and the rewards bestowed by God upon those who served Him faithfully while on this earth. In a day when heaven is spoken of with hesitation and uncertainty even in Protestant pulpits, the Catholic doctrine of the invocation of saints serves as an anchor to the windward and protects the faithful in their unfaltering belief in the teachings of Christ and the Apostles. Heaven is as profound a reality to the Catholic as the earth upon which he lives; the saints and angels, as members of God's heavenly family, are not less real to us than the citizens of our earthly abode.

Discussion Aids

What do you mean by the communion of saints? Explain the honoring of the saints and the praying for the souls in purgatory as reasonable devotions? How does the Council of Trent define the teaching on the invocation of saints? Give instances from the Scriptures of praying for the brethren. How is the non-Catholic objection that praying to the saints makes void the mediatorship of Jesus Christ to be answered? How answer the objection that we should in all cases go directly to God in prayer? What is the value of praying to the saints for both ourselves and our neighbors?

Practices

Meditate on the doctrine of the communion of saints as a

fulfillment of the doctrine of the brotherhood of man under the Fatherhood of God.

Always offer your devotion to the saints through Christ our Lord.

Pray to your patron saint for help in the direction of your life.

NOTES (Chapter 24)

1. *Sess.* 25
2. Gn. 20:7
3. Ex. 32:30-34
4. Job 42:8
5. Rom. 15:30
6. *Ad Riparium*
7. Tb. 12:12
8. Lk. 15:10
9. I Tm. 2:5
10. Gibbons, *Faith of Our Fathers*, p. 162

CHAPTER 25

Images and Relics of Saints

They Are Venerated for What They Represent But Are Not Worshiped

The Catholic Church condemns the worship of images as idolatry but she sanctions reverence for the pictures and effigies of Christ and the saints. She does this not because of the material of which they are composed but because of what they represent. The notion that a Catholic worships a crucifix or an image of Christ is too absurd for serious refutation. Let a traveler ask the humblest Catholic peasant kneeling before a wayside shrine of the crucified Christ if he worships the image itself and he will answer that worship is due to God alone. He merely venerates the crucifix because it represents his Savior dying on the Cross.

The Church's teaching is thus expressed by the Council of Trent: "The images of Christ, and of His Virgin Mother, and of other saints, are to be had and retained, especially in churches; and a due honor and veneration is to be given to them; not that any divinity or virtue is believed to be in them for which they are to be honored, or that any prayer is to be made to them, or that any confidence is to be placed in them, as was formerly done by the heathens, who placed their hopes in idols; but because the honor which is given them is referred to the originals which they represent, so that by the images which we kiss, and before which we uncover our heads or kneel, we adore Christ and venerate His saints, whose likeness they represent. If any abuses have crept in among those holy and salutary observances, the Holy Synod ardently desires that they be utterly abolished."[1]

The penny Catechism states explicitly: "We should give to relics, crucifixes and holy pictures an inferior and relative honor, so far as they relate to Christ and His saints, and are memorials of them. We may not pray to relics or images, for they can neither see, nor hear, nor help us." In other words it is strictly forbidden to pray to a statue or a picture. The use that Catholics make of images is therefore precisely the same as civilized nations make of statues and likenesses of their great statesmen and heroes. Where is the city of any considerable size in the world which has not erected effigies of the nation's heroes and benefactors? Walk through the streets of Washington, London, Paris, Berlin, Vienna, Rome and thousands of other cities, and you will see numerous monuments erected to their illustrious men, seeking thus to honor them and to enshrine them in the abiding memory of their citizens.

Do we denounce this practice as the worshiping of images and accuse those nations of idolatry? To ask the question is to answer it. Then why should any Protestant feel misgivings when he sees the figure of Christ or of His Blessed Mother or of the saints in a Catholic church? They are there to increase the devotion of the faithful, to arouse in them holy sentiments and aspirations and to remind the faithful to imitate their examples of virtue and holiness of life.

The early Christians adorned their catacombs with frescoes of Christ, and of scenes from the Holy Scriptures. Among the most common were Moses striking the rock, Daniel in the lions' den, the birth of Christ, the coming of the Wise Men, the marriage feast of Cana, the raising of Lazarus, and Christ, the Good Shepherd. Statues were uncommon only because they were costly and difficult to make. When the Church emerged from the catacombs, however, she at once proceeded to decorate her churches with mosaics, paintings and sculptures.

It was not until the eighth century that a campaign was waged against images by Leo the Isaurian, Emperor of Constantinople; he ordered the paintings of Christ and His saints to be torn from the church walls and burned. Invading even the homes of people, he confiscated their sacred images, causing all effigies of bronze, silver and gold to be melted down and converted into coins, upon which he had his own image stamped. Like Henry

VIII and Cromwell he pretended to be moved by a zeal for purity of worship, while avarice was the real motive.

The warfare was continued by Constantine Copronymous, his successor. On one occasion, Stephen, an intrepid monk, held before the emperor a coin bearing that tyrant's effigy, with the words: "Sire, whose image is this?"

"It is mine," answered the Emperor.

Whereupon the monk threw down the coin and trampled it. He was seized by the royal attendants and put to a cruel death.

"Alas!" cried the holy religious to the Emperor, "if I am punished for dishonoring the image of a mortal monarch, what punishment do they deserve who burn the image of Jesus Christ?"

The destruction of images was revived by Luther and the other Reformers of the sixteenth century. The churches and monasteries were the great museums of the art of the Middle Ages. Many priceless paintings and statues were demolished, frescoed walls were whitewashed; and gorgeous stained glass windows with figures of Christ and the saints were ruthlessly smashed. The iconoclastic campaign was especially vehement in Germany, Holland and the British Isles. A traveler to these countries, visiting some of the desecrated Catholic churches which are now being used as Protestant houses of worship can scarcely fail to note the mutilated statues of Christ and the saints still standing in their niches.

They stand as grim reminders of a barbarous and fanatical warfare against religious memorials, which was not only a grievous sacrilege but an outrage against the fine arts as well. If the senseless outbursts had extended into Italy, France and Spain, some of the most priceless treasures of art would have been lost forever to the race. It is significant to note that the Lutheran and Tudor princes who encouraged the campaign of pillage had no qualms against confiscating the gold and silver vessels encrusted with precious gems.

"It has always seemed strange to me," says John L. Stoddard, "that Protestants use so sparingly those handmaids of religion — paintings and sculpture. Formerly, indeed, their prejudice against all symbols of Christianity was so intense that they not only stripped old churches, monasteries and cathedrals of their crosses, crucifixes, statues of the Apostles, and pictures of the Blessed Virgin, but actually mutilated sculptured carvings over the portals of the noblest sanctuaries, struck off the noses from the statues of bishops on their tombs, and white-washed frescoes of religious subjects upon cloister walls. Even in our own times some Protestants have thought it consonant with the worship of God to make the walls of their churches as bare and unattractive as possible. . . ."

He then proceeds to seek the cause of this strange hostility. "What is the cause," he asks, "of this aversion to the image of our Lord in those who claim to love Him, and who sing such hymns as 'In the Cross of Christ I glory,' and 'When I survey the wondrous Cross, on which the Prince of Glory died'? Does it not lie in an unreasonable hatred of the Catholic Church, which has for ages held this symbol as the most sacred object in the world? When people tell me that such memorials are unnecessary, they speak the truth perhaps so far as they themselves are concerned, but they assuredly cannot speak for all. Many there are who find such things a blessing. It is a matter of feeling and association, rather than of intellect. I, for example, though an educated man, and having attained an age when life is seldom influenced by sentimental emotions, confess to a feeling of genuine pleasure in seeing near me, when in church or in my home, some beautiful memento of the Son of God, or of His Mother, or the saints. I do not pray to them, of course, yet often during prayer or religious meditation I love to turn my gaze to them, as aids to a devotional frame of mind."[2]

In walking through Westminster Abbey, which was once a Catholic church but is now used as a Protestant church, I saw monuments and statues everywhere. They commemorate the illustrious men and women of England who are buried there. Suppose I were to address myself thus to an English Protestant worshiping in this historic shrine.

"Why, your church is filled with statues. Are you not guilty of idolatry?"

"Not at all," he would reply, "I do not adore or worship the statues; they are simply memorials."

So, too, it is with Catholics. Statues and images in our churches are memorials to Christ and the saints.

The intention in the mind of the worshiper is all important, as Cardinal Gibbons was fond of illustrating with the following story. An English parson once remarked to a Catholic friend:

"Tom, don't you pray to images?"

"We pray before them," replied Tom, "but we have no intention of praying to them."

"Who cares for your intention," retorted the parson.

"Don't you pray at night?" observed Tom.

"Yes," said the parson, "I pray at my bed."

"Yes, you pray to the bedpost."

"Oh, no!" said the reverend gentleman; "I have no intention of doing that."

"Who cares," replied Tom, "for your intention."[3]

After the dedication of our beautiful new church at the campus of the University of Illinois, the writer invited the members of the University Senate, consisting of about 150 professors, and their wives to the church where he explained to them its art and the symbolism of its sacramentals. As educators they were deeply impressed by the generous use which the Church makes of pictures, mosaics, sculptures and effigies in the stained-glass windows to vivify faith and enrich the devotion of her people. Wherever their gaze turned, there was some beautiful sacramental to arrest the attention and turn it to thoughts of God and members of His heavenly family.

"So numerous," observed a professor of educational psychology, as he pointed to the altar with its Calvary group, surmounted by a canopy depicting the scene of the Last Supper, to the Stations of the Cross and to the numerous paintings and sculptured effigies, "are the stimuli to devotion that it should be difficult for a person to think of aught but holy subjects while in this church. Everything that architecture, painting and sculpture can do to interpret religion in terms of beauty and to stir the mind of the worshiper to a vivid realization of Christ's redeeming love for man, has been done. It is an object lesson in the art of reaching the mind through the gateway of the senses; the Catholic Church appeals not only to the ear through the spoken word from the pulpit but she quickens the mind with imagery obtained through the eyes, which is usually the richest in content and remains the longest in memory."

No less significant was the reaction of the professor of English literature. "Father," he said, "I was born of Protestant parents and brought up in a town in New England where something of the Puritanical spirit of the Colonists still held sway. I may be said to be, therefore, a dyed-in-the-wool Protestant; but I can see now that the reformers of the sixteenth century made a great mistake when they demolished statues, destroyed paintings, and exiled beauty from our churches. They have reduced them to buildings with four plain walls and an empty pulpit, thus identifying religion with drab ugliness. I hope that it will not be long until we return to the authentic Christian viewpoint which prevailed up to the Reformation, and which regards all beauty as mirroring the God of beauty, holiness and love. Art should be the handmaid of religion, achieving its highest purpose when it lifts the mind of the creature to the contemplation of the Eternal."

While the great masterpieces of painting and of sculpture have been brought into existence under the inspiration of the religious motive, and adorn our massive cathedrals, we must not minimize the influence of the simpler and less pretentious paintings and statues that adorn the churches of the humble poor. They speak to them in a language which they understand and stir their piety not less effectively than the more artistic works which appeal to the cultured worshiper and the aesthete in our great cathedrals. No one who has entered an adobe chapel in New Mexico and observed Indians at prayer before an altar abounding in the vivid paintings of the suffering Christ, which would not meet the canons of great art, or who has seen the devotion of a Tyrolean peasant kneeling before a wayside shrine with its hand-carved crucifix, can doubt the influence of even the simplest and the humblest representations to kindle the religious fervor of the worshiper.

The Catholic Church is the religious home of the cultured savant and the untutored peasant, of the rich and of the poor; in her mighty family of some 659,000,000 children are found the types and temperaments of the race. Far from looking with disdain upon the lowly poor, she seeks to embellish the commonplace of their lives, to weave through the drab monotony of their routine threads of color and to quicken their imagination with visions of beauty. The memories of paintings and images which they have gazed upon with awe and reverence from their tenderest years often remain with them to the end, exercising a profound influence upon their character.

Perhaps no writer has pointed out with greater penetration the far-reaching character of this influence than the English historian, Lecky: "Associated with the fondest recollections of his childhood," he writes, "and with the music of the church bells . . . painted over the altar where he received the companion of his life, around the cemetery where so many he loved are laid, on the stations of the mountains, on the portal of the vineyard, on the chapel where the storm-tossed mariner fulfills his grateful vows, keeping guard over his cottage door, and looking down upon his humble bed, forms of tender beauty and gentle pathos forever haunt the poor man's fancy, and silently win their way into the very depths of his being. More than any spoken eloquence, more than any dogmatic teaching, they transform and subdue his character, till he learns to realize the sanctity of weakness and suffering the supreme majesty of compassion and gentleness."[4]

In closing this treatment of the veneration of images, a word about the use of *relics* may be appropriate. The Council of Trent teaches "that the holy bodies of holy martyrs and others now living with Christ — which bodies were the living members of Christ and the temples of the Holy Spirit — and which are by Him to be raised to eternal life and to be glorified, are to be venerated by the faithful; for through these bodies many benefits are bestowed by God on men, so that they who affirm that veneration and honor are not due to the relics of the saints, or that these and other sacred monuments are uselessly honored by the faithful, and that the places dedicated to the memory of the saints are in vain visited with the view of obtaining their aid, are wholly to be condemned."[5]

Contrary to the impression of many non-Catholics, the Church does not ascribe any magical virtue or curative powers to the relic itself: she merely states, in accordance with the Scriptures, that relics are sometimes the occasion of God's miracles. The Scriptures record the incident of a woman who was cured by touching the hem of our Lord's garments,[6] of the sick healed by the shadow of St. Peter[7] and of the handkerchiefs and aprons that had touched the body of St. Paul.[8]

The reverence for Christian relics is as old as Christianity itself. Back in the second century we find that the disciples of Polycarp who had been burned at the stake "took up his bones, which were more valuable than precious stones and finer than refined gold, and laid them in a suitable place where the Lord allows us to assemble in gladness and joy to celebrate the birthday of his martyrdom."[9] Writing in the fourth century, St. Jerome thus refutes the charge of idolatry or "cinder-worshiping": "We do not worship, we do not adore, we do not bow down before the relics of the martyrs in order the better to adore Him whose martyrs they are."[10]

Discussion Aids

Why does the Church sanction the giving of reverence to images and relics of saints? What is the teaching of the Council of Trent on the doctrine? Give the catechism definition of the doctrine. Do we honor images of our national heroes? Is this practice idolatry? What was the practice of early Christians in the catacombs in the matter of sacred pictures, etc.? Give a brief history of the campaign against images. Quote John L. Stoddard on this doctrine; Cardinal Gibbons; the historian, Lecky.

Practices

Have the crucifix and pictures of our Lord and the saints in places of honor in your home.

Be enrolled in the scapular and wear a scapular medal as a reminder that it is the livery of our Lady.

NOTES (Chapter 25)

1. *Sess.* 25
2. Stoddard, *Rebuilding a Lost Faith*, p. 199

3. Gibbons, *Faith of Our Fathers,* pp. 201-202
4. *History of European Morals,* Vol. 2, p. 106 (Appleton & Co., N.Y., 1870)
5. Sess. 25
6. Mt. 9:20-21
7. Acts 5:15-16
8. *Ibid.,* 19:12
9. *Mart. Polly.*
10. *Ad Riparium,* 9

CHAPTER 26

Purgatory and Prayers for the Dead

Basis of Devotion Traced
Through Scripture, Tradition and Reason

"Why do Catholics pray for the dead?" is a question frequently asked by our non-Catholic fellow citizens. Since the practice of praying for the souls of the deceased is based upon the doctrine of purgatory which was abandoned by the Reformers in the sixteenth century, and is now practically unknown among their followers, the latter are naturally at a loss to understand the Catholic custom of praying for their departed brethren, or as it is commonly called, "the devotion to the poor souls." The Church keeps this devotion before the eyes of her children by setting aside the second of November as All Souls' Day, permitting her priests to celebrate three Masses on that day for the souls of the departed, and by designating the entire month of November as the month of special devotion for the poor souls. Let us invite our non-Catholic friends then to investigate with us the basis of this devotion in Scripture, tradition and in reason.

The Scriptures encourage us to pray not only for one another on earth, and to invoke the intercession of the saints and angels, but they encourage us to pray for the souls of our deceased brethren as well. In the second Book of Maccabees it is narrated that after Judas had defeated Gorgias, he came with his company to bury the Jews slain in the battle. "Making a gathering, he sent twelve thousand drachmas of silver to Jerusalem for sacrifice to be offered for the sins of the dead." He did not regard their sins to be grievous, "because he considered that they who had fallen asleep with godliness had great grace laid up for them." The sacred writer then expresses the doctrine involved herein: *"It is, therefore, a holy and wholesome thought to pray for the dead, that they may be loosed from their sins."*[1]

While our dissenting brethren do not acknowledge the Books of Maccabees to be inspired, they must at least admit them to be faithful historical records that bear witness to the Jewish faith centuries before Christ. As a matter of fact, they rest upon the same authority as Isaiah, St. John and all the other books in the Bible — the infallible teaching authority of the Church which has declared all the books in the Bible to be inspired.

Our Savior speaks of the forgiveness of sins in "the world to come"[2] which refers to purgatory according to St. Augustine and St. Gregory the Great. In his letter to the Corinthians, St. Paul tells us that "every man's work shall be manifest" on the Lord's day. "The fire," he continues, "shall try every man's work of what sort it is. If any man's work abide," that is, if his works are righteous, "he shall receive a reward. If any man's work burn," that is, if his words are faulty and imperfect, "he shall suffer loss but he himself shall be saved, *yet so as by fire.*"[3] In these words St. Paul tells us that the soul of such a man will ultimately be saved, though he will suffer for a time the purifying flames of purgatory.

This too is the unanimous interpretation of the Fathers of the early Church and the continuing tradition of the intervening centuries. It speaks to us from the tombs of the martyrs and from the catacombs where lie the bodies of the early Christians. In going through the catacombs of St. Callixtus under the plain of the Roman campagna outside the walls of Rome, the writer saw a number of inscriptions echoing still the last words of the dying Christians: "In your prayers remember us who have gone before you." "Mayest thou have eternal light in Christ," was the answering prayer of those who remained behind. Inscriptions such as these are found under the tombs of many Christians in the first three centuries and are reproduced by Monsignor A. S. Barnes in his book, *The Early Church in the Light of the Monuments.*[4]

This Apostolic custom of praying for the dead is frequently

referred to in the writings of the Fathers of both the East and West. Tertullian (160-240) in two different passages speaks of anniversary Masses: "We make on one day every year oblations for the dead, as for their birthdays."[5] "The faithful widow prays for the soul of her husband, and begs for him in the interim repose, and participation in the first resurrection, and offers prayers on the anniversary of his death."[6]

In his funeral sermon over the Emperor Theodosius, St. Ambrose, Bishop of Milan, said: "Give perfect rest to Thy servant Theodosius, that rest which Thou has prepared for Thy saints. . . . I have loved him, and therefore will I follow him into the land of the living; nor will I leave him until by tears and prayers I shall lead him whither his merits summon him, unto the holy mountain of the Lord."[7]

One of the most touching incidents which have come down to us from the writings of the Fathers upon this subject is from the pen of St. Augustine, who lived in the beginning of the fifth century. This scholarly bishop relates that when his mother was dying, she made this last request of him: "Lay this body anywhere; let not the care of it in any way disturb you. This only I request of you, that you would remember me at the altar of the Lord, wherever you be."[8]

The memory of that request drew from her son this fervent prayer: "I, therefore, O God of my heart, do now beseech Thee for the sins of my mother. Hear me through the medicine of the wounds that hung upon the wood. . . . May she, then, be in peace with her husband. . . . And inspire, my Lord . . . thy servants, my brethren, whom with voice and heart and pen I serve, that as many as shall read these words may remember at Thy altar, Monica, Thy servant. . . ."[9] In this incident there is reflected the universal custom of the early Church of praying for the dead as well as her belief in a state called *purgatory*.

The custom of offering prayers and sacrifice for the souls of their departed relatives and friends was deeply rooted among the ancient Jews and in spite of all their dispersions and wanderings has continued down to the present day. Some years ago the writer observed great numbers of them praying for their deceased at the famous Wailing Wall in Jerusalem. An authorized prayer book in common use among the Hebrews in our country contains the following formula of prayers prescribed for funerals:

"Departed brother! mayest thou find open the gates of heaven, and see the city of peace and the dwellings of safety, and meet the ministering angels hastening joyfully toward thee. And may the High Priest stand to receive thee, and go thou to the end, rest in peace, and rise again into life. May the repose established in the celestial abode ... be the lot, dwelling and the resting-place of the soul of our deceased brother (whom the Spirit of the Lord may guide into Paradise), who departed from this world, according to the will of God, the Lord of heaven and earth. May the supreme King of kings, through His infinite mercy, hide him under the shadow of His wing. May He raise him at the end of his days and cause him to drink of the stream of His delights."[10]

"It is indeed strange," observes Father B. L. Conway, C.S.P., "that the Reformers should set aside such a body of testimony, both in Scripture and tradition, for purgatory and prayers for the dead. But doctrine is so interwoven with doctrine in the consistent gospel of Jesus Christ, that the denial of one central dogma logically means the denial of many others. Luther's false theory of justification by faith alone led him to deny the distinction between mortal and venial sin, the fact of temporal punishment, the necessity of good works, the efficacy of indulgences, and the usefulness of prayers for the dead. If sin is not remitted, but only covered; if the 'new man' of the gospel is Christ imputing His own justice to the still sinful man, it would indeed be useless to pray for the dead that they be loosed from their sins. Luther's denial of purgatory implied either the cruel doctrine that the greater number of even devout Christians were lost, which accounts in some measure for the modern denial of eternal punishment, or the unwarranted assumption that God by 'some sudden, magical change' purifies the soul at the instant of death."[11]

While the word *purgatory* does not occur in Scripture, the reality which it symbolizes is referred to both in the Old and the New Testaments and in the writing of the Fathers in the East and in the West. Since the belief in the efficacy of prayers for the dead was universal in the infant Church, it follows that the belief in purgatory was likewise universal; for without a purgatory, prayers for the dead would be meaningless.

Entirely aside, however from the evidence offered by Scripture and tradition, reason alone would suggest and even demand the existence of a midway state between heaven and hell. Since "nothing defiled can enter heaven," it follows that a soul departing this life either with venial sin or with temporal punishment still to be suffered, could not enter heaven. It could not in justice be sent to hell which is everlasting, as such a punishment would be out of all proportion to the offense committed. It is entirely probable that vast numbers of people die with venial sin upon their souls; they are not worthy to enter at once into heaven; they cannot in justice be doomed to hell. There must, therefore, be another state where the punishment is suited to the offense. Such is the imperative dictate of reason. That state which reason thus demands is *purgatory,* where they are cleansed of their venial imperfections and rendered suitable to enter into the august presence of their Lord and Creator in the unspeakable happiness of heaven.

The custom of praying for the souls of our departed friends is not only conformable to Holy Scripture, but is prompted by the instincts of our nature. The doctrine of the communion of saints emphasizes the social and spiritual solidarity of our race by showing how we can help one another in time of need. It goes a long way to rob death of its terrors. In denying this doctrine the Reformers of the sixteenth century did violence not only to the Scriptures and the unbroken tradition of the Christian Church for sixteen centuries, but they halted and jarred also the instincts of our nature and the craving of our hearts. They severed those tender and sacred ties which bind earth with heaven — the soul in the flesh with the soul released from its fleshy tabernacle.

If I may pray for my brother on this earth, why must I not continue to pray for him when he has crossed the border line into eternity? Does he not, therefore, still live and think and remember and love? What earthly reason is there then why I should not continue to remember him in my prayers and prove my love for him not by unavailing tears but by the more potent means of my petitions in his behalf addressed to the God of mercy and compassion? What Christian is there who can stand at the open grave and see the body of a loved one being lowered to its resting place without lifting tear-dimmed eyes to heaven with the cry: "O dear God, have mercy upon the soul of my beloved!"

Regardless of the silence of his Protestant creed upon the efficacy of prayers for the dead, he hearkens to the voice of his heart and responds in that universal language of love and sympathy which all mankind understands. From the mute lips of his deceased friends he hears again the same plea as that uttered by Job in his adversity: "Have pity on me, at least you my friends, because the hand of the Lord hath touched me!" That such an appeal does not fall upon deaf ears is an evidence that the human heart has not allowed prejudice to rob it of its love and sympathy.

Out of his long experience of more than fifty years in the ministry, Cardinal Gibbons narrates an incident which illustrates this point: "I have seen," he relates, "a devoted daughter minister with tender solicitude at the sickbed of a fond parent. Many an anxious day and sleepless night did she watch at his bedside. She moistened the parched lips, and cooled the fevered brow, and raised the drooping head on its pillow. Every change in her patient for better or worse brought a corresponding sunshine or gloom to her heart. It was filial love that prompted all this. Her father died and she followed his remains to the grave. Though not a Catholic, standing by the bier she burst those chains which a cruel religious prejudice had wrought around her heart, and, rising superior to her sect, she cried out: 'Lord, have mercy on his soul.' It was the voice of nature and of religion."[12]

Tennyson reflects alike the Christian tradition and the natural yearning of the human heart when he makes his hero, the dying King Arthur, thus address his surviving comrade, Sir Bedivere:

"I have lived my life, and that which I have done
May He within Himself make pure; but thou,
If thou shouldst never see my face again,
Pray for my soul. More things are wrought by prayer
Than this world dreams of. Wherefore, let thy voice

Rise like a fountain for me night and day."[13]

When John L. Stoddard was groping in the mists of uncertainty for the sure light of religious truth, he received a letter from a Catholic friend calling his attention to the beauty and reasonableness of the Church's teaching on purgatory. The letter which proved so illuminating and helpful to Stoddard states the case with admirable lucidity as follows: "There is hardly a religious system of antiquity in which some similar provision (to purgatory) is not found. It was left for the 'Reformers' of the sixteenth century to reject this immemorial dogma of the Church. When they denied the sanctity of the Mass and many other sacramental features of Catholicism, the doctrine of purgatory went with the rest. If the souls of the dead pass instantly into an eternally fixed state, beyond the efficacy of our intercessions, then all our requiems, prayers and similar practices are vain. But if, on the contrary, we believe in the communion of saints, that is, in the intercommunion of the threefold Church, militant on earth, suffering in purgatory, and triumphant in heaven, then we on earth can influence, and be influenced by, the souls who have crossed the border.

"Few, indeed, quit this life in a state of purity and grace which warrants their immediate entrance into heaven. Still fewer, let us hope, are those to whom the blessed refuge of purgatory, that halfway house of our dead, is closed. I cannot conceive how Protestants can believe as they do on this point, nor is it astonishing that their rejection of purgatory has been followed, in the case of many, by the elimination of a belief in hell; for the latter doctrine, taken alone, is monstrous. In fact, all Catholic doctrines are interdependent; they stand or fall together. You cannot pick stones out of the arch, and expect it to stand, for it will not do so. Purgatory is one of the most humane and beautiful conceptions imaginable. How many mothers' aching hearts has it not soothed and comforted with hope for some dead, wayward son!"[14]

After his conversion Stoddard wrote the story of his religious wanderings in *Rebuilding a Lost Faith,* in which he thus sets forth the reasonableness of this doctrine which made so powerful an appeal to him: "The doctrine of the Catholic Church in reference to purgatory states that there is such a place, in which souls suffer for a time, before they can be admitted to the joys of heaven, because they still need to be cleansed from certain venial sins, infirmities and faults, or still have to discharge the *temporal* punishment due to the mortal sins, which is as yet uncancelled, though the *lasting* punishment of those sins has been forgiven and removed through Christ's atonement. Furthermore the Church declares that by our prayers and by the acceptable sacrifice of the Mass we may still help those souls through the merits of Christ. Beyond this statement the Church's formal doctrine does not go; but it is *not* an article of Catholic faith that there is in purgatory any material fire. It is generally believed that souls in purgatory suffer spiritual anguish from the fact that they then feel acutely, as they could not do on earth, the perfect happiness from which they are for a time excluded, while they must also understand the enormity of the sins which they committed against their heavenly Father and their Savior."[15]

The writer has met many Protestants who, though they have no doctrine of purgatory in their official creed, acknowledge that they often remember their deceased loved ones in their prayers. I remember a devout Protestant woman who stated that she prayed each day for her son who was killed in an automobile accident a few days after his graduation from the university. Though she had never read a line of St. Augustine, and probably never heard even his name, yet out of the unquenchable yearning of her heart and the ineradicable instincts of her human nature, she knew his teaching, that "there are some who have departed this life, not so bad as to be deemed unworthy of mercy, nor so good as to be entitled to immediate happiness."[16]

In constantly increasing numbers our separated brethren are coming to recognize both the reasonableness and the authentic character, in the light of the teachings of Christ and the Apostles, of the doctrine of purgatory. As Mallock well observes: "It is becoming fast recognized that it is the only doctrine that can bring a belief in future rewards and punishments into anything like accordance with our notions of what is just and reasonable. So far from its being a superfluous superstition, it is seen to be just what is demanded at once by reason and morality; and a belief in it is not an intellectual assent only, but a partial harmonizing of the whole moral ideal."[17] In short, the doctrine of purgatory answers the demand of reason, harmonizes with the instinctive yearnings of our nature, and reflects the teaching of Christ and His Apostles.

Discussion Aids

How should you answer the question of a non-Catholic, "Why do Catholics pray for the dead?" What Scriptural references sustain the doctrine? What testimony to the doctrine is found in the catacombs? In the Church Fathers? What was the practice in this matter among the ancient Jews? The modern Jews? What action did the Reformers take on this doctrine? Is the word *purgatory* found in Scripture? Is the reality symbolized by that word found in Scripture? Give examples. How is purgatory a demand of reason? Quote Cardinal Gibbons, Alfred Tennyson, John L. Stoddard and the author Mallock on the reasonableness of the doctrine.

Practices

Have Masses said for your departed ones.
Include in your grace after meals the prayer for the faithful departed.
Include your departed ones in your daily prayers.

NOTES (Chapter 26)

1. II Mc. 12:43-46
2. Mt. 12:32
3. I Cor. 3:13-15
4. *The Early Church in the Light of the Monuments*, pp. 149-157 (Longmans, Green & Co., N.Y., 1913)

5. *De Cor. Mill.* 3
6. *De Monag.* 10
7. *De Obitu, Theod.*, 36, 37
8. *Confessions*, Book 9, p. 215, trans. by J.G. Pelkington (Leveright Pub. Co., N.Y., 1943)
9. *Ibid.*
10. *Jewish Prayer Book*, ed. by Isaac Leeser (Slote & Mooney, Philadelphia)
11. *The Question Box*, pp. 395-396
12. Gibbons, *The Faith of Our Fathers*, p. 224
13. "Morte d'Arthur," in *The Best of Tennyson*, p. 606 (T. Nelson Co., N.Y., 1930)
14. Stoddard, *Rebuilding a Lost Faith*, p. 155
15. *Ibid.*, p. 156
16. *De Civ. Dei.*, 21:24
17. *Is Life Worth Living?*, p. 290 (Belford, Clarke & Co., Chicago, 1879)

CHAPTER 27

The Way of the Cross

Going with Christ to Calvary

The places where Christ was born, lived and died, have always been dear to the hearts of the Christian world; they are redolent with memories of the Savior. Especially sacred in the eyes of Christians is that stretch of ground over which Christ bore His cross on the journey to Calvary. In the early ages vast multitudes of Christians made pilgrimages across Europe over into Asia to visit these sacred places; there they meditated on His sufferings and walked in His footsteps to Calvary.

When the Holy Land fell into the possession of the Mohammedans, pilgrimages to Jerusalem became hazardous; there was danger from the despotic government and from the savage fanaticism of the people. The idea therefore occurred to pious pilgrims who had previously made the journey to Palestine to erect representations of scenes in Christ's journey to Golgotha. They would assist meditation by presenting the sufferings of the Savior in a vivid, realistic manner.

In the early part of the fifteenth century, Blessed Alberez, a pious Dominican who had visited the Holy Land, erected in Cordova, Spain, a series of little chapels, each of which contained a painting of one of the principal scenes in the Passion of Christ. In the fifteenth and sixteenth centuries reproductions of the sufferings of Christ carrying His cross to Calvary were erected in various countries of Europe. The devotion made an instant appeal to the hearts of Christians. At first the number of stations varied; in some places there were erected ten stations; in others twelve, fourteen, twenty, and even more. For the sake of uniformity the Church has specified fourteen as the number of stations to be erected in all the churches of the world.

Some of the scenes depicted in the stations are contained in the gospels; there are others which are not mentioned in Scripture but which have come down to us through an oral tradition from the first century. Thus there is no Scriptural authority for three falls of Christ under the cross, nor for the touching story of Veronica wiping the face of Jesus. They are traceable to that body of written and unwritten testimony that dates from Apostolic times.

In 1694 Pope Innocent XII declared that the same indulgences formerly gained by a visit to the holy places in Palestine could now be secured by all Franciscans and those affiliated with the Order who devoutly made the Way of the Cross. Shortly afterwards Pope Benedict XIII extended these indulgences to all the faithful. The indulgences are very great. The learned theologian, Father Alston says: "It may be safely asserted that there is no devotion more richly endowed with indulgences than the Way of the Cross and none which enables us more literally to obey Christ's injunction to 'take up our cross and follow Him.' "[1] In 1931 Pope Pius XI abolished all previous indulgences and granted these:

1. A plenary indulgence as often as the Way of the Cross is made.

2. A plenary indulgence for all who (a) make the Way of the Cross on a day on which they receive Holy Communion, and (b) for those who have made the Stations ten times and within a month receive Holy Communion.

3. A partial indulgence of ten years and ten quarantines for every station made if the Way of the Cross is not completed.

How are the stations to be made in order to gain the indulgences? What prayers are to be said? Strictly speaking there are no prescribed prayers. All that is necessary is that the person walk around the stations meditating upon the sufferings of Christ, preferably as depicted in each of the stations, or at least upon the sufferings of Christ in general. Prayer books are helpful for the beginner in suggesting suitable reflections for each station. It is well also to say some brief oral prayer such as a Hail Mary and a brief expression of love and contrition at each station, such as: "My Jesus, I love Thee more than myself. Grant that I may love Thee always and never offend Thee again." After one has become familiar with the devotion he will be able to make the stations in a brief time, from five to ten minutes.

Persons who are at sea or sick or are unable for various reasons to go to the church may gain the indulgences by holding in the hand a crucifix specially blessed for this devotion and reciting the Our Father and Hail Mary once for each of the fourteen Stations, then the Our Father, Hail Mary and Gloria five times, followed by one Our Father, Hail Mary and Gloria, for the intentions of our Holy Father. The indulgence may be applied either to one's own soul or to the souls in purgatory. Thus does our tender Mother, the Holy Church, temper her laws to the weakness of her children, allowing us now to gain indulgences which were formerly secured only by long, arduous pilgrimages to the Holy Land made in the face of dangers, privations and many hardships.

What values other than the indulgences are to be derived from this devotion? What spiritual fruits are gained? Spiritual writers tell us that there is no subject upon which meditation is so wholesome and salutary for the soul as upon the sufferings of Christ. This would seem to be confirmed by an incident narrated in the life of St. Bridget. Christ once appeared to her with blood streaming from all the wounds in His hands and feet and side. When asked what had reduced Him to this pitiable condition, our Divine Savior answered: "It is the doing of those who never consider the great love I manifest for them by all I suffered for them on the cross." It was as a perpetuation of His Passion that our Holy Redeemer instituted the Holy Sacrifice of the Mass, placing ever before us in vivid drama the story of His sufferings.

To suffer and to sacrifice for others and then to receive from them no acknowledgment — that is painful indeed. Parents and others who have toiled and sacrificed only to be repaid by ingratitude know how sharp a pang it is. Shakespeare reflects the experience of the ages when he exclaims: "Sharper than a serpent's tongue is base ingratitude."

In the Way of the Cross we have the antidote that will calm

and still our passions. A man once said to a holy priest: "Father, I have an ungovernable temper. I fly into an angry rage at the slightest provocation."

"Go," said the priest, "and make every day the Way of the Cross. When you come to the twelfth station showing Jesus dying on the Cross in the most excruciating torment with a prayer of forgiveness for His executioners on His lips, linger a little longer. See if in the face of such patience and forbearance you can find it in you ever to grow angry or to blaspheme."

The man did so and found that the thought of Christ dying on the cross for his sins smothered in its very beginnings the tendency to anger and to curse. The Way of the Cross is a literal fulfillment of Christ's injunction: "If any man will come after Me, let him deny himself, and take up his cross daily, and follow Me."[2]

Some years ago the writer made a visit to the Blessed Sacrament in Old St. Mary's Church in the business district of Chicago. It was evening. Men and women of all classes on their way home from work were dropping in for a visit to their Eucharistic Lord. As I glanced up from my prayers, my eyes fell upon the countenance of a man making the Way of the Cross. I recognized him as a distinguished jurist, a judge of the Superior Court, universally known and loved. I told him when he came out how edified I was at seeing him, despite the pressure of a multitude of legal duties and other responsibilities, find time for this beautiful devotion.

"Father," he said, "after a busy day at court, listening to lawyers haranguing and arguing and trying one's patience, I find comfort and peace of mind in making the Way of the Cross."

The Way of the Cross is the antidote for the passion of anger, the counteractive of lust, the prophylactic for vice and sin. Make the Way of the Cross daily if possible, or at least weekly. You will then experience the profound truth of those words of the great philosopher of the human heart, Thomas a Kempis, in the "Following of Christ": "For there is no other way unto life and unto true inward peace, but the Way of the Cross and of daily mortification. Go where thou wilt, seek whatsoever thou wilt, thou shalt not find a higher way above nor a safer way below than the Way of the Holy Cross."[3]

Discussion Aids

Where are the original stations of the cross? Where and when did Blessed Alberez erect stations? In what centuries were stations erected in various countries of Europe? Was the number always fourteen? Is there Scriptural authority for all the scenes depicted in the stations? What indulgences were granted by Pope Innocent XII? By Pope Benedict XIII? What are the indulgences now granted? By what Pope were they granted? How does one make the stations? What value other than indulgences are to be derived from this devotion?

Practices

Practice the devotion of the Way of the Cross as an antidote for the vice or fault you are trying to eradicate from your life.

Say the stations for the peace of the world.

Say the stations as part of your preparation for confession.

NOTES (Chapter 27)

1. *Catholic Encyclopedia*, Vol. 15, p. 571
2. Lk. 9:23
3. Book 2, Ch. 12

CHAPTER 28

The Holy Name: Why Reverence It?

The Church Wars Against Profanity

One of the most impressive memorials in Paris, dear to the heart of every Frenchman, and visited annually by thousands of travelers from all parts of the world, is the tomb of Napoleon Bonaparte in the Hotel des Invalides. It rests beneath a majestic dome, erected by the famous architect Mansart, and is strangely reminiscent of St. Paul's in London. Around the central crypt are chapels in which repose the remains of two men intimately associated with the Emperor in his mighty scheme of placing all Europe at the feet of France.

They are his two brothers, Joseph, King of Spain, and Jerome, King of Westphalia. There, too, repose the two great generals, Turenne and Vauban. The martial atmosphere is further enhanced by the scene depicted in the cupola of the dome, showing St. Louis offering to the Savior the sword with which he fought for the Christian faith.

Leaning over a balustrade, the visitor looks down into the open crypt upon a sarcophagus of red Finland granite, the gift of the Emperor, Nicholas of Russia, in which are contained all that is mortal of the great Napoleon. His remains were brought back to France from the island of St. Helena in fulfillment of the dead Caesar's wish, as expressed in his last will, and now inscribed over the bronze entrance to the crypt: "I desire that my ashes repose on the banks of the Seine, in the midst of the French people whom I have loved so much."

Gazing upon the sarcophagus are twelve colossal figures, representing the chief victories of the greatest soldier of France. Between the statues are displayed fifty-four flags, taken from the hands of the enemy and symbolizing the victories of Napoleon at Austerlitz, Jena, the Battle of the Bridges, under the Pyramids in Egypt, and all the other battlefields where the tricolor of France waved in victory.

Tattered and torn, scarred with the holes of bullets, and crimsoned with the blood of dying warriors, these flags stand beside the tomb of the great Napoleon as the mute but eloquent symbols of the dauntless valor and bravery of the soldiery of France. Hither the Frenchman brings his children to feast their eyes upon the memorials of their former greatness, and bathe their minds in an atmosphere redolent with the martial grandeur of a glorious past. History is speaking to the youth of France from that silent tomb and from every bullet hole in those tattered flags. The heart of the Frenchman beats faster and his eyes light up, as he gazes upon these symbols of courage, of heroism, and of victory achieved by his fellow countrymen on the bloody field of battle.

Let us suppose that on the fourteenth of July, when the French are celebrating Bastille Day and while a vast throng of citizens is standing with bowed heads before the ashes of the mighty dead and gazing in silent reverence upon the tattered flags, a vandal should suddenly rush through the door into the open crypt. Raising a huge sledgehammer before the eyes of the amazed throng, he brings it crashing down upon the tomb until he has demolished it. Then he seizes the flags, gathered from all the battlefields where Napoleon's soldiers fought and died, and tearing them to shreds, stomps upon them. Can you not imagine how the indignation of the French people would burst out with fury upon the scoundrel guilty of so heinous an outrage?

Would not the gendarmes have the greatest difficulty in restraining the indignant throng from tearing the profaner limb from limb? Would not the whole population of France from Cherbourg to Marseilles rise up as a single man in protest against such desecration of the name and memory of their honored dead? Would they not say as with a single voice: "The man who desecrates these hallowed symbols of our nation's past insults every son and daughter of France. It is not merely the crime of vandalism. It is the sacrilege of profanation — the desecration of memorials held forever sacred by the chivalrous people of France."

Why should this tomb and these flags be held in such honor and reverence? Is the tomb not simply a piece of granite, and the flags mere tattered rags? Yes, they are such; but they are also something more. They are *symbols* of the valor and the bravery of the soldiery of France; it is because of what they *symbolize* to the people of France that they are held in such reverence.

Words too are symbols. They are the *verbal effigies* of ideas, persons and things. It is because of the realities which they symbolize that they derive any honor bestowed upon them. The person who is deserving of the highest honor and reverence that man can render is Jesus, our Savior. He is the untarnished mirror of the majesty of God. As the God incarnate who redeemed the world from the effects of its own sinfulness by dying for us upon Calvary's cross, Christ is entitled to the love, honor and reverence of all mankind.

Since the name of Jesus stands as the symbol, the verbal effigy of the personality of Christ, it follows that the Holy Name should be enshrined in the hearts of men, and should receive from them the highest honor paid to any name uttered by human lips. In honoring the Holy Name we honor Jesus Christ Himself: in profaning that sacred name we profane Christ Himself.

It is probable that many people who profane the Holy Name do not realize that it stands as the symbol of the divine personality, Jesus Christ Himself, as truly as a painting or a sculptured effigy represents the Savior. It is true that the latter represents Christ in a more visible and graphic manner, but not more really, and even not so intimately as the Holy Name itself does. If people understood more clearly how profanation of the sacred name of Jesus reflects irreverence toward Christ Himself, it is probable that few who call themselves Christians would be guilty of such irreverence. Let us therefore present the following example to illustrate this point so clearly that even the little child can see and understand.

The scene occurs in Chicago in the beautiful Cathedral of

the Holy Name. It has been so designated to hold aloft forever before the eyes of Christian people the great ideal of reverence for the august name of our Savior, Jesus Christ. A vast congregation is assembled to hear holy Mass. His Eminence the Cardinal, with his two auxiliary bishops and the officers of the Mass, preceded by a long line of acolytes in cassock and surplice, has just arrived at the altar. Now let us suppose that a man carrying a sledgehammer suddenly appears, hurrying down the central aisle; he opens the gates of the sanctuary and climbs upon the altar. Then before the horrified eyes of the clergy and laity, he rains blow after blow upon the figure of Christ nailed to the cross until it falls in fragments upon the floor. Then he tramples upon them while he shouts: "This is what I think of your God, Jesus Christ."

Can you imagine the horror that would fill the hearts of priests and people at the sight of such a sacrilege? Can you not imagine the indignation that would sweep over the whole Christian world at the news of such a desecration? Would not the whole of Christendom arise in indignant protest against such a profanation? Would not even the weakest Catholic, careless and negligent though he be in the practice of his holy faith, burn with indignation at the news of such an outrage? More sacrilegious even than the despoliation of Napoleon's tomb and its battle flags would be this desecration of the emblem, sacred to all Christianity, the effigy of Christ dying upon Calvary's cross.

Surely no Christian, even the most indifferent, could fail to perceive the malice of such an act of profanation. He would probably be willing to endure any suffering before he would stoop to so heinous a sacrilege. Yet how does this act differ in character from the action of the man who profanes the Holy Name of Jesus? One tramples in the dust the *sculptured* likeness of Christ; the other tramples in the mire of cursing and profanity the *verbal* effigy of the Savior.

The first symbol was carved by human hands; the second was conceived by the Most High in heaven. It is the name which the angel revealed to the Blessed Virgin: it had been chosen by Almighty God before the child had been conceived in her womb. "Behold thou shalt conceive in thy womb, and shalt bring forth a Son; and thou shalt call His name Jesus."[1]

Nor is the sculptured symbol more expressive or meaningful than the verbal one. For the name Jesus means *Savior*, as was disclosed by Almighty God in revealing the mission of Christ on earth. Thus the angel declared to Mary: "Thou shalt call His name Jesus. *For He shall save His people from their sins.*"[2]

Reason dictates that reverence be shown toward the sculptured likeness of Christ. Not only reason, but also Almighty God speaking through the inspired words of St. Paul, commands us to honor the Holy Name: "He humbled Himself, becoming obedient unto death, even to the death of the Cross. For which cause God also hath exalted Him, and hath given Him a name which is above all names: That in the name of Jesus, every knee should bow, of those that are in heaven, on earth, and under the earth."[3]

We do not strain at any figure of speech or at any forced comparison, therefore, when we ask in calm earnestness: How does the action of the man who takes a name chosen by Almighty God in heaven, the most sacred name that human lips can utter, and tramples it in the mire of cursing and profanity, differ in malice from the action of the man who tramples upon the fragments of the sculptured likeness of Christ? The simple truth is that there is *no substantial difference* in the malice of these two acts. If there be any difference at all, the greater malice would seem to lie in the profanation not of an earth-born symbol but of the heaven-born symbol of the divine personality, the Holy Name of Jesus, at the sound of which "every knee should bow, of those that are in heaven, on earth, and under the earth."

We are all to some extent victims of the tyranny of the senses. We are more easily impressed by what we see with the eyes and feel with the hands than by realities which we discern not with the senses but with the intellect. Hence it is that even the dullest man can see the figure of Christ in the sculptured statue, though he cannot see the Savior in the verbal effigy, but discerns the divine personality behind that symbol only by a process of reasoning.

Once, however, the meaning of that tremendous symbol is made known to him, once it is made clear to him that the *Holy Name is the verbal effigy of Jesus Christ Himself*, then it becomes difficult to understand how he could ever bring himself to the sacrilege of profaning the Holy Name of Jesus any more than he could ever bring himself to the crime of trampling the sculptured image of Christ under his feet. It is difficult to see how Christian people could excuse him more readily for the former than for the latter. We have dwelt at considerable length upon this important point, that the Holy Name is the symbol, *the verbal effigy of Jesus Christ Himself*, because we are convinced that most sins of profanity against the sacred name are traceable ultimately to the failure to understand this truth, and that they will largely cease when their malice is clearly perceived.

True, there is some profanity, particularly on the part of the young, that is traceable to their slavish copying of others. Because some people are foolish enough to render themselves slaves to drunkenness, sensuality and profanity is no reason why we should subject ourselves to the tyranny of such vices. Youth should remember that vulgar and profane speech is an indication of a lack not only of culture and refinement but of character and manhood. "Out of the abundance of the heart," said our Blessed Lord, "the mouth speaketh." It is reasonable to believe that when a youth, who has fallen into the habit of profanity through thoughtless imitation of others, realizes the insult it offers to Almighty God, he will speedily end so vile a practice.

Let us now turn from these considerations, proposed by human reason, to the inspired words of Holy Writ to observe the emphasis it places upon the duty of reverence to the name of God and of His divine Son, our Lord and Savior. In the Book of Exodus we read the words of the divine command: "Thou shalt not take the name of the Lord thy God in vain: for the Lord will not hold him guiltless, that shall take the name of the Lord his God in vain."[4] The first part of this injunction constitutes the second commandment in the decalogue. It commands us to speak with reverence of God and of holy things.

This refrain is sounded frequently in the books of the Old Testament. Thus Ezechiel utters the inspired prophecy: "And I will make my holy name known in the midst of my people Israel, and my holy name shall be profaned no more: and the Gentiles shall know that I am the Lord, the Holy One of Israel."[5]

When we come to the New Testament, which depicts the life and teachings of our Savior, we find an increased emphasis upon the sanctity, power and reverential character of the Holy Name of Jesus. To the name, Jesus, is added that of "Christ," which means the "anointed." This title is expressive of office and honor. Thus under the Old Law it was the custom to anoint priests, prophets and kings with oil, to signify that they were called to play a special role in the relations between God and man. When our Savior came into the world, He was called upon to play the threefold role of Priest, Prophet and King. His anointing, however, was not from man but from on high. This the prophet clearly indicates when he addresses the Redeemer in the words: "Thou hast loved justice, and hated iniquity: therefore God, Thy God, hath anointed Thee with the oil of gladness above Thy fellows."[6]

The efficacy of invoking His name in prayer is thus expressly taught by our Blessed Lord: "And whatsoever you shall ask the Father in My name, that will I do: that the Father may be glorified in the Son. If you shall ask Me anything in My name, that I will do."[7] A striking instance of the efficacy of a petition sought in the name of Christ is narrated in the Acts of the Apostles, when a beggar who was lame from birth entreated them for alms. Whereupon Peter said: "Silver and gold I have none; but what I have, I give thee: In the *name* of Jesus Christ of Nazareth, arise and walk. And taking him by the right hand, he lifted him up, and forthwith his feet and soles received strength. And he leaping up stood, and walked, and went with them into the temple, walking and leaping, and praising God."[8]

Later on Peter and John were asked by Annas and Caiphas and the kindred of the high priest: "By what power or by what name, have you done this?" To which Peter unhesitatingly replied: "Be it known to you all, and to all the people of Israel, that by the name of our Lord Jesus Christ of Nazareth, whom you crucified, whom God hath raised from the dead, even by Him this man standeth here before you whole." Then he added those impressive words which should be written indelibly into the memory of every follower of the Crucified Christ: "Neither is there salvation in any other. For there is no other name under heaven given to men, whereby we must be saved."[9]

Reverence for the name of God and of His divine Son is not therefore a recent development; neither is it of human origin; it is a command of the Most High, repeated through a long line of prophets, and reaching its climactic expression in the words of Christ and of His Apostles. Visitors to the catacombs of St. Calixtus on the outskirts of Rome will find the sacred words *Jesus* and *Christus* carved in the soft limestone over the tombs of the martyrs. The literature of the first four centuries describing the ordeals of Christians in the Roman amphitheatre shows that they met death with a smile lighting their faces and pronouncing with their dying breath the sacred name of our Lord Jesus Christ.

Down through all the centuries of the Christian era, the Church has held aloft before the eyes of her children the glorious name of her divine Founder. She carves that Holy Name upon the cornerstone of her churches, writes it upon her altars, breathes it at the bedside of the dying. It is the name of Jesus which occurs most frequently in her prayers at Mass and in the administration of her sacraments. The Holy Name of Jesus is as music to her ears and as honey to her lips. She encourages her children to invoke that sacred name often, especially in time of danger.

A striking manifestation of the devotion and love, which should burn in every Christian heart for the Savior and His sacred name, is narrated by the learned Dominican, Father Charles J. Callan. A young Catholic man lay on an operating table in a New York hospital. The doctors and nurses were gathered around him, ready to begin the operation. Resting his hand gently upon the patient's shoulder, the chief surgeon said:

"My young friend, I think I should tell you frankly that your malady has been diagnosed as cancer of the tongue. In order to save your life, it will be necessary for us to remove your tongue. If there is anything you wish to say, please do so now, as you will be speechless the rest of your life."

As the full import of the doctor's words sank home to the youth his face paled in a momentary shudder. There was a twitching of the muscles about the mouth. Then, pulling himself together, he looked into the faces of those around him, and said in a calm, earnest voice:

"I want my last words to be: 'Praised be the sacred name of Jesus!' "

In mentioning the incident later, the chief surgeon declared it was the most eloquent sermon ever uttered in his presence, and one he would carry with him to his dying day. Would that it could be placed before the eyes of every man and woman in America.

The Church does not render, however, merely lip service to the ideal of reverence for the Holy Name: she translates this ideal into life and action. She has brought millions of men into a mighty organization known as the Holy Name Society. This society, which is to be found in practically every parish in our land, has as its primary end the inculcation of reverence for the Holy Name and the avoidance of all profanity. Every Catholic man in America should be a soldier in this mighty army which emblazons upon its raised banners the sacred name of Jesus and pledges itself to reverence that name in chastity of speech.

Probably the most impressive of all the gatherings in connection with the Eucharistic Congress in Chicago was the one sponsored by the Holy Name Society. Held at night in Soldiers Field, a vast throng, numbering over 400,000 men from all parts of our country and from every foreign land, assembled to manifest to the world their reverence and devotion to the Holy Name. The climax of the meeting was reached when the great arc lights were extinguished, and every man held aloft in his right hand a lighted candle, as a symbol of his living faith in Christ and his reverence for the Holy Name. Every man then joined in repeating in unison the following pledge of the Holy Name Society:

"In honor of His divine name, I pledge myself against perjury, blasphemy, profanity and obscene speech. . . . I dedicate my manhood to the honor of the sacred name of Jesus, and beg that He will keep me faithful to the pledge until death. . . ."

The voices of the members of this mighty army of almost half a million men rose in volume until their echo could be heard great distances through the streets of Chicago. Non-Catholic journalists, describing the effect of the myriad candlelights shining in the darkness and the surging roar of men's voices rising like thunder from the earth, declared in their papers the next morning that it was the most stirring and impressive demonstration of religious faith and loyalty ever staged in the western hemisphere or probably anywhere in the world.

While pleased with such impressive public demonstrations of faith, which certain occasions render appropriate and wholesome, the Church is far more concerned to see that each individual translates the ideals of faith into proper habits of speech and conduct in his private life. She asks not merely the pledge but its fulfillment. She demands that every man and boy, worthy of the name Catholic, speak with reverence of God and of His divine Son, Jesus Christ. She can scarcely bring herself to think that a woman or a girl would so debase herself as to indulge in profanity.

Not a one of her vast empire of more than 659,000,000 members, speaking every language under the sun, can be unconscious of the daily tug of the Church's teachings upon his habits of speech and conduct — pulling them in the direction of reverence and chastity. Is it not apparent not only to those of the household of the faith, but to our dear non-Catholic friends as well, that the Church's ceaseless insistence upon reverence for the name of God and of His divine Son, our Savior, is but the external reflection of an inward and living faith in these abiding realities?

Today in many a pulpit calling itself Christian, God is spoken of as a vague force somewhere off in the distant sky, a "system of cosmic patterns," the meaning of which no one understands, an impersonal energy that for all practical purposes is lost in the vast reaches of the universe. Other ministers speak of God as though they were none too sure of His very existence. From these same pulpits Christ is pictured as an ethical teacher with the limited outlook of a Palestinian Jew of the first century, with no vestige of the divine about Him. How refreshing to the weary occupants of such depressing pews must it be to discover that in the Mother Church of Christianity, God and His Christ are not exiled as outmoded myths or as threads of tenuous gossamer tangled somewhere off in the cobwebs of the sky, but are living, abiding realities.

How comforting must it be to such members to discover that in the great historic Church of Christendom, the only one which unites the twentieth century with the first, God and His

Christ are still the objects of our love and worship, still the unseen witnesses of our every conversation, the spectators of all the thoughts and aspirations that stir in the silent kingdom of the soul. Will they not accept our outstretched hand and join with us in proclaiming to a world that has lost its moorings and is wandering in the mists of uncertainty that God, our Father, and Jesus Christ, our Lord and Savior, still rule, still reign!

Discussion Aids

How should you explain to a non-Catholic why Catholics revere the Holy Name? What is the meaning of the name *Jesus?* Quote the text in which St. Paul shows that great honor is due to the Name of Jesus. Explain how the Name is the verbal effigy of Jesus Christ Himself. What is the Second Commandment? Quote Ezechiel 29:7. What does *Christ* mean? What did our Blessed Lord promise in His Name? Describe Peter's first miracle. What was Peter's answer to Annas and Caiphas?

Practices

Say "Blessed be the Name of Jesus" whenever you hear the Holy Name profaned.

Join the Holy Name Society and encourage other men to do so.

Avoid all careless or serious taking of the name of God in vain.

NOTES (Chapter 28)

1. Lk. 1:31
2. Mt. 1:21
3. Phil. 2:8-10
4. Ex. 20:7
5. Ez. 39:7
6. Ps. 44:8
7. Jn. 14:13-14
8. Acts 3:6-8
9. *Ibid.*, 4:10-12

CHAPTER 29

Why Catholics Honor Mary

Outside of the Catholic Church the name of Mary is seldom heard. No hymns are sung in her honor; no prayers for Mary's intercession wend their way toward heaven. In her regard, there is only a silence — cold, strange and mystifying to the filial hearts of men. In the various creeds which have fallen away from the Mother Church, Mary has been relegated to a position of such obscurity that she has become almost an outcast. But in the Mother Church of which the Divine Son, Jesus Christ, is the living heart and soul, Mary the Mother is not forgotten but is honored and loved second only to God Himself.

Why do Catholics honor Mary? In the first place, it should be understood that Catholics do not worship Mary in the sense in which they adore Christ. Adoration belongs to God alone; reverence and honor to the saints. But as Mary is the Queen of Saints, the respect and honor shown her surpasses that accorded the other saints of God.

The grounds upon which Catholics honor and love Mary may be said to be fourfold: her divine maternity, her perpetual virginity, her Immaculate Conception, and her Assumption into heaven. First of all, Mary is the Mother of Jesus, the Son of God. She was singled out from among all the women of the universe by the omniscient mind of the Godhead for this unique honor and singular distinction.

Now it is a principle abundantly illustrated in Holy Scripture that when God selects a person for a particular office, He always bestows upon that soul the graces and virtues necessary for the appropriate discharge of its mission. When Moses, for example, was chosen by God to be the leader of the Hebrew people, he hesitated because of "impediment and slowness of tongue"; but Jehovah reassured him by promising to supply him with all the qualifications necessary for that high office: "I will be in thy mouth, and I will teach thee what thou shalt speak."[1]

Likewise was the prophet Jeremiah sanctified from his birth because he was to be the herald of truth to Israel. John the Baptist was filled with the Holy Spirit even from his mother's womb in order that he might be a shining light to blaze the way for the coming of the Messiah. That they might fulfill their high office effectively, the Apostles were endowed with the gift of tongues and other powers. As St. Paul says: "Our sufficiency is from God, who hath made us fit ministers of the New Testament."[2]

Important as were the various roles played by personages in the great drama of our redemption, they pale into insignificance in comparison with the role of Mary. To her was given the most sublime, the most sacred, the most intimate relationship to Jesus that was ever accorded to any human — the relationship of mother to son. For the perfect fulfillment of that sublime office Almighty God lavished upon Mary wondrous and ineffable graces and blessings. She stands, therefore, preeminent among the saints of heaven, as the fairest, the most beautiful, and the most worthy of our love and devotion.

When we say that Mary is the Mother of God, we assert implicitly two truths. First, that Jesus Christ, her Son, is true man; otherwise, Mary could not be His Mother. Second, that her Son, the Incarnate Word, is also true God; otherwise, Mary could not be the Mother of God. "In other words we affirm," as Cardinal Gibbons points out, "that the Second Person of the Blessed Trinity, the word of God who in His divine nature is from all eternity begotten of the Father, consubstantial with Him, was in the fullness of time again begotten, by being born of the Virgin, thus taking to Himself, from her maternal womb, a human nature of the same substance with hers."[3]

One might object that Mary is only the Mother of the

human nature of Christ, and therefore should not be styled the Mother of God. This objection may be best answered by asking the question: Is our mother the mother of our soul? That, the nobler part of man's nature, is created directly and immediately by Almighty God; and yet no one would dream of referring to his mother as the mother of his material nature, or the mother of his body.

"The comparison," observes Cardinal Gibbons, "teaches us that the terms parent and child, mother and son, refer to the persons and not to the parts or elements of which the persons are composed. Hence no one says: "The Mother of my body, the Mother of my soul,' but in all propriety, 'My mother' the mother of me who live and breathe, think and act, one in my personality though uniting in it a soul directly created by God, and a material body directly derived from the maternal womb. In like manner, as far as the sublime mystery of the Incarnation can be reflected in the natural order, the Blessed Virgin, under the overshadowing of the Holy Spirit, by communicating to the Second Person of the Adorable Trinity, as mothers do, a true human nature of the same substance with her own, is thereby really and truly His Mother."[4]

The second great prerogative of Mary which furnishes additional ground for our devotion is her perpetual virginity. Though the Mother of Jesus, she remained ever a Virgin; for the child that was born to her was conceived by the power of the Holy Spirit. Thus St. Matthew states that the angel sent by God said to Joseph: "Fear not to take unto thee Mary thy wife, for that which is conceived in her is of the Holy Spirit."[5] St. Luke likewise testified to her perpetual virginity: "The angel was sent from God to a virgin espoused to a man whose name was Joseph."[6] Thus she alone of all the race united in herself the dual glories of motherhood and virginity.

The third prerogative of the Blessed Virgin is her Immaculate Conception. Not only was she free from the slightest stain of actual sin, but by a singular miracle of divine grace she was free also from original sin, with which all the other children of Adam are born into this world. It was eminently fitting that she who was destined to be the Mother of Christ, who was to give Him flesh of her flesh and blood of her blood, should be undefiled by even that slight shadow of Adam's fall. To her alone, among all the members of the race, was granted this singular immunity. It is to be noted that the Immaculate Conception does not refer to the miraculous conception of Christ in the womb of the Virgin Mother without the intervention of a human father, as many non-Catholics imagine, but to the conception of Mary in the womb of her mother without the stain of original sin.

This dogma of the Immaculate Conception was thus defined by Pope Pius IX: "We define that the Blessed Virgin in the first moment of her conception, by the singular grace and privilege of Almighty God, in virtue of the merits of Jesus Christ, the Savior of the human race, was preserved free from every stain of original sin."[7] While this was not officially proclaimed a dogma of the Catholic faith until 1854, it had actually been held in the Church for centuries. As Cardinal Newman points out in his "Development of Doctrine," not all the doctrines of the Church were fully blossomed in the first centuries. Time was required for their growth and development.

The mustard tree has wide-spreading branches under whose shade many travelers find shelter; but time is required for the tiny mustard seed to unfold its potentialities and reach its mature growth. So it is with this doctrine of the Immaculate Conception and with many other doctrines, such as, the Holy Trinity and the Atonement now held alike by Protestants and Catholics. As W. H. Mallock well says of the Catholic Church: "Her doctrines as she one by one unfolds them, emerge upon us like petals from a half-closed bud; they are not added arbitrarily from without; they are developed from within."

The fourth great prerogative of the Blessed Virgin is her Assumption into heaven. It was eminently fitting that the body of the chaste and Immaculate Mother of God was not permitted to undergo disintegration and putrefaction but was assumed into heaven. This belief of Christians from the earliest times down to the present was formally defined as a dogma of the Universal Church by Pope Pius XII on November 1, 1950.

"After we have poured forth our prayers of supplication again and again to God," declared the Pontiff, "and have called upon the Spirit of Truth, for the glory of Almighty God who has lavished His special affection upon the Virgin Mary, for the honor of her Son, the immortal King of the Ages and the Victor over sin and death, for the increase of the glory of that same august Mother, and for the joy and exultation of the entire Church; by the authority of our Lord Jesus Christ, of the Blessed Apostles Peter and Paul, and by our own authority, We pronounce, declare and define it to be divinely revealed dogma: that the Immaculate Mother of God, the ever Virgin Mary, having completed the course of her earthly life, was assumed body and soul into heavenly glory."

Entirely aside from this fourfold evidence, her four prerogatives, there is another and a more compelling reason why we honor and love Mary; Jesus Christ honored and loved Mary, His Mother. Of the thirty-three years our Savior spent on earth, all but three years were spent in the closest and most intimate association with Mary. Indeed, almost all we know of the first thirty years of our Lord's life is recorded in the verse of the Evangelist; "He went back to Nazareth and was subject to them and grew in age and wisdom before God and man."

Jesus not only obeyed the commands of Mary, He anticipated her every wish. He loved her with all the passionate tenderness and devotion of the warmest and kindest of filial hearts. As a little babe He nestled in her tender arms and drew nourishment from her virgin breasts; and yet that little babe nestling at His Mother's bosom, and breathing the sweet perfume of His breath into the roses of her cheeks, is none other than the almighty and eternal Godhead.

It is the same Infinite and Omniscient Being who called the universe into existence out of the yawning abyss of nothingness and who hung the stars in the heavens as so many lanterns to light our way. It is the Infinite Creator of innumerable worlds whose mathematics is the orbit of the stars, whose chemistry is the rainbow of the skies, who has written the story of creation in the strata of the rocks and folded them up as the pages of a mighty book for the geologists of after ages to read and ponder o'er. If the Incarnate Word, Jesus Christ Himself, bowed His head in obedience, love and devotion to Mary, His Mother, can we frail children of Eve do better than follow the example of the Master and give Mary the humble tribute of our reverence and our love?

"In those who disbelieve in Christ's divinity," observes John L. Stoddard, "the slighting of the Virgin Mother may be comprehensible; but why should evangelical Protestants object to designate as Blessed the Mother of the Savior? Can anyone expect to please even an earthly son by showing a lack of reverence to His Mother? How much less, then, can such a course be pleasing to the Son of God, who, while enduring agony upon the cross, confided His Mother to His beloved disciple?"[8]

The beauty and the glories of Mary's character have been the inspiration throughout the ages of many of the world's greatest masterpieces in art and sculpture. Indeed the painting which is said by many critics to be one of the finest that ever came from human hands is the Sistine Madonna that now hangs in the famous Dresden Gallery. It is the masterpiece of the world-renowned artist, Raphael.

Even as a youth, Raphael had a special devotion and love of the Virgin Mother; she was his ideal of angelic beauty and virgin innocence. Nothing fascinated him so much as the effort to make the canvas glow with the majestic beauty of Mary's countenance as perceived by his mental vision. To express through the gentle play of lights and shadows and the subtle blending of colors those delicate and ethereal beauties of the Virgin Mother that seemed ever to defy the coarse medium of the artist's brush, became the overpowering passion of his life. At last, between 1515 and 1519 Raphael succeeded in imprisoning upon the canvas his spiritual vision of the Madonna's beauty. The result is the flowering of the artistic genius of the Italian race — the climax of the painter's art. It remains to this day one of the masterpieces of all time.

In that face of striking beauty are reflected the powerful strength of a Mother's love combined with the infinite tenderness and delicacy of the Virgin. Through those soft and gentle eyes one perceives the soul within, pure as the angels. Travelers have been so affected by the strange beauty of the painting, that tears have come to their eyes and they have stood transfixed before this vision of celestial loveliness. The things of earth seem to fade away, as they stand enraptured at this glimpse of heaven, this vision from another world.

But just as Raphael found in his devotion to Mary and his

meditation upon the beauties and glories of Mary's character the inspiration to draw from the magic rainbow of his own fancy and to imprison on the canvas colors that were never seen before on land or sea, so will each of us find in our devotion to Mary the inspiration that will give to our souls the urge so to shape our character that its picture will stand out as a masterpiece of beauty on the multicolored canvas of human life.

Not only in art and sculpture, but in literature as well, has Mary's inspiration been felt. She has been the theme of some of the greatest of the world's poetry. Even the non-Catholic poet, Wordsworth, pays tribute to the glory of Mary's character in these beautiful lines:

> Mother! whose virgin bosom was uncrossed
>   With the least shade of thought to sin allied
> Woman! above all women glorified,
>   Our tainted nature's solitary boast
> Purer than foam on central ocean tost,
>   Brighter than eastern skies at daybreak strewn
> With fancied roses, than the unblemished moon
>   Before her wane begins on heaven's blue coast,
> Thy image falls to earth.[9]

One of the most quoted of modern poets, Rudyard Kipling, though not of our faith, has written this touching prayer to Mary:

> Oh Mary, pierced with sorrow,
>   Remember, reach and save
> The soul that comes tomorrow
>   Before the God that gave!
> Since each was born of woman,
>   For each at utter need
> True comrade and true foeman
>   Madonna, intercede!

The eminent historian, William H. Lecky, though not a

member of the Christian faith, found himself compelled by the facts of history to pay the following tribute concerning the influence of the ideal of the Blessed Virgin upon western civilization: "The world is governed by its ideals, and seldom or never has there been one which has exercised a more salutary influence than the mediaeval conception of the Virgin. For the first time woman was elevated to her rightful position, and the sanctity of weakness was recognized, as well as the sanctity of sorrow. No longer the slave or toy of man, no longer associated only with ideas of degradation and of sensuality, woman rose, in the person of the Virgin Mother, into a new sphere, and became the object of a reverential homage, of which antiquity had no conception . . . .

"A new type of character was called into being; a new kind of admiration was fostered. Into a harsh and ignorant and benighted age this ideal type infused a conception of gentleness and purity, unknown to the proudest civilizations of the past. In the pages of living tenderness, which many a monkish writer has left in honour of his celestial patron; in the millions who, in many lands and in many ages, have sought to mould their characters into her image; in those holy maidens who, for the love of Mary, have separated themselves from all the glories and pleasures of the world, to seek in fastings and vigils and humble charity to render themselves worthy of her benediction; in the new sense of honour, in the chivalrous respect, in the softening of manners, in the refinement of tastes displayed in all the walks of society; in these and in many other ways we detect its influence. *All that was best* in Europe clustered around it, and it is the origin of many of the purest elements of our civilization."[10]

Mary is not, however, a cold empty abstraction, an ideal to be reverenced, but reverenced always from afar. She is not a star hung in the distant heavens reaching us only by a light that shines through the realms of infinite space: she is our Mother, near and dear to us, loving us with all the warmth of a mother's love. As the little child frightened by the shadows of night finds safety in his mother's arms so will we in time of temptation find a safe refuge by fleeing to the outstretched arms of Mary our Mother. If we will but clasp the loving hand of our Mother, stretched out to aid us in every danger, our uncertain footsteps will be guided safely to that golden ladder upon whose rungs we will climb step by step, to the very throne of her Son and Savior, Jesus Christ.

Discussion Aids

Explain the honor that Catholics give to Mary, upon three grounds. Explain fully what we mean when we say that Mary is the Mother of God. What is meant by Mary's perpetual virginity? What is the dogma of the Immaculate Conception? Does it refer to the miraculous conception of Christ, or to the so-called Virgin Birth? When was it proclaimed by the Church? Had this dogma been held by the Church before this proclamation? Explain. In addition to her four prerogatives, name a fifth reason why Catholics love and honor Mary. Reproduce the substance of John L. Stoddard's view on this doctrine. What may be said of Raphael's masterpiece on the Madonna? What do Wordsworth and Kipling say of Mary? the historian, Lecky?

Practices

Cultivate a feeling of nearness to the Mother of God because she is really your heavenly mother.

Say especially in time of temptation, "O Mary, conceived without sin, pray for us who have recourse to thee."

Have a picture or a statue of Mary in a conspicuous place in your home.

NOTES (Chapter 29)

1. Ex. 4:12
2. II Cor. 3:6
3. Gibbons, *Faith of Our Fathers*, p. 167
4. *Ibid.*
5. Mt. 1:20

6. Lk. 1:27
7. "Ineffabilis Deus," issued by Pope Pius IX, Dec. 8, 1854
8. Stoddard, *Rebuilding a Lost Faith*, pp. 176-177
9. "The Virgin," in *Complete Works of Wordsworth*, Vol. 7, p. 316 (Houghton Mifflin Co., Boston, 1911)
10. Lecky, *History of Rationalism*, Vol. 1, p. 225 (Appleton, N.Y. 1886)

CHAPTER 30

The Devotion of the Holy Rosary

A Worldwide Prayer

One of the most universal and popular devotions in the Catholic Church is that of the Holy Rosary. It is to be found in all the countries of the world from the frozen stretches of the Yukon to the burning sands of the Sahara and out into the islands in the Indian Sea. It is popular with all classes, poor and rich, illiterate and learned; the untutored peasant in the field, as well as the learned theologian, find in the rosary the manna for their souls.

Tradition ascribes the *popular* use of the rosary to St. Dominic, founder of the Dominican Order. When the Albigensian heresy was spreading through the south of France and the north of Italy in the year 1200, Dominic was commissioned by the Pope to preach against it. His efforts were unavailing. He then besought the aid of Mary. Appearing to Dominic, Mary gave him the rosary bidding him to use it as a weapon against the prevailing heresy. The devotion spread rapidly and in a short time had effected the conversion of more than a hundred thousand heretics.

Later on, when dire calamities loomed up before Christendom, recourse was again had to the rosary. To its efficacy the Christians chiefly attributed the deliverance of Europe from the Turks by the well-nigh miraculous victories at Lepanto (1571), Vienna (1683) and Belgrade. It was in thanksgiving for these victories that the feast of the Holy Rosary was established on the first Sunday of October and the whole month dedicated to the

Holy Rosary. That the Blessed Virgin was highly pleased with this prayer was clearly evidenced by the fact that when she appeared at Lourdes to St. Bernadette, she held in her hand the rosary.

Pope Leo XIII issued no fewer than twelve encyclicals and letters apostolic encouraging this devotion. As it averted the evils threatening the Church in the days of St. Dominic, and later on when the crescent of the Turks seeking to replace the cross of Christ loomed up menacingly against the Christian horizon, so also has it the power to avert the evils threatening the Church, society and the individual soul in this day and age.

The complete rosary consists of fifteen decades. But ordinarily only the rosary of five decades is said at one time. There are three sets of mysteries upon which one meditates while saying the rosary: the joyful, sorrowful and glorious mysteries. The joyful mysteries commemorate the chief events in the lives of Jesus and Mary before the Passion. The sorrowful commemorate the chief events of the Passion, while the glorious recall the principal happenings after the Passion; they thus serve as an epitome of the lives of Jesus and Mary. The joyful mysteries are customarily commemorated on Monday, Thursday and the Sundays during Advent, the sorrowful on Tuesday, Friday and the Sundays during Lent, the glorious on Wednesday, Saturday and the remaining Sundays of the year.

The five joyful mysteries include all the events mentioned in the gospels concerning the birth and the childhood of Christ. The first is the Annunciation. This brings before our minds the scene in the humble home of the Blessed Virgin in Nazareth, when the angel Gabriel brought to her the wonderful message from on high: "Hail, full of grace, the Lord is with thee; blessed art thou among women. . . . Behold thou shalt conceive in thy womb, and shalt bring forth a Son; and thou shalt call His name Jesus. He shall be great and shall be called the Son of the Most High; and the Lord God shall give unto Him the throne of David His father; and He shall reign in the house of Jacob for ever. And of His kingdom there shall be no end. And Mary said to the angel: How shall this be done, because I know not man? And the angel answering, said to her: The Holy Spirit shall come upon thee, and the power of the Most High shall overshadow thee.

And therefore also the Holy Child which shall be born of thee shall be called the Son of God. And behold thy cousin Elizabeth, she also hath conceived a son in her old age; and this is the sixth month with her that is called barren: Because no word shall be impossible with God. And Mary said: Behold the handmaid of the Lord; be it done to me according to thy word."[1]

When the humble Virgin bowed obediently to the will of God and uttered the words, "Be it done to me according to thy word," at that moment Christ became incarnate in Mary.

The second joyful mystery, the Visitation, directs our thoughts to the meeting of the Blessed Virgin with her cousin, St. Elizabeth, the mother of St. John the Baptist. When Mary entered the home of Elizabeth and saluted her, "the infant leaped in her womb. And Elizabeth was filled with the Holy Spirit: And she cried out with a loud voice, and said: Blessed art thou among women, and blessed is the fruit of thy womb. And whence is this to me, that the mother of my Lord should come to me? For behold as soon as the voice of thy salutation sounded in my ears, the infant in my womb leaped for joy. And blessed art thou that hast believed, because those things shall be accomplished that were spoken to thee by the Lord. And Mary said: My soul doth magnify the Lord. And my spirit hath rejoiced in God my Savior. Because He hath regarded the humility of His handmaid; for behold from henceforth all generations shall call me blessed. Because He that is mighty, hath done great things to me; and holy is His name."[2]

The third mystery, the Nativity, brings before us the familiar scene at the stable of Bethlehem where Jesus was born, as the angels sang, "Glory to God in the highest; and on earth peace to men of good will."[3]

In the fourth mystery, the Presentation, we behold Mary presenting Jesus in the Temple and offering Him to the Eternal Father as the Victim that is to be sacrificed in atonement for the sins of the world. When Mary placed Him in the arms of the holy Simeon, the latter uttered the prophetic words that revealed the sublimity of her sacrifice: "Behold this Child is set for the fall and for the resurrection of many in Israel, and for a sign which shall be contradicted; and thy own soul a sword shall pierce, that, out of many hearts, thoughts may be revealed."[4]

377

In the fifth mystery, the Finding of Jesus in the Temple, we contemplate first the desolation that filled the hearts of Mary and Joseph when for three days they were separated from Jesus, and then the ineffable joy and peace that filled their hearts upon finding the Child in the temple, hearing the learned doctors of the law and asking them questions. Whereupon, "He went down with them and came to Nazareth and was subject to them."[5]

The five sorrowful mysteries bring to our minds in rapid succession the moving events of the last hours of our Savior's life, from His agony in the garden to His death on Calvary's cross. The first mystery, the Agony in the Garden, portrays the gloom of Gethsemani, where "being in an agony, He prayed the longer. And His sweat became as drops of blood trickling down upon the ground."[6] Jesus sees the awful sufferings He is to undergo on the morrow, and cries out: "Father, if it be possible, let this chalice pass from Me. Nevertheless, not as I will, but as Thou wilt."[7]

In the second mystery, the Scourging at the Pillar, we see Jesus being whipped with the relentless lashes until His sacred flesh is torn and the blood streams forth. "Then therefore Pilate took Jesus, and scourged Him."[8]

In the third mystery, the Crowning with Thorns, we see the executioners in mockery of Christ's claim to kingship, place upon Him a crown of thorns, that pierced His sacred brow. "And the soldiers, platting a crown of thorns, put it upon His head; and they put on Him a purple garment."[9]

The fourth mystery, the Carrying of the Cross, turns our minds to the journey that our Savior made from the tribunal of Pontius Pilate to Calvary bearing the cross on which He was to be crucified. "And they took Jesus, and led Him forth. And bearing His own cross He went forth to that place which is called Calvary."[10] "And there followed Him a great multitude of people and of women; who bewailed and lamented Him."[11] Tradition tells us that among this pious throng was Mary, whose soul was indeed pierced with a sword of sorrow as she looked upon her Son bearing His cross.

The fifth mystery, the Crucifixion, leads us to the climactic event in the sufferings of Christ — His death after three hours' agony upon the cross. "And they crucified Him." "Now there stood by the Cross of Jesus, His Mother."[12] The words which Christ uttered as He hung upon the cross reach a climax in the prayers for the forgiveness of His executioners: "Father, forgive them for they know not what they do."[13]

The five glorious mysteries turn our thoughts to the glorious events after His death and lead us to hope that we may share in the joys and glories of His heavenly kingdom. The first mystery, the Resurrection, recalls to our minds Christ's triumph over death. This event constitutes the supreme evidence of Christ's divinity as well as of the truth of the religion which He founded; it robs death of its sting and the grave of its victory.

The second mystery, the Ascension, brings before our minds the scene which occurred forty days after the resurrection, when Christ ascended in the presence of the Apostles into heaven.

In the third mystery, the Descent of the Holy Spirit upon the Apostles, we consider the great event which occurred on Pentecost. When the Apostles were gathered together in the upper chamber of a dwelling house in Jerusalem, there came a sound as of a mighty wind, and the Holy Spirit came upon them in the form of tongues of fire. From weak timid men they were transformed into intrepid Apostles who went forth and preached the gospel fearlessly to every creature.

In the fourth mystery, the Assumption of the Blessed Virgin into heaven, we recall the event, not recorded in the Scripture, but attested by authentic Catholic tradition, of the angels taking the body of the Blessed Virgin after her death into heaven.

In the fifth mystery, the Coronation, we contemplate the Crowning of the Blessed Virgin as Queen of the Saints and Angels in heaven. As she went down with Jesus into the depths of sorrow and humiliation, so it is fitting that she should be exalted with Him before all the creatures in heaven.

Thus do the mysteries of the rosary bring before our minds a panorama of the great events in the life of Christ and of His Blessed Mother. They make us familiar with the moving events in our redemption, and intensify our love for our divine Savior and for Mary, His Mother, who played so intimate a role in the drama of atonement.

Concerning the power of the Hail Mary that is recited so

often in the rosary, the saintly Thomas a Kempis said: "When I recite the Hail Mary, heaven rejoices, the earth marvels, Satan withdraws, hell trembles, all sadness vanishes, joy returns, the heart glows, the soul is filled with holy unction; hope animates my bosom and a wonderful consolation gladdens my whole being." Another saintly writer says: "The Hail Mary is small in extent, but great as to the effects; it is sweeter than honey and more precious than gold. It should be frequently on our lips and reecho in our hearts."

Think of the mysteries when saying the rosary. Then it is not like the windmill prayers of India. For the natives there think that they are praying so long as the wind turns the wheel upon which their prayer is inscribed. The material beads serve as counters of the number of prayers said. The practice of using counters, either in the form of small stones or seeds strung on a cord, is a very ancient one. It existed among the hermits in the first centuries.

The rosary may well be called the *thermometer* of Christianity. When it is used, Christianity is flourishing. When it is neglected, Christianity falls to a low ebb. Pope Pius IX was accustomed to say: "In the whole of the Vatican there is no greater treasure than the rosary." This saintly pontiff was most anxious that the rosary be said daily in every family. The legacy he bequeathed to the faithful was the admonition: "Let the rosary, this simple, beautiful method of prayer, enriched with many indulgences, be habitually recited of an evening in every household. These are my last words to you: the memorial I leave behind me."

What memories these words conjure to the minds of many of us — memories of the times when we knelt down together at night with father and mother and brother and sister and said the rosary. How sacred and how inspiring those memories will always be to us! May they be the harbinger of that ultimate reunion with Christ and His saints in paradise.

While one is saying the Our Father and the Hail Mary of a decade he should meditate upon the particular mystery commemorated therein: it is this meditation which constitutes the heart and soul of the rosary. There is no higher form of prayer than that in which the soul is united to Christ in contemplation.

It is through the door of meditation that Christ enters into the kingdom of the soul and ceases to be merely a name and becomes instead a living and abiding reality.

Thus it is seen that there is no force to the objection that there is too much mechanical repetition in the rosary. For while the lips are repeating the words of the Hail Mary the mind is contemplating the various mysteries. Moreover, modern psychology shows us how deeply rooted in human nature is the tendency to repeat over and over again words that spring from the depths of a fervent heart. In the one hundred and thirty-fifth psalm David exclaims twenty-seven times: "His mercy endureth forever." St. Francis of Assisi was accustomed to repeat the phrase, "My God and my all!" through many hours of the night. Well may the words of the rosary be on our lips in life, and its beads clasped in our hands at death.

Discussion Aids

Speak of the Holy Rosary as a universal devotion. Explain the connection that St. Dominic had with the rosary. In what other crises in the history of the Church did the rosary prove most availing? How did the Blessed Virgin show her approval of the rosary to Bernadette? Name a modern Pope who especially encouraged the rosary. Explain the composition of the rosary. What mysteries in the lives of our Lord and His Blessed Mother are commemorated? On what days of the week are the various mysteries said? Name and explain the joyful mysteries, the sorrowful mysteries, the glorious mysteries. Explain what is meant by *meditating* on the mysteries. How should you answer the objection that there is too much mechanical repetition in the rosary?

Practices

Say at least a decade of the rosary, daily.

Learn the mysteries of the rosary and use them on the appointed days of the week.

Meditate with devotion on the religious truth suggested in each mystery.

NOTES (Chapter 30)

1. Lk. 1:31-39
2. Ibid., 1:41-50
3. Ibid., 2:14
4. Ibid., 2:34-35
5. Ibid., 2:51
6. Ibid., 22:44
7. Mt. 26:39
8. Jn. 19:1
9. Ibid., 19:2
10. Ibid., 19:16-17
11. Lk. 23:27
12. Jn. 19:25
13. Lk. 23:34

CHAPTER 31

St. Joseph

Patron of the Universal Church and of the Workingman

The tendency to honor the memory of illustrious men seems to spring spontaneously from one of the deepest instincts of human nature. In all the tribes and races of men, in all the varying stages of civilization, we find the effort always made to rescue the names of their great heroes from complete oblivion. Tombs and mausoleums preserve their mortal remains, monuments are erected to them; their statues are placed in our public squares, while poets enshrine their memory in immortal verse. Indeed all history has been defined as but the biography of distinguished men and women.

Before the admiring eyes of each generation, history unfolds the panorama of their lives, the story ancient yet ever new. To the school children of today, the names of Alexander the Great, of Hannibal, of Julius Caesar, are almost as real and vivid as those of the great contemporaries of the day. Their names have survived the wear and tear of centuries and all the devastation of the blighting finger of time; thus does the world pay ceaseless homage to her heroes.

If we strive to hold in enduring fame the names of those illustrious men who accomplished great temporal successes, or achievements of a material character, with how much greater earnestness should we enshrine in the sanctuary of a deathless memory the names of those who wrought great spiritual and moral victories, the effect of whose work will never die, but will gather into the granaries of heaven the ceaseless harvest of human souls? If we honor earthly heroes whose achievements frequently crumble and perish, how much more should we honor heavenly heroes, the saints of God, the influence of whose lives will continue throughout the ages to inspire the souls of men, and to guide their footsteps safely through the winding labyrinth of life? To the saints can most fittingly be applied those words of the poet Longfellow:

> Were a star quenched on high,
>   For ages would its light
> Still travelling downward from the sky,
>   Shine on our mortal sight.
> So when a great man dies,
>   For years beyond our ken,
> The light he leaves behind him lies
>   Upon the paths of men.[1]

On the nineteenth of March we celebrate the feast of one of the greatest of all the saints of God, St. Joseph. Alone, from among all the sons of men, he was singled out by the omniscient Mind of the eternal Godhead who reads the hearts of men as an open book, to be the spouse of Mary and the foster-father of Jesus. How pure and holy in the sight of Almighty God must Joseph have been to have been deemed worthy of so great an honor! The evangelist characterizes Joseph simply as "a just man." But what volumes of praise are contained therein, when one realizes that such is not simply the judgment of men but the unerring verdict of the Holy Spirit!

Seldom does Joseph appear in the pages of the gospel story. Even on those occasions he seems to stand, as it were, in the background. We see him journeying with Mary to Bethlehem seeking in vain to find for her a place in the inns. With what great anxiety his paternal heart must have throbbed as he went tirelessly from house to house seeking lodging and the needed comforts for Mary who was with child! We find him present in the rude stable at Bethlehem, ministering to Mary, at the birth of the Infant Jesus. With what sentiments of reverence and affection he prostrated himself — the first worshiper of all mankind — before the Incarnate God!

See Joseph again when he is awakened from his sleep by an angel saying: "Arise, and take the child and His mother, and fly into Egypt."[2] Without a moment's hesitation or delay, Joseph set out in the darkness of the night on that long journey into Egypt to save the life of the Infant Jesus from the designing Herod. With what infinite tenderness did he shield Mary and the Child from the dangers, fatigue and hardships of that flight!

The picture which the thought of St. Joseph usually conjures up in our minds, however, is that of the saint toiling humbly as a carpenter in his obscure home at Nazareth. It was thus that he spent nearly all of his life as the spouse of Mary and the foster-father of Jesus, earning by the sweat of his brow the necessities of life for his holy family. With what devotion and love he must have cared for Mary and the Divine Son, Jesus in their little cottage at Nazareth. It is thus that St. Joseph is revealed to us — toiling faithfully, day by day, at the humble trade of a carpenter, providing for the child and His Mother. When at last his work was done he died, according to tradition, some time before the marriage feast of Cana, in the arms of Jesus and Mary; because of the rare beauty of his death, he is invoked as the patron of a happy death.

If one pauses to pass in review the whole earthly life of St. Joseph, he is able to discover therein no single gesture of grandiloquence to mar, for even an instant, the humble tenor of that simple life. The white spotlight is seldom upon him: the dramatic elements are wholly lacking. There are no flourishes of the band; no tumultuous cheering crowds dog his footsteps. He walks not on the mountaintop before the eyes of the world, but labors down below in the darkness and silence of the valley, away from the gaze of the world. And yet the Church honors St. Joseph as the patron of the universal Church — after Mary the greatest among the saints of God. And why? Because of his humility, his holiness, his love, his patience, his sacrifice and self-denial.

When we read of Peter offering himself to the executioner to be crucified, head downward, not considering himself worthy to die like his Master; or of Francis Xavier, leaving all that life holds worthwhile to go as a missionary to win souls to Christ in far-off Hindustan, finally dying on a lonely isle in the South China Sea, with his arms outstretched to China, the land of promise, which he yearned so ardently to bring to the feet of the Crucified; or when we read of Ignatius of Antioch, who, rather than deny his faith, walked bravely into the arena to be torn to pieces by wild beasts, we are thrilled with admiration. We recognize, however, that they were chosen by Almighty God to do extraordinary works, and seem more appropriate models of heroic souls than for ordinary mortals like ourselves. St. Joseph, however, did only the common everyday work of the world. He is better suited, therefore, to serve as a model for the farmer in the field, the laborer in the factory, the clerk in the store, the student in the school, the father in the home — all doing the ordinary duties of everyday life.

St. Joseph may be said, therefore, to be the saint of the commonplace. He reached the heights of heroic sanctity, not by doing extraordinary things, but by doing the little ordinary duties of life supremely well. How fittingly he was chosen as the patron of the universal Church! Most of us are destined to do the ordinary, commonplace work of the world, humbly and obscurely. It is only the few who can scale the heights of extraordinary achievements to the accompaniment of the plaudits of admiring multitudes. But however lowly or obscure may be our lot, the life of St. Joseph teaches us that if we discharge the daily round of our simple duties supremely well, in the eyes of Almighty God we may be placed higher than the kings or generals or statesmen who strut their brief hour in the center of the stage before the limelight of this world's gaze.

In the life of St. Joseph there is found inspiration for the great toiling masses of mankind. There is offered to all of us an antidote for the false philosophy of this world which looks upon a good deed as lost unless it attracts human attention and receives the plaudits of men. From a natural point of view, the words of the poet Thomas Gray may be true, when he says:

Full many a gem of purest ray serene,
    The dark unfathomed caves of ocean bear:
Full many a flower is born to blush unseen,

And waste its sweetness on the desert air.[3]

They are not true, however, from the supernatural or Christian viewpoint; for, every kindly deed, every holy thought, though witnessed by no human being, is seen by the all-seeing eye of God. Regardless of this world's praise or blame, He gives to every one his just reward.

The story is told of an old man who approached the architect in charge of the adornment of one of the great cathedrals of Europe and begged permission to do some work. The architect wishing to get rid of him told him he could go up near the roof and carve upon one of the rafters. Day after day he labored up there in the semidarkness. One day he did not come down. Going up they found him lying dead upon the scaffolding, his sightless eyes turned upward.

There, upon a rafter, they saw the face of Christ wrought with exquisite beauty and wonderful charm. Beneath it were inscribed the words: "God at least will see and understand." Artists and architects and the great men of the earth, bared their heads as they recognized the superb master in him, whose ears were now deaf to all their words of praise.

There are times when a ray of light from a window falls upon this portion of the rafter. When it does, the guide points out to the visitors this exquisite face as the masterpiece of the cathedral which still thrills them with its appealing beauty.

Beneath every kindly word, or holy thought, or virtuous deed, done in the darkness or in the obscurity of the valley, where no human eye is witnessing, could be engraven with equal truth those words of the dead sculptor: "God at least will see and understand." And when the time of the great revealing comes, and the searching white light of eternity plays upon it, that good deed will stand uncovered before the eyes of all mankind to thrill them with its Christlike beauty. Perhaps some humble peasant from the fields or lowly toiler in the factory will then be exalted above the lords of the earth, to occupy one of the highest places in heaven. That is what the life of St. Joseph teaches us in a striking manner.

Devotion to St. Joseph is a powerful means of obtaining

favors, both spiritual and temporal. At the Council of Constance in 1416, when the legates of the Holy See, twenty cardinals, two hundred bishops, besides large numbers of the doctors and theologians of the Church were gathered together to devise the best means to stem the tide of corruption then inundating the Church, there appeared before them Gerson, the learned Chancellor of the University of Paris. He pointed out that as St. Joseph was the guardian of Jesus on earth, he still remains the guardian of the mystical body of Jesus, which is His Church, and as his wishes were obeyed by Christ while on earth, so now, when he is in heaven, will his intercession still be granted. Gerson strongly counseled devotion to St. Joseph as the effective remedy. His counsel was accepted by all, as the counsel of one who had a mission from on high. Within a few years after the spread of this devotion throughout the Church, the schisms were healed and the troubles had all disappeared.

In practically every Catholic Church throughout the land there is a side altar dedicated to the Spouse of Mary. Before that altar or in the solitude of one's own home, or under the vault of the open skies, a person may appeal to St. Joseph for aid in life's struggle. The assistance which thousands of the faithful have secured through their devotion to St. Joseph in the overcoming of moral difficulties is by its very nature not susceptible of external observation but can be vouched for by the introspection of the individual conscience. The attainment of moral and spiritual values and the continued growth of the soul in holiness should be the supreme objectives in the life of every human being, rather than the gaining of temporal favors, which may have no real bearing upon the attainment of the individual's ultimate salvation, his eternal union with God in heaven.

There are instances, however, where the attainment of a temporal good has an obvious bearing upon the moral and spiritual life of the individual. At such times recourse may be had to prayer to supplement the individual's efforts to attain the same through the use of natural means.

So today in all the continents under the sun and in the islands out in the sea, over 659,000,000 Catholics can exclaim as with a single voice: "Holy Joseph, guardian of Mary and the Infant Jesus on that long dark journey into Egypt, guard and guide us safely in the journey across this earthly life. And when our steps falter at the journey's end and the lengthening shadows fall, when life's fitful fever is o'er and the angel of death comes to close our eyes, ah! then take us by the hand and lead us across the frontier of eternity into that heavenly Nazareth, where with thee we shall see the smiling face of Mary, and feel the embrace of Jesus, the Eternal King."

Discussion Aids

Discuss the tendency that exists in human nature to honor greatness. When is St. Joseph's feast day? What do we know from the Scriptures about St. Joseph? Compare St. Joseph with Sts. Peter, Francis Xavier, Ignatius of Antioch. Discuss St. Joseph as the saint of the commonplace. How is he the inspiration for the toiling masses of mankind? Describe the happenings relative to St. Joseph at the Council of Constance. Sum up the reasons why the Church honors St. Joseph.

Practices

Pray to St. Joseph to protect the Church against her fearful modern enemies.

Say a Hail Mary in honor of St. Joseph every day for a happy death.

Recommend yourself to the intercession of St. Joseph when discouraged in your daily work.

NOTES (Chapter 31)

1. W. Longfellow, "Charles Summer," in *The Home Book of Quotations,* p. 809 (Dodd, Mead & Co., N.Y., 1937)
2. Mt. 2:13
3. Thomas Gray, "Elegy Written in a Country Church Yard," in *A Book of Famous Verse,* p. 147 (Houghton Mifflin Co., N.Y., 1920)

PART VI

The Commandments of God

Our Duties to God and to Man

CHAPTER 32

The Way to Holiness of Life

The First Four Commandments

Before explaining the commandments of God, it will be well to review briefly the meaning and the nature of sin. There are two kinds of sin: original and actual sin. Original sin is that state in which we are born as a result of the fall of our first parents, Adam and Eve. By disobeying Almighty God, our parents lost innocence and holiness and became subject to sickness and death; they lost the wonderful supernatural life of grace by which they shared in the very life of God; God simply withdrew from them certain gifts and favors to which they had no strict right. As their descendants, we share in the consequences of their disobedience as we would have shared in their happiness if they had remained faithful to God.

We are like children of a father who has lost a large fortune.

If he had retained it, we would come into possession of it; but since he did not retain it, naturally we cannot inherit it. God has not done us an injustice, as we had no right to the special favors and gifts which He bestowed upon Adam and Eve and which were to be retained only on condition that they obeyed God's holy law. As a consequence of that fall, our understanding was darkened, our will was weakened, and there was left in human nature an inclination to evil. This corruption of our nature remains in us even after original sin is forgiven.

The kind of sin that we ourselves commit and for which we shall be directly punished is called actual sin. It is any willful thought, word, deed, or omission contrary to the law of God. Actual sin may be either mortal or venial.

Mortal sin is grievous offense against the law of God and requires three things: serious matter, sufficient reflection and full consent of the will. Thus, stealing is a sin; but if one steals merely a newspaper, it does not involve serious or grievous matter, and hence would be only a venial sin. If one were to steal a hundred dollars, however, the matter would be serious and the sin would be a mortal one.

This type of sin is termed mortal because it deprives the soul of sanctifying grace which is spiritual life, and thus brings death and damnation to the soul. It is the greatest evil that can come into the soul; it is the greatest evil that can come into human life, and its far-reaching consequences are most tragic.

In contrast to mortal sin, venial sin is a slight offense against the law of God in matters of less importance; or in matters of great importance, it is an offense committed without sufficient reflection or full consent of the will. The effects of venial sin are the lessening of the love of God in our heart, the making us less worthy of His help, and the weakening of the power to resist mortal sin. In other words, venial sins prepare the way for mortal sins. It is important, therefore, to be on our guard against any venial sin, no matter how slight; we will keep from sin if we avoid dangers, temptations and the near occasions of sin. By the latter is meant any person, place or thing that might lead one to sin. Prayer and vigilance are the armor of innocence. "Watch ye and pray," said our divine Savior, "that you enter not into temptation."[1] Our safety lies in the prudent avoidance of danger. "He that loveth danger," warns the author of Ecclesiasticus, "shall perish in it." If these two admonitions are observed we shall employ wise strategy in waging our ceaseless battle against the world, the flesh and the devil.

In reality, the ten commandments can be reduced to two. A doctor of the law asked Jesus: "Master, which is the great commandment in the law?" Jesus answered: "Thou shalt love the Lord thy God with thy whole heart, and with thy whole soul, and with thy whole mind. This is the greatest and the first commandment. And the second is like to this: thou shalt love thy neighbor as thyself."[2]

Those two commandments contain practically all the others. Thus, the first three of the ten commandments relate to the love of God; the last seven refer to the love of our neighbor. If we really love God, we won't fail to give Him our homage and obedience; if we really love our neighbor, we won't injure him, deprive him of his property, nor injure his good name; we shall respect all his rights.

The first commandment is: "I am the Lord, thy God, thou shalt not have strange gods before Me." That is the substance of it; along with the other nine commandments, this one is formulated in the Book of Exodus.[3] The complete statement of the first commandment is: "I am the Lord thy God, who brought thee out of the land of Egypt, out of the house of bondage. Thou shalt not have strange gods before Me. Thou shalt not make to thyself a graven thing, nor the likeness of anything that is in heaven above, or in the earth beneath, nor of those things that are in the waters under the earth. Thou shalt not adore them, nor serve them."

Non-Catholics consider that last sentence. "Thou shalt not adore them nor serve them," as expressing the second commandment: that accounts for the difference between the Catholic and non-Catholic numbering of the commandments. Catholics consider all of that as but an elaboration of the one central thought inculcating the duty of worshiping God and prohibiting the worship of false gods and idols. In giving the commandments to Moses, God did not number them; neither did Moses; this was done centuries after they were published in the Book of Exodus in the Old Testament.

This does not mean, however, that non-Catholics have eleven commandments instead of the traditional ten, as they combine the Catholic ninth and tenth commandments into one — their tenth.

Does this first commandment forbid the making of all statues, images or pictures? No, only when they are to be used for idolatrous purposes, although some non-Catholics think that statues or paintings should not adorn churches or be used at all in religious worship. This notion is untenable. The Hebrews offered divine homage before the Ark of the Covenant which was between graven things, made at God's own direction. In the same book of the Bible in which the commandments are listed, it is recorded that God commanded the making of the images of two angels: "Thou shalt make also two cherubims of beaten gold on the two sides of the oracle."[4]

The catacombs are replete with evidence of the use of images and pictures by the early Christians in prayer, sacrifice and worship. Back in the eighth century, St. John Damascene answered those who objected to the use of images in religious worship. "The image of the king," he said, "is also called the king, and there are not two kings in consequence. . . . Honoring the image is honoring the one who is set forth in the image. . . . Do not reject the veneration of images."[5]

We put statues of our statesmen and heroes in our parks and public buildings. Thus do we honor those men and keep their memory fresh and green; but no one would accuse us of worshiping the statues. In the same manner we place the crucifix before us to remind us of the sufferings and death of Jesus for us; it stirs our memory and kindles our love. How much more helpful it is to pray before a crucifix or a statue of Jesus than to pray before a bare wall, with nothing to help us fix our attention upon Christ to whom we are praying. Sometimes non-Catholics have observed Catholics worshiping *before* a crucifix and have concluded that they were praying *to* the crucifix. There is, of course, a world of difference between the two.

Catholics *honor* the saints but *worship* only God; to Him alone is due the supreme homage of adoration; to give such homage to any creature is forbidden by this commandment. This commandment also forbids all actions which attribute to a creature a perfection which belongs to God alone. That is why it is wrong to make use of spells or charms, to believe in dreams, mediums, spirits and fortunetellers.

Don't Catholics believe in wearing medals around their necks in order to be protected from danger and temptation? Catholics wear medals and scapulars and believe in the devout use of blessed articles to secure God's protection; but they do not expect it infallibly, and they know, of course, that the help can come only from God and not from the material objects. There are medals in honor of the Sacred Heart of Jesus, the Blessed Virgin, St. Anthony, St. Benedict and others. Such medals are blessed by a priest and are worn out of devotion to the ones in whose honor they are carried.

The Church protects her children from all superstitious beliefs and practices: the notion that passing under a ladder, or having three persons light their cigarettes from the same match, or traveling on Friday will bring bad luck. While intelligent people can perceive the folly of such notions, the Church tells her children that it is not only foolish but also wrong and sinful to expect any material object or person to exercise a power which God alone possesses.

What is required by this commandment? It requires us to adore God alone, to worship Him by acts of faith, hope and charity, by prayer and sacrifice. We worship God by faith when we believe what God has revealed to us; when we rely on His goodness and promises and confidently hope to attain eternal life; by charity, when we love him above all things for His own sake and do His will.

All are obliged to pray to God in the morning and at night and also in time of danger and temptation. Upon arising, we should offer to Almighty God all our thoughts, words and deeds of that day. That is what St. Paul means when he says: "Whether you eat or drink, or do anything else, do all for the glory of God."[6] In this way we dedicate all our activities to God's honor and thus sanctify them and make them rich in merit: prayer takes away the raw tang of the world from our lives and unites us more closely to God in love.

We can scarcely claim to be Christians if we don't pray. Faith, too becomes a hollow shell if we ignore God day after day.

We vitalize our faith by daily prayer, by meditation and by spiritual reading, especially the reading of the New Testament; we should increase our knowledge of the great truths revealed to us by Christ and safeguarded and taught by His Church.

We are never allowed to deny our faith and are obliged to profess it when the honor of God, or the good of our neighbor, or lawful authority requires it. We must be on our guard against falling into the attitudes of indifferentism — the notion that all religions are equally good and true; hence we must not take part in the services of a false religion. To do so would imply that one places man-made creed on the same basis as a religion founded by Christ; it would mean disloyalty to His faith and would scandalize the faithful.

It is permitted, however, to attend a funeral or marriage in a non-Catholic church, out of friendship or respect, without taking active part in the service. It is apparent here that our sole purpose is to pay a tribute of respect for a friend and not to express agreement with a different creed. The principle of loyalty — acting consistently with one's faith — is thus safeguarded, while one is permitted to pay a tribute of esteem to a friend, for friendship is precious too.

A person may sin against faith then in three ways: by not trying to know what God has taught, by refusing to believe what God has taught, and by neglecting to profess his belief in what God has taught. No earthly consideration should deter a person from professing his belief in Christ and in the religion which He founded; in all the centuries of the Christian era, the followers of Christ have suffered martyrdom rather than deny Christ or any of His teachings. In their ears there echoed the words of their Redeemer: "Whosoever shall confess Me before men, him shall the Son of man also confess before the angels of God. But he that shall deny Me before men, shall be denied before . . . God."[7]

In other words, a person is bound to investigate which Church is the true Church. When he discovers that the Catholic Church is the true Church, for it alone was founded by Christ and guaranteed His constant protection from error, then he is bound in conscience to become a Catholic. If a person were to fail to profess his faith in the Catholic Church because of business, social or political considerations, he would be comparable to

Judas who sold his Lord for thirty pieces of silver. That is one of the worst sins a person can commit.

The virtue of hope enables us with God's grace to trust firmly in God's promise to give us eternal life and the means to attain it; that virtue may be lost by either of two grave sins — presumption or despair. One would be guilty of presumption if he rejected God's help and relied solely on his own efforts to be saved, or if he relied solely on God's help without giving any personal effort or cooperation. Despair is the complete abandonment of all hope of salvation and the rejection of the means of attaining it.

Lastly, we must worship God by love. Any grave sin is a violation of the love we owe God; we must also love our neighbors for the sake of God and see His image in them. We fail in the love we owe our neighbors by any action calculated to lead them into sin, such as using vulgar or blasphemous language, passing around obscene pictures or immoral books, or by our own bad example. Thus you see how comprehensive is this first commandment and how it serves as a basis for all the others.

The second commandment is: "Thou shalt not take the name of the Lord, thy God, in vain." It requires us to speak with reverence of God, of the saints and of all holy things, and to keep our lawful oaths and vows. "Taking the name of God in vain" means using it without sufficient reason or proper reverence. There are many people who use the name of God in expressions of surprise, emphasis, anger, hatred and cursing; profanity, the irreverent use of God's holy name, is one of the besetting sins of our day; even the girls and women shock us at times with their profanity.

This commandment enjoins reverence for the name of God and for the holy name of Jesus, as well as for the personality suggested by that name. So great was the reverence of the Jews of old for the name of God that they never uttered it: Catholics bow their heads when the sacred name of Jesus is spoken. "From the rising of the sun," said the Psalmist, "unto the going down of the same, the name of the Lord is worthy of praise."[8]

This refrain is frequently sounded in the Old Testament. Thus in Ezechiel we read the inspired prophecy: "And I will make My holy name known in the midst of My people Israel, and

My holy name shall be profaned no more; and the Gentiles shall know that I am the Lord, the Holy One of Israel."[9]

Earnestly did St. Paul inculcate reverence for the holy name of Jesus, saying: "God also hath exalted Him, and hath given Him a name which is above all names: That in the name of Jesus, every knee should bow, of those that are in heaven, on earth, and under the earth."[10] When Peter and John were asked by Annas and Caiphas by what power had the Apostles cured the lame beggar, Peter replied:

"Be it known to you all, and to all the people of Israel, that by the name of our Lord Jesus Christ of Nazareth, whom you crucified, whom God hath raised from the dead, even by Him this man standeth here before you whole." Then he adds the words which should be written indelibly upon the memory of every follower of the crucified Christ: "Neither is there salvation in any other. For there is no other name under heaven given to men, whereby we must be saved."[11]

If one would only recall those words when he is about to take the holy name in anger, the words would die . . . unuttered . . . at the realization of the shocking irreverence he would commit. If people given to profanity would recall those words of the Apostles Peter and Paul, they would speedily cure themselves of this bad habit. It is chiefly a matter of thoughtlessness — with no malice or contempt intended for the holy name; that is what makes profanity usually but a venial sin. Nevertheless, even such thoughtless, non-malicious use should be avoided; it serves no useful purpose; it is offensive to women present, and it is disedifying to all. The Church has organized 5,000,000 of her men into the Holy Name Society to promote reverence for the name of God and cleanliness of speech.

What is meant by cursing? That means invoking evil upon persons or things. When God's name is used in cursing, the sin becomes a greater one. While cursing can be a mortal sin, it is ordinarily only a venial one because the person who curses does not really wish upon others the evil which the words express. Instead of asking God to damn a person or send him to hell, we should invoke God to bless and help him. "For such as bless him," says the Psalmist, "shall inherit the land; but such as curse him shall perish."[12]

What is blasphemy? It is abusive, contemptuous, insulting language against God; by its nature, it is a mortal sin. Under the Old Law it was punished by death: "And he that blasphemeth the name of the Lord, dying let him die; all the multitude shall stone him."[13]

What is a vow? A vow is a free and deliberate promise made to God to do something that is pleasing to Him; it differs from an ordinary promise or a good resolution because it is made to God and binds according to the intention of the one who makes the vow. Men and women in religious communities ordinarily take the three vows of poverty, chastity and obedience.

An oath is the calling upon God to witness to the truth of what we say or promise. Hence unnecessary oaths are forbidden by this commandment. More grievous, of course, is the sin of perjury whereby a person deliberately associates God in his lie. One may take an oath when some important matter is at stake and it is essential that the truth be made known, as in a case in court. Witnesses, before the chair, ordinarily take an oath, swearing with their hand upon the Bible to tell the truth; hence taking an oath is called swearing. "He that sweareth by heaven," says St. Matthew, "sweareth by the throne of God, and by Him that sitteth thereon."[14]

There are societies of men which require their members to take an oath of secrecy. The Church, however, does not regard the reasons assigned for such secrecy as sufficient; hence she does not approve such organizations as enact an oath of secrecy; even from considerations of the welfare of society, such oaths are unwarranted. Why should a man blindly swear to secrecy when he does not know that everything that may take place in a meeting may conscientiously be kept secret?

Don't the Knights of Columbus require, however, an oath of secrecy from its members? No; this organization exacts merely a promise — not an oath — and the promise is not to bind in case it conflicts with one's duty as a citizen or with the dictates of conscience.

There are a number of oath-bound secret societies which are benevolent and social in character and foster good fellowship and the fraternal spirit. It is to be acknowledged that these societies have many fine features and worthy ideals; but the

Church disapproves of these societies for two reasons. The first is the requirement of the blind oath of secrecy; the second is the substitution of their ritual, with chaplain, Bible and ceremonies, for the services of the Church. Frequently they have their own services at burials and at other occasions. Many members declare: "I don't need to go to Church anymore. I get enough religion in the lodge."

Obviously, the Catholic Church, founded by Jesus Christ to minister to all mankind, could not, on principle, sanction the substitution of a man-made lodge ritual with religious ceremonies for the religion given to her by Christ. If the lodges left the Church, where they rightfully belong, and confined themselves to fraternal matters, they would not have the tendency to wean people away from the supernatural religion which Christ commanded His Church to teach to all nations unto the consummation of the world.

Thus it is evident that the second commandment inculcates the duty of showing reverence for the holy name of God and of His Son Jesus Christ; it reminds us that God has given us the faculty of speech to praise and reverence Him, not to abuse and insult Him with profane language. Cultivate a special love for the sacred name of Jesus, the most sacred name human lips can utter; it would be well to memorize the following stanza of the beautiful hymn in honor of the holy name of Jesus:

No voice can sing, no heart can frame
  Nor can the memory find
A sweeter sound than Thy blest Name
  O Savior of mankind!

Say the name of Jesus often with devotion and love: it will be your protection in time of danger and temptation. When the angel of death comes to summon you, say with your dying breath: "Jesus! my God and my all! Into Thy hands I commend my spirit . . . dear Jesus!"

The third commandment is: "Remember thou keep holy the Sabbath Day." Like the first two commandments, this one also concerns our duties to God, particularly the duty to worship

Him on a designated day. The word *Sabbath* means rest, and is Saturday the seventh day of the week.

Why then do Christians observe Sunday instead of the day mentioned in the Bible? In order to make clear to the Jews that they are no longer under the Old Law of Moses, with its requirements of circumcision, abstinence from certain meat and the scrupulous observance of the Jewish sacrifice in the Sabbath; but under the New Law of Christ, the infant Church changed the day to be kept holy from Saturday to Sunday. All the ceremonial laws of the Jews ended with the coming of Christ; but since these ceremonies and practices were enshrined in Jewish tradition for two thousand years, the early Christian Church thought that the most effective way to drive home to them the arrival of the New Law of Christ was to transfer the traditional day of public worship to the Sunday.

This change was made in the early days of Christianity. Thus St. Luke tells us in the Acts of the Apostles: "And on the first day of the week, when we were assembled to break bread, Paul discoursed with them."[15]

Why was Sunday chosen? Because on that day Christ rose from the dead and the Holy Spirit descended upon the Apostles. The Resurrection was the greatest miracle which Christ wrought, and demonstrated in a most striking manner the divinity of Christ and of His Church. On Pentecost the Holy Spirit entered the Church to be the source of its divine life and to abide with it forever.

The Church received the authority to make such a change from her Founder, Jesus Christ. He solemnly conferred upon His Church the power to legislate, govern and administer . . . the power of the keys. It is to be noted that the Church did not change the divine law obliging men to worship, but merely changed the day on which such public worship was to be offered; thus the law involved was merely a ceremonial law.

But since Saturday, not Sunday, is specified in the Bible, isn't it curious that non-Catholics who profess to take their religion directly from the Bible and not from the Church, observe Sunday instead of Saturday? Yes, of course, it is inconsistent; but this change was made about fifteen centuries before Protestantism was born, and by that time the custom was universally observed. They have continued the custom, even though it rests upon the authority of the Catholic Church and not upon an explicit text in the Bible. That observance remains as a reminder of the Mother Church from which the non-Catholic sects broke away — like a boy running away from home but still carrying in his pocket a picture of his mother or a lock of her hair.

What does this commandment specifically require? The commandment itself is rather general — simply requiring the day to be sanctified. The Church defines the manner in which this general obligation is to be fulfilled. First, she declares that one must abstain from unnecessary servile work; this is the physical labor usually performed by artisans, merchants and clerks for pay; of course, she does not forbid such work as is involved in the preparation of meals, caring for the sick and other necessary work.

Secondly, it commands that people assemble to give public homage to God. The Church requires Catholics to sanctify the Lord's Day by attending the Holy Sacrifice of the Mass. This binds under pain of mortal sin all Catholics who have attained the use of reason; they should hear an entire Mass — be present before the priest comes out on the altar and remain in their pews until he has left.

They should guard against the habit of tardiness, which robs God of some of the homage due Him. If one should come after the chalice is uncovered, the tardiness would be so serious as to oblige him to return to another Mass; if the tardiness is less than that, it is a venial sin. All venial sins are not the same, however, and the venial sin would vary with the amount missed — within the limit specified.

In addition to attending holy Mass and abstaining from servile work, it is well to spend some time in reading the Bible and other spiritual books, reciting the family rosary, visiting the Blessed Sacrament and the sick, and performing some of the spiritual and corporal works of mercy.

What excuses one from the obligation of attending Mass? If one is ill, or obliged to care for a sick person, or obliged to work under penalty of losing his job, or is so far from church that a grave hardship would be suffered in trying to reach it, he would be excused. Catholics make every effort, however, to attend Sunday Mass not only because the obligation is a serious one but also because they appreciate the great spiritual treasures they derive from hearing it; the great throngs which pack our city churches from early morning until noon to hear Mass constitute the greatest religious spectacle in America today and show the vitality of the Catholic religion.

This practice of attending Mass faithfully is a great safeguard against a person ever drifting very far from God; it keeps God, eternity, and the thought of his own salvation before one. In fact, many spiritual writers devoutly believe that persons who hear Mass faithfully and devoutly Sunday after Sunday are *almost sure to save their souls.* There is an old saying: "As the tree inclines, so shall it fall." We can paraphrase that by saying that the person who attends Mass devoutly all his life inclines toward God, and when he falls in death, he will fall into God's arms.

How does one best assist at Mass? By following along as closely as possible with the prayers and action of the celebrant, reading from the prayer book the "Prayers at Mass," or the "Ordinary of the Mass," or better still, an English missal. Our endeavor should be to participate in the priesthood of Christ by repeating the words of the priest at the altar, uniting our intentions with Christ's, and offering ourselves with Christ as victims in atonement for the sins of men and as the supreme expression of our love and homage to our heavenly Father.

It is advisable to be present ten or fifteen minutes before Mass begins so we can mark our prayer books and missals at the proper places and prepare our minds by meditation for the devout assistance at the holy Sacrifice. Avoid distractions, refrain from gazing idly at others, and concentrate all your attention upon the tremendous action taking place at the altar — the unbloody renewal of Christ's sacrifice upon Calvary. In this way you will offer God greater praise and homage; you yourself will derive greater spiritual fruits, and you will love the Mass and appreciate it as the greatest act of homage and worship at which you can ever assist.

The fourth commandment is: "Honor thy father and thy mother." This commandment stresses the duty of honoring, obeying and loving one's parents and superiors. God strengthens and stabilizes the love for parents which He has placed in the hearts of children by rendering the expression of that filial piety not merely a matter of capricious sentiment but of strict duty.

Mirroring God's mind in this matter, the Bible frequently inculcates the duty of reverence and obedience to parents. "Hear the instruction of thy father," warns the inspired author of the Book of Proverbs, "and forsake not the law of thy mother."[16] To the same effect are the words of the Apostle Paul: "Children, obey your parents in the Lord, for this is just; 'Honor thy father and thy mother,' which is the first commandment with a promise: 'That it may be well with thee, and thou mayest be long-lived upon earth.' "[17]

This commandment requires children to love, honor and obey their parents in all that is not sin. Parents not only bring their offspring into being, sharing with them their own flesh and blood, but also provide them with food, clothing, shelter, care for them when sick, and make many sacrifices to give them a good education. In return, parents are entitled to the obedience and love of their children.

If the parents in their old age should be in need, children should show their gratitude by providing for their material wants. Far from being stubborn, sullen, or spiteful to their parents, children should be tender, considerate and affectionate toward them and be a joy and comfort for them in their old age.

This commandment requires obedience to other superiors as well: Teachers and guardians are entitled to the respect and obedience of children. Since all legitimate authority comes from God, not only children but also adults should respect and obey their civil rulers and their spiritual authorities; hence obedience to the laws of a country is both a civil duty and a religious obligation.

Citizens should vote for the candidates best qualified for the office regardless of religious affiliation, and should give unstinted support to the city, county, state and federal governments in their efforts to promote the moral health and the general welfare of society. Such magistrates are bound to discharge the duties of their office with conscientious care and scrupulous honesty; graft is not only a crime against the state but also a sin against God.

Parents likewise have duties to their children: they are obliged to instruct children in their moral and religious obligations, to set them the proper example and to watch over them with ceaseless care and diligence. Most juvenile delinquency is traceable to the negligence of parents — their failure to know where their children are at night and with whom they are.

Parents can wipe out juvenile delinquency almost overnight by concerning themselves with the religious growth and moral welfare of their offspring. When parents stand before the judgment seat of Almighty God, they will be required to give a strict account of their stewardship. Imagine what God will say to those parents who allowed their children to run the streets at night, to frequent taverns and dangerous places of amusement, where the seeds of crime and vice were planted in their young minds.

Do parents have an obligation to provide for the religious education of their children? Yes, a strict obligation. Parents are God's representatives in regard to their offspring; consequently, upon them rests the primary responsibility of seeing that their children grow up in the knowledge and the love of God. While teachers may *supplement* the teaching and example of parents in this matter, they can never *supplant* them. Parents are the child's first teachers; he trusts them as he does no others; the lessons that a child learns and remembers longest are those he learned at his mother's knee.

Parents are bound to teach children their prayers, to send them to a school where a Christian education may be received, and to see that they attend Mass regularly and receive the sacraments frequently. Such parents can rest assured that such religious training will bear fruit a hundredfold for the children, for themselves and for society in this life and will prepare them for a happy eternity with God in heaven.

It is clear then the fourth commandment is not a one-sided affair: it binds parents as much as offspring. Parents largely determine the character and the future of their children. Parents are the quarterbacks; they call the signals, and the children but act out the plays. If parents would only call the right signals, the children would do their part. There's an old and true saying: "Like father, like son."

Discussion Aids

What is the difference between original sin and actual sin? Define mortal sin; venial sin. What does the first commandment forbid? Command? Explain the difference between *honoring* the saints and *worshiping* God. Why do Catholics wear medals? How may one sin against faith? What does the second commandment forbid? Require? What is cursing? Blasphemy? Vow? Oath? Why are certain secret societies forbidden? What does the third commandment require? Forbid? Why was Sunday chosen? The fourth commandment requires what? Forbids what?

Practices

Reflect upon the purposes for which God gave us the commandments.

Examine your conscience to see wherein you can keep the commandments more perfectly.

Receive Holy Communion frequently so you will grow daily in the love and service of God.

NOTES (Chapter 32)

1. Mt. 26:41
2. *Ibid.*, 22:36-39
3. Ex. 20:1-17
4. *Ibid.*, 25:18
5. Libr. LV De Fid. Orth.
6. I Cor. 10:31
7. Lk. 12:8-9
8. Ps. 112:3
9. Ez. 39:7
10. Phil. 2:8-10
11. Acts 4:10-12
12. Ps. 36:22
13. Lv. 24:16
14. Mt. 23:22
15. Acts 20:7
16. Prv. 1:8
17. Eph. 6:1-3

CHAPTER 33

The Way to Holiness of Life

The Last Six Commandments

The fifth commandment is: "Thou shalt not kill." It requires us to live in peace and union with our neighbor, to respect his rights, to seek his spiritual and bodily welfare, and to take proper care of our own life and health.

What does it forbid? It forbids all willful murder, fighting, anger, hatred, revenge and bad example. Since God is the author of human life, infusing the rational soul into the physical embryo, He alone has absolute jurisdiction over our lives. They belong to Him; hence we have no right to take the life of another, which is murder, nor to take our own life, which is suicide. Both are offenses, therefore, against the supreme sovereignty of God.

Is killing sometimes justified? Yes, in self-defense, when attacked by an unjust aggressor; but even here one should be content with wounding the assailant if that would suffice to save one's life.

Capital punishment may be inflicted by the civil authority for heinous crimes. Individuals are members of society in much the same manner as our arms and feet are members of our body. To save one's life, one may have a diseased member amputated: to preserve its life, society may execute a member which seriously menaces it. In doing this, society is acting with the authority which God bestows upon a just government.

What about the killing that goes on in war? Whether such killing is justified or not depends upon whether the war is just.

Since war entails a frightful destruction of human life, every effort should be made to prevent it and even to outlaw war as an *institution* of society. This is the supreme task to which men and nations should set themselves — to eradicate the cancer of war from the body of civilization before the cancer kills the whole body. Most wars in the past have been unjustified: they have been the result of greed, hatred, envy and national pride masquerading in the name of "national honor."

Catholic moralists teach that four conditions must be fulfilled before a war can be morally justified. (1) The State which declares war must be morally certain that its rights are being actually violated or are in certain and imminent danger. (2) The cause of the war must be in proportion to the monstrous evils of the war itself. (3) Every peaceful method of settling the controversy must be exhausted. (4) There must be a solidly grounded hope that conditions will be improved by the waging of the war.

With the development of the frightful destructiveness of the instruments of war, such as the atomic bomb, it is difficult, except in the case of being unjustly attacked, to see how the four conditions just mentioned can ever again be fulfilled. Modern war renders both victors and losers vastly worse off than before the conflict and sets back the clock of human progress; all men and women in every nation should struggle to establish a world court and a world sheriff to decide international disputes and thus to do away with the monumental folly and destructiveness of war.

The pontiffs of the Catholic Church have pleaded and worked for peace and have made clear the duty of all nations to settle their disputes by courts of justice. We settle disputes between individuals by such courts. Why can't we do the same for nations? We can, if we have faith, work and pray, and never stop trying.

Isn't a strike much the same as war — only on an industrial plane? Yes. Strikes generate hatred between employers and laborers, and frequently flare forth in violence, destroying property, injuring and beating people, and sometimes even taking life. For many years management acted in a tyrannical manner over its unorganized workers. Now, labor, highly unionized, exercises tremendous power and can act in an equally ruthless manner.

Both labor and capital should settle all their disputes through governmentally established boards of arbitration which mete out economic justice to both sides. Such tribunals will show some concern for the rights of the public so generally disregarded and trampled upon in industrial warfare. Strikes are harmful, wasteful and irrational methods of settling disputes: instead of deciding which side is right, a strike, like war, merely shows which side is more powerful.

Before a strike can be morally justified, the four conditions stipulated for waging a war must be fulfilled. It is doubtful if they can any longer be fulfilled — especially when the government has established tribunals for the peaceful settling of the controversy in accordance with reason and conscience. A strike is warfare on an industrial scale and should be delegated to the same limbo to which mankind is now trying to consign its older brother — military warfare: harmony and friendly relations between labor and capital, with a fair distribution to each of the products of their joint labor, along with consideration for the rights of the general public, will best promote the welfare of all.

Is abortion a form of murder? Yes, it is the murder of the unborn child. Since God infuses a rational soul into the organism at the moment of conception, it is a human being with the right to life. Only God has the right to take that life; hence the physician who assists in the abortion and the person who consents are equally guilty. So heinous is the murder of an unborn babe, unable to utter a cry or raise a hand in its own defense, that the Church inflicts the penalty of excommunication upon those guilty of it. If an unwed girl finds herself with child, she should not add to her guilt the far greater sin — the murder of her unborn babe. Hospitals conducted by nuns will shelter her in her difficulty and provide medical care for her and her child.

Besides forbidding murder, this commandment also forbids actions which would harm a person's health; hence it forbids intemperance, taking needless risks, and all actions which injure the health of the body or of the mind. Drunkenness is far too prevalent today; some persons are allergic to alcohol and once they discover that, they should never touch a drop. Most people, especially the young, would be better off to abstain completely from hard liquor. A glass of beer or a little wine with a meal is harmless enough, but hard liquor is extremely dangerous and has brought untold misery to millions of people and to their families. Wise indeed are they who follow the path of temperance or, better still, of complete abstinence.

Does scandal fall under this commandment? Yes, since it forbids us to injure our neighbor, it must forbid scandal; for scandal, or bad example, damages the supernatural life of the soul and constitutes a more serious injury than a mere bodily one. Hence we must be careful to set a good example to our neighbor and help sustain him in a life of virtue and goodness. We should keep before our minds the stern warning of Christ against scandal: "He that shall scandalize one of these little ones that believe in Me, it were better for him that a millstone should be hanged about his neck, and that he should be drowned in the depths of the sea."[1]

Hatred of others and the desire for revenge are also forbidden by this commandment, as they usually prepare the way for an attack upon a person — an attack by word or deed. "Whosoever hateth his brother," says St. John, "is a murderer." We must root hate and envy out of our souls so that the flowers of kindliness and love may bloom. We do not begin to be true Christians until we strive earnestly to love all men, even our enemies: the willingness to forgive those who have wronged us and to love them for Christ's sake is the unfailing mark of one who professes to be a true Christian.

"You have heard," said Christ, "that it was said to them of old, 'Thou shalt not kill'; and whosoever shall kill shall be in danger of the judgment. But I say to you, that whosoever is angry with his brother shall be in danger of the judgment."[2]

It is clear then that the fifth commandment forbids much more than murder: it even commands us to practice the Golden Rule and to love even our enemies. It forbids us to get angry, to "blow our top," to be sullen and pouty; anger never helps us, but actually harms us, as hatred does, in body, mind and soul. If we could only practice the Golden Rule, Christ's law of universal love, and observe the spirit as well as the letter of this commandment, what a better world this would be and how much happier we would all be. We all need to cultivate a cheerful, pleasant, forgiving disposition and to see Christ in our brothers and to love them as Christ does.

As the sixth and ninth commandments are so closely related, we shall combine them in this discussion of holy purity. The sixth is: "Thou shalt not commit adultery." The ninth is: "Thou shalt not covet thy neighbor's wife." Thus we see that the sixth forbids *acts* of impurity while the ninth prohibits willful *thoughts* and *desires* contrary to the angelic virtue.

The sixth commandment forbids not only adultery but all unchaste freedom with another's wife or husband and all immodesty with ourselves or others in looks, dress, words or actions; it prohibits likewise the reading of suggestive and immodest magazines and books.

God has endowed man with the gift of sex to secure the procreation of the race. "From the beginning of creation," said our Lord, "God made them male and female. For this cause a man shall leave his father and mother; and shall cleave to his wife. And they two shall be in one flesh. Therefore now they are not two, but one flesh."[3]

In order that man will not fail to use that endowment for the purpose indicated, God has planted in man a sex appetite which prompts man to marry and thus to propagate the race. Similarly, God has endowed man with an appetite for food, which prompts him to nourish his body and thus sustain his individual life. Both appetites are of divine origin, and both serve important ends when satisfied in accordance with God's laws. To abuse the faculty of eating by overindulgence is to commit the sin of gluttony: to abuse the faculty of sex is to commit the sin of impurity. The legitimate use of these endowments makes for man's virtue and well-being; their abuse constitutes sin and brings misery and suffering to the individual and to society.

The pleasures of sex in marriage are God's compensations for the burden of child-bearing and child-rearing. The marriage relation is a sacred one and deepens the love of husband and wife; it is God's method of preserving intact the Christian home, and using the husband and wife as His ambassadors in the divinely appointed task of propagating the race.

Indeed they are more than ambassadors: they are cooperators with God in the sublime work of bringing a human being

410

into existence. God creates the human soul while the parents supply the physical embryo into which the soul is infused; thus intimately do parents participate in the creative work of Almighty God.

Our body is the temple of the Holy Spirit, and we should reverence it as such. St. Paul declares: "Do not err; neither fornicators, nor idolators, nor adulterers, nor the effeminate, nor sodomites, nor thieves, nor the covetous, nor drunkards, nor the evil-tongued, nor the greedy will possess the kingdom." Reaching the climax of this theme, the Apostle says: "Know you not that your members are the temple of the Holy Spirit, who is in you, whom you have from God; and you are not your own? For you are bought with a great price. Glorify and bear God in your body."[4]

The best way to preserve one's purity unsullied is to flee the danger. "He that loveth danger," warns Holy Writ, "shall perish in it."[5] Evil thoughts and imaginations will come unbidden into the minds of all; they are sinful only when we consent to them; as long as we withhold consent and try to banish them, we are not only blameless, but we have gained merit as well. The best protection is to turn instantly to God in prayer and then to busy ourselves with other duties.

It is comforting to know that God will always come to our aid if we call upon Him; thus St. Paul assures us that God will never permit us to be tempted above our strength and will always give us grace to resist, if we will but cooperate with that grace.

Is birth control forbidden by this commandment? Birth control by partial or complete abstinence is not forbidden; but birth prevention by contraceptive devices and other unnatural means of frustrating the primary purpose for which the conjugal relation was ordained by God is grievously immoral. Such persons make a mockery of marriage and are guilty of mortal sin; the fact that many people violate this law of God and nature does not lessen the malice of this act any more than the fact that many drink to excess lessens the sin of drunkenness.

Purity is called the angelic virtue because it makes men resemble angels. Everybody admires a clean, wholesome person; purity sheds a fragrance upon the mind and heart of a pure per-

411

son and makes him radiant with the shining splendor of the Holy Spirit who dwells within his body as within a holy temple. Spotless purity can be achieved only as a result of constant vigilance, effort and frequent prayer.

Guarding our senses, choosing good companions, having a special devotion to the Blessed Virgin, receiving Holy Communion frequently, remembering that God sees our every thought and deed, and little acts of self-denial will help all to preserve their purity untarnished. God will bestow upon the pure an exceeding rich reward. "Blessed are the pure in heart," said Jesus, "for they shall see God."

The seventh commandment is: "Thou shalt not steal." The tenth commandment is: "Thou shalt not covet thy neighbor's goods." Since they both concern violations of justice, we shall discuss them together; the seventh commandment forbids external actions, while the tenth prohibits intentions or desires against the virtue of justice.

The seventh commandment forbids all unjust taking, keeping, or damaging what belongs to another; robbery, theft, forgery, cheating in buying or selling, overcharging, using false weights and measures, passing counterfeit money, making excessive profits, and adulterating foods are thus forbidden. Children violate this commandment by stealing from their parents or keeping back change, likewise by the vandalism often perpetrated on Halloween, such as breaking windows or destroying property.

Is it sinful to fail to pay one's bills? Yes, and if not paid after a reasonable time, interest should be added. This commandment likewise forbids the breaking of contracts and the buying or selling of stolen goods.

Graft too would fall under this commandment. An officeholder or politician who accepts bribes for his personal enrichment at the expense of the public is guilty of theft and must make retribution. Our cities are frequently honeycombed with graft; politicians are in alliance with criminals, keeping the police from arresting them or bringing pressure to bear upon prosecutors not to push the case against them. Such actions are a serious threat to the welfare and safety of society and cannot be condemned too vigorously.

Citizens should wage a fearless and unceasing war against every form of racketeering, graft and corruption; they should encourage honest candidates to seek public office and give them their wholehearted support. Grafters should not delude themselves into thinking that stealing from the public treasury is less of a crime because others do it and "get away" with it. God sees them and will hold them to strict accountability for every penny of the taxpayers' money entrusted to their care.

Stealing is either a mortal or a venial sin according to the amount of injury done to an individual or to society. The theft of a day's wages from a person is generally considered a grievous injustice. One should avoid stealing even the slightest object, even a penny, as the principle of justice is violated, and such small thefts usually prepare the way for larger ones.

Must a person restore ill-gotten goods? Yes, either the goods or their value. If the owner is dead, restitution must be made to his heirs; if the owner cannot be located, however, the property must be given to the poor or to some benevolent, charitable or religious purpose.

Inability to make restitution does not excuse one permanently from this duty. One must have the intention of making restitution as soon as possible and must work and save to achieve that goal; restitution may be made secretly through the mail or some agent who keeps the identity of the person undisclosed.

If one finds an article of value, he is obliged to try to locate the owner so the article can be returned to him; frequently an ad in the papers will enable one to find the owner. If one should unknowingly buy an article that was stolen, he would not be permitted to retain it if he could locate the rightful owner. True, such an action would entail a loss for him; but the old principle, "Let the buyer beware," would still hold good. An article cries out for its real owner and it remains his until he gives it up.

What does "covet" mean? It means to desire inordinately, to crave excessively the property of another, and to be envious of the good fortune of another. This is forbidden by the tenth commandment. Unless such desires are forbidden, they are likely to issue forth in action. "Envy not," says the Psalmist, "the man who prospers in his way."[6]

Employees may violate the seventh commandment through neglect and wastefulness — by pilfering the employer's goods, wasting his time and neglecting to perform the duties for which they are being paid. Employees are obliged to do an honest day's work, and to take a personal interest in the property and business of their employers; this means they must be careful of tools and machinery entrusted to them.

Employers also have duties toward their employees. They should pay a living wage — a wage sufficient to support that worker and his family in reasonable comfort, to enable him to educate his children and to lay something aside for the "rainy day." Employers are obliged also to provide decent working conditions, conducive to the health of body and soul; in general, they should regard their workers not as mere money-making machines but as human beings, as their brothers. They should take an interest in them and their families, visit them in sickness, help them to achieve economic security and follow with joy and pride the educational progress of their children. What a world of difference it would make if employers took such a deep personal interest in the workers and their families. It would promote peace and harmony between the two groups and advance the interests of both as well as those of the general public.

Thus powerfully do the seventh and the tenth commandments drive home to all people the truth of the saying, "Honesty is the best policy."

The eighth commandment is: "Thou shalt not bear false witness against thy neighbor." This commandment forbids lying, detraction, slander, uncharitable conversation, rash judgment and rash suspicion. A lie is telling what we know or think is false; lying is sinful, being a misuse of the faculty God has given to us. "Lying lips," warns Holy Writ, "are an abomination to the Lord."[7] A lie about some trivial matter is of course only a venial sin; but a lie which seriously injures another is a grievous sin.

Detraction means the telling of the hidden faults or sins of another; hence to mention something which has been published in the papers or is otherwise generally known is not detraction. Newspapers should not publish private family troubles which do not concern the public; such publication hurts the good name of the parties concerned and serves no useful purpose. Publishers of newspapers are not exempt from this commandment nor from the law of charity. We all should heed the warning of Holy Writ: "Hear not a wicked tongue and make doors and bars to thy mouth."[8]

What is meant by slander? That is the telling of a falsehood about a person; hence it is a more grievous sin than detraction. We are obliged to repair the damage unjustly done to a neighbor's reputation. A person values his reputation more than his pocketbook; if we are obliged to restore goods unjustly taken from him, we are all the more strictly bound to repair the injury done to his good name. In the case of slander we must frankly acknowledge that what we said about a person was a lie: in the case of detraction, we must try by praising the person's good qualities to offset the damage we inflicted by disclosing his hidden faults.

We are allowed to reveal another's faults when the person to whom we tell them has a right to know, when it is for the good of the guilty person, or when it is necessary to protect ourselves or others. Thus it may be necessary to make known certain faults to a parent or teacher in order that they may be properly corrected and thus help the person concerned.

Talebearing, carrying to persons the unfavorable remarks made about them, is wrong and contemptible; it is one of the favorite methods used by gossipers in sowing hatred and discord. "The whisperer and the double-tongued," warns Holy Writ, "is accursed, for he hath troubled many that were at peace."[9]

A good rule to follow is this: "If you can't say something good about a person, keep silent about him." It is wrong not only to speak uncharitably about our absent brother but also to encourage such conversation. The wise and tactful thing to do is to change the topic of conversation whenever you see it veering dangerously in the direction of backbiting or talebearing. "Admonish them," wrote the Apostle Paul to Titus, "to speak evil of no man."[10]

What must we keep secret? Whatever would be harmful to another if disclosed, and whatever is imparted to us in conidence. Young people should not, however, withhold from parents, teachers or superiors what these have a right to know.

To protect oneself or another from harm one may ordinarily disclose a secret. We are sometimes allowed to give a double-meaning answer, when it is necessary to conceal a secret we have a right or duty to keep, or when such concealment is necessary to protect ourselves or others from harm. Thus if a soldier, engaged in a just war, is captured and asked to tell where his companions are hidden, he may reply: "I do not know," meaning "I do not know with the right to tell."

The observance of this commandment brings peace and happiness to people, while its violation inevitably means heartache and suffering. How sensitive we all are to any reflection upon our good name. If we wish others to speak well of us, we ought to do the same for them; moreover, we never talk uncharitably of others without feeling a sense of guilt afterwards. The person who hurts the good name of others steals a treasure from them, but is unable to keep the treasure; in fact, he injures himself as well. Shakespeare gives a memorable expression of this great truth in the lines:[11]

Good name in man and woman, dear my lord,
Is the immediate jewel of their souls:
Who steals my purse steals trash; 'tis something, nothing;
'Twas mine, 'tis his, and has been slave to thousands;
But he that filches from me my good name
Robs me of that which not enriches him,
And makes me poor indeed.

If we would but remember that God has endowed us with the marvelous faculty of speech that we might utter useful, kind and charitable words, we would not abuse it by speaking harsh and injurious words about our absent brother. It is well for us to recall likewise that we shall be required to render an account to Almighty God for the use we have made of this great gift and to account for every idle and uncharitable word. St. James epitomizes it well when he says: "If any man offend not in word, the same is a perfect man."[12]

Thus we end our explanation of the ten commandments of God. They have been given to us by Almighty God for our pro-

416

tection, our welfare and our happiness. People make a mistake when they imagine that the commandments block them off from happiness; true contentment and happiness are never found in the violation of God's holy law but only in its observance.

THE PRECEPTS OF THE CHURCH

The precepts of the Church supplement the ten commandments by giving further detailed guidance for our conduct. There are six such precepts. The first, "To hear Mass on Sundays and holydays of obligation," specifies the manner in which we are to fulfill the third commandment of God. It obliges us under pain of mortal sin to hear Mass on Sundays and holydays of obligation unless excused by sickness or some other serious reason; it also obliges those who have charge of others to see that the latter likewise fulfill this duty. Holydays were instituted by the Church to recall to our minds the great mysteries of religion and the virtues and rewards of the saints.

The second precept is, "To fast and abstain on the days appointed." By fast-days are meant days on which we are allowed but one full meal; days of abstinence are those on which we are forbidden to eat meat but are allowed the usual number of meals. The Church commands us to fast and abstain in order that we may mortify our passions and satisfy for our sins.

The third precept, "To confess at least once a year," requires us under pain of mortal sin to go to confession within the year. Of course, it is recommended that we go more frequently, once a month or once a week, if we wish to advance in virtue and holiness. Children should go to confession when they are old enough to commit sin, which is commonly about the age of seven years. It is preferable to have a regular confessor, that is, a priest to whom we customarily go; he is then in a better position to chart our progress, and to caution us against the danger of falling back into our former sins.

The fourth precept, "To receive the Holy Eucharist during the Easter time," obliges us under pain of mortal sin to receive during that period, which extends in this country from the first Sunday in Lent to Trinity Sunday — fifteen weeks. This does not mean that we should be content with the observance of the minimum requirement. All who wish to grow in holiness and virtue will receive often — each month, each week, or even daily — the Author of all holiness and the Source of all blessings and graces. We can't stress too strongly the wisdom of frequent Holy Communion. The person who will open wide the door of his heart to our Eucharistic Lord every week will find new power and strength to resist even venial sin and will experience a genuine determination to grow in perfection like his divine Master.

The fifth precept is, "To contribute to the support of our pastors." This obliges us to bear our share in the expenses of the Church and school: we should give in proportion to our means, realizing that God will see that, like the bread cast upon the waters, it comes back to us a hundredfold.

What is the sixth and last precept? "Not to marry persons who are not Catholics and who are related to us within the third degree of kindred, nor privately without witnesses, nor to solemnize marriage at forbidden times." The third degree of kindred means the third degree of blood relationship. As brothers and sisters are in the first degree, second cousins are in the third degree. The command not to marry privately means that none should marry without the blessing of God's priests or without witnesses. The meaning of the precept not to solemnize marriage at forbidden times is that during Lent and Advent the marriage ceremony should not be performed with pomp or a Nuptial Mass; the latter is a Mass appointed by the Church to invoke a special blessing upon the married couple. Catholics should be married at a Nuptial Mass because they thereby show greater reverence for the holy sacrament and bring richer blessings upon their wedded life.

We can see that all these precepts are designed to promote the spiritual welfare of the person and to assist him in keeping God's holy commandments. They constitute a beautiful and a touching expression of the Church's solicitude for the welfare and the happiness of her children.

The Church is concerned not only that we believe the truths taught by Christ but also that we keep His commandments. Both are necessary; the person who professes the Christian faith while ignoring the moral precepts makes a mockery of his religion and becomes a stumbling block to those outside the faith. God demands the homage of our minds, demands that we conform our belief to the truth which He has revealed; not less insistently, however, does He demand the homage of our actions, the sweet incense of virtue, the conformity of our conduct to His moral law, expressed in the decalogue and in the six precepts of the Church. It is well to remember the words of Christ: "Not everyone that sayeth Lord, Lord, shall enter into the kingdom of heaven: but he that doth the will of My Father who is in heaven; he shall enter into the kingdom of heaven."[13] On another occasion Christ said: "By their fruits you shall know them."[14] Our Savior demands not only the leaves of words but also the fruit of deeds.

A certain lawyer once asked the Savior: "Master, what must I do to possess eternal life?" Jesus replied by telling him to love God with his whole heart and soul and to love his neighbor as himself. Then the Master turned to the lawyer with the significant words: "This do, and thou shalt live."[15] On this note sounded by our Divine Savior we end the explanation of the commandments of God and the precepts of His Church.

Discussion Aids

What does the fifth commandment require? Forbid? What four conditions are necessary for a just war? Are strikes industrial war? Why? What is abortion? Why forbidden? What is scandal? Why forbidden? What does the sixth commandment forbid? The ninth? Are our bodies temples of the Holy Spirit? Explain. What kind of birth control is forbidden? Why? What does the seventh commandment forbid? The tenth? Explain restitution. What does the eighth commandment forbid? Define detraction, slander, talebearing.

Practices

Recall the commandments of God and the precepts of the Church before going to Confession.

Try each month to fulfill one of the commandments more perfectly.

Ask the aid of St. Joseph to keep the six precepts of the Church and encourage others to keep them.

NOTES (Chapter 33)

1. Mt. 18:6
2. *Ibid.*, 5:21-22
3. Mk. 10:6-8
4. I Cor. 6:9-20
5. Eccl. (Sir.) 3:26
6. Ps. 36:7
7. Prv. 12:22
8. Eccl. (Sir.) 28:24-26
9. *Ibid.*, 28:13
10. Ti. 3:1-2
11. *Othello*, Act 3, Scene 3
12. Jas. 3:2
13. Mt. 7:21
14. *Ibid.*, 7:16
15. Lk. 10:28

CHAPTER 34

Time for Action

You are now familiar with the chief doctrines and practices of the Catholic religion. You have seen how Christ founded the Catholic Church and, giving her complete jurisdiction over the divine deposit of truth, commissioned her to teach His truths to all mankind. She alone traces her origin back to Christ; she alone received from Him the power and the authority to teach and to minister in His name; she alone possesses the marks of unity, sanctity, catholicity and apostolicity — the marks which will guide the wanderer to the Church of Christ. The evidence that the Catholic Church is the true Church of Jesus Christ is so clear that even he who runs can read.

Knowledge alone, however, is not enough. It is necessary to reduce knowledge to action, to translate one's conviction into life and conduct. It is time now to cease being a mere passive spectator, to leave the sidelines to enter the Church of Christ and avail yourself of the sacraments, the divinely established means of sanctification. Cast aside now all doubts and misgivings; Christ cannot deceive us; Christ cannot fail us; neither can He be outdone in generosity. If you are generous in your trust and faith in Him, He will not fail to give you light to see the truth and the strength to follow it.

Let no worldly considerations deter you from following the voice of your enlightened conscience. The breaking of old ties, the leaving of old moorings may entail a temporary hardship, a brief nostalgia; but such is frequently the price of progress. In your new home, peace and serenity will fill your heart and you will taste of that peace which the world cannot give. For a slight and temporary cross you will gain an eternal crown that will never lose its brilliance.

Love is diffusive of itself. Tell others of the joy that is yours; show your gratitude to Almighty God for the grace He has given to you by bringing each year another soul into the Church of Christ. You will prove your love for others most effectively by sharing with them your greatest treasure on earth — your holy Catholic faith. You will be among that shining galaxy of noble souls of whom Daniel, the prophet, said: "They that instruct many unto justice shall shine as the stars for all eternity."[1]

You are called to be not merely another Catholic, another member in the vast army of more than 659,000,000 men and women who in every land find shelter under the mighty expanse of St. Peter's dome. You are called to be an exemplary Catholic whose life squares with your faith. You are called — as indeed are all Catholics — to be a *saint* of God, a just and holy person, proclaiming your Catholic faith through the irresistible eloquence of a virtuous and noble life. This is the language which all mankind can understand and the music which never fails to win the hearts of men.

Discussion Aids

Sum up what you have learned from studying this text. Why is knowledge of the truth not enough? What means of sanctification did Christ in His inestimable love leave us that we might share His divine nature? Does He expect us to be saints? Is it possible for all to be saints? How can we best proclaim that the Catholic Church teaches the truth?

Practices

Thank God fervently that He has made you a member of His Church. Be an ornament to the Church.

Know that the sacraments are the instruments by which Christ welds us to Himself, and use them.

Meditate on the tremendous power of good example and try hard always to give good example.

NOTES (Chapter 34)

1. Dn. 12:3

PART VII

The Movement
For Christian Unity

CHAPTER 35

A New Religious Climate

One of the greatest religious events of the twentieth century was the Second Vatican Council, convoked by Pope John XXIII. Meeting in four sessions, each lasting about a couple of months, the Council opened on October 11, 1962, and closed on December 8, 1965. The Council was pastoral and constructive, issuing no decree of condemnation nor branding anyone a heretic. It sought to bring about the renewal and reform of the spiritual life of the Church, to update her liturgy, to increase the relevance of her ministry to the needs of a world undergoing revolutionary changes and to promote the unity of all Christians.

It was the latter which attracted the attention of the general public, particularly of non-Catholic Christians. The large Protestant Churches were invited to send observers, who were treated with every courtesy. They were provided with the texts of documents under discussion and with translators who interpreted the oral addresses: a favor not extended even to the Council Fathers.

In a friendly little talk to the Protestant observers at the beginning of the Council, Pope John said: "We do not intend to conduct a trial of the past; we do not want to prove who was right or who was wrong. The blame is on both sides. All we want is to say: 'Let us come together. Let us make an end of our divisions.' "

This sounded the keynote of the whole Council. The transparent sincerity of the great Pope and his boundless love won the hearts of all. Much the same note was sounded by his successor, Pope Paul VI, at the second session of the Council when he addressed the observers and said: "After so many years of separation, after such painful polemics, what else can we do but again love one another, listen to one another, and pray for one another?"

The Council brought a new spirit of warmth, friendliness and mutual respect into the relations of Catholics and non-Catholic Christians. It started a dialogue which has already effected new areas of agreement and joint worship and has brought about cooperative action in dealing with the vexing world problems of racism, social justice and peace. While the Council formulated no new dogmas, it has prompted all Christians to try to enlarge their areas of doctrinal agreement so as to reflect the desire of Christ for the unity of all His followers.

Surrounded by the Apostles on the night before He died, Christ uttered the prayer for unity which sounds the keynote of the whole ecumenical movement: "Yet not for these only do I pray, but for those also who through their word are to believe in Me, that all may be one, even as Thou, Father, in Me and I in Thee; that they also may be one in Us, that the world may believe that Thou hast sent Me."[1]

Moreover, Christ instituted the life-giving sacrament of the Eucharist whereby the unity of His Church is both signified and made a reality. He gave His disciples a new commandment to love one another, and promised that the Spirit, their Advocate, would remain with them forever. After His redeeming death and glorious resurrection, the Lord Jesus poured forth the Spirit upon the people of the New Covenant and called them into a unity of faith, hope and charity, as the Apostle Paul teaches us: "There is one body and one Spirit, just as you were called to the one hope of your calling; one Lord, one faith, one baptism."[2]

Recurring to the theme of the unity of Christ's followers, the Apostle reminds us that "all you who have been baptized into Christ have put on Christ ... for you are all one in Christ Jesus."[3] Hence by baptism all Christians are made brothers in Christ.

Dwelling in those who believe and pervading the whole Church, the Holy Spirit brings about a wonderful communion of the faithful. Through the distribution of graces He enriches the Church of Jesus Christ with different functions "in order to equip the saints for the work of service, so as to build up the body of Christ."[4]

"This," declared Vatican II in the *Decree on Ecumenism*, which we draw upon often in this chapter, "is the sacred mystery of the unity of the Church, in Christ and through Christ, the Holy Spirit energizing its various functions. It is a mystery that finds its highest exemplar and source in the unity of Persons of the Trinity: the Father and the Son in the Holy Spirit, one God."[5]

In the course of centuries this unity was marred by serious dissensions which led to the withdrawal of whole communities from full communion with the Catholic Church, "for which, often enough," acknowledges the Council, "men of both sides were to blame."[6] Persons who are born into these communities and who grow up believing in Christ cannot be blamed for the sin involved in the separation, and the Catholic Church, says the Council, "embraces them as brothers with respect and affection."[7]

Men and women who believe in the Lord Jesus and have been truly baptized are in communion with the Catholic Church even though this communion is imperfect. The differences that exist in varying degrees between them and the Catholic Church, in doctrine, discipline or concerning the structure and organization of the Church, create obstacles to complete ecclesiastical communion.

The ecumenical movement is striving to remove these obstacles. But even in spite of them it remains true, declares the Council, "that all who have been justified by faith in Baptism are members of Christ's Body, and have a right to be called Christian, and so are correctly accepted as brothers by the children of the Catholic Church."[8]

Going still further on the path to Christian unity, the Council acknowledges that within the separated Churches there exist many of the significant elements and endowments which enrich the spiritual life of their members: the written word of God; the life of grace; faith, hope and charity, with the other interior gifts of the Holy Spirit.

The Council also admits that our separated brethren use many of the liturgical actions which engender a life of grace and must therefore be regarded as capable of giving access to the community of salvation. Hence the Council concludes that the Spirit of Christ has not refrained from using the separated Churches as "means of salvation."

These are developments of enormous significance for the ecumenical movement and they are, in fact, some of the most remarkable fruit which that movement has already produced. They call for a more gentle and restrained manner in referring to our differences with the separated Churches and a more ready and candid acknowledgment of the means of grace and salvation which they provide for their members. Protestants are to us no longer simply non-Catholics but fellow Christians and our separated brothers in Christ. Hence virtually all books presenting the credentials of the Catholic Church as the sole and exclusive means of salvation, written before Vatican II, need serious revision.

When Catholics refer to Protestants as their "separated brethren," the emphasis now is not on *separated* but on *brethren*. It was Pope John XXIII who was chiefly responsible for this shift of emphasis, and Catholics joyfully follow his example. They cannot forget how his unfailing kindness, understanding, sympathy and love won the heart of the world so that his death brought tears to the eyes of millions of our separated brethren as well as to those of his own children.

Indeed neither side can forget that, during the weeks of the long, drawn-out agony that preceded his death, the gentle and humble servant of Christ declared: "Gladly do I give my life and offer all my suffering to help bring about the unity of Christ's children — a unity for which the Lord Jesus prayed so fervently." Surely he was the means used by Christ to usher in a new era in the relations of Christians to one another. Gone are the days of strife and bitter polemics when the passions were stirred, and kindness, sensitivity for the feelings of others and love were the first casualties.

The new era, marvelous though it be, is not however without its own dangers, particularly the danger of not acknowledging the serious differences which still exist. The ecumenist who blurs such differences in the effort to achieve apparent agreement does not promote true Christian unity but retards it. Hence the first rule in the ecumenical movement is to acknowledge differences which really exist, but to hold out the olive branch of peace and hope that further friendly discussion will lead to well-reasoned and justifiable agreement.

Hence it is that, after joyfully acknowledging that Christ has not refrained from using the separated Churches as "means of salvation," the Council in its *Decree on Ecumenism* immediately adds: "Nevertheless, our separated brethren, whether considered as individuals or as communities and Churches, are not blessed with that unity which Jesus Christ wished to bestow on all those who through Him were born again into one body, and with Him quickened to newness of life — that unity which the Holy Scriptures and the ancient Tradition of the Church proclaim."[9]

The Church believes that her divine Founder confided all the blessings of the Covenant to the apostolic college alone, of which Peter is the head, in order to establish the one Body of Christ on earth, in which "all should be fully incorporated who belong in any way to the People of God."[10]

Though still liable to sin, this People of God is ever growing in Christ during its pilgrimage on earth, and is guided by "God's gentle wisdom" until it shall happily arrive at the fullness of eternal glory in the heavenly Jerusalem.

The Council instructs Catholics to avoid expressions, judgments and actions which do not represent the belief of our separated brethren with truth and fairness and thus render mutual relations with them more difficult. It encourages experts to hold dialogues with representatives of the separated Churches to gain a more accurate understanding and appreciation of the teachings and religious life of the respective communions. Thus the way is prepared for cooperation in promoting the common good of humanity.

This may well be followed by prayer in common so that all may be prompted to examine their own faithfulness to Christ's will for the Church and undertake with vigor the task of renewal and reform. Hence when the obstacles to perfect ecclesiastical communion have been gradually surmounted, the Council expresses the hope that all Christians will at last, in a common celebration of the Holy Eucharist, be gathered into the Church and will thus possess the unity which Christ bestowed upon her from the beginning.

The Council is quick to point out, however, that the reconciliation of individuals to the Church and their preparation for entrance into it constitute an undertaking that is distinct from ecumenical action but not opposed to it, "as both proceed from the marvelous ways of God."[11] This clear, candid statement of Vatican Council II is of the utmost importance, for it removes the widespread misconception that all efforts to spread the faith among *individuals* are to be halted, that now our concern is solely with corporate reunion — the merging of all Churches into one Christian body.

Acting under this misconception, thousands of parish priests have discontinued the practice of conducting inquiry classes and information forums, while many of the laity have ceased to recruit persons for such classes. Thus the missionary activity of the Church on the individual level has been drastically curtailed and almost paralyzed. The result has been tragic. The number of adult baptisms has dropped to new lows. Thousands of churchless and non-churchgoing individuals, who are eager to learn more about the Christian faith, find no hands stretched out to welcome them and are lost to Christ and to His Church.

Experience shows that individuals hesitate to call at a rectory to ask for a course of instruction when they are not sure that they will embrace the Christian faith. But if public inquiry classes are conducted throughout the year and are well advertised, many will enroll in them. Indeed the number of adult baptisms in a parish is generally in direct proportion to the number of its inquiry classes and to the enrollment in each.

As a priest who was privileged to assist some fifty dioceses establish such classes on diocesan and statewide levels, and thus greatly increase the number of persons who embraced the Christian faith, I find it heartbreaking to see this missionary work so widely curtailed with the tragic results mentioned. Instead of being curtailed, such inquiry classes should be doubled and the recruiting intensified. Far from conflicting with the ecumenical movement, such classes are fruitful means of spreading the Christian faith, which is, of course, the goal of that movement.

One of the chief reasons for the misconceptions that evangelical or missionary work among individuals, particularly churchless or non-churchgoing, is to be curtailed or discontinued, is the fact that such activity is totally out of place in: (1) ecumenical dialogues between theologians; (2) formal negotiations between Church officials concerning mergers; and (3) all ecumenical gatherings for study, discussion and prayer for Christian unity through Church mergers. When corporate reunion will take place, God alone knows.

It may require many decades and even centuries. Until that consummation happens, however, we must continue the age-old practice of presenting the teachings and credentials of Christ to all interested persons and particularly to those outside the Christian fold. To do otherwise would be to suspend the missionary work of the Church, which is an essential part of her divine commission and of her very life.

Thus the *Decree* further states: "Catholics, in their ecumenical work, must assuredly be concerned for their separated brethren, praying for them, keeping them informed about the Church, making the first approaches toward them."[12] We must also edify them by our Christ-like lives. In short, we must have the zeal of Christ and the Apostles in seeking in a humble and friendly manner to share the precious treasure of our holy faith, our greatest spiritual heritage, with those outside the fold.

Surveys show that more than 70,000,000 people in the U.S.A. have no Church affiliation, while more than half of the affiliated acknowledge their attendance to be irregular. Careful students of this subject estimate that on the average Sunday more than 100,000,000 people attend no divine service. This is the first step in the process of falling away from organized religion into a merely secular life. Hence it is evident that the United States is one of the great mission fields of the world.

"It should be clear," said the late Cardinal Meyer of Chicago and one of the leaders at Vatican II, "that it would be a great mistake for Catholics to cease to carry on the apostolate to individuals on the grounds that it hinders the ecumenical movement. It would be a mistake because the ecumenical movement itself requires an honest and full witness to the truth which has been given to every Christian. It would be a mistake for Catholics in particular, because we know that the entire revelation of Jesus Christ is preserved by Him in the Catholic Church in its infallible truth, and it is this truth that all men are seeking."[13]

Pointing out how our apostolate should be oriented, Cardinal Meyer continues: "Undoubtedly our apostolate should be especially directed to those who know little of the gospel and who are not affiliated to any Christian group, but we should also make available to Christian inquirers from any Church the opportunity to hear what the Catholic Church teaches. At the same time, we must scrupulously avoid attacking other religious groups. Let us not open old wounds, nor let us drive others away by an attitude of arrogance as if we had nothing to learn from them."

Sounding a similar note Cardinal Heenan of London says: "If we have the spirit of true apostles, we are bound to seek to spread the truth. . . . This is the ideal of truth and charity which Pope John XXIII has set firmly before us. He has not asked us to play down Catholic doctrine nor to disguise our opposition to what is false in the teachings of other religions. He has asked us by prayer and example to strive 'that all may be one.' This is the plea of Christ's vicar as it was the prayer of Christ Himself the night before He suffered."[14]

The statements of Cardinals Meyer and Heenan as well as of Vatican II reflect the traditional teaching of the Church for more than nineteen centuries. This was emphasized also by Pope Pius XII, who spoke so often about the necessity for the laity to participate in the missionary activities of the Church. "We shall regard with special favor," said His Holiness, "all those Catholics who, moved by divine grace, shall strive to help their separated brethren to the true faith, preparing the way for them by dissipating inveterate prejudices, by teaching Catholic doctrine, and, above all, by showing themselves that charity which is the mark of a disciple of Christ."

In his great Encyclical *Fidei Donum* (The Gift of Faith) Pius XII urged the laity to be convert-minded and mission-minded. "The missionary spirit," he declared, "is not a virtue of supererogation, expected of the chosen few. This spirit and the Catholic spirit are one and the same thing. . . . One is not genuinely interested in, and devoted to, the Church unless one is interested in and devoted to its universality; that is, to its taking root and flourishing everywhere on earth." In short, one is scarcely worthy of the name of Catholic if he is not mission-minded and convert-minded.

Pope Pius XI is generally credited with giving the lay apostolate in the twentieth century its great impetus. His Holiness said: "It is necessary that all men be apostles."[15] Pointing out that the first Apostles would have accomplished little without the zealous assistance of the laity, he declared: "What would the Twelve have done, lost in the world's immensity, if they had not called aloud to others — men, women, the aged and children — and said, 'Let us carry forth the treasure of heaven; help us to distribute it'?" Those words might well be framed and placed in all our churches, schools and in every hall where our laity assemble.

As a matter of fact, the whole idea of lay participation in the work of winning souls is just as old as the Church itself. Among the early Christians the faith was spread chiefly by the laity. The seventy-two disciples mentioned in the Scriptures were all laymen, and Christ sent them "two by two before His face into every city and place whither He Himself was to come." Following the example of our Lord, the Apostle Paul made generous use of lay disciples and, in one of his epistles, lists the names of about thirty. In the early centuries it was the laity who not only won most of the converts, but also furnished most of the martyrs. "It is an undeniable fact," declared Cardinal Cag-

432

giano of Buenos Aires at the Congress of Lay Apostles in Rome, "that from the first days of the Church the simple faithful helped the hierarchy of the Church in spreading the Kingdom of God."

Ecumenical-minded as Pope John XXIII was, he did not fail to stress the duty of Catholics to share their faith with others. "Each one," said His Holiness, "must be zealous for the spiritual welfare of his neighbor, for the defense of his own faith, to make it known to him who is completely ignorant of it, or to him who knows it imperfectly."[16]

In an address to the officers of the Pontifical Missionary Societies and the Missionary Union of the Clergy, on May 14, 1965, Pope Paul VI declared that the missionary responsibility to communicate God's message of redemption is more urgent and necessary than ever. While realizing that God has other means of saving those beyond the light of revelation, His Holiness said this does not mean that "the sons of light are permitted to leave it to God Himself to work out His hidden economy of salvation." In similar vein the *Constitution on the Church* declares: "The obligation of spreading the faith is imposed on every disciple of Christ according to his state."[17] That aptly sums up the mind of the Church on this subject.

The thoroughgoing, extensive and careful revisions of *The Faith of Millions* were made to reflect with the utmost accuracy the authentic mind of the post-Vatican II Church on her teachings as well as on the manner and spirit in which they should be presented in this ecumenical era, pregnant with such wonderful possibilities for the advancement of Christian unity. The ecumenical movement has brought a new climate of understanding, friendship, brotherhood and love, and this book endeavors to reflect that climate.

NOTES (Chapter 35)

1. Jn. 17:20-21
2. Eph. 4:4-5
3. Gal. 3:27-28

4. Eph. 4:12
5. DE 2
6. DE 3
7. *Ibid.*
8. *Ibid.*
9. *Ibid.*
10. *Ibid.*
11. DE 4
12. *Ibid.*
13. *New Horizons for Christian Unity*, ed. by J.A. O'Brien, p. 27 (Wichita: The Liturgical Commission)
14. *Ibid.*, p. 28
15. *Ibid.*, p. 28f
16. *Ibid.*, p. 28
17. Art. 21

INDEX

435

St. Thomas Aquinas, on Communion
— 239
    on indulgences — 199
Salvation, outside the true fold — 35 f.
Sanctity of Church — 21
Sin, actual — 20
    mortal and venial — 391
    original — 20
Slander — 414 f.
Spiritual treasury of the Church — 198
Stoddard, John L., on purgatory —
    345 f.
    on use of images — 332 f.
Strikes, when justified — 407 f.
Substance, a mystery — 221
Sunday Mass — 310 ff.
Sunday, observance of — 399 f.
Supreme court and infallibility — 111
    ff.

T

Talebearing — 415
Temporal punishment — 195 f.
Tennyson, on prayer — 202
    on prayers for the dead — 344
Tertullian, on confirmation — 160
Thompson, Francis — 317

Title deed of Church — 52 ff.
Triumph, of early Church — 85

U

Unity of Church — 21
Unity of Faith — 34

V

Vatican Council, Second — 424 ff.
Vicarious satisfaction — 198

W

War, conditions justifying — 407
Washington, George — 38
Way of the Cross — 349 ff.
Wiseman, Cardinal, on Real Presence
    — 210

Z

Zwingli — 146

NOTES

NOTES

NOTES

NOTES

NOTES

NOTES